"A singular book on the Spirit combini
porary literature with imagination and theological creativity. It leads to a suggestive but open-ended exploration of various models for experiencing and understanding the work of the Spirit."

**Justo L. González,** author of *The Mestizo Augustine*

"This is a book I didn't know we needed; but after reading it, I now see how much we did! Leo Sánchez provides a fresh mixture of historical summaries and constructive contributions that will prove helpful to our trinitarian discussions. A somewhat neglected focus for many, Sánchez gives particular attention to the relationship between the Spirit's work in the incarnate Christ and the Spirit's presence in our lives. Ably drawing from the patristics (especially Irenaeus) as well as leaning heavily on Luther, Sánchez seeks to outline five models for understanding life in the Spirit. Rather than imagining these in unavoidable tension, he creatively points out strengths in each, especially looking at them in light of pastoral concerns. Much in this volume can help clarify our thinking and stimulate our Spirit dependent lives."

**Kelly M. Kapic,** Covenant College

"In the winsome spirit we have come to expect from Sánchez, *Sculptor Spirit* is a gentle and timely corrective to a lot of anemic spirituality found on the market today. Using Spirit Christology as the lens through which to examine the sanctifying work of the Spirit, Sánchez puts holiness back on the agenda as he recommends five models of sanctification for Spirit-filled believers today. Listening to voices from the past, Sánchez places before the reader various complementary models on what the Christian life looks like and how we can be further conformed to the image of Christ. It wasn't too long ago that Spirit Christology was a promising area to explore; with *Sculptor Spirit* we have another example of how Spirit Christology is delivering on its early promises. The Spirit gives life and in this work Sánchez clearly shows how the Spirit is at work conforming people to Christ's image for the glory of God."

**Myk Habets,** dean of faculty and professor of theology, Carey Baptist College and Graduate School, Auckland, New Zealand

"One of the theological dangers facing the English-speaking church is its over reliance on Christology, what can be called *hyperchristocentrism*, which means that Christ is emphasized to such a degree that Christian trinitarianism breaks down. What is needed in response to this situation are ways to make Christology more trinitarian, and this is what Sánchez helps achieve in this work. *Sculptor Spirit* emphasizes a Spirit Christology for its implications related to sanctification, spirituality, and the Christian life overall. Through its models and various examples from antiquity to the present, it is a reliable guide that I hope finds resonance with students, preachers, and teachers who are passionate to offer something substantive to a hungry church."

**Daniel Castelo,** professor of dogmatic and constructive theology, Seattle Pacific University and Seminary

"Sánchez's past work on the relationship of the Holy Spirit to Christ provides an effective foundation for this exploration of several views of the ways in which the Holy Spirit creates and forms the holy life of faith in those who trust in Christ. This work draws readers into a world- and church-wide conversation on how the Spirit goes about sanctifying sinners and leading them into a life of faith and obedience that exercises true humanity in the midst of our faltering world. This skillfully constructed, aptly delivered assessment of various models for interpreting the presence and working of the Spirit in believers' lives will stimulate and guide pastors and laity into new perspectives on how to understand and practice the faith."

**Robert Kolb,** professor of systematic theology emeritus, Concordia Seminary, Saint Louis

"In this impressive volume, Leopoldo Sánchez provides a comprehensive and detailed account of Spirit Christology, tracing its development through the ages to offer a robust trinitarian account of Christ as one filled with the power of the Spirit. Having laid the foundation for Christ as the pattern for the Spirit-filled life, he then applies this to a practical, generative, and thought-provoking, models-based approach to sanctification, making the much-needed link between orthodox dogmatic theology and everyday life. Thus this book is a valuable contribution to both the academy and the church."

**Lucy Peppiatt,** principal, Westminster Theological Centre, UK

"With fourth-century church fathers and Luther as foundational resources, in interaction with current scholarship, Sánchez explores five models of sanctification that illumine the ministry of the Spirit of Christ in believers. This creative Latino-Lutheran scholar continues his fruitful work in Christology and pneumatology with a volume that will benefit the broader church in North America. A stellar contribution from a fresh voice, forged as a Latino within a historic tradition. *Un aporte singular.*"

**M. Daniel Carroll R.,** Blanchard Professor of Old Testament, Wheaton College and Graduate School

"Everyone these days wants to be spiritual. They just don't know how or what it really means to be spiritual. Leo Sánchez charts a course that anchors that yearning for spirituality on solid ground. He presents an experience of the Spirit grounded firmly in the theology and practice of the church through the centuries as he provides various models of what it means to be 'in the Spirit.' Spirituality is not so much a feeling or a yearning as it is a way of life worked out in the person of Christ and his work through and in the Spirit in and for us. Sánchez reminds us that the Spirit blows where it wills, but it never blows apart from the will of Christ and the Father. If you're looking for a theological yet pastoral approach to reach those who want to be spiritual but don't know how, this book is a great resource."

**Joel C. Elowsky,** professor of historical theology, Concordia Seminary, St. Louis

# SCULPTOR SPIRIT

## MODELS *of* SANCTIFICATION FROM SPIRIT CHRISTOLOGY

LEOPOLDO A. SÁNCHEZ M.

An imprint of InterVarsity Press
Downers Grove, Illinois

*InterVarsity Press*
*P.O. Box 1400, Downers Grove, IL 60515-1426*
*ivpress.com*
*email@ivpress.com*



*InterVarsity Press® is the book-publishing division of InterVarsity Christian Fellowship/USA®, a movement of students and faculty active on campus at hundreds of universities, colleges, and schools of nursing in the United States of America, and a member movement of the International Fellowship of Evangelical Students. For information about local and regional activities, visit intervarsity.org.*



*The section titled "Avoiding Romantic and Utilitarian Views of the Neighbor" in chapter five uses edited material from Leopoldo A. Sánchez M., "'The Poor You Will Always Have With You': A Biblical View of People in Need," in* A People Called to Love: Christian Charity in North American Society, *ed. Kent J. Burreson, September 2012, http://concordiatheology.org/wp-content/uploads/2012/09/Sanchez-essay1.pdf. Used by permission.*

*The section titled "Crossing Borders: Spiritual Practices and Issues in the Christian Life" in chapter six uses edited material from Leopoldo A. Sánchez M., "Can Anything Good Come Out of ___________? Come and See! Faithful Witness in Marginality and Hospitality,"* Concordia Journal *41, no. 2 (2015): 111-23. Used by permission.*

*The section titled "Martin Luther: Exiles' Plight, Church as Refuge, Stranger Christ, Love of the Cross" in chapter six uses edited material from Leopoldo A. Sánchez M., "The Church is the House of Abraham: Reflections on Martin Luther's Teaching on Hospitality Toward Exiles,"* Concordia Journal *44, no. 1 (2018): 23-39. Used by permission.*

*Cover design and image composite: David Fassett*
*Interior design: Jeanna Wiggins*
*Images: grunge blue background: © belterz / E+ / Getty Images*
*hand and dove graphics: David Fassett*

*ISBN 978-0-8308-5233-8 (print)*
*ISBN 978-0-8308-7317-3 (digital)*

*Printed in the United States of America* ♾

*InterVarsity Press is committed to ecological stewardship and to the conservation of natural resources in all our operations. This book was printed using sustainably sourced paper.*

**Library of Congress Cataloging-in-Publication Data**
*A catalog record for this book is available from the Library of Congress.*

**P** 25 24 23 22 21 20 19 18 17 16 15 14 13 12 11 10 9 8 7 6 5 4 3 2 1
**Y** 38 37 36 35 34 33 32 31 30 29 28 27 26 25 24 23 22 21 20 19

TO MY STUDENTS

AND COLLEAGUES IN MINISTRY

for giving me the joy of teaching

in service to the church

# CONTENTS

*Foreword by Oscar García-Johnson* ix
*Preface* xiii
*Acknowledgments* xix
*Abbreviations* xxi
Introduction 1
1 Sculptor Spirit: Spirit Christology and the Sanctified Life 15
2 Voices from the Past: Patristic Images of the Sanctifying Spirit 42
3 Baptized into Death and Life: The Renewal Model 66
4 Facing Demons Through Prayer and Meditation: The Dramatic Model 89
5 Sharing Life Together: The Sacrificial Model 115
6 Welcoming the Stranger: The Hospitality Model 144
7 Work, Pray, and Rest: The Devotional Model 169
8 I Want to Tell the Story: North American Spirituality and the Models 194
Conclusion 235
*Appendix* 249
*Bibliography* 253
*Author Index* 267
*Subject Index* 269
*Scripture Index* 275

# FOREWORD

## OSCAR GARCÍA-JOHNSON

We welcome *Sculptor Spirit: Models of Sanctification from Spirit Christology* written by Leo Sánchez, a fine theologian of the church and dear colleague. Sánchez's fresh exploration into the subject of sanctification by means of Spirit Christology represents a timely step forward in theological studies and ecclesial imagination. The disciplines of practical theology and pneumatology, in particular, should feel grateful for this work.

I receive this work with consideration, for I am an ordained minister who does critical ecclesiology, appreciates desert and patristic spirituality, and, as an activist, exercises decoloniality. Where to find sources that can nurture my spirit, call attention to my pastoral practice, give me access to a patristic theologian who makes sense to me, and illustrate ways to identify the character of Christ being shaped in me without having to convert me into a white-male-Western subject? I suspect we are in the presence of such a source.

Although the Spirit of God has no particular season (though we do), some have claimed that we are living in the Age of the Spirit (e.g., Harvey Cox, *The Future of Faith*; Leonardo Boff, *O Espírito Santo*). This pneumatological shift in theological studies responds in part to centuries of epistemic, ethical, and theological neglect of the Spirit as a primary historical agent in the context of the hegemonic West. Until recently, in the Westernized sectors of the academy, the Spirit of God has been regulated and consigned to the suspicious areas of esoteric (noumenal) experiences and popular religion as illustrated by marginal communities of the

Global South, such as those found in the Renewal movements. Of course, these are perceptions funded by the epistemic machine of the hegemonic West, that is, by colonial modernity with its instrumental (i.e., Enlightenment) rationality and occidentalizing ethics.

It has taken about five centuries for people of the Global South to have access to literary channels such as this to express independent theological thoughts. In this regard, the level of achievement of a work such as *Sculptor Spirit* must be noticed. First of all, it dares to name and portray the Spirit in fresh ways from within the canonical imagination of Western sources. It does it with a muscular pastoral conscience that maintains a robust conversation with patristic sources and Martin Luther, thereby educating the illiterate modern mind that tends to be dismissive of premodern wisdom. Secondly, it utilizes a contextual (and contested) methodology, namely, Spirit Christology, to document how sanctification has been and may be experienced by various communities within and outside the West (i.e., renewal, dramatic, sacrificial, hospitality, and devotional models). This is significant when we realize that in the West, models, paradigms, categorizations, and methodologies have been normative and exclusive parts of the Western epistemic machine. Every model proposed combines scholarship, contextuality, and practicality. Finally, it shows its independent contribution to the field of practical theology/pneumatology by critically embracing classical postures of Western traditions and demonstrating how communities of the Global South and millennials, for instance, may embed sanctification. In short, what is fresh and transformational in *Sculptor Spirit* is the place from *where* classical traditions are accessed, namely, from another social location that bears witness to the Spirit of Life (Moltmann), the Wild Child of the Trinity (Zaida Maldonado Perez), and the Decolonial Healer of the American Global South (García-Johnson).

Sánchez has been able to actualize his vision of exploring the implications of Spirit Christology and a practical theology of sanctification to foster Christian practices within the canonical imagination of the West. His most obvious contribution is the interlacing of multiple normative voices in West under the logic of practicing communities of the margin. This shows one of the transformations happening nowadays to Western approaches, as we have noticed, the reassessment of theoretical resources and the rerouting of praxis in the service of ecclesial practice, holistic liberation, and multidimensional sanctification. Perhaps because of Sánchez's own social location, we begin to anticipate, in his work, new pathways that stand before, across, and beyond our Westernized Christian imagination. We are left with the desire for more witnessing to the sculpting activity of the Spirit of Life and more models of the sanctified life beyond white-male-Western-modern-colonial normativity.

Come, Holy Spirit!

# PREFACE

In an often-quoted statement on the need for revitalizing the doctrine of the Trinity in the Western church, Karl Rahner argues that "despite their orthodox confession of the Trinity, Christians are, in their practical life, almost 'mere monotheists.'"[1] By a "mere monotheist," Rahner means a Christian who thinks and speaks about "God" in general, with little or no thought or mention of any of the *persons* of the Trinity in particular. When hearing such a person praying to, speaking for, or teaching about "God," one is left to wonder *who* exactly this "God" is and what this "God" will *do* in our lives. Rahner's point is that without a trinitarian anchor or narrative in place, answers to such questions are not only elusive in some theoretical sense but also unsatisfying from an existential point of view. As Catherine LaCugna observes, the doctrine of the Trinity becomes a second thought, buried under the abstract and esoteric idea of a "generic Godhead," instead of the tri-personal story of the Father, the Son, and the Holy Spirit acting for us in creation and new creation.[2] Rahner's indictment of "mere monotheism" in the West remains a salutary warning: "We must be willing to admit that, should the doctrine of the Trinity have to be dropped as false, the major part of religious literature could well remain virtually unchanged."[3]

---

[1]Karl Rahner, *The Trinity*, trans. Joseph Donceel (New York: Crossroad, 1998), 10-11.

[2]"The mission of the Son to become incarnate belongs properly to the Son as Son. The Spirit is the one sent to make the creature holy. Each of these is a *proprium*, an identifying characteristic of a unique person, and as such cannot be appropriated. The Father's role in *sending* the Son and Spirit belongs to the Father alone and cannot indifferently be appropriated either to the Son or Spirit *or* to a generic Godhead." Catherine Mowry LaCugna, *God for Us: The Trinity and Christian Life* (San Francisco: HarperCollins, 1991), 100.

[3]Rahner, *Trinity*, 10-11.

Much has happened since Rahner wrote those words. On the positive side, repeated calls for a revival of trinitarian theology have yielded so many treatises on the Holy Spirit that the third person can no longer be called "the Cinderella of Western theology."[4] Yet linking descriptions of the Spirit to everyday life has remained a challenge for theologians. Heribert Mühlen warned of a "practical atheism" of the third person of the Trinity, namely, a formal belief in the Spirit's divinity that is accompanied by a practical denial of the experience of the Spirit.[5] A popular book on the Holy Spirit claims that "if we woke up tomorrow and discovered that it is not true the Holy Spirit lives inside of us, most likely our lives wouldn't look much different."[6] Be that as it may, and acknowledging the need to "test the spirits to see whether they are from God" (1 Jn 4:1) when dealing with spiritual experiences and claims, the challenge remains to articulate a theology of the Holy Spirit in a trinitarian key that is deeply linked to people's lives.

Two moves in Spirit (and spirituality) talk are to be avoided. One danger is adopting a "Spirit only" non-trinitarian approach to life, which sees the Holy Spirit as a "free agent" acting in isolation from the Father and the Son. Such an isolationist view severs the inseparable connection between the Spirit and the Word, failing to see the Spirit at work in our lives in light of biblical narratives bearing witness to God's commands and his promises in Christ.[7] Another danger lies in holding a more subtle "Spirit void" move that reduces the Holy Spirit to a past idea disconnected from us rather than seeing it as a living person who shapes us to make us God's own

---

[4]Jürgen Moltmann, *The Spirit of Life: A Universal Affirmation* (Minneapolis: Fortress, 1992), 1. Relatively recent works available in English include Michael Welker, *God the Spirit*, trans. John F. Hoffmeyer (Minneapolis: Fortress, 1994); Clark H. Pinnock, *Flame of Love: A Theology of the Holy Spirit* (Downers Grove, IL: InterVarsity Press, 1996); Yves Congar, *I Believe in the Holy Spirit*, trans. David Smith, 3 vols. (New York: Crossroad, 1997); Kilian McDonnell, *The Other Hand of God: The Holy Spirit as the Universal Touch and Goal* (Collegeville, MN: Liturgical Press, 2003); Sergius Bulgakov, *The Comforter*, trans. Boris Jakim (Grand Rapids: Eerdmans, 2004); Amos Yong, *The Spirit Poured Out on All Flesh: Pentecostalism and the Possibility of Global Theology* (Grand Rapids: Baker Academic, 2005); David Coffey, *"Did You Receive the Holy Spirit When You Believed?": Some Basic Questions for Pneumatology* (Milwaukee: Marquette University Press, 2005); Eugene F. Rogers Jr., *After the Spirit: A Constructive Pneumatology from Resources Outside the Modern West* (Grand Rapids: Eerdmans, 2005); Anthony C. Thiselton, *The Holy Spirit—In Biblical Teaching, Through the Centuries, and Today* (Grand Rapids: Eerdmans, 2013); Leonardo Boff, *Come, Holy Spirit: Inner Fire, Giver of Life and Comforter of the Poor* (Maryknoll, NY: Orbis, 2015); and Myk Habets, ed., *Third Article Theology: A Pneumatological Dogmatics* (Minneapolis: Fortress, 2016).

[5]Heribert Mühlen, *Espíritu. Carisma. Liberación. La renovación de la fe cristiana*, trans. Luis Artigas, 2nd ed. (Salamanca: Secretariado Trinitario, 1975), 53-54.

[6]Francis Chan and Danae Yankoski, *Forgotten God: Reversing Our Tragic Neglect of the Holy Spirit* (Colorado Springs: David C. Cook, 2009), 34-35.

[7]Leopoldo A. Sánchez M., "Pneumatology: Key to Understanding the Trinity," in *Who Is God?: In the Light of the Lutheran Confessions*, ed. John A. Maxfield (St. Louis: Luther Academy), 124-27.

holy people now.[8] Such a static view of the Spirit reduces spirituality to an experience attained only by a few historic spiritual heroes in some golden age or to a humanly conceived and enacted way of life attained in the present without reference to God's ongoing work in the world. The mysterious wind of the Spirit surely "blows where it wishes" (Jn 3:8), but it still remains the Spirit of the Father who rests on the Son (Jn 1:33) and whom the Son breathes on his disciples (20:22). Spirit talk must embrace its organic christological and ecclesial trajectories.

So what is the Holy Spirit up to in our lives? The question is deceptively simple to pose, and answers abound. In theological circles, descriptions of life in the Spirit often come under the heading of sanctification, holiness, or the Christian life. Although much has been written to describe biblically and theologically what sanctification entails, Gerhard Forde has noted that it is one thing to explain holiness and its goals but quite another to be made holy and live by faith in that reality. As Forde puts it, appealing to Romans 6, "The Word does not merely tell *about* sanctification; it sanctifies through its power to end the old and raise up the new."[9] Otherwise stated, it is one thing to talk *about* the Spirit as "an object of faith, an article of the creed, or a church dogma."[10] It is another thing "to *do* the Holy Spirit" to hearers of the Word, bringing them into the story of Christ through proclamation and teaching.[11] As secondary or explanatory discourse, theological descriptions of sanctification have their place, but these do not yet shape or form Christians to become certain kinds of persons—indeed, holy persons. For that to happen, a move needs to be made from secondary to primary discourse, from explication to formation.[12]

Like a sculptor who molds a mass into its desired shape, the Spirit's sanctifying work lies in shaping Christ's image in persons. A theology of the Spirit strives at fostering the sanctified life in others by making them participants by grace in the

---

[8]Sánchez, "Pneumatology," 127-29. To distinguish properly between the persons of the Holy Spirit and the Son, I will use neuter pronouns for the former throughout the book.

[9]Gerhard O. Forde, "A Lutheran Response," in *Christian Spirituality: Five Views of Sanctification*, ed. Donald L. Alexander (Downers Grove, IL: InterVarsity Press, 1988), 122. Forde's argument in his response to the Wesleyan view here is echoed in his assessment of other essays, namely, that the use of language (even biblical language!) about sanctification ceases to be helpful when such language subtly displaces the biblical witness to the Holy Spirit's work of making the Christian holy in favor of the Christian's response to the Holy Spirit's action in him.

[10]Sánchez, "Pneumatology," 123.

[11]Sánchez, "Pneumatology," 122.

[12]On the distinction between proclamation and explanation, or primary and secondary discourse, see Gerhard O. Forde, *Theology Is for Proclamation* (Minneapolis: Fortress, 1990), 1-9.

Spirit's manifold ways of forming persons after the "image" or "likeness" of Christ (Rom 8:29; 2 Cor 3:18). The one Spirit works in many ways. Holiness and holy persons are not homogeneous realities. Reflecting on 1 Corinthians 12, Cyril of Jerusalem, an early church father known for his teaching, speaks beautifully of the grace of the Spirit in the saints, which like water from heaven falls equally on all created things while adapting uniquely to the color of each recipient.

> For one fountain watereth the whole of Paradise, and one and the same rain comes down upon all the world, yet it becomes white in the lily, and red in the rose, and purple in violets and hyacinths, and different and varied in each several kind: so it is one in the palmtree, and another in the vine, and all in all things; and yet is one in nature, not diverse from itself; for the rain does not change itself, and come down first as one thing, then as another, but adapting itself to the constitution of each thing which receives it, it becomes to each what is suitable. Thus also the Holy Ghost, being one, and of one nature, and indivisible, divides to each His grace, *according as He will*.[13]

There is not merely one way to describe what the Spirit accomplishes in us, but a diversity of configurations of Christlikeness that the Scriptures and theologians across time have bequeathed to us.[14] What approach to sanctification might be most conducive for mining the implications of this multidimensional action of the Spirit for people groups in North America who indicate a hunger for a spiritually compelling and meaningful life?

In this work, I argue that a Spirit Christology, which looks at the role of God's Spirit in Jesus' life and mission, provides a theological framework for articulating a models-based approach to sanctification that can assist pastors and church leaders to engage the spiritual hopes and struggles of neighbors in and outside the church, especially in a North American context. By Spirit Christology, I mean a trinitarian framework or lens that interprets created life in terms of God's action in Jesus, and through him on others, by the power of the Spirit.[15] An inquiry into the church's biblical and historic witness to the Spirit's role in Jesus and his saints yields a number of models of the sanctified life, each painting a unique picture of

---

[13]Cyril of Jerusalem, *Catechetical Lecture* 16.12 (*NPNF*[2] 7:118).

[14]Leopoldo A. Sánchez M., "Sculpting Christ in Us: Public Faces of the Spirit in God's World," in Habets, *Third Article Theology*, 297-318.

[15]Leopoldo A. Sánchez M., *Receiver, Bearer, and Giver of God's Spirit: Jesus' Life in the Spirit as a Lens for Theology and Life* (Eugene, OR: Pickwick, 2015).

how the Spirit forms Christ in persons. Due to their foundational use of pneumatology as a link between Christology and the life of the saints in a trinitarian context, I focus on images of Christlikeness in fourth-century church theologians Athanasius, Didymus the Blind, Cyril of Jerusalem, Basil of Caesarea, and Ambrose of Milan. Given that I am also writing shortly after the quincentenary of the Protestant Reformation, I explore how Martin Luther appropriated images of the sanctified life in his own teaching and preaching. Moreover, I engage a number of contemporary authors from various Christian traditions whose work can assist us in further describing and illustrating the sanctified life. I offer these theologians not to be exhaustive, but to give readers a taste of how a Spirit Christology opens a space for communicating what life in the Spirit looks like. Theologians, students of theology, pastors, and other church leaders from various church families are encouraged to dig into their own tradition's sources for similar or perhaps different pictures of life in the Spirit of Christ. Although I come from an evangelical perspective informed especially by the Lutheran tradition, the reader will recognize that my proposal engages and aims for an audience beyond that of my own ecclesial family.

For the purposes of my project, a model can be defined as a cohesive yet flexible account of life whose productivity for addressing certain questions or needs can be tested.[16] Accordingly, each model of the sanctified life in this book describes different aspects of the Spirit's work, finds its roots in various biblical narratives and sources in theological traditions past and present, and fosters particular spiritual practices or ways of being in the world today. Moreover, each model seeks to address particular issues in life such as the need for identity, reconciliation, security, purpose, community, belonging, and balance.

My investigation will focus on the formation dynamics of the Spirit of Christ at work in persons according to five models:

1. Renewal model (death and resurrection)
2. Dramatic model (vigilance and resistance)
3. Sacrificial model (service and sharing)

---

[16] Theologians have made use of a models-based approach in similar ways. For example, see Stephen B. Bevans, *Models of Contextual Theology*, rev. ed. (Maryknoll, NY: Orbis, 2002); Avery Dulles, *Models of the Church*, expanded ed. (New York: Doubleday, 1987); and Avery Dulles, *Models of Revelation* (New York: Doubleday, 1983).

4. Hospitality model (marginality and welcome)
5. Devotional model (work, rest, and play)

Although these models describe in their own ways what holiness looks like, no single model accounts for the totality of the Spirit's work in the lives of God's saints, either individually or collectively. Because models are porous and interactive in everyday life, people may resonate with themes across different models simultaneously or at different times in their life journeys. Nevertheless, as a starting point for ongoing reflection and conversation, these models are dealt with separately in order to assist pastors and other church leaders in their task of discerning and speaking to the spiritual needs and hopes of people in their churches and communities.

Can these models offer us a lens for awareness of our own spiritual condition at particular times in our lives and foster ways to grow more deeply in our trust in God and love of neighbor? Are these models helpful to inculcate in hearers of the Word a Spirit-shaped lived witness in the world that opens doors for conversations with North American neighbors about their spiritual struggles and aspirations? Moreover, do these models contribute ways of understanding what life in the Spirit and growth in sanctification entail? These are some of the questions the following work explores.

# ACKNOWLEDGMENTS

THE COMPLETION OF this project would not have been possible without the financial and moral support of institutions and individuals. I wish to acknowledge the Louisville Institute and its director, Dr. Edwin David Aponte, and the leadership staff he leads for partnering with Concordia Seminary by awarding me a prestigious Sabbatical Grant for Researchers, which allowed me to set one full year aside to complete the writing of this project. I also thank my fellow Louisville awardees who offered valuable feedback on my project and encouragement during an intensive winter seminar gathering.

I would like to express my thanks to Concordia Seminary, St. Louis, its former Provost, Dr. Jeff Kloha, its Systematic Theology Department chairman, Dr. Joel Okamoto, as well as Prof. Mark Kempff, my assistant at the Center for Hispanic Studies, for making it possible for me to have the blessing of an uninterrupted research sabbatical to complete this book. The partnership between Concordia Seminary and the Louisville Institute allowed me to spend some weeks for sustained writing at Vision of Peace in Pevely, Missouri. A word of thanks to the staff at Vision for their hospitality. A special word of appreciation goes to David McNutt, my editor at InterVarsity Press, for his counsel, encouragement, and assistance in bringing this manuscript to publication.

The ideas in this book have been tested over a number of years among diverse audiences, in different cultural settings and languages, and in different pedagogical formats. A significant amount of field testing took place among theologians, students of theology, pastors, and lay church workers through theological dialogues, presentations in lecture halls and conference rooms, workshops in church basements, pastoral and deaconess formation courses, and graduate-level seminars. Although they are too many to mention individually, I would like to thank all participants in these sessions over the years for their generous feedback. Their constructive criticism and, above all, their desire to find ways of making the Spirit and sanctification both a lively teaching and everyday reality in their lives and the lives of those entrusted to their care, has greatly nourished my spirit and helped me refine my arguments, particularly in terms of their application to the work of churches in North America. A special word of thanks to the managing editor of the *Concordia Journal* of Concordia Seminary for granting permission to use revised versions of previously published essays.

Last but certainly not least a special word of thanks to my wife, Tracy Lynn, and my children, Lucas Antonio and Ana Victoria, for allowing me to spend many hours in the completion of this work, often sacrificing their own time with me. I see in their unconditional and undeserved love for me a beautiful picture of the Spirit's work in their lives. I see in them the likeness of Christ the servant, who in teaching true discipleship to his followers reminded them that "the Son of Man came not to be served but to serve, and to give his life as a ransom for many" (Mk 10:45). Through their outpouring of love and support, and by sharing burdens and joys with me every day, Christ himself has come into my life in the persons of his precious saints by the power of his Spirit. And I rejoice in John's words, "If we love one another, God abides in us and his love is perfected in us. By this we know that we abide in him and he in us, because he has given us of his Spirit" (1 Jn 4:12-13).

# ABBREVIATIONS

*ANF* *The Ante-Nicene Fathers: Translations of the Fathers down to A.D. 325.* Edited by Alexander Roberts and James Donaldson. 10 vols. Peabody, MA: Hendrickson, 1994.

*BC* *The Book of Concord: The Confessions of the Evangelical Lutheran Church.* Edited by Robert Kolb and Timothy J. Wengert. Minneapolis: Fortress, 2000.

*Ap* Apology of the Augsburg Confession

*CA* The Augsburg Confession (Confessio Augustana)

*FC* Formula of Concord

*LC* Luther's Large Catechism

*SD* Solid Declaration of the Formula of Concord

*LW* *Luther's Works*. American Edition. Edited by Jaroslav Pelikan and Helmut T. Lehmann. 55 vols. Philadelphia: Muhlenberg and Fortress Press, St. Louis: Concordia, 1955–.

*NPNF* *Nicene and Post-Nicene Fathers*. Edited by Philip Schaff. 28 vols. Grand Rapids: Eerdmans, 1983–1987.

*ST* Thomas Aquinas, *Summa Theologiae: Latin Text and English Translation, Introductions, Notes, Appendices, Glossaries*. 61 vols. New York: McGraw-Hill, 1964–1980.

# INTRODUCTION

THAT THE SPIRIT is both *from* God and *for* us stands as a foundational theme in Scripture.[1] The Spirit who is from above, sent by God to rest on the Son, can also be received by humans below. The Spirit is holy and makes holy.[2] With one accord, early church fathers such as Athanasius, Didymus the Blind, Cyril of Jerusalem, Basil, and Ambrose taught that because the Spirit is from God and thus divine with the Father and the Son our human sharing in the Spirit by the grace of adoption effects nothing less than our sanctification or holiness. The Spirit who rests on the Son comes to dwell in us.

Athanasius notes that partaking of Christ (and God the Father) through the Spirit cannot refer to a sharing in a created reality, because "the anointing and the seal which is in us does not belong to the nature of created things which have been brought into existence, but to the Son, who joins us to the Father through the Spirit that is in him [i.e., in the Son]."[3] The Son gives the Spirit to us because

---

[1]"The Spirit of God is *Derived from Another*, that is, he is *One who can be Shared out among Participants*. . . . The importance of this will become clearer in the NT, when Paul stresses that our experience of the Holy Spirit is *derived from Christ*, just like our adoption as sons and daughters, and our dying and being raised with Christ. Resurrection in the NT is by the Holy Spirit (Rom 8:11), because we are in Christ. The OT pattern of participation in a derived Gift anticipates the possibility of this." Anthony C. Thiselton, *A Shorter Guide to the Holy Spirit: Bible, Doctrine, Experience* (Grand Rapids: Eerdmans, 2016), 10; cf. Anthony C. Thiselton, *The Holy Spirit—In Biblical Teaching, Through the Centuries, and Today*, 5, 18-21, 70-72.

[2]"With regard to God Himself, holiness implies transcendence, uniqueness, and purity. With regard to God's people, holiness means *being set apart for a relationship with the Holy One, to display his character in every sphere of life*." David Peterson, *Possessed by God: A New Testament Theology of Sanctification and Holiness* (Downers Grove, IL: InterVarsity Press, 1995), 24.

[3]Athanasius, *Letters to Serapion on the Holy Spirit* 1.24.2, in *Works on the Spirit: Athanasius the Great and Didymus the Blind*, trans. with an introduction and annotations by Mark DelCogliano, Andrew Radde-Gallwitz, and Lewis Ayres (Crestwood, NY: St. Vladimir's Seminary Press, 2011), 90; cf. Athanasius, *Letters*

he has the Spirit by nature as God, even as the Son also gives the Spirit to us through his flesh.

But what does life in the Spirit of God look like for the Son, and what does life through him look like for those who have shared in his Spirit by grace? Otherwise stated, what is the christological pattern of a life shaped by the Spirit of God? Or in more biblical terms, how are humans "conformed to the image of his [God's] Son" (Rom 8:29), who is himself "the image of God" (2 Cor 4:4)? How are new creatures "being transformed into the same image" through the Spirit's sanctifying work in their lives (2 Cor 3:18)? And what difference does it make to pursue this question for ourselves in general and in our North American context in particular?

## MAKING THE CASE: SPIRIT CHRISTOLOGY AND SANCTIFICATION

In this work, I argue that a Spirit Christology, which focuses on the role of God's Spirit in Jesus' life and mission, serves as a constructive framework for articulating a models-based approach to sanctification that can assist students of theology, pastors, and other church leaders in discerning and addressing some of the main spiritual concerns of various North American groups. There are at least two issues that call for this type of research.

First, the field of Spirit Christology has focused mainly on methodological questions related to Christology proper, trinitarian theology, and soteriology. With some exceptions, the field has been developed in a North Atlantic/European context around the question of whether Spirit Christology should be a replacement for, a parallel alternative to, or mutually complementary with the classic Logos-oriented (two natures) Christology of the ecumenical councils.[4] In terms of exploring the connections above, the field has already come of age.[5]

*to Serapion* 2.12.3, p. 121. See also Atanasio, *Epístolas a Serapión sobre el Espíritu Santo*, trans. Carmelo Granado (Madrid: Editorial Ciudad Nueva, 2007), I, 24, 2, p. 107; cf. Atanasio, *Epístolas*, III, 3.2, p. 15.

[4]For a summary and proposal, see Cornelis van der Kooi, "On the Identity of Jesus Christ," in *Third Article Theology*, ed. Myk Habets (Minneapolis: Fortress, 2016), 193-206. The same methodological concern defines significantly the work of authors across theological traditions writing in a North American context, such as Ralph Del Colle, *Christ and the Spirit: Spirit-Christology in Trinitarian Perspective* (New York: Oxford University Press, 1994); Sammy Alfaro, *Divino Compañero: Toward a Hispanic Pentecostal Christology* (Eugene, OR: Pickwick, 2010); and Leopoldo A. Sánchez M., *Receiver, Bearer, and Giver of God's Spirit* (Eugene, OR: Pickwick, 2015).

[5]"This turn to Spirit Christology in a robust Trinitarian context is welcome and has produced an increasing amount of suggestive and significant works. However, it is also, I suggest, a discipline come of age, and with that, it is poised to move from its preoccupation with definition and methodology—that is, with prolegomena—to constructive and systematic integration." Myk Habets, "Prolegomenon," in Habets, *Third Article Theology*, 14.

However, there is a general consensus among scholars working in Spirit Christology that this area of study has yet to bear its fruits more fully in tackling questions related to more immediately practical or existential concerns, including the areas of spirituality and sanctification.[6] Although accounts of spirituality and the implications of pneumatology for the Christian life are many and varied, the use of a Spirit Christology as a theological lens for engaging these areas remains largely unexplored.[7]

A number of North American authors have begun to assess the usefulness of a Spirit Christology for dealing with practices such as proclamation and prayer and issues ranging from social justice to interreligious dialogue.[8] However, the field has yet to interact significantly with the growing number of studies in spirituality and religion among rising demographics in North America such as the millennial generation (born ca. 1981–2001), the religiously unaffiliated (or "Nones"), and groups such as the US Hispanic population, engaging their understanding of and interest in spiritual questions from a Christian perspective.[9] My project seeks to contribute to this largely neglected trajectory in the field.

---

[6]In one of his theses for developing a third article theology (TAT), Habets includes the area of sanctification: "TAT emphasizes the sanctifying work of the Spirit, who moves believers into further holiness or christification—thus it is existentially viable and apologetically effective in today's postmodern milieu." Habets, "Prolegomenon," 18. In the same volume, see Joseph McGarry, "Formed by the Spirit: A Third Article Theology of Christian Spirituality," 283-96.

[7]For a historical survey of spirituality, see Cheslyn Jones, Geoffrey Wainwright, and Edward Yarnold, eds., *The Study of Spirituality* (New York: Oxford University Press, 1986). At times, pneumatology covers aspects of the Spirit's work in the believer such as forgiving guilt, enabling prayer, and witnessing in word and deed. As an example, see W. Curry Mavis, *The Holy Spirit in the Christian Life* (Grand Rapids: Baker Books, 1977). Other times, a theology of sanctification is framed around a broad thematic locus such as grace. See Kent Eilers and Kyle C. Strobel, eds., *Sanctified by Grace: A Theology of the Christian Life* (New York: Bloomsbury T&T Clark, 2014). Such treatments do not yet deal with how a Spirit Christology in particular shapes or advances discussions on the spiritual life.

[8]On proclamation and prayer, see Sánchez, *Receiver, Bearer, and Giver of God's Spirit*, 181-218; on culture and experience, social justice, and interreligious dialogue, see Del Colle, *Christ and the Spirit*, 195-216; on nonviolence, contentment and sharing, and racial unity, see Andréa Snavely, *Life in the Spirit: A Post-Constantinian and Trinitarian Account of the Christian Life* (Eugene, OR: Pickwick, 2015), 154-89; on liberative praxis vis-à-vis the Hispanic Pentecostal experience of marginality, see Alfaro, *Divino Compañero*; on interreligious dialogue with the Jewish tradition, see Michael E. Lodahl, *Shekinah/Spirit: Divine Presence in Jewish and Christian Religion* (Mahwah, NY: Paulist, 1992).

[9]As an example, consider some of the Pew Research Center demographic reports available on the subject: "U.S. Public Becoming Less Religious," November 3, 2015, www.pewforum.org/2015/11/03/u-s-public-becoming-less-religious; "The Shifting Religious Identity of Latinos in the United States," May 7, 2014, www.pewforum.org/2014/05/07/the-shifting-religious-identity-of-latinos-in-the-united-states; "'Nones' on the Rise," October 9, 2012, www.pewforum.org/2012/10/09/nones-on-the-rise; and "Changing Faiths: Latinos and the Transformation of American Religion," April 25, 2007,

Second, the theology of sanctification has developed mostly around an apologetic tone and orientation, inquiring into how sanctification relates to justification and grace and sorting out the proper tension of divine agency vis-à-vis human response in holiness talk.[10] Within these parameters, authors reflect considerably on the implications of the doctrine in relation to the reality of sin (old self) in the life of the believer (new self), the Word (including law and gospel, sacraments) and faith as means of sanctification, and at times the place of the theological virtues (faith, hope, and love) and the Holy Spirit in the life of the saints.

With some exceptions, what is lacking in the literature is a multidimensional account of sanctification or holiness that does not merely argue *about* life in the Spirit, but invites hearers of the Word to be brought *into* stories of the Spirit in God's economy of salvation that in turn address some of their spiritual yearnings, needs, and struggles. Although the apologetic approach has its place and benefits, it often has a hard time setting the stage for painting vivid pictures of what holiness looks like and fostering spiritual practices. Still, there are some authors who have attempted to bridge this gap between the *what* and the *how* of holiness either in the literature on sanctification itself or by moving toward related and broader areas of inquiry such as Christian spirituality and the spiritual disciplines.[11] I

www.pewforum.org/2007/04/25/changing-faiths-latinos-and-the-transformation-of-american-religion-2.

[10]See Donald L. Alexander, ed., *Christian Spirituality: Five Views of Sanctification* (Downers Grove, IL: InterVarsity Press, 1988), which offers Lutheran (Forde), Reformed (Ferguson), Wesleyan (Wood), Pentecostal (Spittler), and Contemplative (Hinson) views; and Melvin E. Dieter, ed., *Five Views on Sanctification* (Grand Rapids: Zondervan, 1987), which presents Wesleyan (Dieter), Reformed (Hoekema), Pentecostal (Horton), Keswick (Spittler), and Augustinian-Dispensational (McQuilkin) accounts; for a Roman Catholic treatise, see Antonio Royo Marín, *Teología de la perfección Cristiana* (Madrid: BAC, 2012); for other Lutheran approaches, see Oswald Bayer, *Living by Faith: Justification and Sanctification*, trans. Geoffrey W. Bromiley (Grand Rapids: Eerdmans, 2003); and Adolf Köberle, *The Quest for Holiness: A Biblical, Historical and Systematic Investigation*, trans. John C. Mattes (Minneapolis: Augsburg, 1938; Evansville, IN: Ballast, 1999); for Reformed contributions, see *Sanctification: Explorations in Theology and Practice*, ed. Kelly M. Kapic (Downers Grove, IL: InterVarsity Press, 2014); for a Wesleyan approach, see Thomas Jay Oord and Michael Lodahl, *Relational Holiness: Responding to the Call of Love* (Kansas City, MO: Beacon Hill, 2005).

[11]In terms of pastoral and homiletical reflections within the theme of sanctification, see Kelly M. Kapic, "Faith, Hope, and Love: A Theological Meditation on Suffering and Sanctification," in Kapic, *Sanctification*, 212-31; Peter Moore, "Sanctification Through Preaching: How John Chrysostom Preached for Personal Transformation," in Kapic, *Sanctification*, 251-68; and Jonathan W. Rusnak, "Shaped by the Spirit," *LOGIA* 24, no. 3 (2015): 15-20; for treatises on Christian spirituality or spiritual disciplines, see Frank C. Senn, ed., *Protestant Spiritual Traditions* (New York: Paulist, 1986), which includes Lutheran (Senn), Reformed (Hageman), Anabaptist (Erb), Anglican (Marshall), Puritan (Hinson), Pietist (Weborg), and Methodist (Lowes Watson) views; see also Ronald Rolheiser, *The Holy Longing: The Search for a Christian Spirituality* (New York: Doubleday, 1999); Gene Edward Veith, *The Spirituality of the Cross: The Way of the First*

welcome these contributions. Although my goal is not to offer an account of spirituality or the spiritual disciplines, the models of sanctification I draw from a Spirit Christology will at times intersect with some of the themes and questions raised in those works. My hope is to enrich the broader conversation already going on concerning the nature and purpose of the Christian life, doing so specifically from a Spirit Christology angle.

## A MODELS-BASED APPROACH TO THE SANCTIFIED LIFE

Through a models-based Spirit-oriented approach to the sanctified life, my project seeks to integrate and complement the common conceptual and theoretical approach in sanctification studies with a more devotional and narrative orientation and tone.[12] At its best, the church's theological legacy includes both concept and image, the philosophical and the rhetorical, explanation and proclamation, study and prayer. My overall intention is to help the reader appreciate the interaction between these modes of theological reflection and assist them in moving from secondary to primary theology, from explication to formation, from description to participation.

Over the years, I have looked into the potential implications of a Spirit Christology and a theology of sanctification for fostering Christian practices such as proclamation, missions, prayer, justice, vocation, and ecumenism.[13] In

---

*Evangelicals* (St. Louis: Concordia, 1999); John H. Kieschnick, *The Best Is Yet to Come: 7 Doors of Spiritual Growth* (Friendswood, TX: Baxter, 2006); and Philip Nation, *Habits for Our Holiness: How the Spiritual Disciplines Grow Us Up, Draw Us Together, and Send Us Out* (Chicago: Moody, 2016); on the missional implications of spirituality and holiness, see Nathan A. Finn and Keith S. Whitfield, eds., *Spirituality for the Sent: Casting a New Vision for the Missional Church* (Downers Grove, IL: InterVarsity Press, 2017), and Andy Johnson, *Holiness and the* Missio Dei (Eugene, OR: Cascade, 2016).

[12] I am aware that my systematic approach to the sanctified life tends to place biblical themes on holiness in a broader pneumatic framework, and thus can be construed as making sanctification—as an exegete has wryly stated—"the basket into which every theme related to Christian life and growth has been placed." Peterson, *Possessed by God*, 13. Notwithstanding the need for a biblically informed theology of sanctification, my response is simply that a *theological* interpretation of biblical themes, as well as its constructive *use* in response to various areas of inquiry (e.g., spirituality in North America), cannot be taken for granted and remains an important task for the systematic theologian. In that sense, sanctification or holiness must be interpreted within the wider scriptural witness to the Spirit's work in creation and new creation and in conversation with the spiritual questions of people today.

[13] See Leopoldo A. Sánchez M., "God Against Us and for Us: Preaching Jesus in the Spirit," *Word & World* 24, no. 2 (2003): 134-45; "A Missionary Theology of the Holy Spirit: The Father's Anointing of Christ and Its Implications for the Church in Mission," *Missio Apostolica* 14, no. 1 (2006): 28-40; "Praying to God the Father in the Spirit: Reclaiming the Church's Participation in the Son's Prayer Life," *Concordia Journal* 32, no. 3 (2006): 274-95; "Individualism, Indulgence, and the Mind of Christ: Making Room for the Neighbor and the Father," in *The American Mind Meets the Mind of Christ*, ed. Robert Kolb (St. Louis: Concordia

*Teología de la santificación*, I began to explore more earnestly the idea of a models-based approach to sanctification grounded in a Spirit Christology.[14] The impetus for an expanded work in this area in the English language follows from many interactions with students of theology, pastors, church leaders, and scholars who continuously ask for ways to link sanctification not only to Christian growth in faith and love but also to Christian practices such as preaching and teaching, prayer and worship, spiritual care, mercy and justice, vocation, and missional engagement with individuals and communities. In preliminary field-testing of the ideas laid out in this book, the overwhelming majority of audiences have reacted positively to the assumption behind our models-based approach, namely, that there is no homogeneous way to describe holiness.[15] Instead, sanctification stands as a rich, complex, multidimensional reality that Christians experience differently at various points in time, depending on the spiritual struggles they are going through in life and their spiritual needs and hopes.

Models are broad yet cohesive in scope. On the one hand, a model tends to be more encompassing or comprehensive than any single biblical narrative or theological source describing life in the Spirit. A medley of pictures, themes, and life applications adds to the richness and complexity of each model. On the other hand, the variety of images and motifs a model provides requires interpreting through a theological foundation—in my case, a Spirit Christology—that can bring focus to their potential usefulness in articulating a relatively

Seminary Press, 2010), 54-66; and "More Promise Than Ambiguity: Pneumatological Christology as a Model for Ecumenical Engagement," in *Critical Issues in Ecclesiology: Essays in Honor of Carl E. Braaten*, ed. Alberto García and Susan K. Wood (Grand Rapids: Eerdmans, 2011), 189-214.

[14]See Leopoldo A. Sánchez M., *Teología de la santificación: La espiritualidad del cristiano* (St. Louis: Concordia, 2013), 75-147, where I present baptismal, dramatic, and eucharistic models of sanctification. A brief summary of these models in English followed in "Life in the Spirit of Christ: Models of Sanctification as Sacramental Pneumatology," *LOGIA* 22, no. 3 (2013), which was revised as the final chapter of *Receiver, Bearer, and Giver of God's Spirit*, 219-37. More recently, I began to explore a hospitality model in "Sculpting Christ in Us," 315-17.

[15]Similarly, McGarry has argued that the theological interpretation of the content of biblical metaphors dealing with the Spirit's work of christoformation (such as being imitators of Christ, being clothed with Christ, having the mind of Christ, Christ being formed in us, and following Christ) is open for discussion and elaboration. McGarry does offer the unique ancient Near Eastern interpretation of the "image of God," signifying the human representation of God on earth, as the best theological content in the Hebrew Bible behind the New Testament idea of Christlikeness. Yet his observations suggest the freedom to lay out various expressions of this content while remaining flexible in the options offered. This approach has an affinity with what we seek to do in our models-based approach to the sanctified life. See McGarry, "Formed by the Spirit," 293-96.

cohesive vision of the spiritual life one might embody or employ to address spiritual concerns.

My goal is not to develop a full pneumatology, but to show how a Spirit Christology can yield some models of sanctification. Such accounts correspond to ways in which the Holy Spirit conforms humans to the image and likeness of Christ. Within that narrower scope, my models still aim at a degree of comprehensiveness without becoming totalizing or prescriptive. They strive to become something like quilts that, in seeking to portray a theme or idea, reflect many colors and evoke a variety of images. A particular model's description of life in the Spirit may resonate with some people and not with others. In everyday life, models do not stand alone but are complementary. People may especially identify with aspects and narratives of a particular model, but they may also see a combination of motifs from various models operating in their lives at once. Given their permeability and flexibility, models can accommodate many types of experiences. Such dynamic comingling or interweaving among models reflects the complexity and richness of the spiritual life itself. And yet, given the Spirit's freedom to work in manifold ways, the models should not be seen as inflexible categories that reduce or domesticate the third person's sphere of operation. Indeed, the Spirit could work in other ways outside the scope of these models, but the ones offered in this work give us a solid point on which to build.

My models-based approach to the sanctified life seeks to assist North American pastors in understanding their own spiritual conditions and those of their flocks at particular moments in time, so that through the pastoral application of God's Word all are cared for and encouraged to grow in their love for God and neighbor. Moreover, by showing how the models' narratives and images intersect with the spiritual hopes and needs expressed by North American neighbors, my project seeks to test or discern their capacity for interacting with and addressing these neighbors' interests in religious questions or in a spiritually informed life. By assisting Christians in their own grasp of and growth in the sanctified life, my hope is that they will be able to dialogue with, model or embody, and invite others with spiritual questions into the Christian story.

## OUTLINE OF CHAPTERS

Given the interest of North Americans in spirituality,[16] church leaders can benefit from a theological work that can assist them in interpreting and engaging their own and their neighbors' spiritual conditions from the vantage point of a robust Christian framework with the capacity to foster discussions about spirituality and nurture spiritual practices. In chapter one, I argue that the field of Spirit Christology offers a contemporary theological framework with the capacity to link discourse on the Spirit with the spiritual life. Laying out main themes, methodological contributions, and contemporary trajectories of a Spirit Christology, with special attention to North American authors working from a trinitarian framework, the chapter explores what the literature on Spirit Christology offers to reflection on the shape of the Christian life. The chapter sets the stage for the need to develop more explicitly a theology of the sanctified life on the basis of a Spirit Christology.

In chapter two, I argue that, given their classic exploration of human participation in the Spirit whom the Son bears and gives to others, early church theologians such as Irenaeus and Athanasius offer the foundations and building blocks for the development of a Spirit Christology. Reflecting on the Spirit's presence in the Son, while preserving the Son's divine identity and incarnation, these theologians show ways in which a pneumatic account of Christ can be pursued in a trinitarian key. These theologians also reflect on the significance of the Spirit's presence in Christ for our sanctification. In doing so, they not only use apologetic language, but offer a rich variety of pictures of the Christian life, giving us a sense of the devotional and catechetical impulse in their theology. In preparation for articulating a more illustrative approach to the sanctified life, readers are invited to journey along with these voices of the past and see the array of images they employ to describe the mystery of the Spirit's presence in Christ and his saints. The chapter will offer a historico-theological foundation for our models-based approach.

The next five chapters lay out a comprehensive, though not exhaustive, models-based approach to the Spirit's work of sanctification, with attention to the Christlike pattern of such work in the lives of the saints. In this section as a whole,

[16]"Americans may be getting less religious, but feelings of spirituality are on the rise," January 21, 2016, www.pewresearch.org/fact-tank/2016/01/21/americans-spirituality.

I argue that a Spirit Christology yields at least five portrayals of life in the Spirit of Christ, namely, renewal, dramatic, sacrificial, hospitality, and devotional models of the sanctified life. Each model finds inspiration in particular biblical narratives as well as in catechetical, homiletical, and theological sources in Christian traditions.

To illustrate each model, I will explore images from fourth-century church theologians, who combine apologetic and devotional modes of theological expression in their portrayals of the mystery of the Spirit in Christ's life. Moreover, given that I am pursuing the writing of this project as a Lutheran theologian and am doing so soon after the Christian world's commemoration of the quincentenary of the Protestant Reformation, I will look at ways in which Martin Luther's depictions of the Christian life in his teaching and preaching share an affinity with the models. To be sure, the voices I use as examples of each model in the next five chapters are not intended to be limiting but rather illustrative and evocative of the possibilities of the use of a Spirit Christology for reflection on the sanctified life. Therefore, readers are encouraged to think about other voices from other times in Christian history and in their own theological traditions who might illumine further these models or perhaps offer new ones.

I will show how each of the models lends itself to dealing with certain issues in the Christian life and how each model fosters certain spiritual practices or ways of being in the world. In each of the five chapters, I will also test the productivity of these models for dealing with some theological questions that arise in a theology of the Christian life, such as the relationship between justification and sanctification and the nature of the Spirit's agency in relation to the saints' response to the Spirit's impulses in their lives. To accomplish the aforementioned goals, I interact with contemporary authors, including North Americans, whose work suggests a certain embodiment of each of the models.

Chapter three presents sanctification as God's *renewal* of the old self into the newness of Christ or as the Spirit's work of conforming us to Christ in his death and resurrection through a life of daily repentance that seeks reconciliation with God and neighbor. Chapter four sees the Christian life in *dramatic* terms, as a struggle in the wilderness, or as the Spirit's work of making us vigilant, resistant, and resilient children of God in the midst of spiritual attacks through prayer, meditation on the Word of God, and other disciplines. Chapter five approaches sanctification through *sacrificial* language, focusing on the Holy Spirit's work of shaping us after Christ's servanthood and forming us as an interdependent community where Christ's joys and burdens are shared among brothers and sisters. Chapter six looks at the sanctified life through the lens of *hospitality*, highlighting the Spirit's leading of the saints to reach out and extend the hand of welcome to marginalized and often forgotten neighbors. Chapter seven presents the Christian life in *devotional* terms—namely, as a participation in the rhythm of movement and repose for which we were created as stewards of God's creation. Here the Spirit shapes us after Christ's life of labor and prayer, bringing us into a sharing in God's gifts of work, rest, and play.

Despite doom-and-gloom scenarios about the end of religion, spirituality, or even Christianity in North America, studies done by sociologists of religion, demographers, generational studies gurus, as well authors who interpret such data for churches, exhibit a great degree of interest in spirituality among North Americans. This is the case even among groups such as the Nones or religiously unaffiliated. Descendants of Global South peoples such as US Hispanics also show interest in spiritual practices. As an example, millennials in both of the aforementioned groups value a spirituality that, while at times suspicious of institutional religion, is open to a socially conscious and active form of belief. By taking stock of these studies, which quite often include interviewees with various degrees of involvement in Christian denominations, church leaders can hear anew the spiritual cries of persons who compose various demographics in the US. These persons include Christians and other neighbors with little to no connection to the church.

In chapter eight, I test the missional usefulness of the models of sanctification for engaging the diversity of attitudes toward faith and religion represented in the aforementioned studies, focusing on how each model can address, to some degree, a number of spiritual yearnings and needs that surface across the literature. In short, North Americans are looking for right relations and reconciliation, security or safety in a broken world, purpose or meaning in life, a socially active faith that makes a difference in the world, community and interdependence, hospitality and belonging, reaching out to vulnerable neighbors and strangers, and a healthy lifestyle or rhythm that balances work and leisure. I argue that a Spirit Christology and the models of sanctification it yields offer church leaders compelling narratives that have the capacity to engage both Christians and non-Christians in conversations about the spiritual life through dialogue, modeling, and invitation.

By the end of my constructive proposal, my hope is that the reader will see how a models-based approach to sanctification offers a resource for pastors, preachers, teachers, spiritual caregivers, and others to base spirituality talk on the story of God's multidimensional action in persons through the Spirit of Christ. The reader should also see how a models-based approach can assist theologians, pastors, students of theology, and other church workers in illustrating what life in the Spirit looks like, not only personally in the interior life but publicly in social networks, thus inviting people to reflect on and embody forms of life in the Spirit. Our intention is to move readers from a merely apologetic and conceptual approach that talks *about* sanctification toward a deeper appreciation and desire for the Spirit's *forming* of persons to be or become holy in the world.

## A FINAL NOTE TO THE READER

Although the arguments in this book and its development of models of sanctification from a Spirit Christology can be read successively from beginning to end, readers must not feel compelled to do so. This book is neither a novel nor a how-to manual requiring a progressive reading of its contents. It is more like a catalogue of testimonies and a toolbox of resources for thinking about the pastoral and missional implications of a theology of sanctification grounded in a Spirit Christology. The reader should feel free to skip around. Those interested in the field of Spirit Christology are welcome to begin with chapter one, which at times does use technical language depending on the author discussed. Others with a greater interest in the church fathers' building blocks toward the development of a trinitarian Spirit Christology can begin in chapter two and then move to hear their voices as they describe various images of life in the Spirit in chapters three through seven. Still others with an interest in the Protestant Reformation's contribution to models of the Christian life may skip to Martin Luther's development of narratives of the sanctified life in chapters three through seven.

Some readers may have a pressing desire to go right to the end of the book in chapter eight, take stock of the spiritual yearnings of North Americans laid out in the literature, and see how a models-based approach to the sanctified life can foster conversations about spirituality with our neighbors. To better grasp the final chapter, one could benefit from at least a basic familiarity with the five models presented in the book, which readers can find by either looking at the brief introduction to each chapter, where a model's basic definition is laid out or, for those who are more visual, by checking out the table summarizing the main characteristics of each model after the conclusion of the book (see appendix). Those interested in the implications of each model for a theology of sanctification in relationship to justification, the Word of God (including law and gospel), the believer's growth in holiness, good works, or the problem of sin, death, and the devil, may want to go both to the final application section of each model and to the conclusion of the book where such matters are variously addressed.

The structure of each chapter dealing with a model includes a biblical section, a catechetical section that focuses on patristic voices and on Luther as an example of a Reformation voice, and a final section on contemporary applications of the model. As I stated earlier, my choice of early church fathers follows from their foundational role in linking the Holy Spirit's presence in Christ to human participation in the Spirit's sanctification and in their doing so in a way that is not only rich in theological concepts but also in catechetical images. Besides other reasons already mentioned, my focus on Luther comes from an interest in showing how his depictions of the Christian life are often in continuity with earlier patristic traditions, offering us an important Reformation source for reflection on the sanctified life grounded in the greater tradition. Moreover, given the typical criticism that Luther's teaching on justification leaves little to no room for sanctification, I hope to show that his understanding, narratives, and images of the Christian life remain an untapped evangelical resource for teaching sanctification and reflecting on its implications for spiritual care and missional engagement.[17]

Keeping in mind the threefold structure of each chapter dealing with a model, the reader could approach the book devotionally by first delving into models of the sanctified life and the biblical narratives that inspire each of them and then perhaps skipping to the very end of each chapter to see how each model addresses different issues in our lives. Since there is always room for learning from those saints who have gone before us, I highly recommend returning to the church fathers in the second section at some point in the reading of the book. Regardless of

[17]It is often thought that Luther's emphasis on justification did not allow him to develop a theology of sanctification. It is more accurate to argue that, for Luther, sanctification is indissolubly linked to justification. See Carter Lindberg, "Do Lutherans Shout Justification but Whisper Sanctification?," *Lutheran Quarterly* 13 (1999): 1-20.

the starting point, all readers are encouraged to pay special attention to the images and narratives of each model and to ponder how these stories have shaped or could shape their lives. Pastors, students of theology, church leaders, and scholars are welcome to consider how each model can be useful in their own lives; in teaching, preaching, praying, worship, spiritual care, and other tasks given to them in the body of Christ; and in interacting with other neighbors in the community with an interest in spirituality who may or not be Christians.

# 1

# SCULPTOR SPIRIT

## SPIRIT CHRISTOLOGY *and* *the* SANCTIFIED LIFE

A Spirit Christology focuses on the presence and activity of the Holy Spirit in the life and mission of Jesus. It asks what the identity of Jesus as the receiver, bearer, and giver of God's Spirit contributes to our theological reflection and Christian living. Thinking about the Spirit in relation to the Son lends itself to reflection on the theology of God, Christology, and pneumatology itself. As a field of theological inquiry, Spirit Christology has focused precisely on such questions. But how does a Spirit-oriented account of Christ operate as a framework for exploring sanctification or holiness? This question needs further development in the field and will be the focus of this chapter. Our guiding thesis is that the same Spirit in whom Jesus lived shapes the lives of his disciples today.

Because a Spirit Christology points to Christ as the locus or privileged place of the Spirit, it gives us a variety of pictures of Christlikeness we can draw from to discern the Spirit's work of forming Christ in human persons. Indeed, the Spirit of God blows where it wills, and there is a certain hiddenness and anonymity to its works in the world; and yet, the Scriptures also reveal rich images of the Spirit's activity in the world that help us discern its presence in our midst. A Spirit Christology offers us a theological lens to explore how the identity of Jesus as the receiver, bearer, and giver of God's Spirit assists us in that discernment. In chapters one and two, we make the case for Spirit Christology as a robust trinitarian framework, grounded in Christian traditions of the East and the West, with the capacity to promote discussions about the Spirit's indwelling of persons. In chapter two, we will delve into contributions from the early church to the development of a Spirit Christology, looking at their apologetic arguments for the unity of Christ and the Spirit but also at the rich variety of catechetical images they use to tell the story of the Spirit in Christ and his saints.

In chapter one, we focus on Spirit Christology today. Our presentation proceeds in two stages. First, we offer a bird's-eye view of the field by looking at two contrasting contemporary examples of Spirit Christologies, namely, a revisionary and a complementary approach. British scholar G. W. H. Lampe represents an example in the field of the revisionary route, which sees Spirit Christology as a replacement for the Logos (or two-natures) Christology inspired by the ecumenical councils. French theologian Yves Congar represents an example of the other method, which sees Spirit Christology as a complement to Logos Christology. Though distinct in fundamentally different ways, both theologians show how a Spirit Christology functions as a lens to reflect on the doctrine of God, the identity of Christ, and life in the Spirit. With these two authors, we also give readers unfamiliar with the field a taste of its European contributions.

Second, we survey a bit more in-depth two North American systematic theologians who exemplify narrative and historical approaches to the field of Spirit Christology and ask how these two authors have tested constructively the implications of the theological framework in response to various issues. Focusing significantly on Eastern Christian sources, Eugene Rogers Jr. represents a narrative approach that tracks the acts of the Spirit in the Gospels in order to suggest how humans participate in Christ's life through the same Spirit. Focusing mainly on Western sources, Ralph Del Colle represents a historical approach that tracks the development of Roman Catholic neo-scholastic (and post-neo-scholastic) ideas on the Spirit's presence in Christ in order to establish a coherent trinitarian account of the incarnation and grace. By looking at these two constructive contemporary trajectories in the field by North American authors, we are in a better position to assess what has been done on this side of the Atlantic and what needs further attention. Our exploration will expose a gap in the field, leading to our proposal for the constructive yet underutilized use of a Spirit Christology as a trinitarian narrative for articulating a models-based approach to the sanctified life and as a theological lens for addressing the spiritual needs and hopes of North Americans with an interest in spirituality and religion.

## TWO STORIES OF THE SPIRIT IN CHRIST: A BRIEF INTRODUCTION TO EUROPEAN SPIRIT CHRISTOLOGIES

In the last half of the twentieth century, events such as the revival of trinitarian theology across theological traditions, the rise of the ecumenical movement (including the interest of Western churches in Eastern Christian traditions), and the growth of Pentecostalism across the globe led to a renewed commitment to reflect on the person and work of the Holy Spirit. Parallel to this development, a number of theologians in the North Atlantic began to explore ways of thinking about the place of the Spirit in the life of Christ. Roughly speaking, two schools of thought surfaced. Some argued for Spirit Christology as a replacement for the classic Logos (or two-natures) Christology of the ecumenical councils, offering a revisionary view of trinitarian theology and the incarnation. Others argued for a Spirit Christology as a complement to Logos Christology, looking for ways to add or integrate a strong pneumatological trajectory into the mystery of the incarnation, while avoiding an adoptionist view of Christ as a mere man endowed with the Spirit.

My work tends toward the complementarity of Spirit- and Logos-oriented aspects of Christ's identity as a methodological basis for exploring models of the Christian life or sanctification. But before taking a closer look at North American contributions and setting the stage for my own argument, let us explore some of the basic contours of a revisionary and a complementary approach to Spirit Christology by looking at two European authors.

***G. W. H. Lampe: Jesus acts divinely by God's Spirit.*** Anglican scholar G. W. H. Lampe exemplifies a revisionary Spirit Christology.[1] Against notions of the Holy Spirit as a personal agent or hypostasis (person) distinct from God, Lampe defines "Spirit" in more general terms as God's simultaneously other-worldly (transcendent) and worldly (immanent) presence in all creatures. Consider the following definition, where "Spirit" functions as a metaphor for describing divine presence and activity:

> In speaking now of God as Spirit we are not referring to an impersonal influence, an energy transmitted by God but distinct from himself. Nor are we indicating a divine entity or hypostasis which is a third person of the Godhead. We are speaking of God himself, his personal presence, as active and related.[2]

[1]Other brief examples of the revisionary approach from Europe and North America include P. J. A. M. Schoonenberg, "Spirit Christology and Logos Christology," *Bijdragen* 38 (1977): 350-75; and Roger Haight, "The Case for Spirit Christology," *Theological Studies* 53 (1992): 257-87.

[2]G. W. H. Lampe, *God as Spirit* (New York: Oxford University Press, 1977), 208; cf. Lampe, *God as Spirit,* 37, 115-16.

Although Lampe highlights the divine identity of "Spirit" in functional terms or according to its activity and presence in creation, the framing of his proposal in a non-trinitarian monotheistic mold leaves him open to some objections. Lampe shows awareness of the historic problem of modalism, according to which God is said to be one only in Godself (Lat. *ad intra*) but appears as (or is named in) three modes only in his relationship to us in history (Lat. *ad extra*). Yet his proposal still tends to depersonalize Spirit due to his preference for an absolute monotheism that admits no difference or distinction in God. Lampe does not think in terms of "the" Spirit, but in terms of "Spirit."

The theology of God at work in Lampe's view of Spirit shapes his Christology. The author speaks of Jesus' divinity in terms of his unique possession of Spirit as a man. In doing so, he redefines the incarnation so that the subject or agent of the union is not the person or hypostasis of the divine Logos per se, but the man Jesus who bears Spirit. In distinction from the Logos Christology of the ecumenical councils, a goal of Lampe's Spirit Christology is "to acknowledge that the personal subject of the experience of Jesus Christ is a man. The hypostasis is not the Logos incarnate but a human being."[3] Therefore, Jesus is not God "substantivally," but because of the Spirit's presence in him "such a unity of will and operation with God" takes place that he can be called God in an adverbial sense, namely, in "that in all his actions the human Jesus acted divinely."[4] It is not the divine Logos who acts humanly to save us, but rather the human Jesus who acts divinely as our spiritual example.

Although Lampe is eager to recapture a strong sense of the true human reality and personality of Jesus as determined by God's Spirit in order to make him more relatable to other Spirit-bearing humans like us, his interpretation of Jesus' divinity as a function of Spirit-led actions makes one wonder whether a strong sense of Jesus' divine identity in distinction from his acts in creation remains possible. The problem does not lie in the preference for a more relational conception of Jesus' divine identity, but rather in whether there is a ground for such relationality in God as such, as opposed to in an act external to God. Without such ontological ground, even if penultimate in an overall account of Jesus, one ends up with a Spirit Jesusology more than a Spirit Christology. While aware of the problem of

[3]G. W. H. Lampe, "The Holy Spirit and the Person of Christ," in *Christ, Faith, and History*, ed. S. W. Sykes and J. P. Clayton (London: Cambridge University Press), 124.
[4]Lampe, "The Holy Spirit and the Person of Christ," 124.

adoptionism, Lampe's option for a non-ontological or non-substantival approach to Jesus' divinity still moves in the direction of an ontology driven by an "anthropological maximalism," one in which the human response of Jesus to the influence of God's Spirit in him overshadows the divine transfiguration of his own human life and ours through the power of the Spirit.[5] Otherwise stated, Lampe's focus on Jesus as a superlative Spirit-bearing man can at best give us a picture of an ideal spiritual person to emulate, but cannot show us how the transformative presence of the Spirit in the man Jesus reveals and defines him as the divine mediator of the Spirit of God to human persons.

As noted above, Lampe in his own way desires to make Jesus more relatable to us and like us, and finds in the reality of Spirit a bridge between Jesus and other saints. As a man of Spirit, Jesus can serve as a paradigm for others. To be a true model for imitation, however, Lampe suggests that Jesus' identity as Son must be seen in terms of the "degree" to which his bearing of Spirit makes him both unique from and similar to other humans.[6] Because Jesus is the fullest expression of the cooperative interaction between God's Spirit and the human spirit, Jesus' human acts as one possessed of Spirit makes him an unparalleled pattern of divine self-giving to the creature and human self-transcendence toward the divine that others can to some extent aspire to and replicate.

Lampe's approach allows him to posit both pneumatic discontinuity and continuity between Jesus and others. Yet in keeping with the author's anthropological maximalism, Jesus does not actually shape us into his likeness internally through the Spirit in order to bring us to communion with God. Instead, Jesus

---

[5]Orthodox theologian Georges V. Florovsky used the term "anthropological maximalism" to describe a soteriological error in which human freedom relativizes divine freedom. With reference to Theodore of Mopsuestia's teaching that "Christ had need of the Spirit to defeat the evil, to perform miracles and to receive (divine) instruction as to the activities he should undertake," Bobrinskoy defines Florovsky's term as "the tendency to make of Christ, in his humanity, the simple receptacle of the Spirit, thereby obscuring the truth that the Savior is above all the 'royal dwelling-place,' the living and unique locus of the full presence of the Spirit who belongs to him alone." Boris Bobrinskoy, "The Indwelling of the Spirit in Christ: 'Pneumatic Christology' in the Cappadocian Fathers," *St. Vladimir's Theological Quarterly* 28, no. 1 (1984), 61; Rosato's summary of the dangers of early adoptionist Spirit christologies is also helpful: "The generalization can be made that this Christology was in effect no Christology at all, but rather a blend of Father theology and Spirit theology to the exclusion of Son theology. . . . Emphasis on a strict monotheism on the one hand and on a theology of grace on the other made any assertion about Jesus Christ's unique ontological role in the very nature of God superfluous. Instead, God's absolute transcendence and man's universal participation in grace through the Spirit reduced the Messiah to the model of man's own relationship to God, to the paradigm of man's own adoption as son of God." Philip J. Rosato, "Spirit Christology: Ambiguity and Promise," *Theological Studies* 38, no. 3 (1977): 435.

[6]Lampe, "The Holy Spirit and the Person of Christ," 124.

merely points us in an external way to the human life he lives divinely as an example of divine likeness through human obedience in the hope that others can act divinely as humans, though in a lesser degree than Jesus. Although Lampe's proposal for a continuity of degree between Jesus and us depends heavily on an account of his identity as receiver and bearer of God's Spirit, it does not consider just as fully the strong discontinuity between Jesus and us inherent in the former's identity as the unparalleled giver of the Spirit. Jesus' receiving and bearing of Spirit is not adequately seen in light of his giving of the Spirit. Practically speaking, the former aspect is disconnected from the latter or simply overshadows it. Yet the author's attempt to describe Jesus' Spirit-led life in the context of human participation in his Spirit deserves attention in the development of a Spirit Christology.

***Yves Congar: Decisive moments of the Spirit in the Son's life.*** Roman Catholic theologian Yves Congar illustrates a complementary approach to Spirit Christology that takes into account the concerns of a Logos (two-natures) Christology. In continuity with the ecumenical councils, Congar holds to the Son's identity as the only-begotten of God, of the same divine substance with the Father. Avoiding an adoptionist Christology that reduces Christ to a Spirit-bearing man, while also giving the Spirit its important place in his human history, Congar states that Jesus "was ontologically the Son of God by a personal (hypostatic) union from the moment of his conception and that he was also from that moment onwards the Temple of the Holy Spirit and made holy in his humanity by that Spirit."[7] Congar allows for the place of both the Logos and the Spirit in an account of the incarnation.

Congar acknowledges that, due to the influence of Thomas Aquinas's theology of created grace in Western Christology, the Son is said to have the fullness of grace, the Holy Spirit, and its gifts already from the moment of conception.[8] Although this assertion remains true from the ontological perspective of the Word's "descent" to assume a full humanity, such a move makes it difficult to give full weight to "the action of the Holy Spirit" in God's economy at various special moments or "*kairoi*" of Christ's human life and mission.[9] The testimony of the Scriptures to the Holy

---

[7]Yves Congar, *The Word and the Spirit*, trans. David Smith (San Francisco: Harper & Row, 1986), 92; for a similar account of Spirit Christology, see Congar, *I Believe in the Holy Spirit*, 3:165-73.
[8]Congar, *The Word and the Spirit*, 85-86.
[9]Congar, *The Word and the Spirit*, 86-87.

Spirit's role in the life of Christ requires the introduction of a more robust pneumatic trajectory in the description of the divine Son's incarnation.

Lest the movements of the Spirit in the history of the incarnate Son become reduced to a mere "manifestation for others" of the Spirit's prior presence in the Son from the time of conception, a need arises for complementing Thomas's Logos-oriented Christology with a more economic Spirit Christology that accounts adequately for "the successive comings of the Holy Spirit over Jesus in his quality as 'Christ the Saviour.'"[10] Two events receive particular attention in the economy of Jesus' sonship, namely, his anointing at baptism and his resurrection from the dead.

Congar sees these events as special times in which, according to God's plan of salvation, the Holy Spirit's descents or actions on Jesus did "something new" to him.[11] Anointed at the Jordan, he was "declared" to be Christ, but in a sense he was also "made" Christ by the Spirit in view of his being placed into the office of servant.[12] Moreover, he was not only declared but "constituted" Son of God in power in the body "according to the Spirit of holiness by his resurrection from the dead" (Rom 1:4).[13] Thus the Spirit determines the economic form or identity of Christ, namely, that of God's faithful Son and suffering/glorified servant.

Bringing the Spirit back into Christology also yields a soteriological benefit. The presence of the Spirit in the incarnate Son brings about our participation by grace in his Spirit. In other words, the Son bears the Spirit in his humanity in order to bestow the Spirit on humanity. A Logos Christology highlights the Son's distinction from us as the only-begotten Son (Lat. *unigenitus*) of the Father, and thus the sole incarnation of God in a hypostatic union. A Spirit Christology, on the other hand, points to the Son's identity as the firstborn (Lat. *primogenitus*) among many brothers and sisters (Rom 8:29), and thus lends itself more readily to reflection on our human sharing in the Son's filial life through the Spirit whom he bears and gives to us.[14]

---

[10]Congar, *The Word and the Spirit*, 86-87.

[11]Congar, *The Word and the Spirit*, 87; for Congar, Jesus' baptism and resurrection are "authentic qualitative moments in which God's communication of himself . . . to Jesus Christ was accomplished" (Congar, *The Word and the Spirit*, 87).

[12]Congar, *The Word and the Spirit*, 88.

[13]Congar, *The Word and the Spirit*, 91.

[14]Congar, *The Word and the Spirit*, 91-92. Ladaria writes, "The Spirit first has to fulfill its work in Jesus so that it might then fulfill it in us and configure us according to the pattern of Christ. . . . [Jesus] gives us

By going the way of complementarity, Congar articulates a Spirit Christology within an incarnational Logos Christology, but in doing so also sets the latter in a stronger historical, soteriological, and trinitarian trajectory.[15] In assuming a human nature, the Logos assumes a human history in which the Spirit accompanies him. Receiving and bearing the Spirit of God in the flesh for our sake, the Logos bestows the Spirit on the flesh to bring us into communion with God. In his anointing and resurrection, the Logos does not merely reveal his individual constitution as the God-man, but his trinitarian identity as the Son of the Father in whom the Spirit rests and through whom the Spirit is given to others. Complementarity allows us to posit both our discontinuity and continuity with Christ without falling into modalism, adoptionism, or anthropological maximalism, and thus without the need to radically revise basic trinitarian and christological teachings in the great tradition of the East and the West. Although Congar gives us rich insights into the action of the Spirit in the incarnate Logos, his complementary approach tends to speak of the Spirit and the Logos as parallel realities and does not yet completely integrate the pneumatic and incarnational dimensions of Christology. Such integration remains an important task in articulating a trinitarian Spirit Christology.

## IN OUR NECK OF THE WOODS: SPIRIT CHRISTOLOGY IN NORTH AMERICA

In the last quarter century, Spirit Christology has become an international field of study, moving from its European inception to new developments in other parts of the world. In the English-speaking world, a number of works have appeared outside of North America.[16] In this section, we explore contributions to the field of

as the Spirit of filiation the Spirit of the Father who has rested upon him . . . so that we too might cry out 'abba Father.' The Spirit thus works in us what it has worked in the humanity of Jesus. . . . The status of only Son of God cannot be communicated [to others]. . . . The Spirit whom he has because of his unique relationship with the Father can be communicated [to others]." Luis F. Ladaria, "La unción de Jesús y el don del Espíritu," *Gregorianum* 71, no. 3 (1990): 568-70 (translation mine). Similarly, Wong asserts that Romans 8:29 highlights our conformity to Christ by sharing in his sonship or filial identity, and therefore, in his communion with both the Father and his adopted children. See Joseph H. P. Wong, "The Holy Spirit in the Life of Jesus and of the Christian," *Gregorianum* 73 (1992): 84-87.

[15]For other Roman Catholic authors writing in a European context, see John J. O'Donnell, "In Him and over Him: The Holy Spirit in the Life of Jesus," *Gregorianum* 70, no. 1 (1989): 25-45; and Luis F. Ladaria, "Cristología del Logos y cristología del Espíritu," *Gregorianum* 61 (1980): 353-60.

[16]Outside of Europe and North America, English-speaking authors include Australian Roman Catholic theologian David Coffey, *Deus Trinitas: The Doctrine of the Triune God* (New York: Oxford, 1999), and "Spirit Christology and the Trinity," in *Advents of the Spirit: An Introduction to the Current Study of Pneumatology*, ed. Bradford E. Hinze and D. Lyle Dabney (Milwaukee: Marquette University Press, 2001), 315-46; and New Zealand Reformed theologian Myk Habets, *The Anointed Son: A Trinitarian Spirit*

Spirit Christology by two North American authors working from different theological traditions: Episcopalian theologian Eugene F. Rogers Jr. and Roman Catholic theologian Ralph Del Colle.

Given my interest in articulating a Spirit Christology as a complement to the Christology of the ecumenical councils, I chose these two systematic theologians because they operate within a solid trinitarian tradition, and therefore with an implicit or explicit concern for maintaining elements of a Logos-oriented Christology. Moreover, given my interest in articulating models of sanctification from Spirit Christology in a North American context, my interest in these authors lies primarily in the way they use Spirit Christology to pave the way for or contribute to discussions on the shape of the Christian life in the world.

***Eugene F. Rogers Jr.'s narrative approach: The resting of the bodily Spirit in the Son, the church, and the world.*** In *After the Spirit*, Eugene F. Rogers Jr. looks for images and narratives of the Spirit that bring the third person into the closest possible association with bodies, namely, Christ's own physical body, the church as his body, and the bodies of his members.[17] Because the Spirit "rests" on the body of the Son, the Spirit also rests on the creature not only to inhabit human nature but to do so "in excess of nature, or 'paraphysically' . . . in a way that redeems, transfigures, elevates, and exceeds" human nature to bring it into communion with God.[18] The Spirit also rests on the world, whether that is in the waters of creation, the womb of Mary, or baptism.[19] These theses are attempts to move beyond what the author sees as a main problem in Western pneumatology, namely, that "the Spirit had grown dull because unembodied, and bodily experience unpersuasive because un-Spirited."[20]

After assessing how contemporary theology arrived at a bodiless pneumatology, Rogers offers a Spirit Christology in dialogue with sources in the great tradition (especially, from the East) that explores the dynamics of the Spirit's resting on the Son at his resurrection, annunciation, baptism, transfiguration, and ascension,

---

*Christology* (Eugene, OR: Pickwick, 2010), and "Spirit Christology: Seeing in Stereo," *Journal of Pentecostal Theology* 11, no. 2 (2003): 199-234.

[17]For instance, Rogers's thesis no. 5 reads: "The Spirit proceeds from the Father to rest on the Son. This happens (1) in the life of Jesus as recorded in the New Testament, (2) in the life of his body the Church, as recorded in the liturgy, and (3) in the bodies of his members, as they are liturgically constructed in sacraments and prayer." Eugene F. Rogers Jr., *After the Spirit* (Grand Rapids: Eerdmans, 2005), 14.

[18]See theses no. 6 and no. 7. Rogers, *After the Spirit*, 14-15.

[19]See thesis no. 9. Rogers, *After the Spirit*, 15.

[20]Rogers, *After the Spirit*, 3.

and at Pentecost. Throughout his exposition of Spirit Christology, the author incorporates narratives from Scripture and church theologians (including liturgical or devotional images) that illumine ways in which the resting of the Spirit on the Son at various events of his life gives us insight into our own human participation in the Spirit of the Son.[21] In an epilogue, Rogers also offers some reflections on human sharing in the prayer of the Son in light of Romans 8.

*Is there something the Spirit can do better than the Son?* Drawing on Robert Jenson's critique of Barth's mechanistic tendency to depersonalize the Spirit as either the "power" of Christ subsumed under the latter's work or a "third mode of being of the one divine Subject" in the eternal Trinity, Rogers sees Barth as a salient Western example of a view of the Spirit that, in seeking to be linked to Christ, nevertheless takes away the Spirit's own unique personhood in the story of salvation.[22] In particular, Rogers notes that no significant place is given in Barth's theology to the Spirit's acts in the various events of Christ's life.[23] The danger lies in thinking that, as Rogers often puts it, there is nothing the Spirit can do that the Son cannot already do better.[24]

As a rhetorical device, the author asks whether the Spirit is "superfluous" by looking at two ways in which the third person has been rendered practically unnecessary. One is by way of seeing the Spirit as a "distance-crosser," the final bridge in God's outreach to the human heart. At first, the image of "crossing a distance" sounds good and pious until the Spirit is either replaced by Christ, who can cross the same distance anyway, or replaced by the will of the person who makes a decision for Christ.[25] The other way to make the Spirit superfluous is by

---

[21]Rogers describes his methodology as typological: "In Part II, I will consider how the Spirit rests on the Son in the New Testament narratives about Jesus. I consider commentary that works typologically to incorporate other (often earlier) narratives into that pattern, and liturgy that works typologically to incorporate the community and the material world into it." Rogers, *After the Spirit*, 71. "In the foreground, I want to recover the way in which some Christian doctrines speak of the destiny of the human being as fellowship with God, variously called vocation (among Protestants), consummation (among Catholics), or deification (among the Eastern Orthodox): the sense in which human beings become 'participants in the divine nature' (II Peter. 1:4)." Rogers, *After the Spirit*, 9. Or as Rogers states in thesis no. 2: "Interactions among the Persons recorded in the New Testament give glimpses of the intratrinitarian life as it dilates—delays and opens up—to include human beings within it. These interactions occur at the annunciation, baptism, temptation, and crucifixion of Jesus, and at the institution of the Lord's Supper. Most important among them is the resurrection of Jesus as described in Romans 8." Rogers, *After the Spirit*, 11; cf. thesis no. 3. Rogers, *After the Spirit*, 13.

[22]Rogers, *After the Spirit*, 19-23.

[23]Rogers, *After the Spirit*, 23.

[24]Rogers, *After the Spirit*, 9, 20, 33.

[25]Rogers, *After the Spirit*, 33-34.

way of "gratuitous incorporation," according to which the Spirit becomes the "what" or thing that the Father gives through the Son (e.g., "grace as a quality" in man).[26] Otherwise stated, the Spirit becomes a "what" and not a "who," and this in the end makes him less than a person and therefore an unnecessary step toward our gracious incorporation in the Father-Son relationship.

Either way one chooses to speak, the Spirit is rendered a dispensable surplus in the trinitarian economy, and therefore becomes a suspicious addition to an already complete reality in a way similar to how economic surpluses become a matter of suspicion when associated with material excesses.[27] Add to this mix the church's suspicion of Spirit talk that appears to replace Christ, and the typical strategy has been to retreat to Christ.[28] Such a move, however, has sidestepped dealing closely with the uniqueness of the Spirit as a person in its own right. Moving too quickly away from the Spirit toward Christ has also resulted in avoiding dealing with the Spirit in Christ himself. In Bulgakov's insight that Christ's resurrection by the Spirit makes fruitful human labor a sign of God's renewal of creation, and in Schmemann's thesis that in eucharistic food humans are linked to God's transfiguration of creation in Christ by the Spirit, Rogers finds helpful images that link the Spirit to the renewal of our bodies in Christ's mystical body (church) through Christ's own body.[29] Rather than sidestepping the Spirit to get to Christ, biblical pneumatology moves us instead to see the Spirit in Christ, and through him, in others.

Like other contemporary authors, Rogers points to the problem of the anonymity of the Spirit. Because God is one, it follows that all persons of the Trinity work indivisibly in the world. Even though this statement is true at the level of the unified collaboration of the divine persons in history, the axiom raises the question of what is unique to the person of the Holy Spirit that the other two persons do not already do.[30] By reflecting on biblical stories where the Spirit reveals his particular narrative character in relation to the Father and the Son, but also to humans and things, we arrive at the Spirit's proper personhood.[31] The

---

[26]Rogers, *After the Spirit*, 35.

[27]Rogers, *After the Spirit*, 36-39.

[28]As an example, Rogers notes how Barth sees Schleiermacher's confusion of the Holy Spirit with the subjectivity of the human spirit as a consequence of a lack of christological objectivity in theology. Rogers, *After the Spirit*, 34.

[29]Rogers, *After the Spirit*, 41-44.

[30]Rogers, *After the Spirit*, 45-47.

[31]Rogers, *After the Spirit*, 52-60.

author's thesis that "the Spirit befriends matter" arises from a christological way of reading Scripture, namely, that "the Spirit has befriended matter for Christ's sake on account of the incarnation."[32] Therefore, the Spirit's work has an incarnational and sacramental trajectory:

> It is the Spirit whom Christians call down to sanctify people and things: deacons, priests, believers, water, wine, oil, incense, churches, houses, and anything that can be blessed. Oil, water, bread, wine, the bodies of human beings to be baptized, married, or ordained: in many and various ways the matter of the world becomes the element of a sacrament. To think about the Spirit it will not do to think "spiritually": to think about the Spirit you have to think materially.[33]

Inspired by John of Damascus, the author describes the Spirit's unique personhood as its active resting on bodies and things on the grounds that it rests on the Son in the economy of salvation and in the trinitarian life.[34] By doing so, the Spirit brings to fulfillment not only the incarnation of the Son, but also its fruits in our lives. Otherwise stated, the Spirit rests on the physical body of the Son so that the Spirit "might rest also on the body of the Son in the Church, . . . and on the body of the Son in the bread and wine, and the body of the Son in whatever other places she conceives it."[35] The materiality of the Spirit is evident.

To show how the Spirit rests on us in a way that human diversity is not dissolved but also brought into unity in Christ, Rogers picks up on Staniloae's argument that the Spirit's procession from the Father to rest on the Son highlights both the Spirit's uniting of the Father and the Son and the Spirit's unitive function to take diversity in creation up into communion with the divine persons.[36] Therefore, the Spirit is not superfluous and can actually do something better than the Son, namely, "rest."[37] Not because the Son lacks something, but because the Son makes the Spirit his own by receiving, bearing, and giving it to others. Resting becomes the author's primary pneumatic lens to articulate a Spirit Christology.

---

[32]Rogers, *After the Spirit*, 58.

[33]Rogers, *After the Spirit*, 56.

[34]"In the world, the Spirit is not Person *or* thing, because the Spirit is Person *on* thing. And the Spirit is Person on thing *because* the Spirit is Person on Person. The Spirit rests on material bodies in the economy, because she rests on the Son in the Trinity." Rogers, *After the Spirit*, 62; cf. 69.

[35]Rogers, *After the Spirit*, 62; cf. 70.

[36]Rogers, *After the Spirit*, 63-69.

[37]Rogers, *After the Spirit*, 71.

*The narrative pattern of the Spirit's resting on the Son and us.* Beginning with Romans 8:11, Rogers argues that the Son's resurrection from the dead, which is preceded by the Spirit's resting on the Son's body in his crucifixion, reveals the life of the Trinity and the free mystery of the incorporation of human beings into such life by the Spirit of the Son.[38] The passage reveals a trinitarian logic according to which the Father appears as the one who by the Spirit "raises human, mortal bodies," thus showing the Spirit as one "who assimilates other human beings to Christ, stamps or seals Christ's character on them."[39] Even though the crucifixion appears as a failure from a human perspective, the author argues that Christ underwent it in his humiliation so that he might allow room for the repentance of the Gentiles and their incorporation into the household of God.[40] On the basis of Philippians 2:5-11, the author interprets the crucifixion as the climax of Christ's receiving "the forebearance the Spirit teaches and the excess with which the Spirit vindicates [at the resurrection],"[41] revealing a christoform pattern of death and resurrection into which the Gentiles are likewise assimilated "by the surprising excesses of the Spirit."[42]

Similar to the Spirit's fruitful "excess" of divine freedom and love through which the Gentiles are made the firstfruits of the Son's resurrection, the Spirit surprisingly consummates God's plan of salvation in the womb of Mary (Lk 1:35).[43] Highlighting God's philanthropic becoming flesh in solidarity with the flesh as the Spirit's fruitful "excess" in Mary's womb, Rogers observes that "the virgin birth, like the salvation of the Gentiles, is neither merely physical nor anti-physical: it is strictly paraphysical; it accompanies and exceeds nature."[44] In an analogical ladder going up, the Spirit's resting on Mary's womb is an icon of the Spirit's resting on the Son in "the Father's womb" (a metaphor for the Father's begetting of the Son).[45] Coming down the same ladder, the Spirit's resting on Mary's womb

[38]Rogers, *After the Spirit*, 75-97.

[39]Rogers, *After the Spirit*, 76.

[40]Rogers, *After the Spirit*, 95-97.

[41]Rogers, *After the Spirit*, 96. Such forbearance is also evident in Christ's temptation. See Rogers, *After the Spirit*, 94.

[42]Rogers, *After the Spirit*, 97. The author's argument for the Gentiles as the firstfruits of the resurrection is made in the broader context of a critique of supersessionism.

[43]Rogers, *After the Spirit*, 99.

[44]Rogers, *After the Spirit*, 103.

[45]Rogers, *After the Spirit*, 111. The reference comes from the 11th Council of Toledo (AD 675): "One must believe that the Son is begotten *and born* not from nothing, nor from some other substance, but *from the womb of the Father* [*de Patris utero*], that is, from his substance." Cited in Rogers, *After the Spirit*, 116.

anticipates the Spirit's resting on the crucified Christ, whose side wound (see Jn 19:34) is portrayed in Syrian theology and Cistercian thought as an opening through which humans enter into the life of the triune God.[46] Along the same tradition of interpretation, some authors suggested that just as the Holy Spirit descended on the womb of Mary to create the body of Christ, so also the Spirit descended on "the womb of the wine" as the sacramental opening through which the body of Christ (church) enters into communion with his eucharistic body.[47] Rogers's use of patristic images to link the Spirit's presence in Christ's physical, sacramental, and ecclesial bodies is representative of his overall narrative approach to Spirit Christology.

At the Son's baptism, a trinitarian event in which the Holy Spirit bears witness to the Father's love for the Son, the Jordan waters signal the Spirit's celebration of the Father's election of adopted children through his Son in the waters of their baptismal fonts.[48] In the Syriac tradition, the baptized went into the waters of baptism to receive the robe of Christ, which their father Adam had lost in Paradise, so that they might be clothed anew with the bridal garment and attend the eschatological wedding feast (Mt 22).[49] Although the Son does not need holiness or sanctification for himself in baptism, "the Spirit overshadowed Christ's baptism, and Christ received what he did not need as gift, in that he is baptized by John," so that "other human beings may be sanctified by God in baptism."[50] Through the use of these baptismal images, Rogers sums up the patristic theme of human sharing in the Spirit of Christ through participation in his baptismal anointing.

At the Mount of Transfiguration, the Spirit in the form of the cloud rests on the Son as he prays to the Father.[51] Through the same Spirit, a human being

---

[46]Rogers, *After the Spirit*, 111, cf. 119-24; Rogers notes that in the Syriac tradition "the wound in the side of Christ reopens the door to Paradise, found inside his body (which is also the membership of the church). Not only is the womb of Mary a *felix dilatio*, but the body of Christ is a tissue of openings, a way into the triune God, itself held open by the Spirit for the accommodation of others into its communion." Rogers, *After the Spirit*, 124.

[47]Rogers, *After the Spirit*, 125-34; Rogers cites Brock: "Just as the Holy Spirit descended to the womb of Mary . . . and made the body of God the Word from the flesh of the Virgin, so too the Spirit descends on the bread and wine on the altar and makes them into the Body and Blood of God the Word which originated from the Virgin." Rogers, *After the Spirit*, 125.

[48]Rogers, *After the Spirit*, 135, 140-48.

[49]Rogers, *After the Spirit*, 146.

[50]Rogers, *After the Spirit*, 137-40.

[51]Rogers, *After the Spirit*, 172.

can participate by grace in the prayer of the Son to the Father, and thus become "a liturgical being, a glorifying being, a blessing being, a thanks-giving being, a being that not only receives, but receives also the permission to give back and again."[52] By bringing them into communion with the Father through a sharing in the Son's Abba prayer, the Spirit displays his role as one who transfigures or perfects humans in their glorification of God. The Spirit nourishes humans even now so that they might glorify God in time and space through embodied forms of life in community, such as marriage and friendships—forms of life that Rogers refers to as "the external fostering of the Spirit's habituation of the human being, the external correlate to the Spirit's internal habituation."[53] Life in the Spirit of the Son is oriented toward the other because the Son's own life in the Spirit is oriented toward the Father.

In Rogers's account of Spirit Christology, the Son receives humanly from the Spirit for our sake what he already has by nature. At the resurrection, for instance, the Son "makes room for the Spirit to gift him with renewed life for his mortal body" so that humans might share in the Son's resurrection through the life-giving Spirit.[54] From the Spirit, the Son also receives "renewed life for his churchly body (at Pentecost) after his ascension," which includes "the gift of the Gentiles."[55] Placing Ascension and Pentecost in an ascent and descent deification pattern, the author asserts that at his ascension "the Son presents the Father with a body, so that in the Spirit those with bodies may be present to the Father."[56] At Pentecost, "the Spirit descends as a foretaste of heaven, to rest by anticipation on the bodies that will be deified."[57] The Spirit's resting on the Son has a goal, namely, the Son's return to the Father and our return to the Father through the Son.

***Ralph Del Colle's historical approach: The presence of the Spirit in the incarnation and grace.*** In his published dissertation *Christ and the Spirit*, Ralph Del Colle argues for a "Spirit Christology . . . that attempts to inform christology with an equally important pneumatology, while at the same time preserving the integrity of the doctrine of the trinity."[58] Working within a Western/

---

[52]Rogers, *After the Spirit*, 178.
[53]Rogers, *After the Spirit*, 184.
[54]Rogers, *After the Spirit*, 201.
[55]Rogers, *After the Spirit*, 201.
[56]Rogers, *After the Spirit*, 207.
[57]Rogers, *After the Spirit*, 206.
[58]Ralph Del Colle, *Christ and the Spirit* (New York: Oxford University Press, 1994), 4.

Latin paradigm of trinitarian relations inspired by Augustine and consolidated by Thomas Aquinas, the author explores the creative ways in which later neo-scholastic Catholic theologians attempted to make greater room for the Holy Spirit in the mystery of the incarnation, salvation, and sanctification than what was allowed by traditional scholastic categories. Del Colle shows how neo-scholastic writers such as Scheeben, Mersch, and de la Taille paved the way for a Spirit Christology by offering extensions or revisions of themes in the scholastic theology of grace (see especially his chapters two and three). The author then moves beyond the neo-scholastics by adopting David Coffey's approach to Spirit Christology and offers ways to test the model's usefulness in various areas of contemporary interest.

The benefit of Del Colle's work lies in his rigorous historical study of neo-scholastic contributions toward a Spirit Christology and his constructive attempt at a cohesive account of the model within a Latin trinitarian paradigm. For our purposes, his nuanced exploration of how the neo-scholastics incorporated the Spirit more boldly in the humanity of Christ and through him in the sanctification of our humanity remains insightful. In the Latin scholastic paradigm, God acts *indivisibly* in the world through efficient causality, that is to say, in a way that God as the originating cause of all things remains *unaffected* by creatures in his self-giving to them. Otherwise stated, God has a logical (in the mind) relation to the creature, but not a real relation to it, since no change occurs in the originating cause, only in the one who receives from God.

*Making room for a proper work of the Spirit.* Two issues arise in the scholastic way of framing the relationship between God and the world that make it difficult to give the Holy Spirit a strong or defining role in the mysteries of the incarnation of the Logos (Son) and the triune God's indwelling of the human creature in deification and sanctification. First, if God works indivisibly in the world, how can we assign both the Son and the Holy Spirit *distinctive* personal properties? The traditional scholastic answer became the theology of appropriations, according to which each person of the Trinity is appropriated a particular work even though all three persons are involved in the same works. For example, even though the Creed appropriates or assigns creation to the Father, the first person of the Trinity, as his special work, the greater reality is that, given the unity of the Trinity, all the persons are in the end equally involved in creation.

But what of the incarnation? Since only the Son (Logos), and not God in general, became incarnate, as Rahner observed in his critique of neo-scholastic theology, the incarnation (personal or hypostatic union) cannot be merely "appropriated" to the Son but must be an act "proper" to his person.[59] When speaking of God's indwelling of the creature by grace, could a similar point be made about the Holy Spirit, namely, that such work is not merely appropriated to the third person but says something about the Spirit's *unique* person? Moreover, in the scholastic tradition, God's indwelling of the creature was described as an effect on the creature of the *one* God's undifferentiated efficient causality in the world. Yet the biblical data also allow for a *differentiated* unity of the one God. For instance, in the baptism at the Jordan, did not the Son (Logos) himself receive the Holy Spirit in his created humanity (as opposed to receiving the Father or receiving himself)? Scripture points to distinctions among persons not only in the intra-divine life but also in the economy of salvation. How then can the Latin West make the *person* of the Holy Spirit as such more prominent in an account of God's self-donation to the creature in the incarnation of Christ and in his indwelling of the saints?

Del Colle suggests that the neo-scholastics moved toward a solution to the problem of an implied subordination of the third person to God's general causality in the world by assigning the Holy Spirit a proper work (Lat. *proprium*) unique to his person. Through the use of the pneumatic language of "anointing" and "spiration," Del Colle asserts that theologians like Scheeben and Mersch succeeded to some extent in linking the presence of the Holy Spirit in Christ's humanity to that of his saints in his mystical body, the church. Positing such pneumatic continuity between the incarnation and the church could only happen if the Spirit was given a *proprium*.[60] In doing so, these theologians were providing

[59] "Jesus is not simply God in general, but the Son. The second divine person, God's Logos, is man, and only he is man. Hence, there is at least *one* 'mission,' *one* presence in the world, *one* reality in salvation history which is not merely appropriated to some divine person, but which is proper to him." Rahner, *The Trinity*, 23. Del Colle explains that the Latin trinitarian paradigm, according to which the distinction of the persons is only spoken of in their intradivine or *ad intra* relation to each other, "has led to the dominance of appropriation theory relative to *ad extra* divine activity. . . . According to this paradigm, the distinct hypostatic identity of a divine person is not properly revealed *ad extra*—i.e., in reference to that person alone—except in the term of the incarnation, the man Jesus Christ." Del Colle, *Christ and the Spirit*, 57.

[60] "Unless the Holy Spirit is given a proper mission (even if non-exclusive) relative to the divine inhabitation and sanctification as is the case with Scheeben and Mersch, then the grounds for the inclusion of the Spirit in the christological locus are limited. For Scheeben, Mersch, Donnelly, and others, the propriety of the Holy Spirit's indwelling establishes a fundamental link with Christ's own person. In other

building blocks toward the development of a Spirit Christology in a Latin trinitarian framework.

*Not only the gifts of the Spirit, but the Spirit itself dwells in us.* The second issue raised by the Latin trinitarian paradigm in the construction of a more robust pneumatology relates to the nature of God's self-giving to the creature. If God only acts toward the creature in a way that the relation remains rational on the side of the Creator as the efficient cause of all things, but real only on the side of the creature as the affected term of the relation, then, how can we say that God as such truly became incarnate and truly dwells in creatures? The Logos would seem untouched by his own flesh and thus only *appear* to be human, and in a similar way the Spirit would seem untouched by those in whom he dwells and thus only *appear* to dwell in us.

The category of efficient causality rightly serves to make a clear distinction between God and creation, but it does not seem equipped to deal with the notion that God as such (and not merely God's effects or created gifts) became flesh in the person of the Logos and analogously dwells in the believer by grace through the Holy Spirit. Positing that human nature is assumed by the person of the uncreated Logos (and thus assumed not only by acts *external* to his person), or analogously that the humanity of saints is inhabited by the person of the uncreated Spirit (and not merely by the Spirit's created gifts), requires that the divine person who assumes or inhabits created reality have some real relation to it beyond that which efficient causality allows.

Although the language of formal causality (that which makes a thing what it is) could be invoked, its use would wrongly suggest that in God's self-giving to created reality the creature itself becomes divine. At this point, the distinction between God and creation would be removed, jeopardizing the freedom of God to relate to us out of the gratuity of divine love and not out of ontological necessity. The problem requires a reformulation of the available scholastic categories of causality. Del Colle argues that the neo-scholastics moved in such a direction by appealing to the less commonly used category of "quasi-formal causality," according to which God's self-giving to the creature in a hypostatic union (incarnation) and in sanctifying indwelling is such that God gives not only his external *gifts* but his own

words, the manifestation of hypostatic identity in the Spirit's temporal mission in the indwelling relates directly to the pneumatic dimension of Christ's person, and this would be the decisive link to any Spirit-christology." Del Colle, *Christ and the Spirit*, 78-79.

*self* to the creature without the creature becoming ontologically divine.[61] Quasi-formal causality allows us to speak of the uncreated Logos himself becoming incarnate without making his human nature into a divine nature. In an analogous way, we can speak of the uncreated Spirit's deifying and sanctifying indwelling of a human person without the latter becoming a person or hypostasis of the Spirit or ontologically divine.

*The Spirit as the agent of the incarnation and our sanctification.* Del Colle introduces the trinitarian synthesis of David Coffey as the most cohesive example of a Spirit Christology set in the context of the Latin tradition but also moving beyond its neo-scholastic limitations. Del Colle shows how Coffey moves even beyond other post-neo-scholastic theologians such as Rahner, Mühlen, and Kasper, who in various ways attempted to bring a more robust pneumatology into Christology with various levels of success. Unique to Coffey is his proposal for a "bestowal" model of the Trinity in which he highlights the uniqueness of the Spirit in the trinitarian outworking of salvation by arguing for the identity of the third person as "the formative agent for both the incarnation and grace."[62] In other words, and logically speaking, the Holy Spirit creates and sanctifies the human nature that the Son assumes, and this makes possible the Spirit's sanctification of human persons (and sinners) by making them adopted sons and daughters (children) of God through union with the Son who bestows the Spirit on them.[63]

This bestowal (or ascent) model, where the Spirit's sanctification of the Son's human nature (also known as his habitual grace) is the economic ground for the hypostatic union (or grace of union), does not do away with but complements the more traditional procession (or descent) model of the Trinity.[64] In the more

---

[61]Del Colle shows that applying the notion of quasi-formal causality and real relation to the incarnation opens the way for applying a similar argument to the Spirit's inhabitation of the creature. The author notes that "a proper temporal mission of the Holy Spirit is dependent on a real relation of the sacred humanity to the divine Son in the hypostatic union. . . . Only by arguing for a 'created actuation by uncreated act' or a 'quasi-formal causality of grace' as the means by which a human nature is assumed by the divine Word in the incarnation is it possible to posit an analogous relationship between the believer and the Holy Spirit in the grace of sanctification effected by the divine indwelling." Del Colle, *Christ and the Spirit*, 84; for Rahner's use of quasi-formal causality, see *The Trinity*, 36, 77.

[62]Del Colle, *Christ and the Spirit*, 119.

[63]Del Colle, *Christ and the Spirit*, 120.

[64]As Thomas Aquinas explains: "The grace of union is precisely God's free gift to the human nature of having personal existence in the Word, and that is the term of the assumption. Habitual grace, forming part of the special holiness of this man, is an effect following upon the union." *ST* 3a, q. 6, a. 6. Beginning with these categories of "habitual grace" (Lat. *gratia habitualis*) and "grace of union" (Lat. *gratia unionis*),

familiar procession model, all three persons of the Trinity act indivisibly by efficient causality in creating the human nature assumed by the Logos and in indwelling the human person by grace. This model highlights the Son's descent from the Father in the Spirit to us in his incarnation, but does not yet speak to our ascent in the risen Son to the Father by the Spirit through our becoming sons and daughters (children).[65]

*The presences of Christ and the Spirit in faith, hope, and love.* Against Christologies of presence, which Del Colle sees as identifying the risen Christ and the Spirit functionally and thus without much distinction between them, he employs the triad of faith, hope, and love as a framework for exploring the distinct though related missions of the Son and the Spirit as they make themselves present among us today.[66] In regard to faith, the presence of Christ (Lat. *Christus praesens*) is received corporately by his body, the church, in the proclamation of the Word and in his sacramental body through belief in him and the memory of his words.[67] Although the presence of the Spirit (Lat. *Spiritus praesens*) mediates Christ's presence in Word and sacrament to us by reminding us of Christ's words, the Spirit does not come to us bodily as Christ does and thus retains a certain anonymity by

---

Roman Catholic theologians today have argued for the logical priority of either one in describing the missions of the Son and the Holy Spirit in relation to Christ's human nature. Mühlen, following Thomas, argued for the grace of union as the basis for habitual grace, and Kasper argued the opposite. Coffey's distinction between processional and bestowal models of the Trinity helps us to see that, generally speaking, Mühlen was operating from the processional side and Kasper from the bestowal side of the argument. For Mühlen's position, see Heribert Mühlen, "El acontecimiento Cristo como acción del Espíritu Santo," in *Mysterium Salutis*, ed. J. Feiner and M. Löhrer (Madrid: Cristiandad, 1992), 3:960-84 (esp. 3:973); for a full treatment of the topic, see Mühlen, *Una Mystica Persona: Die Kirche als das Mysterium der Identität des Heilegen Geistes in Christus und den Christen: Eine Person in vielen Personen*, 2nd ed. (Munich: Schöning, 1967); for a brief study of Mühlen in English, see Congar, *I Believe in the Holy Spirit*, 1:22-25; for Kasper's position, see Walter Kasper, *Jesus the Christ*, trans. V. Green (New York: Paulist, 1976), esp. 251.

[65]David Coffey develops his proposal in several writings such as *Deus Trinitas*; "*Did You Receive the Holy Spirit When You Believed?*"; and "Spirit Christology and the Trinity," 315-46.

[66]Del Colle points to the work of James Dunn as an example of functional modalism. See Del Colle, *Christ and the Spirit*, 141-47, 169-74. For Dunn's position, and, at times, evolving or shifting views, see James D. G. Dunn, *Jesus and the Spirit: A Study of the Religious and Charismatic Experience of Jesus and the First Christians as Reflected in the New Testament* (Grand Rapids: Eerdmans, 1975); "Jesus—Flesh and Spirit: An Exposition of Romans 1:3-4," in *Christology*, vol. 1 of *The Christ and the Spirit* (Grand Rapids: Eerdmans, 1998), 126-53; "Rediscovering the Spirit (1)," in *Pneumatology*, vol. 2 of *The Christ and the Spirit* (Grand Rapids: Eerdmans, 1998), 43-61; "Rediscovering the Spirit (2)," in *Pneumatology*, 62–80; and "2 Corinthians 3:17," in *Christology*, 115-25; Del Colle argues, by contrast, that "faith, hope, and love are the responses of human agency to the divine initiative. The latter is actualized in christological and pneumatological modalities." Del Colle, *Christ and the Spirit*, 175.

[67]Del Colle, *Christ and the Spirit*, 174-76.

pointing us to him by faith.[68] In the Eucharist, Christ comes to us bodily and is also remembered; on the other hand, the Spirit is not remembered but "invoked" in prayer for faith and love.[69]

Concerning hope, Christ's presence comes to us in his promise of a redemption that is to be fully expected, which means that the risen Christ "is yet to be fully known" since we still live in expectation of his return or parousia and our own bodily resurrection.[70] The Spirit's presence "is yet to be fully experienced," because, although the Spirit dwells in us as the firstfruits of the resurrection and we experience a foretaste of its gifts, we are still in a sense expecting the fullness of the Spirit in our resurrection in the likeness of Christ.[71] In the case of Christ, he has already entered that resurrection life in all fullness. We have yet to know him fully in his glory and to experience fully his likeness by the Spirit at the end.

Finally, regarding love, Christ's presence comes to us in his self-giving love to the Father on the cross and his self-giving love to the church by sending the Spirit.[72] By dwelling in our hearts, the Spirit makes us aware of Christ's self-giving to the Father and to us and makes possible our participation in such Christlike self-giving through love of God and neighbor.[73] By distinguishing the modalities of the Son's and the Spirit's presences in the church's faith, hope, and love, Del Colle averts a collapse of the Spirit's mission into that of the Son, but also offers us a way to articulate how the two persons are present to us and with us even today.

*Dealing with human culture, social praxis, and interreligious dialogue.* In his final chapter, Del Colle suggests ways in which a Spirit Christology can offer a lens to deal with three contemporary concerns, namely, human experience, social justice, and religious pluralism. Here the author argues for discerning the distinct, though related, missions of Christ and the Spirit in the church through

---

[68]Del Colle, *Christ and the Spirit*, 176-77.
[69]Del Colle, *Christ and the Spirit*, 177.
[70]Del Colle, *Christ and the Spirit*, 177.
[71]Del Colle, *Christ and the Spirit*, 177-78; Del Colle sums up the distinctions by arguing that "in the ecclesial witness to the divine agency and presence the distinction between the *Christus praesens* and the *Spiritus praesens* is preserved by recognition of the corporeal and anamnetic dimensions of the former and anonymous and epiclectic dimensions of the latter. 'Inseparable but non-identical' was the formula I utilized to describe the relationship between these aspects of the divine presence that was intended to preserve the integrity of the hypostatic distinctions in God and, therefore, the uniqueness of each of the temporal missions." Del Colle, *Christ and the Spirit*, 196.
[72]Del Colle, *Christ and the Spirit*, 178.
[73]Del Colle, *Christ and the Spirit*, 178-79.

her mission and witness in the world. In terms of human experience, Del Colle appeals to Walter Kasper's argument that all humans ultimately find in Jesus Christ and his life the truth about their created identity, their sin before God, and their divinization.[74] He then adds the pneumatological aspect to the argument by correlating Kasper's christological anthropology with Franz Jozef van Beeck's thesis, according to which the Holy Spirit acts as "the agent of inclusion, conversion, and transfiguration" who leads humans respectively to confess Jesus as Lord, to follow him, and to share in his resurrection hope.[75] Based on their own relation to the risen Lord, believers speak in the Spirit by pointing out how all human aspirations are met in "the temporal and (eschatological!) missions of the Son and the Spirit."[76]

Concerning social justice, Del Colle argues for a soft or indirect relationship between salvation from God and liberation in history grounded in the Son's historical redemption of humanity from sin and death through his cross and resurrection. By making us children of God, the Spirit gives us a foretaste of our final redemption from sin and death in the resurrection.[77] When the people of God act in the Spirit through their witness in word and deed on behalf of suffering and oppressed people, who experience in various ways the effects of sin and death in the world, the Spirit brings a foretaste of the age to come into the present.[78] In that sense, human actions in history, especially those mediated by God's people, that seek liberation from oppressive socioeconomic or psychological structures may potentially function as a sign that invites all people to see their hopes for freedom realized ultimately in God's redemption from sin, death, and evil through Christ.[79] In general, Del Colle hesitates to speak in a definitive dogmatic sense about the Spirit's presence in the world, preferring to speak of the Spirit's presence in the church for the sake of the world.

Regarding religious pluralism, Del Colle takes as his starting point Aloysius Pieris's method of dialogue between Christians and people of other religions, in which the parties in conversation learn about and share each other's religious or "primordial experiences" and their "collective memories" of the same in their

[74]Del Colle, *Christ and the Spirit*, 204.
[75]Del Colle, *Christ and the Spirit*, 205.
[76]Del Colle, *Christ and the Spirit*, 205.
[77]Del Colle, *Christ and the Spirit*, 209.
[78]Del Colle, *Christ and the Spirit*, 208.
[79]Del Colle, *Christ and the Spirit*, 210.

traditions' guiding narratives.[80] In this process of dialogue, the church always interprets theologically what she hears and says. Del Colle suggests that in that process of interpretation, Christians will inevitably seek to correlate collective experiences of neighbors from other religions with those of the Christian tradition. This negotiation happens when Christians look for "christological analogues" in other religions, and by so doing implicitly acknowledge the uniqueness and normativity of Christ's identity as the Son who bears and gives the Spirit for the sake of the world.[81]

There is also another way to dialogue, which is complementary to the first, where the Christian adapts a certain "christological kenosis" (Pieris's term) and looks for more implicit "central motifs" that religions might share apart from an explicit mention of Christ.[82] Del Colle associates the latter move with a different type of methodology in which the work of the Spirit is not yet spoken of "in relation to Christ and his work," but more generally in terms of "the Spirit's work in creation, Israel, the secular order, and in other religions even as we still confess the unique work in Jesus Christ."[83] Even though Del Colle does not elaborate on the second approach, one sees in his methodology a desire to strike a delicate balance between ecumenism in a pluralistic world and Christian uniqueness. He does so through a type of interreligious dialogue that seeks to neither fit the other's views into Christian views nor move away from the traditional Christian claim to the centrality of Christ and the normativity of the Christian story for the world.

## PREPARING THE WAY AHEAD: A BRIEF ASSESSMENT OF SPIRIT CHRISTOLOGY IN NORTH AMERICA

We have looked at two North American theologians' distinct approaches to Spirit Christology in a trinitarian key. Framed around the thesis that the Holy Spirit rests on the Son's body in order to rest on human bodies, Anglican theologian Eugene Rogers articulates a narrative approach to the field that tracks the biblical dynamics

---

[80]Del Colle, *Christ and the Spirit*, 210-11.

[81]Del Colle, *Christ and the Spirit*, 212. Although Del Colle does not give specific examples, a search for christological analogues might include questions about whether other religions have concepts similar to divine incarnation or redemption through sacrifice and death.

[82]Del Colle, *Christ and the Spirit*, 212. Del Colle does not offer examples, but some might include questions about other religions' views on life and death, salvation or redemption (from something or someone), or holiness and spirituality.

[83]Del Colle, *Christ and the Spirit*, 212.

of the Spirit's resting on the Son throughout various events of his life. As he tells the Spirit's story in the resurrection, annunciation, baptism, transfiguration, and ascension of Christ, the author interweaves into the rich biblical accounts complementary liturgical, sacramental, and ecclesial images from a number of church fathers (especially from the Eastern church).

Tracking the place of the Spirit in the Western scholastic tradition, particularly in the neo-scholastic development of the theology of the incarnation and grace, Roman Catholic theologian Ralph Del Colle offers a more historical approach to Spirit Christology. Like Rogers, the author tells a story of the Spirit in such a way that the Spirit's role in the humanity of the Son allows for human participation in the grace of the same Spirit. To do so, the author gathers building blocks from neo- and post-neo-scholastic theologians to offer his own constructive proposal for recovering a robust Spirit Christology in a Western trinitarian framework.

While Rogers tends to stress biblical and patristic images in his narrative approach to the Spirit in bodies, Del Colle works closely with Western systematic concepts in his historical tracking of the trinitarian nuances of the neo-scholastic theology of grace and the incarnation. Both types of presentation have their merits. Generally speaking, the former appeals more to our visual imagination through a feast of multiple images of the Spirit at work in our lives, and the latter requires more of our capacity for abstract engagement with a few specific concepts and specialized philosophical frameworks employed among some Western theologians working out the place of the Spirit in Christ and in us. At the end of the day, both approaches complement one another.

As we shall see in the next chapter, early church theologians have generally used both of these approaches in their portrayals of the divinity of the Spirit, the Spirit's role in Christ's life, and the place of the Spirit in the life of the saints. Some are more devotional or narrative-oriented in their catechesis. Others are more apologetic or concept-oriented. Most bring these orientations together in their preaching, teaching, and spiritual care.

My own work in the field has attempted to bring together concept and image, apologetic and narrative approaches, in the formulation of a trinitarian Spirit Christology. Along the lines of constructive theology, I have proposed the addition to Lutheran Christology of a way of speaking about the incarnation that highlights the role of the Holy Spirit in making the humanity of the

Logos a suitable instrument for the latter's work of salvation and for our sharing in the gift of his Spirit.[84] Shaped significantly by the Alexandrian christological tradition, Lutheran Christology asserts a way of speaking or "kind" (Lat. *genus*) of statement about the incarnation—known as the *genus maiestaticum*—according to which the Logos communicates his divine majesty (Lat. *maiestas*) and power to and through his human nature. Otherwise stated, as the subject of his own actions, the Logos sanctifies, exalts, and glorifies his own humanity through his divine power. Although this insight takes seriously the unity of Christ's person and the communication of divine and human attributes in his person, it does not yet address Christ's relationship to the Father and to us in the Spirit.[85] The pneumatic aspect of the mystery of Christ is missing or at least underdeveloped.

To complement a Logos-oriented Christology with a pneumatic trajectory, I drew insights from the Western side of Lutheran Christology and its use of the scholastic category of habitual grace (Lat. *gratia habitualis*), which deals with the holiness of Christ or, more broadly, the Spirit's presence and activity in Christ's life and mission. I argued for a *genus habitualis* or *genus pneumatikon*, namely, a kind of statement about the Spirit's role in the mystery of the incarnation that draws out more clearly the identity of the incarnate Logos as the receiver, bearer, and giver of God's Spirit.[86] From a trinitarian angle, this *genus* of the Spirit is useful for distinguishing the Logos's work through his human nature (Logos Christology) from the indwelling of the Spirit in him (Spirit Christology). Deploying a *genus* of the Spirit in Christology yields some theological benefits.

First, in terms of soteriology, a *genus pneumatikon* shows that "the divine Logos allows the Holy Spirit to sanctify and perfect his humanity, to make it holy,

---

[84]Sánchez, *Receiver, Bearer, and Giver of God's Spirit*, 170-80.

[85]In Reformed Christology, the unity of the two natures of Christ and his work are mediated by the person and work of the Spirit; in Lutheran Christology, the work of the Spirit in Christ's life and work is mediated by the Logos's work in and through his assumed humanity. For an assessment of how a Spirit Christology in a trinitarian key can deal constructively with the ecumenical challenge of differences in Reformed and Lutheran Christologies and their corresponding views of Christ's presence in the Lord's Supper, see Leopoldo A. Sánchez M., "More Promise Than Ambiguity: Pneumatological Christology as a Model for Ecumenical Engagement," in *Critical Issues in Ecclesiology*, ed. Alberto García and Susan K. Wood (Grand Rapids: Eerdmans, 2011), 198-207.

[86]For the development of my work in this area, see Leopoldo A. Sánchez M., "Sculpting Christ in Us: Public Faces of the Spirit in God's World," in Habets, *Third Article Theology*, 302-5; "The Holy Spirit in Christ: Pneumatological Christology as a Ground for a Christ-Centered Pneumatology," in *Propter Christum: Christ at the Center*, ed. Scott Murray et al. (St. Louis: Luther Academy, 2013), 347-52; and "Pneumatology: Key to Understanding the Trinity," in *Who Is God? In the Light of the Lutheran Confessions*, ed. John A. Maxfield (St. Louis: Luther Academy, 2012), 137-39.

so that it may be the Logos's instrument of salvation for all humanity."[87] In more biblical language, the Holy Spirit orients the whole work of Christ as God's faithful Son and anointed servant toward his death and resurrection, and therefore toward our redemption from sin, death, and the devil. The Western scholastic category of habitual gifts also has the potential to link Christ's holiness to the sanctification of his saints, while making Christ's holiness unique. Since the divine Logos freely sanctified his humanity through the Spirit for our sake, or allowed the Spirit to sanctify his humanity for us from the time of the personal union, the Son's humanity becomes "not only 'a' but 'the' suitable instrument for our salvation."[88] In that sense, the presence of the Spirit in Christ is qualitatively different from ours, and there is a pneumatic discontinuity between Christ and us.

Second, in the mystery of salvation, Christ gives us his Spirit through the grace of adoption. A *genus pneumatikon* highlights this continuity between the Spirit in Christ and his saints, inviting us to reflect more deeply about the pneumatic link between Christology and areas such as ecclesiology, sacraments, and mission. Rogers's narrative approach asks what the resting of the Spirit on the body of Christ means for his sacramental body and for his mystical body (church). Del Colle's historical approach explores what the distinct yet related presences of the Spirit and the Son in the church mean for the church's witness in a religiously pluralistic and socially conscious culture. Yet a need arises in the field for mining the various forms of Christ's holiness displayed in his saints by the formative work of his Spirit.

To fill this gap, I have inquired into the fruitfulness of a Spirit Christology for articulating a theology of the sanctified life, paying special attention to Martin Luther.[89] The current work paves the way for expanding on this work in a more

[87]Sánchez, *Receiver, Bearer, and Giver of God's Spirit*, 176. In the Catholic tradition, Ladaria states a similar thought: "Jesus is always the Son of God and is so also as a man from the first moment of his conception; yet nothing prevents us . . . from seeing this truth, which the theology of the incarnation considers with reason to be acquired from the beginning, as one that is developed in time, in the growth of his humanity, in the succession of different moments that bring to fulfillment his saving work, and in the intensity of his relationship with the Father (with respect to his assumed humanity)." Luis F. Ladaria, "La unción de Jesús y el don del Espíritu," 557 (translation mine); "Therefore, the Holy Spirit acts on this Jesus, personally identical with the Logos, in distinct moments of his existence for the fulfillment of his life as Son, the perfection of his filiation already possessed from the beginning (cf. *Heb* 5, 9). If the divine filiation of Jesus has its basis in that he is the Logos of God, the historical fulfillment of his filial life for the salvation of humanity . . . must be attributed to the action of the Spirit of God in him." Ladaria, "Cristología del Logos y cristología el Espíritu," 355-56 (translation mine).

[88]Sánchez, *Receiver, Bearer, and Giver of God's Spirit*, 177.

[89]Sánchez, *Receiver, Bearer, and Giver of God's Spirit*, 219-37.

ecumenical direction, showing how early church theologians also used a Spirit Christology to paint a variety of images describing the Holy Spirit's formation of the saints after the likeness of Christ. The heart of this book lies in my proposal for five models of sanctification, each dealing with different issues in the Christian life. At the end of my proposal, in a final chapter, I also deal with another question that has not received attention in North American expressions of Spirit Christology, namely, how a models-based approach to life in the Spirit of Christ can address the spiritual needs and hopes of North Americans.

2

# VOICES FROM THE PAST

## PATRISTIC IMAGES *of the* SANCTIFYING SPIRIT

To show how a Spirit Christology in a trinitarian key offers a suitable framework for discussing what human participation in the Spirit of God entails, this chapter explores early Christian writers' insights into the relationship between Jesus and the Spirit and its implications for the sanctified life. These theologians from the past are worth listening to because they faced the same questions we continue to ask today about the relationship between Christ and the Spirit and because they thought at length about the Holy Spirit's role in our lives. Moreover, by focusing on Irenaeus and later fourth-century writers Cyril of Jerusalem, Athanasius of Alexandria, Basil of Caesarea, Dydimus the Blind, and Ambrose of Milan, we can see how they laid out key building blocks for a Spirit Christology that does not replace but complements the classic Logos (two natures) Christology articulated more formally in the aftermath of the Council of Nicaea (AD 325).

To various degrees, these theologians wanted to safeguard the Son's preexistence and incarnation, while giving his life and mission a pneumatic trajectory. Given our interest in sanctification, we will pay special attention to how they reflected on and expressed with rich imagery the link between the Spirit's presence and activity in and through Jesus and the Spirit's action in the lives of the saints. Their use of a devotional bent in parts of their apologetic works will prepare us for developing a models-based approach to holiness that fosters the use of an array of narratives and images for telling the story of the Spirit's work of christoformation, that is, of conforming humans to the image of Christ.

We will conclude the chapter with a sketch of basic theological themes and related questions often dealt with in the field of Spirit Christology that these church fathers already reflected on in their own day. These themes are the place of the Spirit in an account of God's salvation, the relationship between the Son's incarnation and the presence of the Spirit in him, and the degree of continuity and discontinuity between the Spirit's presence in Christ and the saints.

## MINING PATRISTIC TRADITIONS: SPIRIT CHRISTOLOGY IN EARLY CHURCH THEOLOGIANS

In this section, we explore primarily the contributions of fourth-century theologians toward a Spirit-oriented Christology in a trinitarian key. Because our approach assumes the complementarity of Spirit- and Logos-oriented readings of the identity of Jesus, we focus our investigation on thinkers working in a Nicene framework. As we journey with Christian writers from the East and the West, we pay special attention to the arguments and images they use to integrate the Spirit into the life of Christ and Christians, seeing how they handle the pneumatic continuity between Christ and the saints.

But first, as an entrée to their thoughts, let us begin with an important figure who precedes them. Irenaeus, Bishop of Lyons (ca. AD 130–200), was an influential ante-Nicene theologian, whose thinking about the significance of the baptism of Jesus at the Jordan laid down key building blocks for later expressions of Spirit Christology. Listening to voices from the past, let us see how our authors weave apologetic and devotional language in their presentation of the Christian story from a pneumatic angle.

***Irenaeus of Lyons: Redoing Adam's history, God's hands in flesh, Spirit's engrafting.*** Despite being a diverse group with a spectrum of ideas and practices, the "Gnostics" (from Gk. *gnōsis*, meaning knowledge), a second century movement espousing a spiritual salvation obtained through special or secret knowledge, shared the assumption that "matter is incapable of salvation."[1] Given their disdain for material, created, or bodily substance, they proposed a "spiritual" form of redemption transcending the body and achieved through "perfect knowledge."[2] Applying this dualism

[1] Irenaeus, *Against Heresies* 1.6.1 (*ANF* 1:324).
[2] Irenaeus, *Against Heresies* 1.6.2 (*ANF* 1:324).

between material and spiritual realms of existence to their reading of Scripture, some Gnostics taught that a "spiritual being" called Christ (also known as Spirit) descended in the form of a dove on the mere human being called Jesus in order to use the latter as a temporary earthly channel or funnel "to proclaim the unknown Father" (or spiritual gnosis) to others before eventually departing from him at his death.[3]

Two problems arise with the Gnostic reading of the Jordan event that take aim at God's story of salvation. First, Christ and Jesus are split into two different beings, effectively denying their union or the reality of the incarnation. Second, since Christ and Spirit are synonymous metaphors for describing spiritual presence in a general way, the Holy Spirit loses its own distinctiveness (its personhood) in the life and mission of Jesus. Driving the Gnostic reading as a whole is the principle that neither the Son (Lord) nor the Spirit associate with the body. The principle applies both to the body of Jesus and his mystical body, the church. This raises a question: How does God save and sanctify that which God does not take on? A major contribution to the answer comes from Irenaeus's response to the Gnostics, which also shapes later thinking about the relationship between the Son's incarnation, his anointing with the Holy Spirit, and human sharing in Christ's redemption and sanctification through his Spirit.

Here is how Irenaeus tells the story of God's redemption.[4] Through his two "hands," the Logos (Word) and the Holy Spirit, God the Father vivifies humans by restoring in them the image and likeness of God lost by their forefather Adam in the fall.

> The Word of the Father and the Spirit of God, having become united with the ancient substance of Adam's formation, rendered man living and perfect, receptive of the perfect Father, in order that as in the natural [Adam] we all were dead, so in the spiritual we may all be made alive. For never at any time did Adam escape the *hands* of God, to whom the Father speaking, said, "Let us make man in Our image, after Our likeness." And for this reason in the last times (*fine*), not by the will of the flesh, nor by the will of man, but by the good pleasure of the Father, His hands formed a living man, in order that Adam might be created [again] after the image and likeness of God.[5]

---

[3]Irenaeus, *Against Heresies* 1.26.1 (*ANF* 1:352). On the varieties of Gnostic positions on Jesus' baptism, see Antonio Orbe, "El Espíritu en el bautismo de Jesús (en torno a San Ireneo)," *Gregorianum* 76, no. 4 (1995): 663-68, 680-86.

[4]For a fuller assessment of Irenaeus's Spirit Christology, see Leopoldo A. Sánchez M., *Receiver, Bearer, and Giver of God's Spirit: Jesus' Life in the Spirit as a Lens for Theology and Life* (Eugene, OR: Pickwick, 2015), 12-20.

[5]Irenaeus, *Against Heresies* 5.1.3 (*ANF* 1:527); "Now shall God be glorified in His handiwork, fitting it so as to be conformable to, and modelled after, His own Son. For by the hands of the Father, that is by the Son

In this theology of recapitulation, whereby God saves humanity by doing the history of Adam over again for our sake, both the incarnation of the Word and his anointing with the Holy Spirit at the Jordan are indispensable events.[6] Irenaeus describes these episodes in such a way that God's two "hands" truly touch and become intimately involved with the body, becoming accustomed to inhabiting material and creaturely existence. Because the Word (Logos) of God, the spiritual Adam, assumed the formation (human substance) of the natural Adam, and the Holy Spirit anointed his body at the Jordan, the race of Adam (humanity) can now receive the indwelling of the Spirit of life. Such indwelling by the Spirit vivifies the dead Adam in us through our sharing in the likeness of the risen Son.

Irenaeus anticipates Athanasius's theology of deification (Gk. *theosis*), a view of salvation according to which God becomes human so that humans can be deified or share by the grace of adoption in God's nature or life (cf. 2 Pet 1:4). The mystery of the incarnation reveals that God works through (not outside of) creation in order to restore creation to fellowship with the Father: "The Word of God . . . dwelt in man, and became Son of man, that He might accustom man to receive God, and God to dwell in man, according to the good pleasure of the Father."[7] Yet for God to dwell in humans, the Holy Spirit must also get involved with the material body, first the body of the incarnate Son and, through him, the body of those baptized into him. After the incarnation, Christ's reception of the Spirit in the flesh serves as a condition in God's plan of salvation for his giving of the Spirit to all flesh.

> Wherefore He [i.e., the Spirit] did also descend upon the Son of God, made the Son of man, becoming accustomed in fellowship with Him to dwell in the human race, to rest with human beings, and to dwell in the workmanship of God, working the will of the Father in them, and renewing them from their old habits into the newness of Christ.[8]

Against the Gnostic identification of Christ and the Spirit with the same spiritual being, the Spirit's role at the Jordan is not primarily to reveal to others that

---

and the Holy Spirit, man, and not [merely] a part of man, was made in the likeness of God." Irenaeus, *Against Heresies* 5.6.1 (*ANF* 1:531).

[6]On recapitulation, see Irenaeus, *Against Heresies* 3.21.10, 3.22.1-2 (*ANF* 1:454-55).

[7]Irenaeus, *Against Heresies* 3.20.2 (*ANF* 1:450).

[8]Irenaeus, *Against Heresies* 3.17.1 (*ANF* 1:444).

the Son is God or that the Spirit is God with the Son, but rather to highlight the Spirit's distinction from and relationship to the Son. The name "Christ" reminds us that the Father anoints the Son, and the Son "is anointed by the Spirit, who is the unction."[9] In this sense, it was at the Jordan that the Word, already united to human nature, "was made Jesus Christ."[10] At his baptism, the Spirit descends on Jesus to anoint him for his mission to preach the gospel, heal the sick, and forgive sins.[11] After carrying out his messianic mission, the Lord gives the Spirit, whom he received at the Jordan, to the church through baptism.[12] Having received the Spirit "as a gift from His Father," the Lord does "confer it upon those who are partakers of Himself, sending the Holy Spirit upon all the earth."[13]

The Spirit's resting on human beings means their restoration to the image and likeness of God, and thus a transformation from the old Adam to the new creature, "from their old habits to the newness of Christ." Bringing together 1 Corinthians 15 and Galatians 5, Irenaeus pairs our bearing of the image of the natural Adam with the works of the flesh and our bearing of the image of the heavenly Adam (Christ) with the works of the Spirit.[14] The Gnostics interpret flesh to mean exclusively body, and thus teach that God cannot save it because "flesh and blood cannot inherit the kingdom of God" (1 Cor 15:50). Irenaeus notes that "flesh" in this text does not refer to God's material handiwork but to a human life without the life-giving Spirit, and thus being "spiritual" does not refer to an existence outside the body but to the indwelling of the vivifying Spirit in the human creature.[15]

Without losing "the substance of its wood," a wild olive tree can still be dead, barren, cut off, and thrown into the fire. Likewise, humans do not lose their

---

[9]Irenaeus, *Against Heresies* 3.18.3 (*ANF* 1:446).

[10]Irenaeus, *Against Heresies* 3.9.3 (*ANF* 1:423); cf. Irenaeus, *Against Heresies* 3.16.1-2 (*ANF* 1:440-41).

[11]Irenaeus, *Against Heresies* 3.9.3 (*ANF* 1:423); cf. Irenaeus, *Against Heresies* 3.18.3 (*ANF* 1:446).

[12]Irenaeus, *Against Heresies* 3.17.1 (*ANF* 1:444). Here Irenaeus cites Mt 28:19 and alludes to Acts 2:17 (cf. Joel 2:28).

[13]Irenaeus, *Against Heresies* 3.17.2 (*ANF* 1:445).

[14]Irenaeus, *Against Heresies* 5.11.1-2 (*ANF* 1:536-37).

[15]Irenaeus, *Against Heresies* 5.9.1-2 (*ANF* 1:534-35). "When we were destitute of the celestial Spirit, we walked in former times in the oldness of the flesh, not obeying God; so now let us, receiving the Spirit, walk in newness of life, obeying God;" Irenaeus, *Against Heresies* 5.9.3 (*ANF* 1:535). "Rightly therefore does the apostle declare, 'Flesh and blood cannot inherit the kingdom of God;' and, 'Those who are in the flesh cannot please God:' not repudiating [by these words] the substance of flesh, but showing that into it the Spirit must be infused [Lat. *sed infusionem Spiritus attrahens*]." Irenaeus, *Against Heresies* 5.10.2 (*ANF* 1:536). In this section, Irenaeus cites 1 Corinthians 15:53 and Romans 8:9-10, 13.

creaturely identity and composition as God created them ("the substance of flesh"), even though they can live in the flesh (that is, without the Spirit), bearing no fruits of righteousness and losing God's kingdom.[16] Yet an old, beat-up, wild olive tree can also be grafted into a good one, and, by drawing life from it, it can become a fruit-bearing tree (see Rom 11:17). So also those who by faith receive the indwelling of the life-giving Spirit have partaken of "the engrafting of the Spirit" and "the Word of God as a graft," becoming spiritual and bearing good fruit.[17] Enlivened by the Spirit, God's restored creatures are like olive trees "being planted in the Paradise of God" and thus heirs of God's kingdom.[18]

God's first hand, his Son, dwelt with Adam by becoming one of us. God's second hand, his Spirit, dwelt with Adam by anointing the incarnate Son at his baptism so that we too might be made sons and daughters of the Father through anointing at baptism. Like other church fathers, Irenaeus teaches that in losing the image of God, the first Adam also lost spiritual fellowship with God and the Holy Spirit. In his account of the fall, Irenaeus puts these words in the mouth of sinful Adam: "I have by disobedience lost that robe of sanctity which I had from the Spirit."[19] Yet in these last days, through the Father's anointing of the incarnate Word, there is a sense in which the Holy Spirit returns to the race of Adam, resting on or clothing humans once again with his sanctity, so that they can enter into communion with God by faith in Christ and by sharing in the likeness of Christ's incorruptible and resurrected life.[20] Against the Gnostics' conception of the Spirit and the spiritual life in opposition to material creation, God's Spirit moves toward the bodily and indwells it, shaping it after the likeness of the anointed and risen Christ.

***Cyril of Jerusalem: Aromatic anointing, sanctified waters, little christs.*** The historic Christian practice of applying the chrism or anointing with oil on the baptized signifies their reception of the Holy Spirit and, therefore, a share by grace in its divine nature, sanctification, and life. In an early description of the rite of chrismation, Cyril of Jerusalem (ca. AD 313–386), a bishop of Jerusalem

---

[16]Irenaeus, *Against Heresies* 5.10.2 (*ANF* 1:536).

[17]Irenaeus, *Against Heresies* 5.10.1 (*ANF* 1:536).

[18]Irenaeus, *Against Heresies* 5.10.1 (*ANF* 1:536).

[19]Irenaeus, *Against Heresies* 3.23.5 (*ANF* 1:457).

[20]"Now the final result of the work of the Spirit is the salvation of the flesh. For what other visible fruit is there of the invisible Spirit, than the rendering of the flesh mature and capable of incorruption?" Irenaeus, *Against Heresies* 5.12.4 (*ANF* 1:538).

(beginning ca. AD 349) known for his catechetical writings, tells us that the oil was applied to "thy forehead and other senses" in a symbolic way in order to express the reality of the Spirit's shaping of the baptized after the likeness of Christ.[21] Otherwise stated, by putting on Christ in baptism, Christians are "conformable to the Son of God" and therefore "made Christs" or "images of Christ" by the action of the Holy Spirit.[22] We become, as it were, little Christs in the world. The Spirit's resting on Jesus at the Jordan anticipates this formative advent of the Spirit on us in the little Jordan of our baptism into Christ.

Cyril uses the language of imitation or partaking as a synonym for the Spirit's work of conforming us to the likeness of Christ as we share in his unction or Spirit, and thus in his death and resurrection.[23] Washed in the Jordan river, Christ sanctifies the waters with the pleasant aroma of his divine presence and with the Spirit resting on him as his equal, so that we, coming out of the baptismal waters, might partake of his anointing or Spirit.[24] Cyril's teaching on the rite of chrism or anointing illustrates how liturgical practice was informed by a Spirit-oriented Christology, which in turn invited hearers of the Christian story to see themselves as beneficiaries of the Spirit who first existed with Christ in the trinitarian life and then descended on him in the economy of salvation for our sake.

***Athanasius of Alexandria: Anointed for us, deifying grace, imaging the Son.*** Athanasius (ca. AD 296–373), bishop of Alexandria (beginning ca. AD 328) and a key player in the articulation of Nicene orthodoxy in response to the Arian controversy, set the major trinitarian and soteriological foundations for responding to the Arian argument that Christ was a son of God by "grace," "adoption," or "only by participation . . . through the Spirit," but not the Son of God by nature or "existing one in essence [Gk. *homoousios*] with the very Father."[25] Central to the Arian teaching was an adoptionist reading of the anointing of Jesus (Ps 45:7), according to which he, being a human creature of "an alterable nature," received from God at his baptism something he "needed" and eventually earned, namely, the grace of adoption "as a reward . . . gained from virtue and promotion" or "as the prize of works done."[26] When describing the relationship between God and

---

[21] Cyril of Jerusalem, *On the Mysteries* 3.3 (*NPNF*[2] 7:150).
[22] Cyril of Jerusalem, *On the Mysteries* 3.1 (*NPNF*[2] 7:149).
[23] Cyril of Jerusalem, *On the Mysteries* 3.1-2.
[24] Cyril of Jerusalem, *On the Mysteries* 3.1.
[25] Athanasius, *First Discourse Against the Arians* 3.9 (*NPNF*[2] 4:311).
[26] Athanasius, *First Discourse Against the Arians* 11.37 (*NPNF*[2] 4:328).

his Son, Arius highlights the upward movement to God of an exemplary Spirit-indwelt man.

Against the subordinationist proposal that Jesus was a mere Spirit-anointed man who was promoted to a divine-like status on the basis of his obedience, Athanasius notes that the Word "was not man, and then became God, but He was God, and then became man, and that to deify us."[27] The purpose of the anointing does not lie in the Son's becoming God (since he is already the unalterable divine Word), but rather in the Son's becoming one of us in the flesh in order to sanctify and exalt us through his Spirit. The end goal of the Son's anointing is thus not ontological, but soteriological. In the end, the anointing does not take place for the Son's benefit, but for our sake.

Due to the Arian interpretation of the baptism of Jesus, Athanasius seems hesitant at first to say that the Son receives "grace" from God, and prefers instead to speak of the Son as the "Giver of grace."[28] His point is that the anointing at the Jordan does not affect or sanctify the Son as God, confirming instead for others that the Son "is not the sanctified, but the Sanctifier."[29] As the divine Word, the Son does not "become holy"; instead, the Word became flesh "that He himself may in Himself sanctify all of us."[30] By his resurrection from the dead, those who are united to the Son's life-giving flesh become adopted sons and God's living temples through the reception of his grace and Spirit.[31] In God's plan of salvation, the Word becomes flesh to deify the flesh by his Spirit, raising it from the dead and bringing it into the Father's presence.

In Athanasius's theology, the deification of the flesh does not take place without the graced creature's participation in (or reception of) the Spirit. Such reception of the Spirit entails a sharing not only in the Son's humanity in general, but in his Spirit-anointed humanity in particular. This leads Athanasius to argue that, according to his humanity, the Son may be said to have "received grace" and been "deified" through his incarnation and exaltation; similarly, it is proper to state that the Son "was anointed with the Spirit."[32] Although Athanasius relates the anointing of the Son's flesh to his baptism at the Jordan, it is finally an

[27] Athanasius, *First Discourse Against the Arians* 11.39 (*NPNF*² 4:329).
[28] Athanasius, *First Discourse Against the Arians* 11.40 (*NPNF*² 4:329).
[29] Athanasius, *First Discourse Against the Arians* 12.46 (*NPNF*² 4:333).
[30] Athanasius, *First Discourse Against the Arians* 11.41 (*NPNF*² 4:330).
[31] Athanasius, *First Discourse Against the Arians* 11.42-43 (*NPNF*² 4:330-31).
[32] Athanasius, *First Discourse Against the Arians* 12.45-46 (*NPNF*² 4:333).

anointing that takes place before the Jordan at the time of his incarnation. "I, being the Father's Word, I give to Myself, when becoming man, the Spirit; and Myself, become man, do I sanctify in Him, that henceforth in Me . . . all may be sanctified."[33] The Son does not receive the anointing of the Spirit from the Father at the Jordan. Rather, the Son gives to himself the Spirit—and thus sanctifies and anoints his own flesh—at the time of his incarnation. Anointing functions as a synonym for the incarnation.

Given Athanasius's greater interest in the soteriological significance of the incarnation for humanity as a whole than in the import of particular events in the Son's own human becoming, the Alexandrian does not distinguish between the holiness of the Son from the moment of the union and his anointing at the Jordan.[34] More simply, sanctification and anointing point to the singular action of the Spirit whom the Son has in the flesh from the moment of the union. Still, Athanasius's soteriology offers a Spirit-oriented Christology as a ground for human reception of the Spirit, in which the baptism of Jesus at the Jordan functions as a revelatory instance of the Son's prior bearing of the Spirit and also of his identity as giver of the Spirit to the church.

> But the Saviour . . . being God, and ever ruling in the Father's kingdom, and being Himself He that supplies the Holy Ghost, nevertheless is here said to be anointed, that, as before, being said as man to be anointed with the Spirit, He might provide for us men, not only exaltation and resurrection, but the indwelling and intimacy of the Spirit.[35]

Setting the Jordan event in an ecclesial trajectory, Athanasius argues that "the Spirit's descent on Him in Jordan was a descent upon us, because of His bearing of our body."[36] The Spirit's descent on the Son "did not take place for the promotion of the Word, but for our sanctification, that we might share His anointing" and

---

[33]Athanasius, *First Discourse Against the Arians* 12.46 (*NPNF*[2] 4:333). "For I the Word am the chrism, and that which has the chrism from Me is the Man; not then without Me could He be called Christ, but being with Me and I in Him." Athanasius, *Fourth Discourse Against the Arians* 36 (*NPNF*[2] 4:447).

[34]For a study of Athanasius's view of the anointing, see Sánchez, *Receiver, Bearer, and Giver of God's Spirit*, 21-27. Bobrinskoy argues that, in distinction from Basil and Chrysostom, Gregory of Nazianzus's handling of the Spirit's relationship to Christ is closer to the Alexandrian tradition (represented by Athanasius), since "he seems more reluctant . . . to investigate the mystery of Christ's humanity and the mode of the Spirit's presence within that humanity. The Spirit, he affirmed, is present but not acting: a formula that expresses his fear of diminishing the personal role of the divine Word-become-man." Boris Bobrinskoy, "The Indwelling of the Spirit in Christ," *St. Vladimir's Theological Quarterly* 28, no. 1 (1984): 64.

[35]Athanasius, *First Discourse Against the Arians* 12.46 (*NPNF*[2] 4:333).

[36]Athanasius, *First Discourse Against the Arians* 12:47 (*NPNF*[2] 4:333).

become God's temples through the Spirit's indwelling.[37] In Christian baptism, the Holy Spirit unites us to the Son in his baptism, so that "when He is baptized, we it is who in Him are baptized."[38]

Christian baptism signifies that the Spirit sanctifies humans by giving them the shape of Christ, the anointed one. To the language of anointing (see 1 Jn 2:7), Athanasius adds the Pauline image of the Spirit as the "seal" who "makes an imprint of the Son, so that whoever has been sealed by the Spirit has the form of Christ" (Eph 1:13; 4:30).[39] The anointed ones have the "breath of the Son," and thus spread "the sweet fragrance and the good odor of the anointer" (2 Cor 2:15).[40] They become deified, or sharers in the divine nature, not in a way that they become God by nature but by receiving the form of the Word (Son) "in the Spirit" (see 2 Pet 1:4).[41]

Since the Spirit "receives from the Son" what is his (Jn 16:14) and conforms the saints to the image of the firstborn among many brethren (Rom 8:29), Athanasius refers to the Spirit as the icon or "Image of the Son."[42] This description of the Spirit has implications for trinitarian theology and the theology of sanctification. Just as the Son exists "in the Spirit as in his own image" and the Father exists "in the Son" in their unity with one another, "there is one holiness which comes from the Father through the Son in the Holy Spirit" in their communion with us.[43] The Spirit is not foreign to the Son, but proper to him, both in relation to one another and in relation to us.

Through the Spirit of the Son, humans are sanctified after the image of the Son with whom the Spirit marks them in baptism. In Athanasius's theology, sanctification serves as an inclusive term that can describe various works of the Spirit. Having said that, a key hermeneutical lens that unlocks the function of sanctification language in Athanasius's soteriology is his appeal to an economic or incarnational Spirit Christology. This theological framework serves as the basis for telling the biblical story of our human participation in the divine life through conformity to Christ's human anointing, life and mission, resurrection, exaltation, and presence before the Father.

---

[37]Athanasius, *First Discourse Against the Arians* 12.47 (*NPNF*[2] 4:333).

[38]Athanasius, *First Discourse Against the Arians* 12.48 (*NPNF*[2] 4:335).

[39]Athanasius, *Letters to Serapion on the Holy Spirit* 2.12.3, in *Works on the Spirit: Athanasius the Great and Didymus the Blind*, trans. Mark DelCogliano, Andrew Radde-Gallwitz, and Lewis Ayres (Crestwood, NY: St. Vladimir's Seminary Press, 2011), 121; cf. 1.23.4-6, pp. 89-90.

[40]Athanasius, *Letters to Serapion on the Holy Spirit* 1.23.7, p. 90; 2.12.2, p. 121.

[41]Athanasius, *Letters to Serapion on the Holy Spirit* 1.23.7, 1.24.4, p. 90.

[42]Athanasius, *Letters to Serapion on the Holy Spirit* 1.20.6, p. 85; 1.24.7-8, p. 91.

[43]Athanasius, *Letters to Serapion on the Holy Spirit* 1.20.4, pp. 84-85.

***Basil of Caesarea: Inseparable companions, God's breath returns, paradise restored.*** As part of his defense of the Spirit's divine identity against the pneumatomachians ("Spirit deniers" or "Spirit fighters"), Basil of Caesarea (AD 330–379), one of the Cappadocian fathers (with Gregory of Nazianzus and Gregory of Nyssa) known for his defense of Nicene orthodoxy, argues that the inseparability of the Holy Spirit and the Son in God's plan of salvation reveals the Spirit's divine communion and union with the Son and the Father. When the Lord commanded trinitarian baptism (Mt 28:19), he included the Holy Spirit in the divine name along with the other two persons (hypostases).[44] The unity of their names and their works toward creation corresponds to their communion in nature. In the mystery of the incarnation, for instance, the Holy Spirit "was made an unction, and being inseparably present was with the very flesh of the Lord."[45] In the wilderness, his working of miracles, and resurrection, the incarnate Son's "every operation was wrought with the co-operation of the Spirit."[46] This Spirit-oriented description of the incarnation, which bears witness to the joint mission of the Son and the Spirit, makes room for a theology of sanctification, that is, an account of human sharing in the Spirit whom Christ bears and gives to others.

When the risen Son breathes the Spirit on the disciples, he renews them in the image of God, "restoring the grace, that came of the inbreathing God, which man had lost" in Paradise (Jn 20:22-23, cf. Gen 2:7).[47] An inclusive term, sanctification involves "our restoration to paradise," as well as "our ascension into the kingdom of heaven, our return to the adoption of sons, our liberty to call God our Father, our being made partakers of the grace of Christ, our being called children of light, our sharing in eternal glory."[48] Seen from below, in terms of its works, the Spirit's sanctification reveals its divine majesty.[49] Or conversely, seen from above, because the Spirit is "of God," "proceeding out of God . . . as Breath of His mouth," as well as the "'Spirit of Christ,' as being by nature closely

---

[44]Basil of Caesarea, *On the Spirit* 10.24 (*NPNF*$^2$ 8:16); cf. Basil of Caesarea, *On the Spirit* 18.44-45 (*NPNF*$^2$ 8:27-28).

[45]Basil of Caesarea, *On the Spirit* 16.39 (*NPNF*$^2$ 8:25).

[46]Basil of Caesarea, *On the Spirit* 16.39 (*NPNF*$^2$ 8:25).

[47]Basil of Caesarea, *On the Spirit* 16.39 (*NPNF*$^2$ 8:25).

[48]Basil of Caesarea, *On the Spirit* 15.36 (*NPNF*$^2$ 8:22). Basil describes these and other sanctifying or perfecting works of the Spirit such as the resurrection from the dead, the renewal of our present life against the passions of the flesh, communion with God, heavenly citizenship, as well as being deified by grace. Cf. Basil of Caesarea, *On the Spirit* 9.22-23 (*NPNF*$^2$ 8:15-16), and 19.49 (*NPNF*$^2$ 8:31).

[49]Basil of Caesarea, *On the Spirit* 19.49 (*NPNF*$^2$ 8:30-31).

related to Him," the Holy Spirit is glorified not as a creature but as the "supreme power of sanctification."[50] Moreover, since the Spirit shares the "holy" name with the other two persons, the Spirit "is described not as being sanctified, but as sanctifying."[51]

Basil's account of the sanctifying work of the Holy Spirit depends on the cooperation of the Spirit with the Son in their joint work of bringing people to communion with God the Father. In God's plan of salvation, the possibility of such sanctification is grounded in the incarnate Son's identity as the bearer and giver of the Spirit. Those who share in the Spirit of the Son through baptism are united to Christ in his death and resurrection, and by taking the form of Christ are restored to the image of God lost by Adam in Paradise.[52] Through the Spirit's work of christoformation, the baptized are initiated into the "pattern life" or "imitation" of Christ's life, which besides a participation in his future resurrection from the dead includes living as new creatures according to his example of gentleness or lowliness, endurance or long-suffering, and freedom from the power of sin.[53] Deification and sanctification go hand in hand in patristic accounts of the Christian life.

For Basil, the Holy Spirit's work of sanctification, broadly speaking, is anchored in a pneumatologically-informed Christology, which in turn reveals the unity of the Trinity. As the work of the Father through the Son in the Spirit, sanctification does not reveal a Spirit that is less than divine, but a Spirit who receives our worship with the Son and the Father in the trinitarian doxology. To worship the Father through the Son "in" the Spirit in their communion with us (economy) is to worship the Spirit "with" the Son and the Father in their communion with one another (theology).[54] To receive the breath of God by faith and baptism into Christ is to be brought into the true worship of God and thus into fellowship with the Father and the Son.

***Didymus the Blind: Partaken but not partaking, indwelling wisdom, master teacher.*** Beginning with the divine identity of the Spirit as "immutable sanctifier . . . and bestower of divine knowledge," Didymus (ca. AD 313–398), an ascetic lay person favorably approved by bishop Athanasius and others for his gifts

---

[50]Basil of Caesarea, *On the Spirit* 18.46 (*NPNF*[2] 8:29).
[51]Basil of Caesarea, *On the Spirit* 19.48 (*NPNF*[2] 8:30).
[52]Basil of Caesarea, *On the Spirit* 15.34-35 (*NPNF*[2] 8:21-22).
[53]Basil of Caesarea, *On the Spirit* 15.35 (*NPNF*[2] 8:21-22).
[54]Basil of Caesarea, *On the Spirit* 26.63 (*NPNF*[2] 8:39-40), and 27.68 (*NPNF*[2] 8:43).

as a teacher of theology, speaks of the economic work of the Spirit who "indwells the soul and the mind as the producer of speech, wisdom and knowledge."[55] Echoing Athanasius's distinction between the divine Son's ontological being of the same essence (Gk. *homoosious*) as the Father and our human participation in the Spirit by the grace of adoption, Didymus argues that the Holy Spirit's indwelling in the graced creature distinguishes the Spirit from the rest of God's creatures. As God and the source of holiness, the Spirit is not capable (Lat. *non capax*) of partaking in "another's sanctity," but through its sanctifying work "others are capable of participating in him" (Lat. *capabilis*).[56]

Didymus picks up on the Pauline image of the Spirit as the "seal" of redemption who imprints its image and wisdom on those whom it inhabits (Eph 1:13-14; 4:30). Since the Spirit is inseparable from Christ, who is the Wisdom of God (1 Cor 1:24), the Spirit "seals those who receive the form and image of God and leads them to the seal of Christ, filling them with wisdom, and knowledge, and above all faith."[57] Being marked with the Spirit, the saints become practitioners of its wisdom, acquiring a spiritual form of life and conduct. In that way, Christians are like apprentices who hone their craft in everyday life by applying themselves to the training of the master Spirit.

> For just as someone, who takes up a practice and a virtue, receives into his mind, as it were, a seal and an image of the knowledge which he takes up, so too the one who is made a sharer in the Holy Spirit becomes, through communion in him, simultaneously spiritual and holy.[58]

A life of witness to Christ illustrates how sanctification is linked to a sharing in the Spirit's wisdom, one of its great gifts to the church (1 Cor 12:8). As the anointing who reveals Christ to the Gentiles, the Holy Spirit spreads Christ's wisdom far and wide. Filled with the Holy Spirit, the apostles speak the Word of God with confidence (Acts 4:31). Like orators who learn their rhetorical skills from wise teachers and perfect the knowledge received over time, so also preachers learn to grasp and speak the wisdom of God from the Spirit who dwells

---

[55]Didymus, *On the Holy Spirit,* in *Works on the Spirit* 2.10, p. 146. I also consulted Dídimo el Ciego, *Tratado sobre el Espíritu Santo,* trans. Carmelo Granado (Madrid: Editorial Ciudad Nueva, 1997).

[56]Didymus, *On the Holy Spirit* 2.19, p. 149. "For this reason it is possible to participate in him but not for him to participate [Lat. *Unde et ipse capabilist est, et non capax*]." Didymus, *On the Holy Spirit* 2.17, p. 148; cf. Didymus, *On the Holy Spirit* 2.54-55, p. 160.

[57]Didymus, *On the Holy Spirit,* 3.95, p. 173; cf. Didymus, *On the Holy Spirit* 3.91-94, pp. 172-73.

[58]Didymus, *On the Holy Spirit* 2.20, p.149.

in them.[59] Didymus presents Stephen, the first martyr, as a witness whose wisdom could not be resisted because he was full of the Holy Spirit who spoke through him (Acts 6:10; cf. Lk 12:11-12).[60] The Spirit of truth acts as the teacher of the saints, making them spiritual by leading them to "understand the Lord and what pertains to the will of God," and to "preach the doctrines of truth."[61] In his glorification, Christ breathes the Spirit on the disciples so that the Spirit might dwell in the hearts of believers, lifting the veils from their eyes to grasp the meaning of the Scriptures.[62]

With the effusion of "the gift of the Holy Spirit" from the risen Christ to the nations, "the fragrant name of Christ," the anointed one, spreads liberally throughout the world.[63] Though the Spirit is different in nature (Lat. *substantia*) from us, God distributed or dispersed the Spirit "by communion with those on whom God decided to bestow him."[64] To have the Spirit of Christ means to have Christ dwell in the saints (Rom 8:9-10) and shows that "the Holy Spirit is inseparable from Christ because wherever the Holy Spirit is, there also is Christ."[65] The inseparable link of Christ and the Spirit becomes evident from the very beginning of Christ's own human life. Commenting on the Creator Spirit in Luke 1:35, Didymus notes that "when the Holy Spirit came upon the virgin Mary, the creating power of the Most High fashioned the body of Christ: using it as a temple."[66] In his human life, the Lord also "received communion with the Holy Spirit," since he was full of the Holy Spirit and acted in the power of the Spirit (Lk 4:1, 14).[67] The unity of Christ and the Spirit in God's plan of salvation—in the incarnation of the Son and the indwelling of the Spirit—reveals their unity with the Father in the Godhead.

***Ambrose of Milan: Spirit fillings, oil of gladness, fragrant flower.*** In the preface to his Latin translation of Didymus's treatise on the Holy Spirit, Jerome unfairly gives Ambrose (AD 339–397), the bishop of Milan (beginning AD 374) known for his influence on Augustine of Hippo (AD 354–430), a bad reputation

---

[59]Didymus, *On the Holy Spirit* 2.32, p. 153.
[60]Didymus, *On the Holy Spirit* 2.37, 39, pp. 155-56.
[61]Didymus, *On the Holy Spirit* 3.146-152, pp. 189-91.
[62]Didymus, *On the Holy Spirit* 3.143, p. 188; cf. Didymus, *On the Holy Spirit* 3.140-142, p. 187.
[63]Didymus, *On the Holy Spirit* 2.51-52, pp. 159-60.
[64]Didymus, *On the Holy Spirit* 2.64, pp. 162-63.
[65]Didymus, *On the Holy Spirit* 3.188, p. 200.
[66]Didymus, *On the Holy Spirit* 3.144, p. 188.
[67]Didymus, *On the Holy Spirit* 3.229, p. 214.

as an unoriginal thinker who plagiarized everything he wrote about the Spirit from Didymus.[68] Carmelo Granado notes that Ambrose's contribution lies in being the first Latin writer to offer a precise and original synthesis of Greek pneumatology to the Western church.[69] Although the Latin bishop echoes many of the themes we have already explored in other Greek writers, he also contributes reflections of his own on the Spirit's work, including its presence and activity with Christ.

Like others before him, Ambrose frames his pneumatology in the Nicene context of a defense of the Spirit's divinity. Echoing Irenaeus and Basil, Ambrose sees the anointing of Christ at the Jordan as an instance of the communion of the three persons also revealed in Christian baptism. Because of "the oneness of the Name" of the three in one baptism, mentioning Christ, the one anointed, implies calling on God the Father who anointed him, "and the Holy Spirit with Whom He was anointed."[70] Possessing an attribute shared with the Lord, who in his omnipresence fills heaven and earth, the Holy Spirit shows its goodness by filling people such as the virgin Mary with its grace. The Spirit also "filled Jesus the Redeemer of the whole world," since Jesus is "full of the Holy Spirit" (Lk 4:1).[71] Yet the Spirit did not only fill Christ "according to the flesh" as other saints but as an equal, since the works Christ did through his flesh healed people as only God can do.[72]

Although the saints receive "of the Spirit," only in the Son "abides forever the fulness of the Spirit."[73] The difference does not lie in the nature of the Spirit, who fills the flesh of both the Son and the sons (and daughters) of God, but

---

[68]Without mentioning him by name, Jerome called Ambrose "a hideous little crow with colors from another [bird]," and described his work as "devoid of logical structure, completely lacking the force and rigor that would draw the reader even unwillingly to agreement." Jerome's Prologue to Didymus, *On the Holy Spirit*, 140-41. In his introduction to Ambrose's treatise, Granado sees Jerome's assessment as unfair and notes that the Latin bishop's systematic synthesis of Greek thinkers on the Spirit ended up becoming more influential in the West than Jerome's translation of Didymus (or than Didymus's own Greek original, which is now lost). See Granado's comments in Ambrosio de Milán, *El Espíritu Santo*, trans. Carmelo Granado (Madrid: Editorial Ciudad Nueva, 1998), 13.

[69]See Ambrosio, *El Espíritu Santo*, 10-11.

[70]Ambrose, *On the Holy Spirit* 1.43-44 (*NPNF*[2] 10:98-99).

[71]Ambrose, *On the Holy Spirit* 1.86 (*NPNF*[2] 10:104). "For what is the Spirit but full of goodness? Who though because of His nature He cannot be attained to, yet because of His goodness can be received by us, filling all things by His power, but only partaken of by the just, simple in substance, rich in virtues, present to each, dividing of His own to every one, and Himself whole everywhere." Ambrose, *On the Holy Spirit* 1.72 (*NPNF*[2] 10:102-3).

[72]"But lest they should object that this was said according to the flesh, though He alone from Whose flesh went forth virtue to heal all, was more than all." Ambrose, *On the Holy Spirit* 1.87 (*NPNF*[2] 10:104).

[73]Ambrose, *On the Holy Spirit* 1.93 (*NPNF*[2] 10:106).

rather in the nature of the recipient of the Spirit's presence. The saints partake of the Spirit as creatures, or "according to the capacity of our nature," but the Son has the Spirit's resting on him in view of the Son's giving of the Spirit unto others (Jn 1:33).[74] In his humiliation, the Son made room for the Spirit to abide in him in the flesh so that, upon his exaltation, he might become the "Giver" of the Spirit "in abundant provision" to us and bestow on us with "liberality" what he "deemed to be sufficient for us."[75] Ambrose portrays the Spirit as the shared link between Christ and the saints, while also distinguishing the Spirit's presence in both.

With anointing texts from both testaments (e.g., Ps 45:7-8; Acts 10:37-38; and Lk 4:18), Ambrose paints a picture of the Holy Spirit as the "ointment of Christ," whose graces or charisms spread "a sweet fragrance" from Christ to others.[76] The blood of sacrifices for the purification of the flesh under the Old Testament law was but a type of the bloody sacrifice of Christ, "who through the eternal Spirit offered Himself without spot to God" (Heb 9:14) as the anointed "prince of Priests."[77] Superseding the old priestly office and its sacrifices, Christ's anointing with the fullness of the Spirit "above his fellows" stands as a reality "above the law."[78] Attentive to the difference between God and creation, the bishop uses the analogy of oil that does not "mingle" with water but "rises" above it in order to illustrate how Christ's anointing with the Spirit at his baptism reveals the Spirit's divinity.[79] The Jordan reveals a salvific event of a higher order whose origin is trinitarian.

Nevertheless, in the New Testament, Christ was born under the law and anointed with "the oil of gladness" (i.e., the Spirit), and through the pleasing aroma of his sacrifice "made those about to die rejoice, put off sadness from the

---

[74]Ambrose, *On the Holy Spirit* 1.93 (*NPNF*[2] 10:106).

[75]Ambrose, *On the Holy Spirit* 1.93 (*NPNF*[2] 10:106). Granado observes that, depending on the manuscript in view, Christ may be said to give us of the Spirit's abundance with "freedom" (Lat. *libertas*) or "generosity" (Lat. *liberalitas*). See Ambrosio, *El Espíritu Santo*, 80n269.

[76]Ambrose, *On the Holy Spirit* 1.100 (*NPNF*[2] 10:107).

[77]Ambrose, *On the Holy Spirit* 1.99-100 (*NPNF*[2] 10:106-7).

[78]Ambrose, *On the Holy Spirit* 1.100-101 (*NPNF*[2] 10:107).

[79]Ambrose, *On the Holy Spirit* 1.102 (*NPNF*[2] 10:107). The Holy Spirit's descent on Jesus at the Jordan is to testify to its own divinity and anticipate its unified working with the Son and the Father in Christian baptism. The Spirit descends in the likeness of a dove "that by the appearance He might manifest that He had a share of the one honour in authority, the one operation in the mystery, the one gift in the bath, together with the Father and the Son." Ambrose, *On the Holy Spirit* 3.4 (*NPNF*[2] 10:136); cf. Ambrose, *On the Holy Spirit* 3.96 (*NPNF*[2] 10:149).

world, destroyed the odor of sorrowful death."[80] Because the saints are united to Christ in his anointing, they receive his Spirit and stand before God as Christ's good aroma in the world (2 Cor 2:15).[81] The Latin theologian shows how the theme of fragrant anointing in the Old Testament finds its fulfillment in Christ's reception of the Spirit for his office as a sacrificial priest and for his giving of the Spirit of gladness to make others a fragrance pleasing to God. In this way, the Spirit shapes saints in the likeness of Christ.

As Creator, the Holy Spirit is "the Author of the Lord's incarnation."[82] The Spirit brings about the birth of Jesus and creates the fruit of Mary's womb.[83] In the mystery of the incarnation, Isaiah's prophecy concerning the appearance of the messianic flower from the root of Jesse comes to fulfillment (Is 11:1). Like a flower that "keeps its odour, and when bruised increases it," so also the good smell of Christ did not yet go out until he was bruised and pierced on the cross.[84] The Spirit "rested" on this fragrant flower from his incarnation onwards, and upon its budding in the resurrection Christ "spread the good odour of faith throughout the world" and breathed "forth upon the dead the gift of eternal life."[85] Ambrose gives the mystery of Christ a marked pneumatic trajectory, moving from the Creator Spirit's resting on the Son to the Son's breathing of the Creator Spirit throughout the world.

## BUILDING BLOCKS: A SKETCH OF EARLY SPIRIT CHRISTOLOGY THEMES

In contemporary theology, Spirit Christology functions as a systematic theological framework and interpretative lens for exploring problems in areas such as trinitarian theology, Christology, pneumatology, soteriology, and ecclesiology. Although such a Spirit Christology does not exist in the early church as a separate christological model per se, we have shown how early church theologians offer building blocks that bear witness to the implications of the presence and activity of the Spirit in and through Christ for our formation after the pattern of Christ's likeness. In this section, we look at major themes or questions arising from their

[80]Ambrose, *On the Holy Spirit* 1.103 (*NPNF*[2] 10:107).
[81]Ambrose, *On the Holy Spirit* 1.103 (*NPNF*[2] 10:107).
[82]Ambrose, *On the Holy Spirit* 2.41 (*NPNF*[2] 10:120).
[83]Ambrose, *On the Holy Spirit* 2.38 (*NPNF*[2] 10:119).
[84]Ambrose, *On the Holy Spirit* 2.39 (*NPNF*[2] 10:119).
[85]Ambrose, *On the Holy Spirit* 2.38-39 (*NPNF*[2] 10:119).

writings as they relate to the use of a Spirit Christology for developing a theology of the sanctified life.

There are at least three questions often asked in the field of Spirit Christology today that were, in some form, already in the minds of saints who came before us. They too wrestled with the best ways to articulate: 1) the place of the Spirit in an account of God's plan of salvation, 2) the relation between the Son's incarnation and the presence of the Spirit in him, and 3) the discontinuity and continuity between the Son of God and the adopted children of God in an account of sanctification.

***If the Spirit makes holy, then the Spirit is holy.*** Nicene theologians often argued for the Spirit's divinity from below, namely, on the basis of the Spirit's works. What the Spirit does in relationship to us (Gk. *oikonomia*) reveals who the Spirit is in relation to the Father and the Son (Gk. *theologia*). If the Spirit *makes* holy, an act attributed to God, then it follows that the Spirit *is* holy and thus equal in honor with the Father. Bishop Basil's inclusion of the doxology, "Glory to the Father *with* the Son, *together with* the Holy Spirit," in the congregations under his care, assumed the co-equality of rank of the three persons.[86]

To justify the use of the doxology in worship against those who denied the Spirit's equality of glory with the Father and the Son, Basil employed two kinds of strategies. The first approach was to argue for the Spirit's divinity on the basis of its sharing in the divine attributes, titles, or names. When Scripture uses titles like "Spirit of God" or states that "God is Spirit" (Jn 4:24), the term *spirit* points to attributes of a "nature" that is indivisible, omnipresent, immutable, and omnipotent.[87] There are also other attributes of which the Spirit partakes that do not merely distinguish its nature from that of created beings, but allows others to partake of it by grace. The Holy Spirit is thus "generous in goodness," "gives life to all things," and is "the source of sanctification."[88]

> He is called holy, as the Father is holy and the Son is holy. For creatures, holiness comes from without; for the Spirit, holiness fills His very nature. He is not sanctified, but sanctifies. . . . The Spirit shares titles held in common by the Father and the Son; He receives these titles due to His natural and intimate relationship with them.[89]

---

[86]St. Basil the Great, *On the Holy Spirit* 1.3, trans. David Anderson (Crestwood, NY: St. Vladimir's Seminary Press, 1980), 17.

[87]St. Basil the Great, *On the Holy Spirit* 9.22, pp. 42-43.

[88]St. Basil the Great, *On the Holy Spirit*, 43.

[89]St. Basil the Great, *On the Holy Spirit* 19.48, p. 48.

Basil's second strategy is to argue for the Spirit's divinity from below. Not only the Holy Spirit's sharing in divine titles, names, and attributes, but also "the greatness of His deeds, and the multitude of His blessings" allows us "to understand at least partially the greatness of His nature and unapproachable power."[90] Reflecting on the Spirit's works, such as the forgiveness of sins, fellowship with God, the resurrection from the dead, and citizenship in heaven, Basil asks, "Understanding all this, how can we be afraid of giving the Spirit too much honor?"[91] When looking at the works of the Spirit, Basil also looks at the Spirit's inseparability from the Son in salvation history as an icon of their unity of honor and nature with the Father.[92] Their joint mission gives witness to their joint rank.

Bringing together Basil's arguments for the Spirit's divinity is the Lord's command to baptize in the name of the Trinity (Mt 28:19) and the church's trinitarian experience of salvation in her worship practice. By including the Holy Spirit in the divine name, the Lord "did not disdain His fellowship with the Holy Spirit.[93] Receiving the Spirit of adoption, the baptized confesses Jesus as Lord and worships the Father.[94] By being initiated into the Christian life through faith and baptism, catechumens receive the Lord's teaching and express it in the profession of faith in the Trinity and the trinitarian doxology.[95] Since baptism brings catechumens into the sanctified life, the church's experience of baptism leads her to confess the Spirit as divine with the other two persons.[96] Because the Spirit makes us holy, we glorify the Spirit as holy and are thus able to sing, "Glory to the Father and to the Son and to the Holy

---

[90]St. Basil the Great, *On the Holy Spirit* 19.48, p. 76.

[91]St. Basil the Great, *On the Holy Spirit* 19.49, pp. 77-78. "He is divine in nature, infinite in greatness, mighty in His works, good in His blessings; shall we not exalt Him?; shall we not glorify Him? I reckon that this 'glorifying' is nothing else but the recounting of His own wonders?" St. Basil the Great, *On the Holy Spirit* 23.54, p. 46.

[92]St. Basil the Great, *On the Holy Spirit* 16.39, p. 65; cf. St. Basil the Great, *On the Holy Spirit* 18.46, pp. 73-74. "He comes in the flesh, but the Spirit is never separated from him." St. Basil the Great, *On the Holy Spirit* 19.49, p. 77.

[93]St. Basil the Great, *On the Holy Spirit* 10.24, p. 45.

[94]"It is impossible to worship the Son except in the Holy Spirit; it is impossible to call upon the Father except in the Spirit of adoption." St. Basil the Great, *On the Holy Spirit* 11.27, p. 48.

[95]St. Basil the Great, *On the Holy Spirit* 10.26, p. 47; cf. St. Basil the Great, *On the Holy Spirit* 27.68, p. 102.

[96]"For if He is not to be worshipped, how can He deify me by Baptism? but if He is to be worshipped, surely He is an Object of adoration, and if an Object of adoration He must be God; the one is linked to the other, a truly golden and saving chain. And indeed from the Spirit comes our New Birth, and from the New Birth our new creation, and from the new creation our deeper knowledge of the dignity of Him from Whom it is derived." Gregory Nazianzen, *Oration* 31.28 (*NPNF*[2] 7:327).

Spirit."[97] Lest the holiness of the baptized be put into question, early church fathers anchored it in the action of the divine Spirit through Word and sacrament and in the church's response to the same in creed and song.

***The Spirit sanctifies through the flesh of the Son.*** How does one speak of the Spirit's presence in the Son without minimizing the Son's divine identity or his incarnation? The question had to be dealt with already in the early church. Interpretations of the baptism of Jesus are illustrative of the dangers at hand. As we noted earlier, the Gnostics used the Jordan to separate the spiritual Christ (sometimes equated with the Spirit) and the man Jesus into two distinct beings, a reading shaped by a dualistic view of the world in which God cannot enter into contact with the flesh in order to assume, redeem, and sanctify it. Their interpretation of what took place at the Jordan followed from their denial of the incarnation, the union of the divine and the human in Christ.

We also observed that the Arians offered a subordinationist reading of the baptism of the Son, which denied his equality with the Father. The Jordan becomes proof that the Son, being a human creature of a mutable nature, needs to receive the Spirit to be exalted as a god-like saint in accordance with his obedience to the Father. Driving this reading is the Arian principle that since God is immutable, God cannot enter into contact with human nature, and thus cannot become flesh in order to save the flesh. Although quite different in their overall systems of thought, Gnostics and Arians shared a view of divine impassibility that made the incarnation of the spiritual or divine Word impossible. Both groups shared a disdain for God's association with the body.

In Gnostic cosmology, the Spirit being who descended on Christ at the Jordan only uses his body as a vessel to pass on spiritual knowledge to others, but does not actually anoint his humanity. The impassible nature of the spiritual dove makes the anointing of the flesh of the Son impossible. Against this vision, Irenaeus upholds the rule of faith (Lat. *regula fidei*), which confesses the creation of the world, the incarnation of the Word, and the resurrection of the body as nothing less than God's own handiwork.[98] God is not afraid to "get his hands dirty," as it were, in the real world of flesh and blood (the world of lost Adam) in

[97]Today's more common use of the formulation, "Glory to the Father and to the Son and to the Holy Spirit," was already considered by Basil as equivalent to the one used in his day, namely, "Glory to the Father with the Son, together with the Holy Spirit." See St. Basil the Great, *On the Holy Spirit* 27.68, p. 103.

[98]Irenaeus, *Against Heresies* 1.10.1 (*ANF* 1:330-31).

order to restore it to the image and likeness of his Son, the last Adam. To do so, God gets his two "hands," the Son and the Spirit, in the game. In God's recapitulating of the story of Adam, the Son assumes our human nature unto himself, and the Holy Spirit anoints it in and through the Son. The intimacy of the Spirit with the humanity of the Son opens the way for the Son's gifting of the Spirit to sanctify humanity.

According to the Arians, God exists in splendid isolation from the mutable world and only becomes a Father when he creates a Son.[99] Like the rest of God's creatures, Christ is made an adopted son of the Father by receiving the Spirit. But since the Spirit is also a creature in Arian thinking, God as such still remains still isolated from his created Son. At best, Spirit is a power from God that enables the Son to live a virtuous life, on account of which the Son eventually earns an exalted status before God. Since the Son and the Spirit remain creatures, God as such never comes into contact with the flesh of the Son. Other humans may partake of the Spirit and become adopted sons if, like the Son, they follow his example of obedience. The impassible God of Arianism does not only render the incarnation of the divine Word impossible, but also the divine Spirit's sanctification and anointing of the Word's humanity for our sake.

Although Athanasius does not deny that the Son, considered as God, is indeed impassible and thus distinct from creation, this assertion stands as a penultimate reality. The ultimate point for him lies in the soteriological trajectory of the mystery of God, which brings us to the gratuity of the Word, who became flesh so that he might sanctify and deify the flesh and bring it into the Father's presence. The Holy Spirit, who is God, also comes directly into contact with the flesh of the Son from the moment of the incarnation and as revealed in his anointing at the Jordan, so that the Son might make us adopted sons by partaking of his Spirit-sanctified and exalted flesh.

Rather than minimizing the Son's divine identity and his incarnation, early church theologians like Irenaeus and Athanasius understood that situating the Holy Spirit in the life of the Son actually maximized the reach of God's story of salvation in several ways. Despite having to navigate through the dangers of Spirit Christologies of an adoptionist bent, they began to see that imbuing Christology

[99]Athanasius attributes to Arius these sayings: "'God was not always a Father;' but 'once God was alone, and not yet a Father, but afterwards He became a Father.'" *First Discourse Against the Arians* 2.5 (*NPNF*[2] 4:308).

with a pneumatic dimension enriched the trinitarian foundation, economic ground, and ecclesial trajectory of the mystery of Christ. Key in their thinking was the conviction and confession that God truly entered our human history in the person of the Son, the bearer and giver of the Spirit, in order to save us and sanctify our lives.

***The Spirit gives humans the form of the Son.*** Early attempts to think of Jesus Christ merely as a Spirit-indwelt man, prophet, or saint adopted or elected by God for a special task led theologians to be especially careful in handling texts dealing with the Holy Spirit in Jesus' life and mission. Adoptionist accounts of Jesus tended to make him too much like us, though still in some ways unique from us. For instance, Arians showed a high degree of continuity between Jesus and the rest of humanity, while maintaining his discontinuity from us. Even though the Son remains a special instrument whom God uses in the creation of the rest of the creatures, the Son is still only a son by grace like the rest of the saints because he partakes of the Spirit.

A further example of discontinuity between Jesus and other saints lies in how Arians thought of Jesus' exalted godlike status—a degree of closeness to God without becoming God by nature—as the highest a creature could attain. Jesus becomes unique as an ideal paradigm of sonship for others to behold and aspire to and, therefore, an example to be followed through imitation of his life of obedience, virtue, and works. Could this prospect of achieving godlike status through human efforts in order to be what Jesus became explain, in part, why Arianism became so popular among the people? A certain way to connect to Jesus, to partake of his adoptive and exalted sonship, is embedded in Arian teaching. Yet bringing Jesus closer to us as an example to follow put the entire burden of closeness to God in human hands. The Arian scheme made Jesus so much like us as a man of the Spirit that it put into question his power to save us and bring us closer to the Father.

Given the adoptionist principle in Arianism, one can see why early church theologians carefully distinguished between the role of the Spirit in Jesus and its work in others. One strategy was to relativize the idea that the Spirit-anointing did something to the Son, even in his humanity, by making the anointing at the Jordan only a revelatory instance of the Son's prior possession of the Spirit from the time of the incarnation. In his anti-Arian polemic, Athanasius, for instance, makes the sanctification and anointing of the Son simultaneous realities, and can even speak of the Word's christening of his humanity with his divinity or Spirit from the moment of the incarnation. Discontinuity between Jesus and the saints lies in that the former is sanctified in the flesh from the moment of the union or birth, whereas the latter receive the Spirit and are made holy through their anointing with the Spirit in baptism.

Another way to highlight discontinuity was to focus on the Son's natural unity with the Spirit, seeing the latter as the Son's own Spirit, that is, as being of the same nature with him—a point often made in Athanasius's teaching. In the case of saints, they partake of and are empowered by the Spirit whose nature is not their own. In the case of the Son, however, he partakes of and thus receives the Spirit in the flesh, but not merely as a power external to him as in the case of prophets and saints. Rather, the Son lives in the Spirit, whose nature he shares as God. The Spirit's presence with the Word in the flesh is not denied, but Athanasius finally highlights the Word's identity as Giver of the Spirit.[100] Inspired by Athanasius and others, Ambrose, as we noted earlier, distinguished between the saints who partake of the filling of the Spirit as creatures, and the Son who alone has the fullness of the Spirit in view of his unique giving of the Spirit to others.[101] Cyril of Jerusalem gets at the same point by stressing that the Spirit descends on Christ as his equal at the Jordan, so that we might share in his anointing and become little Christs at our little Jordan. Even though the Son and the saints both have the Spirit in their humanity, only the former stands as the divine source of the Spirit.

Ultimately, none of the aforementioned strategies for preserving the discontinuity between the unbegotten Son and the adopted sons and daughters obstructs the basic patristic teaching that the latter share in the former's life through the gift of the Spirit. Although the Arians also held to the notion of a human sharing in the Spirit of the Son, they could not anchor such participation in the life of Christ in a gratuitous act of an immutable God to take on our mutable flesh in order to save and sanctify the flesh. Drawing the pneumatic distinction between Christ and us puts the possibility of our sharing in his likeness by the Spirit on more solid

[100]"And if . . . the Spirit is His, and takes of His, and He sends It, it is not the Word, considered as the Word and Wisdom, who is anointed with the Spirit which He Himself gives, but the flesh assumed by Him which is anointed in Him and by Him; that the sanctification coming to the Lord as man, may come to all men from Him . . . the Word is He who gives It to the worthy." Athanasius, *First Discourse Against the Arians* 12.47 (*NPNF*[2] 4:334).

[101]Concerning the anointing/sanctification of the Word in the flesh, Athanasius writes, "For the flesh being first sanctified in Him, and He being said, as man, to have received for its sake, we have the sequel of the Spirit's grace, receiving 'out of His fulness.'" *First Discourse Against the Arians* 12.50 (*NPNF*[2] 4:336).

footing, grounding such sharing by adoption not in a human act driven by the external example of a man but in an act of divine redemption from sin and death.

The church's struggle against Arianism sharpened her theology of the Spirit and life in the Spirit. Critical in the church's response was the conviction that human sharing in the Spirit could not simply be a partaking in some power external to God, but an indwelling of the divine Spirit itself in the creature. As God, the Holy Spirit is thus capable of conforming creatures to the likeness and image of God in Christ. What such conformity to Christ's likeness means will be explored in the next five chapters, where we lay out five models of sanctification or life in the Spirit.

3

# BAPTIZED INTO DEATH AND LIFE

## THE RENEWAL MODEL

WHAT DOES LIFE in the Spirit look like? By arguing that the privileged place of the Spirit of God is Jesus himself, a Spirit Christology provides for the otherwise abstract notion of spirituality a christological center and orientation. In the Christian story, humans get a sense of what a spiritual life looks like by seeing Jesus' own life in the Spirit. Receiving the Holy Spirit from the Father through the Son, adopted children of God now reflect in their own lives the life of Jesus. The Spirit gives them the form of Christ, or conforms them to the image of Christ, and their lives acquire a Christlike pattern. In one of his baptismal catecheses, Cyril of Jerusalem gives an example of the multiplicity of gifts and virtues the one Spirit brings about in the saints:

> And though He is One in nature, yet many are the virtues which by the will of God and in the Name of Christ He works. For He employs the tongue of one man for wisdom; the soul of another He enlightens by prophecy; to another He gives the power to drive away devils; to another He gives to interpret the divine Scriptures. He strengthens one man's self-command; He teaches another the way to give alms; another He teaches to fast and discipline himself; another He teaches to despise the things of the body; another He trains for martyrdom.[1]

---

[1]Cyril of Jerusalem, *Catechetical Lecture* 16.12 (*NPNF*$^2$ 7:118). I also consulted Cirilo de Jerusalén, *El Espíritu Santo (Catequesis XVI-XVII)*, trans. Carmelo Granado (Madrid: Editorial Ciudad Nueva, 1998).

Some may find an affinity with certain gifts or virtues of the Spirit at certain times in their lives or see a combination of these operating throughout their spiritual journeys. When thinking of the Spirit's shaping of a Christlike pattern in our lives, it might be helpful to think of a decorative quilt displaying an array of shapes, colors, and lines that, though distinct from each other, intersect at various points to make the whole artifact a wonderful work of art. The indivisible Spirit shapes us after the likeness of Christ in several ways that, though unique in their own configurations of the one Spirit's work in and through us, often interact with each other.

The first two chapters introduced readers respectively to the field of Spirit Christology in North America and to patristic images bearing witness to Christ as the receiver, bearer, and giver of God's Spirit. Chapter one showed the potential use of a Spirit Christology as a trinitarian narrative and framework for developing a theology of the Christian life. Chapter two showed how early church fathers set the trinitarian foundation for the use of a Spirit Christology in a way that linked their apologetic discourse on the Spirit's divinity to a devotional image-based account of the Spirit in the life of Christ and the saints. The next five chapters test the productivity of a Spirit Christology for articulating a models-based approach to sanctification or holiness. Traditionally, some accounts of sanctification have dealt at least partly with the Spirit's formation of the believer after the likeness of Christ. Yet such treatments have not always appealed to a robust pneumatic basis for establishing an account of the sanctified life that encompasses the Spirit's multiple ways of shaping Christ in the saints. Functioning as a relatively comprehensive yet flexible account of life in the Spirit, a model of sanctification can be inclusive of various biblical narratives and theological sources without becoming exhaustive descriptions of the whole Christian life. Each model can also deal with particular problems or needs in life and be embodied by fostering certain spiritual practices.

In this chapter, the *renewal* model of sanctification receives our attention. This model presents life in the Spirit as a cycle of death and life. Killing the old sinful creature and raising the new creature in the waters of baptism, the Spirit conforms us to Christ's death and resurrection. By making us participants in a life of daily repentance, this model can assist church leaders in fostering among people the personal and corporate practice of confession and absolution, mutual consolation and forgiveness, and reconciliation among those who have hurt each other. This model deals with issues such as guilt and the need for right relations, avoiding both fatalistic and perfectionistic solutions to the problem of sin in the life of Christ's saints.

## BIBLICAL PICTURES: DEATH AND LIFE, GROWN UP CHILDREN, AND NEW CLOTHES

At the waters of the Jordan, Jesus is anointed with the Holy Spirit to begin his public mission as Yahweh's suffering servant (Lk 3:21-22; cf. Is 42:1). Jesus' life in the Spirit takes on a cross-shaped orientation and trajectory. As one of my students once put it: "At the Jordan, Jesus is anointed to die." Jesus' anointing becomes a baptism unto death. His baptism anticipates and comes to fulfillment on the cross. So inextricably linked are these events that Jesus calls his own future death a baptism (Lk 12:50) and asks his disciples if they are willing to drink the cup of his suffering or, synonymously, "be baptized with the baptism with which I am baptized" (Mk 10:38). For Jesus, life in the Spirit leads from the baptism of water at the Jordan to the baptism of blood at Golgotha.

Echoing the Spirit's hovering over the waters of the first creation in Genesis, the Spirit's descent on Jesus in the waters of the Jordan signals the beginning of a new creation. Because the Spirit remains immeasurably on the Son who is from above (Jn 1:33; 3:34), the Son will speak Spirit-breathed words of life that bring people to belief in the Son and a share in his resurrection life (6:63, 40). Through belief in the Son, those who are born of water and the Spirit are born anew or from above and brought into the kingdom of the Son (3:5). Because the Son bears the Spirit, he will baptize his disciples with the Spirit (1:33) by breathing on them the life-giving breath first bestowed on Adam in the first creation (cf. Gen 2:7), and he will send them out into the world to forgive the sins of the penitent (Jn 20:22-23).[2] In short, through the incarnation of his preexistent Son, by whom all things were made (1:3), and through the gift of the Creator Spirit who comes from the Father through the glorified Son (7:37-39; cf. 4:10-15), God restores his creation anew. Life in the Spirit of the Son leads to a share in the new creation, which includes resurrection and eternal life.

The lives of the disciples are, in some ways, patterned after Christ's own life. They are anointed with the Spirit in baptism, becoming sharers in Christ's death and resurrection. Like Jesus, their lives take on a cruciform shape. Paul offers the classic description of the Christian life as being buried with Christ in his death and

---

[2]Sosa has shown that, although John stands in continuity with prior Jewish interpretations of Gen 2:7 which identify God as the one who breathes on Adam, he also seems to be the first Jewish writer who in Jn 20:22 attributes the Creator's breathing on others to a different person (namely, Jesus), thereby including him in the divine identity. See Carlos Raúl Sosa Siliezar, *La Condición Divina de Jesús: Cristología y Creación en el Evangelio de Juan* (Salamanca: Ediciones Sígueme, 2016), 91-104.

being raised with him in his resurrection (Rom 6). Through baptism, we are united to Christ "in a death like his" so that "our old self was crucified" and we might no longer be "enslaved to sin" but rather "free from sin" (Rom 6:5-7). The old sinful way, though present still, is in a sense dead and no longer reigns over the saints. As in a burial in a cemetery, the saints have definitively been buried with Christ—their old self lying underground.

Yet from the tomb they wait eagerly to be awakened into the beauty of Paradise, a future hope traditionally reflected in the lush green gardens of a cemetery. This means that the new creation, though still coming in its fullness at the final resurrection and in a new heaven and earth, has also arrived in part and begun to break into our lives from the future. For those who are in Christ, the old has gone, and the new has come (2 Cor 5:17). They have a new identity. Having died with Christ, their "life is hidden with Christ in God," and upon Christ's final revelation, they will "appear with him in glory" (Col 3:3-4). Because we are united to Christ "in a resurrection like his" (Rom 6:5), "we will also live with him" (v. 8); yet even now, death has no dominion over us, and we are alive to God (vv. 9-11). Therefore, we also "walk in newness of life" (v. 4).

In Paul's eschatological view, an interplay between the old and the new ages, the past and the future, occurs in the present. The old self is dead, yet its ugly arms reach us from the past and its effects are felt now. The new creature will live forever with Christ, yet this resurrection promise reaches us from the future, making us alive to God now. In our baptismal union with Christ, these ages intersect so that everyday life takes on a cyclical rhythm of death and life. Believers crucify the old self with all its sinful passions, so as not to live as "instruments for unrighteousness," and are raised to newness of life to live as "instruments for righteousness" (Rom 6:13). Dying to sin, Christians no longer present their lives to God as "slaves of sin," no longer become "slaves to impurity and to lawlessness" (vv. 17, 19).

Walking in newness of life means living today before God under the reign of the risen Christ. The apostle uses a number of imperatives to exhort believers to stop sinning according to the sinful flesh and live joyfully according to their new status: "*Let not* sin . . . *reign* in your mortal body. . . . *Do not present* your members to sin . . . but *present yourselves* to God . . . as instruments for righteousness" (Rom 6:12-13).[3] As it is typical in the Pauline corpus's use of exhortation, "the indicative

[3]"The New Testament speaks of sanctification both in the imperative and indicative moods. It is described as a divine gift and at the same time as a result of our obedient choice." Adolf Köberle, *The Quest for*

is the necessary presupposition and starting point for the imperative. What Christ has done is the basis for what the believer must do."[4] Otherwise stated, the believers' righteousness before God (passive righteousness) results in their righteousness before others (active righteousness or righteousness of obedience).[5] The "free gift of righteousness . . . through the one man Jesus Christ" (Rom 5:17) energizes and fosters believers' responses to God's free gift in their becoming "slaves to righteousness leading to sanctification" (Rom 6:19).

Living in Christ, believers strive to no longer idolatrously worship their own sinful selves and its desires, but rather honor with their bodies the God and Father who created us all (cf. Col 3:5). Therefore, they offer their members to God "as those who have been brought from death to life" (Rom 6:13), being slaves of "obedience, which leads to righteousness" (v. 16), adhering to the apostolic "teaching" (v. 17), and becoming "slaves to righteousness leading to sanctification" (v. 19). Under the sign of baptism, the Christian life is about being brought from death to life. It is a daily baptism unto death, but also unto new creation. The same waters that drown the old self bring a new self safely ashore. Insofar as sanctification is described as the "fruit" (v. 22) of such baptismal life, one can speak of sanctification itself as a recurring cycle of dying with Christ and being raised with him.

Pauline images of children growing up and new clothes being put on also get at this cyclical dynamic of death and life. Called by the one God to the one body of Christ in the unity of the Spirit (Eph 4:1-6), Christians share in common "one Lord, one faith, one baptism" (v. 5). They have been made anew in Christ. Therefore, they must no longer act as children, who are easily deceived by false teaching (v. 14), or as Gentiles whose minds are darkened by ignorance and hardened hearts (vv. 17-19). Rather, those who have learned Christ (v. 20) must grow up in the knowledge of him to become mature humans (adults), even "to the measure of the stature of the fullness of Christ" (v. 13). Otherwise stated, from the one "grace" and full "measure" of the ascended Christ, the members of his mystical

---

*Holiness: A Biblical, Historical and Systematic Investigation*, trans. John C. Mattes (Evansville, IN: Ballast, 1999), xii. For a discussion of the third use of the law in the Formula of Concord (1577) within the framework of the Holy Spirit's negative and positive use of exhortations or imperatives, see Mark P. Surburg, "Speaking like Paul and Luther: Pauline Exhortation and the Third Use of the Law," *LOGIA* 27, no. 2 (2018): 15-25.

[4]James D. G. Dunn, *The Theology of Paul the Apostle* (Grand Rapids: Eerdmans, 1998), 630.

[5]For a fuller discussion of the distinction between the two kinds of righteousness, see my discussion of Martin Luther's use of the distinction in chapter five dealing with the sacrificial model of the Christian life.

body receive many "gifts" (or graces) until they "grow up in every way into him who is the head, into Christ" (vv. 7-8, 15).

In this life, maturity into the unity of the faith or knowledge of Christ, which causes growth in love among members of his body (Eph 4:16), remains a work in progress. We act like immature children, returning to a "former manner of life" (v. 22) that is no longer suitable for us. Like adults who discard clothes that no longer fit, Christians are called to "put off your old self" (v. 22), the old childish garments that no longer befit their new identity in Christ. Rather, like new creatures growing into full maturity, they "put on the new self, created after the likeness of God in true righteousness and holiness" (v. 24). Joined to Christ, the head, by faith and baptism, the members of his body put on Christ's righteousness and holiness. The likeness or image of God, which is none other than the likeness of Christ, is renewed or restored in the saints (see Col 3:9-11). In this life, they are called to "be renewed in the spirit of your minds" (Eph 4:23; cf. Col 3:2), to claim over and over again their new status in Christ, to put on those new clothes that reflect the image of Christ in their everyday walk, to look, or better yet, to act the part, as it were. A key way Christians model their new wardrobe, their new look and life in Christ, is by "forgiving one another, as God in Christ forgave you" (Eph 4:32).

The Holy Spirit comes into this picture of renewal since "God's chosen ones" put on "compassionate hearts, kindness, humility, meekness, and patience, bearing with one another and . . . forgiving each other" (Col 3:12-13a, cf. Eph 4:1-2). The holy ones have "put on love," which binds them to Christ and to one another in the one Spirit (Col 3:14; cf. Eph 4:2-3, 13). Like models walking down the runway in a fashion show, the saints display before the world a glorious new wardrobe. Through faith and baptism into Christ, they have "put on Christ" (Gal 3:27). As a result, they have put on "the fruit of the Spirit" (Gal 5:22), and thus "walk by the Spirit" (v. 16; cf. v. 25). Exhibiting such "fruit" in life becomes an answer to Paul's hope that "Christ is formed in you" (Gal 4:19), since Christ alone lived according to the fruit of the Spirit in the fullest measure. And again, "those who belong to Christ Jesus" also live and walk by the Spirit by sharing in his death and resurrection (Gal 5:24-25). They put on the form of Christ. If asked, "who are you wearing?" they respond "Christ!"

The Spirit renews the image of Christ in the saints. Like old leaves in winter time, the sinful self dies with Christ, and the "works of the flesh" are put to death too (Gal 5:19-21, 24). Yet winter is not forever. Spring comes, and signs of life appear. New leaves display their beauty. Christ is risen! And so are his saints. The fruit of the Spirit comes forth in their lives, and they reflect the image and likeness of Christ in the world: "love, joy, peace, patience, kindness, goodness, faithfulness, gentleness, self-control" (vv. 22-23).

## CATECHETICAL IMAGES: THE SPIRIT RETURNS, JORDAN BOUND, COURTS AND SINNERS

What can we learn from the wisdom of church theologians who, through various images and forms of discourse, link the sanctifying work of the Spirit to Jesus and his disciples? In this section, we hear from patristic figures Cyril of Jerusalem, a catechist; Basil of Caesarea, an apologist; and John Chrysostom, a preacher. We will close with Luther's baptismal catechesis, which deals with the theme of renewal and where he appropriates some patristic themes.

***Cyril of Jerusalem: Second breath, purifying fire, little Pentecost.*** In the patristic tradition, Jesus' baptism becomes the condition in God's economy of salvation for the communication of the Spirit to others in Christian baptism. Pointing to a common interpretation of the Jordan event in his day, Cyril of Jerusalem teaches that it was fit in God's plan that the firstfruits of the Spirit promised to humanity first come on the humanity of the Lord, the giver of the Spirit.[6] When the Lord first gave his breath of life to Adam (Gen 2:7), it was "stifled through willful sins"; but when the Lord came in the flesh and rose from the dead, he breathed a second time on the human race, bestowing the Holy Spirit on his disciples (Jn 20:22).[7] "The likeness [of God] is the Spirit" restored to the human person, freeing him from his affliction, namely, "from his sins and the subsequent loss of the Spirit."[8] With the descent of the Spirit-Breath on the disciples, Pentecost fulfills the Jordan promise that the bearer of the Spirit will also baptize with the Spirit (Jn 1:33).

The Spirit arrives on the disciples as a purifying fire. Descending on them on Pentecost, the cleansing fire of the Spirit penetrated "the very inmost recesses of

---

[6]Cyril of Jerusalem, *Catechetical Lecture* 17.9 (*NPNF*$^2$ 7:126). Referring to Joel 2:28-29; Acts 2:16-18; and John 3:34-35, Cyril notes that the Father "has given Him [the Son] the power also of bestowing the grace of the All-holy Spirit on whomsoever He will." *Catechetical Lecture* 17.19 (*NPNF*$^2$ 7:129).

[7]Cyril of Jerusalem, *Catechetical Lecture* 17.12 (*NPNF*$^2$ 7:127).

[8]Granado, "Pneumatología de San Cirilo de Jerusalén," *Estudios Eclesiásticos* 58 (1983): 434.

the soul."[9] The house where the disciples were staying became "the vessel of the spiritual water," and they were "invested soul and body with a divine garment of salvation."[10] These promises are not the unique possession of the apostles, but are available to disciples of all times and places.

> They partook of fire, not of burning but of saving fire; of fire which consumes the thorns of sins, but gives lustre to the soul. This is now coming upon you also, and that to strip away and consume your sins which are like thorns, and to brighten yet more that precious possession of your souls, and to give you grace; for He gave it to the Apostles. . . . A fiery sword barred of old the gates of Paradise; a fiery tongue which brought salvation restored the gift.[11]

Consuming thorny sins with the descent of the Holy Spirit and fire, baptism becomes the little Pentecost of catechumens where their souls are purified like a precious metal and graced with a shiny brightness unlike any. Upon entering the waters of baptism, Cyril's disciples receive the same promised Spirit who fell on the apostles and others at Pentecost, and in so doing receive the forgiveness of sins and reentry into Paradise.

***Basil of Caesarea: Baptismal exodus, tomb, and safe passage.*** Basil of Caesarea interprets Israel's crossing of the Red Sea as "a shadow and type" of Christian baptism.[12] In their exodus of old, God's people "were baptized into Moses in the cloud and the sea" (1 Cor 10:2; cf. Ex 13:21; 14:22), foreshadowing an "imitative anticipation of the future" exodus of all believers through baptism into Christ.[13] Though bearing the image of the "first-formed" Adam in whom all die, God graciously preserves his firstborn son Israel from the destroyer by placing on the people the saving blood of the Passover Lamb.[14] The sea became a baptism of death for God's enemy, represented by Pharaoh and his army, and signifies that "in baptism too dies our enmity towards God."[15] Because the waters of baptism become the death of sinful Adam in us and the end of the devil's tyranny against us, we also come out of the waters "unharmed . . . we too . . . alive from the dead, step up from

---

[9]Cyril of Jerusalem, *Catechetical Lecture* 17.14 (*NPNF*[2] 7:128).
[10]Cyril of Jerusalem, *Catechetical Lecture* 17.15 (*NPNF*[2] 7:128).
[11]Cyril of Jerusalem, *Catechetical Lecture* 17.15 (*NPNF*[2] 7:128).
[12]Basil of Caesarea, *On the Spirit* 14.31 (*NPNF*[2] 8:19).
[13]Basil of Caesarea, *On the Spirit* 14.31 (*NPNF*[2] 8:19). For Gregory of Nazianzus, the Spirit is the "cloud" that guided Israel. Gregory of Nazianzus, *Oration* 39.17 (*NPNF*[2] 7:358).
[14]Basil of Caesarea, *On the Spirit* 14.31 (*NPNF*[2] 8:19).
[15]Basil of Caesarea, *On the Spirit* 14.31 (*NPNF*[2] 8:19).

the water 'saved' by the 'grace' of Him who called us."[16] For those who are vivified with Christ, the baptismal sea turns from being an instrument of fear to being a means of preservation and passage to new life.

Basil sees God's plan of salvation with baptismal eyes. Reading Israel's experience of Moses and the sea through Paul's teaching in Romans 6, Basil speaks of baptism as an initiation into the "pattern life" of Christ and thus as an "imitation of Christ" in his death and burial as well as in his resurrection.[17] The baptismal waters become an instrument of death, a "tomb," because "the bodies of the baptized are, as it were, buried in the water," which signifies an end to the former way of life and "the putting off of the works of the flesh" (see Col 2:11-12).[18]

However, since baptism is no mere water, but rather water "associated with the Spirit" (see Jn 3:5), it offers the grace and presence of the Spirit, whose power is "renewing our souls from the deadness of sin unto their original life."[19] The Spirit's work of conformation to Christ in his death and resurrection amounts to the restoration of the image of God in the creature through Christ.[20] As a result of the Spirit's work, the baptized no longer "bear fruit unto death," but rather "fruit in holiness" (see Rom 7:5; 6:22).[21] Baptism gives way to a new life embodied in the fruit of the Spirit.

***John Chrysostom: Courts and judges, self-accusation, and father conscience.*** Delivering a series of homilies on the parable of the rich man and Lazarus (Lk 16:19-31), John Chrysostom (AD 350–407), the famous preacher and orator known as "the golden-mouthed," contrasts the life and destiny of both men. The former's self-indulgence revealed his spiritual idleness and led to his tragic end in Hades. The latter's perseverance and patience in the midst of great adversity revealed his trust in God and led to his blessed reward in the hereafter. Lest hearers

---

[16]Basil of Caesarea, *On the Spirit* 14.31 (*NPNF*[2] 8:19).

[17]Basil of Caesarea, *On the Spirit* 14.31 (*NPNF*[2] 8:19); 15.35 (*NPNF*[2] 8:21); cf. Basil of Caesarea, *On the Spirit* 14.32 (*NPNF*[2] 8:20).

[18]Basil of Caesarea, *On the Spirit* 15.35 (*NPNF*[2] 8:21-22). "For this cause the Lord, who is the Dispenser of our life, gave us the covenant of baptism, containing a type of life and death, for the water fulfils the image of death, and the Spirit gives us the earnest of life." Basil of Caesarea, *On the Spirit* 15:35 (*NPNF*[2] 8:22).

[19]Basil of Caesarea, *On the Spirit* 15:35 (*NPNF*[2] 8:22). "It follows that if there is any grace in the water, it is not of the nature of the water, but of the presence of the Spirit." Basil of Caesarea, *On the Spirit* 15:35 (*NPNF*[2] 8:22).

[20]Citing passages such as 1 Corinthians 15:49 and Colossians 3:9-10, Basil portrays Christian baptism, prefigured in Israel's crossing of the Red Sea, as initiation into the creature's renewal into the image of God and Christ. See Basil of Caesarea, *On the Spirit* 14.32 (*NPNF*[2] 8:20).

[21]Basil of Caesarea, *On the Spirit* 15:35 (*NPNF*[2] 8:22).

meet the fate of the rich man in the final judgment, the homilist reminds the saints to make use of one of God's greatest gifts, namely, their conscience.

Chrysostom describes the Christian life in the forensic language of the courtroom. God has given each one of us a conscience to be "a continuously watchful and sober judge."[22] Unlike the courts and judges of the world that can be corrupted and give "false judgments," the "court of conscience" does not fail to condemn the sinner.[23] Acting as a "vehement accuser," conscience acts as a "sleepless" judge who "never forgets what has happened" and leads the sinner to repentance.[24] We can almost hear the preacher say: If the rich man had only listened to his conscience!

Although the language of "self-accusation" and "self-condemnation" may sound a bit judgmental to modern ears, Chrysostom likens the conscience to a loving "father" who does not neglect his duty to correct his children.[25] Through father conscience, God the Father leads his children along the narrow gate. To this paternal image, the preacher adds a medical one. Knowing his ailment, a sick person reveals his wounds to the doctor in order to receive the appropriate remedy and healing.[26] Similarly, listening to the voice of conscience leads to the salutary confession of sins; then, God deals with the wounded soul with the gift of pardon. In the end, God "wishes you to confess, not in order to punish you, but in order to forgive you."[27] In light of the benefits of conscience, Chrysostom notes that God has "set up such a court in us here . . . as evidence of His love for mankind."[28]

When Chrysostom speaks of killing sinful desire through confession and repentance, he has in mind sins of commission and omission. This focus is in line with his sermons' broader denunciation of the abuse of wealth and possession and the neglect of neighbors in want. In God's providential wisdom, the Creator made the censure of sin "a kind of holy anchor of our conscience, which does not allow us finally to be submerged in the depths of sin."[29] The divine wisdom

---

[22]John Chrysostom, *On Wealth and Poverty*, trans. Catharine P. Roth (Crestwood, NY: St. Vladimir's Seminary Press, 1984), 88.

[23]Chrysostom, *On Wealth and Poverty*, 88.

[24]Chrysostom, *On Wealth and Poverty*, 88.

[25]Chrysostom, *On Wealth and Poverty*, 89-90.

[26]Chrysostom, *On Wealth and Poverty*, 89.

[27]Chrysostom, *On Wealth and Poverty*, 89.

[28]Chrysostom, *On Wealth and Poverty*, 95.

[29]Chrysostom, *On Wealth and Poverty*, 91.

also made conscience's "rebuke to be continual but not continuous"; that is to say, "continual, so that we may not lapse into carelessness, but may be kept always sober and mindful until the end; but not continuous or in close succession, so that we may not fall, but may recover our breath in periods of relief and consolation."[30]

The works of conscience reflect the cyclical movement of the life of repentance, with a time for contrition and tears and a time for forgiveness and comfort. Little accusation leads to spiritual idleness, the rich man's problem. Yet Chrysostom also notes that too much condemnation leads to spiritual discouragement and defeat with no good news in sight to comfort the troubled soul. For the preacher, becoming spiritually virtuous, or "a flute and a lyre for the Holy Spirit," involves sharing in this cyclical life of repentance and forgiveness.[31]

In later chapters, we will look at other ways in which Chrysostom's preaching fosters a Christlike disposition in the saints by incorporating them into stories of life in the Spirit embodied by Christ and other biblical characters.[32] Underlying Chrysostom's portrayals of the sanctified life is his pneumatic understanding of Christ. As Bobrinskoy reminds us:

> He did not hesitate to proclaim that "Christ is everywhere covered by the Holy Spirit" . . . "filled with the Spirit from the beginning" . . . "entirely anointed by the Spirit" . . . and that "Jesus is spiritual, for the Spirit himself has fashioned him (in the flesh), thus God the Word and the whole energy of the Spirit dwells in him."[33]

Because of the inseparable unity of Jesus and the Spirit, which also means that the Spirit "acted in and through his humanity," the Spirit, after Pentecost, can dwell in the baptized person "by leading him from the 'image' in which he was created to

[30]Chrysostom, *On Wealth and Poverty*, 90.

[31]Chrysostom begins his sermon series by praising his hearers for being "filled with spiritual instruction" and becoming "a flute and a lyre for the Holy Spirit." He continues by saying, "You allowed the Holy Spirit to play on your souls and to breathe His grace into your hearts. Thus you sounded a harmonious melody to delight not only mankind but even the powers of heaven." Chrysostom, *On Wealth and Poverty*, 19. The whole series then moves on to speak about what life in the Spirit or spiritual virtue and discipline looks like.

[32]Moore argues that, despite Chrysostom's synergism, his preaching is not merely moralistic but seeks to reorient hearers toward a "chosen life trajectory" by helping them see themselves in stories of spiritual virtue "embodied in Christ's sacrifice, Scripture and the lives of biblical characters and saints." Peter Moore, "Sanctification Through Preaching: How John Chrysostom Preached for Personal Transformation," in *Sanctification: Explorations in Theology and Practice*, ed. Kelly M. Kapic (Downers Grove, IL: InterVarsity Press, 2014), 263.

[33]Boris Bobrinskoy, "The Indwelling of the Spirit in Christ: 'Pneumatic Christology' in the Cappadocian Fathers," *St. Vladimir's Theological Quarterly* 28, no. 1 (1984): 61.

the ultimate 'likeness' of God."[34] Therefore, the Spirit who fashioned Christ as a spiritual being in the flesh now fashions others after the likeness of Christ, who is the definitive bearer and giver of the Spirit to the flesh.

***Martin Luther: Saving flood, blessed exchange, daily garment.*** Martin Luther, the German theologian known for his seminal role in the Protestant Reformation, serves as an example of a major figure in the Western church whose teaching on the Christian life builds on some of the aforementioned biblical and patristic themes. For instance, in his revised *Baptismal Booklet* (1526), included in the second edition of the *Small Catechism* (1529), Luther locates baptism into Christ under the theme of God's use of the waters as a means of judgment and safe passage from death to life. To do so, Luther's "Flood Prayer" brings together a number of biblical events and patristic images:

> Almighty, eternal God, who according to your strict judgment condemned the unbelieving world through the flood and according to your great mercy preserved believing Noah and the seven members of his family, and who drowned Pharaoh with his army in the Red Sea and led your people Israel through the same on dry ground, thereby prefiguring this bath of your Holy Baptism, and who through the baptism of your dear child, our Lord Jesus Christ, hallowed and set apart the Jordan and all water to be a blessed flood and a rich washing away of sins: we ask for the sake of this very boundless mercy of yours that you would look graciously upon N. and bless him with true faith in the Holy Spirit so that through this same saving flood all that has been born in him from Adam and whatever he has added thereto may be drowned in him and sink, and that he, separated from the number of the unbelieving, may be preserved dry and secure in the holy ark of the Christian church.[35]

At the font, Adam, Noah, and Israel lay out a trajectory for the baptized. To enter the waters means to drown and sink the old self inherited from our first father, Adam, navigate with Noah and his family through a saving flood in the security of God's ark (church), and be led with Israel in her exodus through the waters of the Red Sea unto dry ground.

In all these images, baptism becomes "a saving flood," a sign of the death of the old and the beginning of the new, the voyage and exodus of the people of God from unbelief to belief. In Luther's catechesis, we see how baptism signifies the death of Adam in us, an image that Gregory of Nazianzus used to explain what it

---

[34]Bobrinskoy, "The Indwelling of the Spirit," 65.

[35]Luther, "The Baptismal Booklet," 14, *BC*, pp. 373-74.

means for Jesus to purify or sanctify the Jordan waters for us.[36] One also hears in Luther echoes of the patristic theme of baptism as a little exodus from God's judgment of death against sin, as seen for instance in Basil's treatise on the Holy Spirit.[37] Moreover, Luther employs the theme of the church as an ark that brings believers to safe harbor, which is used by Cyril of Jerusalem in his catechesis on the Holy Spirit.[38]

Although God's salvation through water in the days of Noah and Israel "prefigured this bath of your Holy Baptism," it is only through the baptism of Christ that God "hallowed and set apart the Jordan and all water to be a blessed flood and a rich washing away of sins." As noted above, Luther picks up on the patristic theme of the sanctification of the Jordan waters. We see this theme in Cyril of Jerusalem's description of Christ as one who makes baptismal waters holy with his divinity in order to anoint us with his Spirit and also in Gregory of Nazianzus's image of Jesus' sanctifying of the Jordan as the place where the old Adam not only dies but is also restored to Paradise.[39] For Luther, the Jordan stands as an important event in God's economy of salvation, marking the transition from the Old to the New Testament and making possible our participation in Christ's death and new life through baptism. But how?

In his homiletical writings, the Reformer reflects on Christ's sanctification of the Jordan through his humanity and blood, thus linking baptism and the cross. In his sermons at the baptism of Bernard, the son of Prince John of Anhalt (1540), Luther interprets Matthew's account of the Jordan in substitutionary language. Because Christ's baptism anticipates his cruciform destiny as the servant of Yahweh (see Isa 53:6), he goes to the waters in the place of sinners and for their sake.

> Because He has become the Sinner who has all of our sin placed upon Him, He truly does need Baptism and must be baptized for the forgiveness of sins—not with

---

[36]"But John baptizes, Jesus comes to Him . . . perhaps to sanctify the Baptist himself, but certainly to bury the whole of the old Adam in the water; and before this and for the sake of this, to sanctify Jordan; for as He is Spirit and Flesh, so He consecrates us by Spirit and water." Gregory Nazianzen, *Oration* 39.15 (*NPNF*[2] 7:357).

[37]See Basil's imagery earlier in this chapter.

[38]For Cyril's imagery, see chapter four on the dramatic model.

[39]For Cyril's imagery, see chapter two. Gregory of Nazianzus speaks of Jesus' purification at the Jordan River as a mystery of salvation that occurs "for my Purification, or rather, sanctifying the waters by His purification" in order to bring about "my perfection and return to the first condition of Adam." *Oration* 38.16 (*NPNF*[2] 7:350-51).

> respect to His own person, which is innocent and spotless, but for the sake of us, whose sins He bears. He plunges them into His Baptism and washes them away from Himself (that is, He washes them from us, since He has stepped into our person) so that they must be drowned and die in His Baptism.[40]

In liturgical time, the baptized are united to Christ in his Jordan waters and thus their sins are "drowned and die in His baptism," but also washed away.[41] Although Christ does not need baptism because of an ontological need in his own person, he still "truly does need" to go to the waters "for the benefit of you, of me, and of all the world, in order to cleanse us from sins and to make us righteous and blessed."[42] This basic distinction between Christ's own person and his person "for us" echoes many fourth-century theologians' descriptions of the baptism of Jesus.[43] The Jordan is thus set in a soteriological trajectory, opening the way for human participation in Christ's righteousness and holiness. By receiving John's baptism for us, Christ does not only command or confirm Christian baptism, but already "institutes" it.[44] By being "immersed in the water, touching it with His holy body," Christ sanctifies and blesses our baptism.[45]

To highlight the benefits of baptism, how Christ sanctifies it for our sake, Luther uses, along with Paul's clothing imagery (see Eph 4:24), his famous description of salvation in Christ as a "blessed exchange," in which Christ takes on himself our sin and guilt and in exchange clothes and adorns us with his righteousness and purity.

---

[40]Luther, *First Sermon at the Baptism of Bernard of Anhalt*, *LW* 58:45. "That is why He, too, undergoes Baptism and confesses by that deed that He is a sinner—not with respect to Himself, but with respect to us. For here He steps into my person and yours and stands in the place of all of us who are sinners." *First Sermon*, *LW* 58:44. "His Baptism is my Baptism and my Baptism is His Baptism." *A Sermon of Dr. Martin Luther, Delivered in Halle on the Day of Christ's Epiphany*, *LW* 58:362.

[41]Referring to the Father's voice at the Jordan, Luther writes: "For this Son, who stood there and allowed himself to be baptized by John, pleased him [the Father] so well that even though he were bearing the sins of a thousand worlds, they would all be drowned and destroyed in his baptism." *Sermon on Matt. 3:13-17 at the Baptism of Bernhard von Anhalt*, *LW* 51:318.

[42]Luther, *First Sermon*, *LW* 58:45. Implicit in Luther's cruciform approach to Christ's baptism at the Jordan and our participation in it lies Paul's teaching that even though Christ did not sin, he became sin for us so that in him we might become the righteousness of God (2 Cor 5:21).

[43]See chapter two.

[44]Luther, *First Sermon*, *LW* 58:48.

[45]Luther, *First Sermon*, *LW* 58:48-49. "Therefore baptism was instituted by God primarily *for Christ's sake* and then afterwards also *for the sake of all men*. For first he must sanctify baptism through his own body and thereby take away the sin, in order that afterwards those who believe in him may have the forgiveness of sins" (italics mine). *Sermon on Matt. 3:13-17*, *LW* 51:318. Luther speaks of "the Son standing there in his manhood and allowing himself to be baptized for our benefit." *Sermon on Matt. 3:13-17*, *LW* 51:320.

> Is not this a beautiful, glorious exchange, by which Christ, who is wholly innocent and holy, not only takes upon himself another's sin, that is, my sin and guilt, but also clothes and adorns me, who am nothing but sin, with his own innocence and purity? And then besides dies the shameful death of the Cross for the sake of my sins, through which I have deserved death and condemnation, and grants to me his righteousness, in order that I may live with him eternally in glorious and unspeakable joy. Through this blessed exchange, in which Christ changes places with us (something the heart can grasp only in faith), and through nothing else, are we freed from sin and death and given his righteousness and life as our own.[46]

The preacher's "blessed exchange" image highlights the vicarious character of God's economy of grace, in which "Christ changes places with us."[47] Seen from the perspective of the cross, Christ sanctifies baptism—both his, and through his, ours—"through His blood" because there he was "cleansed from sins" in our stead and there those who are "baptized into Christ shall have their sins washed away."[48] In God's economy of salvation, baptism acquires a passive dimension in that it truly affects Christ in his humanity for our sake, as well as an active one in that Christ himself sanctifies through it.[49] Both dimensions are included in Luther's statement that "Christ's Baptism is my Baptism."[50]

In his catechesis, Luther makes use of Romans 6 to describe the significance or daily use of baptism, linking the text's reference to dying and being raised with Christ to the biblical theme of the waters as God's instrument of judgment and salvation we saw earlier in Luther's Flood Prayer. Baptism "signifies that the old creature [i.e., the old Adam] in us with all sins and evil desires is to be drowned and die through daily contrition and repentance and on the other hand that daily a new person is to come forth and rise up to live before God in righteousness and purity forever."[51] As the Reformer puts it in his *Large*

---

[46]Luther, *Sermon on Matt. 3:13-17, LW* 51:315.

[47]In chapter five, we will look to the sacrificial model for further implications of Luther's "exchange" metaphor.

[48]Luther, *A Sermon . . . on the Day of Christ's Epiphany, LW* 58:364.

[49]"But first I must believe that Christ was born and baptized for my benefit, that He washed my sin away through Baptism, indeed, washed it away through His blood." Luther, *A Sermon . . . on the Day of Christ's Epiphany, LW* 58:366.

[50]Luther, *A Sermon . . . on the Day of Christ's Epiphany, LW* 58:366.

[51]Luther, "The Sacrament of Holy Baptism," *LC* IV 12, *BC*, p. 360. "These two parts, being dipped under the water and emerging from it, point to the power and effect of baptism, which is nothing else than the slaying of the old Adam and the resurrection of the new creature, both of which must continue in us our whole life long. Thus a Christian life is nothing else than a daily baptism." Luther, "Fourth Part: Concerning Baptism," *LC* IV 65, *BC*, p. 465.

*Catechism* (1529), the baptismal pattern of the Christian life amounts to the life of repentance, that is, of contrition and absolution: "If you live in repentance, therefore, you are walking in baptism."[52] In baptism, Christ gives us the Holy Spirit "to suppress the old creature so that the new may come forth and grow strong."[53] The Holy Spirit forms Christ in his saints by conforming them to his death and resurrection.

Early church writers also used robe images to link Christ's baptism to ours.[54] We noted how Luther preached that, by clothing himself in our humanity, Christ takes on himself our sins, descending to the Jordan waters in our place to drown our sins with him. Similarly, Ambrose speaks of Christ washing his robe (that is, human nature) at the Jordan for our sake, so that he might also cover us with the "robe of joy" and clean our "filth."[55] As Christ emerges from the waters of the new creation, he leaves his robe of righteousness in the waters for sinners to pick up as they come out of their little Jordan. Repentance signifies a daily descent and ascent with Christ in baptism, a contrite putting off of our filthy rags and a joyful picking up of Christ's holiness.

In the *Large Catechism*, Luther echoes Paul's exhortations to put off the old flesh and put on Christ (see Gal 3:27; Eph 4:22-24; Rom 13:14) by teaching Christians they must see their baptism "as the daily garment that they are to wear all the time. Every day they should be found in faith and with its fruits, suppressing the old creature and growing up in the new."[56] Since the Christian life is a continuous return to the cross and Easter, and thus a daily baptism into Christ's death and resurrection, one must return to it often to turn in one's dirty rags and be clothed anew with the cleansed robe promised to the saints in baptism.

> If I stumble and fall into sin, then I should repent and crawl to the cross, go there and fetch my pure and white robe with which I was clothed in Baptism, where all my sins, if they are not all completely washed away, are nonetheless forgiven, because the forgiveness is altogether pure. That is what I cling to![57]

---

[52]Luther, "Fourth Part: Concerning Baptism," *LC* IV 75, *BC*, p. 466.

[53]Luther, "Fourth Part: Concerning Baptism," *LC* IV 76, *BC*, p. 466.

[54]McDonnell offers many examples from the Syrian fathers. See Kilian McDonnell, *The Baptism of Jesus in the Jordan: The Trinitarian and Cosmic Order of Salvation* (Collegeville, MN: Liturgical Press, 1996), 128-44.

[55]Ambrose, *De patriarchis* 4.24. Cited in Carmelo Granado, *El Espíritu Santo en la teología patrística* (Salamanca: Ediciones Sígueme, 1987), 232.

[56]Luther, "Fourth Part: Concerning Baptism," *LC* IV 84, *BC*, p. 466.

[57]Luther, *A Sermon . . . on the Day of Christ's Epiphany*, *LW* 58:368.

## A MATTER OF LIFE AND DEATH: SPIRITUAL PRACTICES AND ISSUES IN THE CHRISTIAN LIFE

At the entrance to the chapel of the seminary campus where I teach, the community is met by a baptismal font located up front in the narthex area. You cannot miss it. Some familiar faces dip their fingers in the water and make the sign of the cross on their heads and chests in remembrance of their baptism. Less frequent visitors and guests are not quite sure what to make of it. Though beautiful in its simplicity, the sturdy font seems to get in the way of travelers, since one must go around it or avoid it altogether to see the rest of the chapel. And yet, that is precisely the point of the font—to stare us right in the face, make us stop, and interrupt our routine.

The structure's architectural position, the liturgical space it occupies, embodies an invitation to enter into God's presence by dying with the Christ who goes down to the waters in our place to drown our sins with him. If we look closely, with the eyes of the Holy Spirit who hovers over the suffering servant at the Jordan, those murky waters reflect the image of Christ crucified. United to Christ in his death, we see Adam's filthy rags enveloping us, and a guilty conscience calls us to confess our iniquities. Drowning the old Adam and its childish ways in us, we lose the breath of God. And the chasm between the Creator and creature widens, like the distance between the rich man and Lazarus. The font becomes our tomb and burial. We die with Christ.

On the way out of the chapel, the font meets us once again. But this time, we look in its waters as in a mirror and see the risen Christ coming out of the waters in our stead, picking us up with him on his way up. A sign of God's new creation, the heavens open and the Spirit hovers over us like it hovered over the waters of the first creation. United to Christ at our little Jordan, we see ourselves raised from the waters as new and grown-up creatures, clothed with Christ's righteousness and purified of all sins with Christ's Spirit. A second chance: God's breath returns to the race of Adam, a little Pentecost of the Spirit and fire that opens the way to Paradise. Our consciences relieved and comforted before the Judge, we are declared and made righteous for Christ's sake and reconciled to God. Self-accusation and self-condemnation turn into the gift of divine acceptance, and the dark chasm between God and us vanishes in Christ. The font is no longer a tomb, but our exodus from death to life; the flood waters no longer harbingers of divine judgment, but a saving flood that brings Noah's ark to God's safe harbor.

***Embracing the cycle and avoiding extremes.*** The renewal model of the Christian life fosters the spiritual discipline of confession and absolution, the continual return to baptism and the foot of the cross. Because of its cyclical movement, our dying and being raised with Christ daily, this model avoids two potential extremes in sanctification language, namely, perfectionism and fatalism. There is, of course, as in every heresy, a grain of truth in both extremes. Christ does exhort the "blessed" of the Beatitudes to "be perfect, as your heavenly Father is perfect" (Mt 5:48) in fulfilling the law of love by showing mercy to others (see Lk 6:36: "Be merciful, even as your Father is merciful"), especially one's enemies and persecutors. Surely, Christ's blessed disciples heed his call, trying their very best to be merciful, even though they fall short of the gold standard. When a Samaritan village did not receive Jesus as he set his face to Jerusalem, his disciples James and John, the sons of Zebedee, suggested a way to deal with their rejection: "Lord, do you want us to tell fire to come down from heaven and consume them?" (Lk 9:54). Jesus rebukes them. So much for loving your enemies! Even those who have been blessed by Jesus often fail to live according to his words.

As Paul reflects realistically on his own struggle with sin, the apostle notes that in this life the Christian will not always fulfill the law of God on account of the flesh: "So then, I myself serve the law of God with my mind, but with my flesh I serve the law of sin" (Rom 7:25). Yet, Paul does not give up in his fight against the flesh, which still clings to the sinner in us. Paul holds firmly to his new identity as a son of God who has been freed from "the law of sin and death" in order to live by "the law of the Spirit of life" (Rom 8:2). Despite their struggles in this life, Paul does not address Christians according to the flesh (that is, the old creature still hanging around them), but as adopted sons and daughters in whom the Spirit of the God who raised Christ from the dead dwells (Rom 8:9-11). While acknowledging the remaining traces of the old creature in the present, Paul is far from dwelling on the past and invites fellow children of God to live according to their status as new creatures who already now have "the firstfruits of the Spirit"—a status that is yet to be fully revealed in their final adoption and bodily redemption (v. 23). In the meantime, the apostle reminds the "sons of God," namely, those who "are led by the Spirit of God" and "have received the Spirit of adoption," not to give in to "the spirit of slavery to fall back into fear" (vv. 14-15). Why act as a slave to the sinful flesh if you are already an adopted son of God by the Spirit? Why live today with fear if you can instead live with hope as an heir of God's promises of adoption and redemption from sin and death? Thus, the apostle reminds the adopted sons and daughters to live according to their new spiritual reality by dying to the old in order to live anew: "For if you live according to the flesh you will die, but if by the Spirit you put to death the deeds of the body, you will live" (v. 13). If there is no room in sanctification for being overly confident or unrealistically optimistic, there is also no room for being pessimistic or giving up.

Rather than pushing life in either direction, swinging back and forth like a pendulum in the search for some perfect balance, the renewal model of the Christian life simply helps us to embrace life in the Spirit according to the circular rhythm of life and death. If the perfectionist has an overly realized hope in the possibility of expelling sins from his or her life, the fatalist holds to an under-realized hope in the same prospect and does not even try to overcome them. One raises the holiness bar too high, the other one barely raises it. Both moves end up keeping people bound in their sins. The perfectionist dismisses the everyday struggle with sin in the already now, and when no one is looking tends to brush certain sins under the rug—as one would a stubborn pile of dust that refuses to go away even after our best efforts at cleaning up the mess. The fatalist does not claim that in Christ the old has gone and the new creation has already broken in from the not yet, and when everyone is looking tends to proudly pity himself as the most sinful creature who ever lived—as old men of chivalry spoke poetically of their unworthiness to be loved by their one and only, turning their sorry state into a mark of great virtue!

When facing the font, the perfectionist becomes a great swimmer, avoiding his death with Christ in the waters at all costs, paddling his way away from the mirror that reveals his sins instead of facing up to them. The fatalist goes deep into the font and building herself a house down under from which no one can pull her out, avoids coming out of the waters with Christ to live as a new creature. One goes in kicking and screaming, the other one comes out likewise. The perfectionist and fatalist in all of us need to die to sin and be raised a forgiven person, confess sins and be pardoned; we need contrition and absolution. Whether we enter this rhythm of death and life individually before God, privately with a confessor, or in public worship with the whole people of God, the renewal model fosters a view of holiness that promises neither inevitable progress and triumph over sins nor inevitable failure and apathy toward them. Embracing and focusing on our continual death and life in and with Christ, the renewal model keeps us from harboring unrealistic expectations, from raising the holiness bar too high or setting it too low.

***Cyclical growth.*** The Spirit's sanctifying work of conforming sinners after the pattern of Christ's death and resurrection differs logically from the Spirit's justifying work of declaring the sinner righteous or not guilty before God through the forgiveness of sins. If the latter deals with the sinner's guilt before God on account of Christ, the former deals with the recurrent power of sin in the everyday life of the justified sinner. The renewal model of sanctification, which the Holy Spirit brings about in the justified through death and resurrection (through killing and making the sinner alive; see Deut 32:39), highlights sanctification's indissoluble link to justification, since the saints are always returning to the cross to deal with the guilt brought on them by their everyday sins through the reception of God's pardon. Since sanctification finds its source and power in the gospel of justification, it cannot be seen as moving beyond justification but rather as moving with it. Though distinct aspects of the Holy Spirit's work, they are joined together in everyday life.

The sanctified life does not consist in achieving something greater or better than justification, but rather in living out one's identity as the justified in the world. In that sense, sanctification can be thought of as "*the art of getting used to justification*,"[58] or as "the institutional side of the event of justification."[59] Rather than thinking of holiness as a one-directional, linear movement away from justification, we can think of it instead as a circular, cyclical movement, toward justification.[60] In a NASCAR race, cars start their engines with a full tank of gas and go around the circuit several times before they reach the finish line. As cars go through the circuit, they get beat up by other cars, tires falter, and more fuel is needed to keep going until reaching the goal. The justified are initiated on the race to life eternal in their baptism and are filled with the power of the gospel to run the race until they reach the promised goal at the last day. Along the circuit, they

[58]Gerhard O. Forde, "The Lutheran View," in *Christian Spirituality: Five Views of Sanctification*, ed. Donald L. Alexander (Downers Grove, IL: InterVarsity Press, 1988), 13.

[59]Oswald Bayer, *Living by Faith: Justification and Sanctification*, trans. Geoffrey W. Bromiley (Grand Rapids: Eerdmans, 2003), 59.

[60]For Lutheran critiques of approaches to sanctification that do not adequately link it to the power of the gospel and justification, see Köberle, *Quest for Holiness*; David P. Scaer, "Sanctification in the Lutheran Confessions," *Concordia Theological Quarterly* 53, no. 3 (1989): 165-81, and "Sanctification in Lutheran Theology," *Concordia Theological Quarterly* 49, nos. 2-3 (1985): 181-95; and Harold L. Senkbeil, *Sanctification: Christ in Action. Evangelical Challenge and Lutheran Response* (Milwaukee: Northwestern, 1989).

lose focus and get beat up by their sins. They need to be refueled to complete the race, receiving over and over again the comfort and power of the gospel. Life is a continual return to the power of the cross until the race is finished and the prize of life eternal is won.

In the renewal model, growth is not denied. The new creature does grow in holiness, but such maturity is not understood in some straight, undeterred upward sense. Rather, progress happens more modestly in the cyclical movement of daily repentance as the sinner in us dies with Christ and a new creature is raised with Christ to new life. With every sin forgiven, every day affords us a new beginning, a fresh start. When the old creature raises its ugly head in our lives, it opposes the Holy Spirit's work of formation, as the perfectionist or fatalist in us tries to get his way. Yet as the creature emerges with Christ from the waters and claims his new identity, it does respond in the power of the gospel of forgiveness to the Spirit's work of formation in his heart and mind, delighting in God's law, embodying the law of the Spirit of life, and bearing the fruit of the Spirit.

***Fostering right relations.*** Lest one conclude that the renewal model only fosters the life of repentance with God at a personal level, we should note that there is also a more public dimension to it, an embodiment of Christlikeness in the world in practices of reconciliation. Stories of reconciliation abound, even in the movies. A powerful cinematic depiction of the rise and fall of Jesuit missions among Amerindians in eighteenth-century colonial South America, *The Mission* follows the story of Rodrigo Mendoza, a ruthless mercenary at whose hands the natives were murdered and captured for the profitable slave trade, and whose life takes a tragic turn after killing his half-brother Felipe in a sword duel after finding out about his kin's affair with his assumed fiancée Carlotta. In a self-imposed prison of guilt and self-accusation, convinced that God cannot forgive him, the murderer is visited in the solitude of a cell by Father Gabriel, who dares him to stop feeling sorry for himself and to come with him to the mission above the majestic waterfalls in the land of the Guaraní people.

Making his journey more arduous than the rest of his companions, Rodrigo carries around his neck and shoulders the weight of his armor and sword—the instrument of his many transgressions against others—as a guilty sinner carries on himself his more-than-deserved penance. Upon reaching the top of the cliff above the falls, Rodrigo falls to his knees exhausted. The natives recognized their enemy, the perpetrator of many inhumanities against their people, and one of their own runs toward him with a knife, placing it around his neck while yelling at him as if asking for final words before exacting vengeance on the guilty. Suddenly, the former victim moves his knife away from the enemy's neck, and instead of punishing him with death, cuts the thick rope around Rodrigo's neck which had tied him to his past iniquities. Releasing a contrite Rodrigo from the mighty weight of his sins, the persecutor with a heart of stone begins to weep like a little child and his spiritual father Gabriel runs to hug him, even as a fellow Jesuit looks in disbelief at such a miracle of love. In a moving scene, the forgiven man's uncontrollable tears of joy mingle with the unequaled laughter of the natives, as if a choir of angels were rejoicing over a single sinner who repents. Fruits of repentance follow as Rodrigo takes vows to work in the mission, serving and defending those whom he had formerly persecuted.

Viewers of the story are invited to behold the power of forgiveness and seek the tough road of reconciliation with neighbors whom they have hurt and who have hurt them. In North America, there are many who embody the life of daily repentance either in personal or corporate ways, saints among us who give us a powerful witness and picture of the Holy Spirit's work in their lives. A collective example of a community of clergy and laity in North America working together to bring young people into a participation in Christ's death and resurrection is the Teens Encounter Christ (TEC) movement. Originating after Vatican II through the efforts of Fr. Matthew Fedewa, TEC held its first weekend retreats in Battle Creek, Michigan in 1965 with the goal of helping youth focus their lives around Christ's Paschal Mystery.[61] Although its origins are Roman Catholic, some Protestant versions of their three-day weekend retreat format can be found in various states.

A community of youth and adults gathers for a series of talks, small group discussions, large group activities, fellowship, and worship. This takes place in the theological framework of a three-day journey that incorporates disciples of Christ into his death, resurrection, and the new life that ensues from his cross for the sake of the world. Each day focuses respectively on three aspects of the Christian life, namely, contrition (death), absolution (resurrection), and the change and renewal of the mind (*metanoia*) that follows from dying with and living in Christ (fruits of repentance).

---

[61]For a comprehensive guide to TEC's history and mission, go to their website: www.tecconference.org.

Without trying to become normative for all youth, the TEC experience serves as a microcosm of the daily life of repentance, an ongoing cycle of life to which all Christians are called by virtue of their baptismal identity. Throughout the weekend, young people center their lives on the cross, becoming deeply sorrowful for their sins, rejoicing in their reconciliation with God and others through the power of Christ's forgiveness, and seeing their lives anew as forgiven creatures empowered to be forces for reconciliation in the world. Due to their collective embodiment of life in the Spirit as a cycle of death and new life, the intergenerational TEC community offers us a North American example of the renewal model of sanctification.

And yet in the Holy Spirit's work of conforming persons to Christ crucified and risen, TEC is only one of many wonderful instances of ongoing renewal the Spirit continues to bring about in the lives of God's people across generations. My hope is that our journey through Scripture and selected writings of church theologians past and present on the significance of the baptismal life, of our daily dying and living anew in Christ, has offered us a catholic and ecumenical sense of the rich variety of images pastors and other church leaders have at their disposal to teach and invite people into practices of renewal today.

4

# FACING DEMONS THROUGH PRAYER AND MEDITATION

## THE DRAMATIC MODEL

Seeing reality as a cosmic drama in which God fights against the evil one for the lives of people, the *dramatic* model of sanctification depicts life in the Spirit as a battle against the evil spirit or a struggle amid spiritual attacks. This model bears an affinity with an important early church account of God's work of salvation according to which "Christ—Christus Victor—fights against and triumphs over the evil powers of the world, the 'tyrants' under which mankind is in bondage and suffering, and in Him God reconciles the world to Himself."[1] In a contemporary revival of this "classic" account of the atonement, Gustaf Aulén describes its dominant soteriological theme as "a cosmic drama" in which Christ's "victory over the hostile powers brings to pass a new relation, a relation of reconciliation, between God and the world . . . because in a measure the hostile powers are regarded as in the service of the Will of God the Judge of all, and the executants of His judgment."[2] Paradoxically, in a dramatic account of salvation, God establishes a new relationship with a humanity in bondage to evil powers by submitting them to Christ's power over all things.

What is lacking in Aulén's account is a place for the role of the Spirit of God in the work of Christ as the Victor over the powers of the anti-kingdom.[3] Nor does

[1]Gustaf Aulén, *Christus Victor: An Historical Study of the Three Main Types of the Idea of Atonement* (Eugene, OR: Wipf & Stock, 2003), 4.
[2]Aulén, *Historical Study*, 5.
[3]For a critical engagement with views of the atonement from the perspective of a Spirit Christology, see Leopoldo A. Sánchez M., *Receiver, Bearer, and Giver of God's Spirit* (Eugene, OR: Pickwick, 2015), 76-84.

Aulén's proposal consider how God places such evil powers under the Spirit's greater power in the time between the now and not yet in which we live and have to face them. In this chapter, we will attend to the significance of the dramatic model for sanctification from the perspective of a Spirit Christology. Leading people under attack to the Word of God and prayer and to discernment about one's spiritual condition in light of the Word, the Holy Spirit conforms us to Christ's temptation and testing in the desert and the garden. By drawing attention to our perilous journey in the wilderness, this model can assist church leaders in promoting vigilance in areas of vulnerability to temptation that might bring harm to self and others or in cultivating resilience to stand firm in God's promises when the evil one uses difficult circumstances in life to bring us down.

To stand firm in the midst of the attacks, the spiritual disciplines of meditation on the Word and prayer are central. Forms of external discipline, such as fasting or support groups, are also beneficial as boundaries and safe spaces. Such disciplines can keep the tempted in check or offer those who feel abandoned amid struggles much needed encouragement. The dramatic model deals with issues such as security and the need for vigilance. It also addresses the importance of accountability and support when dealing with personal bondage to sinful desires or habits or with the fear of abandonment, hopelessness, and death amid sufferings such as poverty and sickness.

## BIBLICAL PICTURES: DESERT JOURNEYS, GARDEN PRAYERS, AND ATHLETIC ARENAS

Life in the Spirit is often associated with some pursuit of happiness or an easy and comfortable state in life. In the renewal model of sanctification, there is resurrection but not without death. That life in the Spirit is difficult can also be seen in Jesus' own mission, marked by constant opposition to his kingdom. It is precisely when Jesus is "full of the Holy Spirit" and "led by the Spirit" that he is most under attack (Lk 4:1). The wilderness is often the place of prayer, of solitude with God, but it also stands as the place of struggle where Jesus is "being tempted by the devil" (v. 2). In the desert, the devil offers not only bread to hungry Israel, now represented by Jesus (see Deut 8:1-3), but more temptingly, dominion over "all the kingdoms of the world" to anyone hungry enough for such power, if he should worship him (Lk 4:3-7). For forty years unfaithful Israel, the firstborn of God, worshiped idols in the desert—the golden calf incident being a most memorable instance of a recurrent problem (Deut 9:13-21). Now, Jesus, in his forty desert days (Lk 4:1), recapitulates or does over the failed history of Israel, becoming the faithful Son of God, obedient to his Father alone, despite seemingly more attractive calves available for worship (Lk 4:8; cf. Deut 6:13).

In the wilderness, Jesus' sonship or filial trust is put to the test. Temptation and testing are two sides of the same coin. While the devil tempts God's firstborn Israel to be a disobedient son, God tests his firstborn son in order to humble him in the way of obedience to his Word, teaching him that "man does not live by bread alone, but man lives by every word that comes from the mouth of the LORD" (Deut 8:3). In his baptismal anointing, God's "beloved Son" humbles himself as Yahweh's servant (Lk 3:22) and is led by God's Spirit into the desert to be tempted (Lk 4:1). Verbs like "led" and "tempted" reflect the passivity of the Son in his humiliation, allowing the Spirit of God to have free course in his life as he faces the devil's attacks. Yet the same devil whose goal is to make the Son fail the test of filial obedience ends up being God's instrument of filial testing: "If you are the Son of God . . ." (vv. 3, 9). Unlike disobedient Israel, however, Jesus becomes obedient to the Father's words and will and stays the course. Rather than putting God's will for his life and mission to the test, the obedient Son puts himself under God's command (v. 12; cf. Deut 6:16). In the midst of the attacks, Jesus speaks and stands firm in God's Word.

Jesus' wilderness experience highlights the conflict between God's kingdom and the anti-kingdom. Such experience can be described in pneumatic terms as a battle between the Holy Spirit and the evil spirit, and it characterizes much of Jesus' ministry. When Jesus begins his teaching and preaching ministry in Galilee, he goes to his hometown "in the power of the Spirit" (Lk 4:14), and there proclaims himself to be the one on whom the Lord put his Spirit-anointing to proclaim the Lord's favor, heal the blind, and set captives free (vv. 18-19; cf. Is 61:1-2)—all signs of God's merciful rule among his people. Yet Jesus encounters not a welcoming reception but opposition to the Word of God, and eventually the crowds want to "throw him down the cliff" (Lk 4:29). In cosmic terms, the crowds act as representatives of the anti-kingdom. The fulfillment of God's will brings about opposition to the Messiah.

After Jesus heals a demon-possessed man who was blind and mute, the Pharisees dare to suggest that his work is being done by the power of Beelzebub (Mt 12:22-24). Jesus notes that he does not drive out demons by Beelzebub

(v. 27), but "by the Spirit of God" (v. 28; cf. "finger of God" in Lk 11:20). If Jesus healed and set captives free by the power of the devil, Satan's kingdom would be "divided against itself" and indeed Satan would be "divided against himself" (Mt 12:25-26). An absurd conclusion. Instead, Jesus notes that his healing-exorcism is a sign of God's kingdom brought about by the Spirit of God working in him (v. 28). Jesus warns against a blasphemous opposition to God's kingdom, a definitive denial or rejection of God's work through his Spirit that will not be forgiven (vv. 31-32). Like the crowds mentioned earlier, the Pharisees represent the powers of the anti-kingdom, always in battle against Jesus who acts in the power of the Holy Spirit. The fulfillment of God's will in Jesus' messianic kingdom brings on attacks. Life in the Spirit leads Jesus to conflict but also to his establishment of God's reign.

When the seventy-two return from their mission, they tell Jesus with joy that even the demons were subdued in his name (Lk 10:17). Jesus attests to the fall of Satan and speaks of his "authority . . . over all the power of the enemy" (v. 19). The word of God, the name of Jesus, drives out demons—a sign of the kingdom that has come into human history. In the midst of this encounter, Jesus "rejoiced in the Holy Spirit" and offered a prayer of thanksgiving to the Father for revealing the kingdom to his disciples (v. 21, "little children"). Prayer in the Spirit becomes part of the fabric of Jesus' life, and here includes a prayer of praise and thanksgiving for God's deliverance of his people from evil. But prayer can also be a petition for God's will to be done as Jesus faces spiritual attacks. Jesus utters the latter as the devil returns for another "opportune time" to tempt him (Lk 4:13) later in his ministry, as Jesus set his face to Jerusalem to encounter opposition and death.

Like the wilderness, the garden is the place of prayer and communion with God, as well as the place of temptation and testing. At the Mount of Olives, Jesus teaches his disciples to "pray that you may not enter into temptation" (Lk 22:40, see v. 45). Jesus also prays in a time of intense struggle against evil depicted in strikingly human terms. He asks the Father to "remove this cup from me," even if he also asks "not my will, but yours, be done" (v. 42). On his knees, Jesus receives strength from an angel, is in agony, prays more earnestly, and his sweat drops are thick like blood (vv. 43-44). At the garden of Gethsemane, Jesus says that his "soul is very sorrowful, even to death" (Mk 14:34). It is precisely in the midst of an intense battle with the devil that the Son prays "Abba, Father" in the Spirit, trusting in God (Mk 14:36; cf. Rom 8:15; Gal 4:6).

At Gethsemane, a contrast is suggested between the first Adam and Jesus. In the Garden of Eden, the first Adam fell into the devil's deception and failed to live under God's command (Gen 3). In the garden of Gethsemane, Jesus is the last Adam (cf. Lk 3:23-38) who reverses the failed history of Adam, submitting to the Father's will even unto death for our sake. In his prayer, "yet not what I will, but what you will" (Mk 14:36), Jesus places his life in the Father's hands as he faces the last test of his sonship. He will utter a similar prayer of surrender from the cross as he prepares for his imminent death (Lk 23:46).

What the Son went through in the desert and the garden is paradigmatic for the adopted sons, his brothers and sisters, who mirror in their own lives his drama with the evil one. The Son alone is the image of God, "the radiance of the glory of God and the exact imprint of his nature" (Heb 1:3). Yet for the sake of "bringing many sons to glory" (2:10), the Son shared in their "flesh and blood" and suffered death in order to "destroy the one who has the power of death . . . and deliver all those who through fear of death were subject to lifelong slavery" (2:14-15). Through his incarnation, suffering, and entrance into glory, the Son, who is the exact likeness of God, was made like those whom he sanctified when he made them his brothers and sisters, as well as beneficiaries of his salvation from the devil, the fear of death, and sins (vv. 10-11, 17).

Sanctification becomes a sharing in Jesus' resurrection glory (Heb 2:10-11), but also a partaking in his suffering. The Son was made "perfect through suffering" (v. 10), which included his temptations. The Son "has been tempted as we are," yet he was "without sin" (Heb 4:15), so that "through the eternal Spirit" he might offer his life "without blemish to God" and cleanse our consciences to serve God (9:14). Because Jesus truly suffered temptations, he can "sympathize with our weaknesses" (4:15) and "help those who are being tempted" (2:18). The Christian life does not make us immune to the attacks of the devil but the objects of those attacks. The point is not to avoid temptations, since they are inevitable, but rather to "run with endurance the race that is set before us, looking to Jesus, the founder and perfecter of our faith" so that we, like him, might endure our cross and finally share in his glory (12:1-2).

To share in God's holiness is not merely to be tempted, but to receive such attacks and afflictions as God's own testing of his children. Christians are called to endure discipline (Heb 12:7), not in some masochistic way, but as a form of training so that they might grow strong and healthy to withstand further attacks, make it out alive, and finally share in God's righteousness and peace (vv. 9-13). To the familial image of children receiving unpleasant discipline from their loving parents (vv. 5-11), the writer of Hebrews superimposes the image of the disciplined athlete who requires proper strength training to endure the race of life with perseverance and without becoming weary, feeble, or weak, until he crosses the finish life and receives the crown of glory (vv. 1-3, 12-13; cf. Heb 2:9-10).

It is in this broader eschatological scheme that God's children should approach their struggles with temptation, namely, as often-painful instances through which a loving God tests his children to make them humble and receptive to his Word. By submitting to God's discipline in the midst of spiritual attacks, we are formed into the likeness of his obedient Son, who in his submission to the Father was made "perfect through suffering" (Heb 2:10) so that at last we might partake of the Son's resurrection glory, which is the same as a "share in his [God's] holiness" (Heb 12:10). Holiness is the goal of the race in the beatific vision, since without holiness "no one will see the Lord" (v. 14). Holiness includes the path of temptation and testing along the journey of life through which God makes his children perfect and thus brings to their proper end those whom the Son has sanctified by his suffering, death, and glory.

Life is like a race track or a boxing ring where Christians receive training to become athletes who discipline their bodies to receive the winner's wreath (1 Cor 9:24-27). Life is like a grand sports event where runners do not "run aimlessly" and pugilists do not box "beating the air," but they remain focused on the opponent and the prize waiting at the end of the contest. Along the journey, one is to be prepared, not to be caught off guard, but keep one's eyes on the prize, lest one "should be disqualified" (v. 27). Paul sets these images from the world of sports into an even greater story, that of God's deliverance of Israel from Egypt, which is also the story of the dangerous wilderness where Israel was once tempted and fell into idolatry (1 Cor 10:1-13). The example of Israel in her desert wanderings serves now as a warning to God's children of all times and places to be vigilant lest they grow overly confident and fall (vv. 11-12). Yet the same God who delivered Israel through the sea, fed them manna, and gave them drink in the desert (vv. 1-4) will not let his children "be tempted beyond [their] ability" and "will also provide the way of escape, that [they] may be able to endure it" (v. 13). In their days through the wilderness, God's children heed his warnings, but also receive his promises.

Lest they become vulnerable to the attacks of their opponents, gladiators must "stand firm" in the arena as they face battle (Eph 6:13). In the grand arena of life, Christians too must "be strong in the Lord and in the strength of his might" and "put on the whole armor of God" to "stand against the schemes of the devil" (vv. 10-11). In this spiritual warfare against evil, the saints rely not on themselves but on God's armor for protection (vv. 13-17). Like Jesus in the desert, they are resilient and hold on to "the sword of the Spirit, which is the word of God" (v. 17) to withstand the devil's attacks in all life circumstances. They learn to rely on God and his Word and will, his commands and promises, especially during difficult times of suffering that the evil one uses to bring them down. Like Jesus in the garden, the saints put their lives in God's hands, "praying at all times in the Spirit, with all prayer and supplication" (v. 18). They learn to rely on God, praying "Abba, Father," an expression of filial trust (Rom 8:15; cf. Gal 4:6).[4] They pray as their Lord taught them: "Your will be done, on earth as it is in heaven. . . . Lead us not into temptation, but deliver us from evil" (Mt 6:10, 13). Through struggle and testing, the Spirit forms the saints to be Christlike, making them vigilant, strong, and resilient in the face of spiritual attacks, and shaping them to anchor their lives in the Word of God and prayer as they journey through life.

## CATECHETICAL IMAGES: EXORCISMS AND FORTRESSES, ENDURANCE IN AFFLICTIONS

How do prominent church theologians portray the Christian's struggle against the powers of the evil one and God's work of deliverance from evil? How do they prepare their catechumens, pastors, and hearers of the preached word for this cosmic drama between God's kingdom and the powers of the anti-kingdom? In this section, we look at the pictures Cyril of Jerusalem, Ambrose of Milan, and John Chrysostom paint for us to describe the Holy Spirit's work of forming the saints in the face of temptation and testing. Drawing from a rite of baptism, a preface to a set of his writings, and a pastoral treatise, we also look at some of Martin Luther's contributions to the care of people under spiritual attacks. While Luther shares with earlier voices a deep sense of the church's struggle against the evil one and Christ's victory over Satan, the Reformer also develops these emphases in the service of a more comprehensive approach to pastoral care. Luther does so by

[4]On prayer as a form of participation in Christ's filial identity, see Sánchez, *Receiver, Bearer, and Giver of God's Spirit*, 195-218.

appropriating evangelically and extending congregationally the medieval monastic tradition's focus on the habituation of the person in a community of the Spirit shaped by prayer and the Word.

***Cyril of Jerusalem: Spiritual fortress, pilot of the church, exorcist's seal.*** For Cyril, Jesus' driving out demons by the Spirit of God (Mt 12:28) shows that the Holy Spirit is divine in nature—a teaching that admits no blasphemy against the Spirit.[5] In their baptism, catechumens receive the same Spirit by whom Jesus drove out demons.[6] By descending to the Jordan, Jesus frightens, defeats, and ties up the sea dragon, so that we could step on serpents and scorpions.[7] Baptism anticipates Christ's descent into hell to reveal his victory over Satan and his release of captives from the enemy's bondage.[8] Like the disciples on Pentecost, the saints are fully vested with the power from on high (Lk 24:49), so that "he who is clothed, is completely enfolded by his robe."[9] Investing the disciples with his power, the Holy Spirit becomes a sort of spiritual fortress, serving as their protector against the devil's weapons: "'Fear not,' He [Christ] says, 'the weapons and darts of the devil, for ye shall bear with you the power of the Holy Ghost.'"[10]

By bestowing the Holy Spirit on the saints, the exalted Lord gives them a defender and exorcises the devil from their lives. Each day, the baptized "wrestles with many fiercest demons," but these are driven away "with words of prayer, through the power which is in him of the Holy Spirit."[11] Christians must not be afraid, because they have "a mighty ally and protector . . . a mighty Champion" on their side, "for mightier is He who fighteth for us."[12] Christians journey through life as in a tempestuous sea, but the Spirit, "the Guardian and Sanctifier of the Church," leads them to safe harbor as "the Pilot of the tempest-tossed, who leads the wanderers to the light."[13] The same defender Spirit who leads the ark of the church to safe land "presides over the combatants, and crowns the victors" at the end of the journey.[14]

---

[5]Cyril of Jerusalem, *Catechetical Lecture* 16.1-3 (*NPNF*[2] 7:115).
[6]Cyril of Jerusalem, *Catechetical Lecture* 17.11 (*NPNF*[2] 7:126-27).
[7]Granado, "Pneumatología de San Cirilo de Jerusalén," 449.
[8]Granado, "Pneumatología de San Cirilo de Jerusalén," 449.
[9]Cyril of Jerusalem, *Catechetical Lecture* 17.12 (*NPNF*[2] 7:127).
[10]Cyril of Jerusalem, *Catechetical Lecture* 17.12 (*NPNF*[2] 7:127).
[11]Cyril of Jerusalem, *Catechetical Lecture* 16.19 (*NPNF*[2] 7:120).
[12]Cyril of Jerusalem, *Catechetical Lecture* 16.19 (*NPNF*[2] 7:120).
[13]Cyril of Jerusalem, *Catechetical Lecture* 17.13 (*NPNF*[2] 7:127).
[14]Cyril of Jerusalem, *Catechetical Lecture* 17.13 (*NPNF*[2] 7:127).

The catechist picks up on the Pauline image of the Christian life as a spiritual fight in the perilous arena where the devil attacks. Sealed with the promised Spirit before God and the company of angelic hosts, the baptized belong to Christ and thus are "enrolled in the army of the Great King."[15] The promised Spirit endows their souls with "the Seal at which evil spirits tremble."[16] Christians are warned to keep the Spirit-Seal on their souls, so that they may not fall in the hour of trial. Exhorting the catechumens to hold on to the heavenly seal in their spiritual warfare, Cyril assures them that the same Spirit by whom Jesus drove out demons belongs to them (cf. Mt 12:28).

> Thou wilt receive a power which thou hadst not, thou wilt receive weapons terrible to the evil spirits; and if thou cast not away thine arms, but keep the Seal upon thy soul, no evil spirit will approach thee; for he will be cowed; for verily by the Spirit of God are the evil spirits cast out.[17]

***Ambrose of Milan: Rain from above, thirsty pilgrims, watching the soul's heel.*** In the homiletical prologue to his treatise on the Holy Spirit, Ambrose of Milan creatively mines the biblical association of the Spirit with water. The advent of Christ prepared the way for his pouring of the rain of the Spirit on the world.[18] Like a "health-giving shower of salutary grace" flowing from the Lord, the "heavenly drops" of the Spirit fall on the thirsty desert of the soul in time of draught.[19] Evoking images of deserts turning into verdant lands, the theologian prays for the Holy Spirit's descent on his flesh, "that through the moisture of this rain the valleys of our minds and the fields of our hearts may grow green."[20] To the picture of redemption as the Spirit's renewal of the world and restoration of the individual from death to immortality, Ambrose adds the image of life as redemption from the evil one.

Inviting readers to place themselves in the aftermath of the Garden of Eden, Ambrose asks for the Spirit's help to withstand the serpent's seduction. The note of vigilance in the midst of temptations comes through in his prayer to Jesus for the protection of his Spirit.

---

[15]Cyril of Jerusalem, *Catechetical Lecture* 3.3 (*NPNF*[2] 7:14).
[16]Cyril of Jerusalem, *Catechetical Lecture* 17.35 (*NPNF*[2] 7:132).
[17]Cyril of Jerusalem, *Catechetical Lecture* 17.35 (*NPNF*[2] 7:133).
[18]Ambrose, *On the Holy Spirit* 1.8 (*NPNF*[2] 10:94).
[19]Ambrose, *On the Holy Spirit* 1.8 (*NPNF*[2] 10:94).
[20]Ambrose, *On the Holy Spirit* 1.16 (*NPNF*[2] 10:95).

> May the drops from Thee come upon me, shedding forth grace and immortality. Wash the steps of my mind that I may not sin again. Wash the heel of my soul, that I may be able to efface the curse, that I feel not the serpent's bite on the foot of my soul.[21]

The waters of the Spirit serve both a cleansing and protective function, pouring life on the soul and keeping it from sin, away from the curse of the serpent's bite.

If struck in the right place, a heel can be particularly susceptible to falling. Yet with the protection Christ gives through his Spirit, those whom he redeems "may tread on serpents and scorpions with uninjured foot."[22] The journey of the saints occurs on a dry and dangerous desert, a harsh life outside Eden, where the refreshing rain of the Holy Spirit gives much needed strength to thirsty pilgrims experiencing spiritual struggles.

***John Chrysostom: Job-like endurance, theodicy silence, wounded fighter.*** In his homilies on the rich man and Lazarus, Chrysostom presents the poor man Lazarus as an example of spiritual virtue for hearers to embody. In light of Lazarus's blessed end in heaven, the preacher extols his righteousness before God and reflects on the ways he remained faithful to God in the face of tremendous adversity. Given his great suffering in this life, the orator portrays Lazarus as a Job-like figure whose endurance amid poverty and illness revealed the strength of his character.

Lazarus's condition raises the old theodicy problem, namely, why the rich man "who lived in wickedness and inhumanity enjoyed every kind of good fortune, while the righteous man who practiced virtue endured the extremes of ill fortune."[23] Why do the unjust prosper and the just suffer? And where is God's own justice in this odd state of affairs? Chrysostom makes it clear that Lazarus's virtue does not lie in a rational attempt to justify his state according to some divine-human scheme, such as blaming himself for his bad fortune or making God look just and good when bad things happen.[24] Without sugarcoating the

---

[21]Ambrose, *On the Holy Spirit* 1.16 (*NPNF*[2] 10:95).

[22]Ambrose, *On the Holy Spirit* 1.16 (*NPNF*[2] 10:95).

[23]John Chrysostom, *On Wealth and Poverty*, trans. Catharine P. Roth (Crestwood, NY: St. Vladimir's Seminary Press, 1984), 23.

[24]Chrysostom portrays Lazarus as someone who, like Job and Paul, suffered not only physically but also spiritually at the hand of foolish theologians: "For most people, when they see someone in hunger, chronic illness, and the extremes of misfortune, do not even allow him a good reputation, but judge his life by his troubles, and think that he is surely in such misery because of wickedness. They say many other things like this to one another, foolishly indeed, but still they say them: for example, if this man were dear to God, He would not have left him to suffer in poverty and the other troubles. This is what happened both to Job and to Paul." The preacher goes on to cite Job 4:2-6 and Acts 28:4 as examples of bad theodicy. *On Wealth and Poverty*, 31-32.

situation, Chrysostom calls the poor man's poverty "truly a dreadful thing," and notes that on top of his indigence he had a chronic "illness yoked to it, and this to an excessive degree."[25]

What then makes Lazarus virtuous? Or to use the preacher's language in his introduction to the sermon, what makes such a person someone "filled with spiritual instruction" or "a flute and a lyre for the Holy Spirit," projecting the sounds of "a harmonious melody to delight not only mankind but even the powers of heaven"?[26] His virtue lies in that, amid great and unexplainable suffering, the man "did not become discouraged, blaspheme, or complain" to God.[27] Upon death's arrival, God finally reveals his justice and gives each man in the story what he deserves. Accounts are settled, as it were. Their works do follow them into the hereafter, revealing their true spiritual disposition as they journeyed in this life. The unrighteous receives the torments of Hades, and the righteous is taken by an angelic caravan to Abraham's bosom.

Paradoxically, Lazarus cannot even move his body to drive away the dogs licking his sores, yet he stands as an example of spiritual discipline, displaying great perseverance, patience, and wisdom in the midst of trials.[28] He is resilient in the face of adversity. Nevertheless, the rich man, though quite active and healthy in the eyes of the world, embodies spiritual idleness and by his own self-indulgence harms his spiritual health.[29] The preacher invites hearers to listen to Christ's words concerning Lazarus and learn from the poor man's example of faith.

> For this reason Christ set him before us, so that whatever troubles we encounter, seeing in this man a greater measure of tribulation, we may gain enough comfort and consolation from his wisdom and patience. He stands forth as a single teacher of the whole world, for those who suffer any misfortune whatever, offering himself for all to see, and surpassing all of them in the excess of his own troubles.[30]

---

[25]Chrysostom, *On Wealth and Poverty*, 29.

[26]Chrysostom, *On Wealth and Poverty*, 19.

[27]Chrysostom, *On Wealth and Poverty*, 28.

[28]Chrysostom, *On Wealth and Poverty*, 29. "Do not tell me that he was afflicted with sores, but consider that he had a soul inside more precious than any gold—or rather not his soul only, but also his body, for the virtue of the body is not plumpness and vigor but the ability to bear so many severe trials." Chrysostom, *On Wealth and Poverty*, 35.

[29]"For as the rich man lived in such wickedness, practiced luxury every day, and dressed himself splendidly, he was preparing for himself a more grievous punishment, building himself a greater fire, and making his penalty inexorable and his retribution inaccessible to pardon." Chrysostom, *On Wealth and Poverty*, 28.

[30]Chrysostom, *On Wealth and Poverty*, 38.

Chrysostom uses a variety of images to describe the spiritual strength of Lazarus and those who emulate him today. Like a wounded fighter carried on his fans' shoulders to receive "the wreath of victory" in the arena, so also suffering Lazarus is carried by angels to receive the crown of glory.[31] The preacher makes use of Ephesians 6 to describe the Christian life as a war in which "the full armor of the Scriptures" offers protection in the midst of "the multitude of missiles" that come our way.[32] Being spiritually disciplined is to receive "the divine medicines to heal the wounds" of battle, or "quench the darts of the devil by continual reading of the divine Scriptures."[33] In the arena of life, the fighter "cannot enjoy relaxation" when tribulation comes, but must take up "the hard and laborious life" of a dedicated athlete so that "he may enjoy lasting honor hereafter."[34]

***Martin Luther: Little exorcism, becoming a doctor of theology, fighting together.*** In his "Baptismal Booklet" (1526), Luther speaks of baptism as the beginning of the Christian's lifetime struggle against the evil one. Baptism is like a little exorcism that brings the baptized into conflict with the devil. It signals definitive "action against the devil . . . not only to drive him away from the little child but also to hang around the child's neck such a mighty, lifelong enemy."[35] Prior to becoming "a child of God," there is no struggle with the enemy, since the sinner is already in the devil's grip as his possession.[36] The struggle begins with baptism and faith and continues throughout life, thus making it all the more necessary to entrust the baptized to God with our prayers, so that "God would not only free the child from the devil's power but also strengthen the child, so that the child might resist him valiantly in life and in death."[37]

The rite of baptism employs an indirect epiclesis or prayer for the Spirit's descent on the baptized to drive the evil spirit away from his or her life: "The baptizer

---

[31]Chrysostom, *On Wealth and Poverty*, 43.

[32]Chrysostom, *On Wealth and Poverty*, 59. "Reading the Scriptures is a great means of security against sinning." Chrysostom, *On Wealth and Poverty*, 60.

[33]Chrysostom, *On Wealth and Poverty*, 59.

[34]Chrysostom, *On Wealth and Poverty*, 68. "The rich man's death was death and burial; but the poor man's death was a journey, a change for the better, a run from the mark to the prize, from the sea to the harbor, from the battle to the victory, from the sweat of the contest to the crown." Chrysostom, *On Wealth and Poverty*, 108.

[35]Luther, "Baptismal Booklet," 3, *BC*, p. 372.

[36]Luther, "Baptismal Booklet," 2, *BC*, p. 372. Through our new birth, "we, being freed from the devil's tyranny and loosed from sin, death, and hell, become children of life, heirs of all God's possessions, God's own children, and brothers and sisters in Christ." Luther, "Baptismal Booklet," 8, *BC*, p. 373.

[37]Luther, "Baptismal Booklet," 3-4, *BC*, p. 372.

shall say: 'Depart, you unclean spirit, and make room for the Holy Spirit.'"[38] A practice that Luther includes in the rite and still remains to this day in some churches is the renunciation of the devil, "all his works . . . and all his ways."[39] An act of resistance against evil and a statement of trust in God. Although "external ceremonies" such as making the sign of the cross on the baptized, putting salt on their mouths, and anointing the head and shoulders with oil may be used to "embellish baptism," Luther makes clear that these medieval practices linked to baptism "are not the actual devices from which the devil shrinks or flees."[40] That honor goes to God's Word alone, accompanied by the prayer of God's saints for the baptized.[41]

In the *Preface to the Wittenberg Edition* of his German writings (1539), Luther lays out "three rules" inspired by David in Psalm 119 to become a faithful theologian, namely, *oratio*, *meditatio*, and *tentatio*.[42] By bringing theologians—a concept Luther applies to all Christians—into these three aspects of life, the Holy Spirit shapes them after the likeness of Christ in his humility, which includes his experience of *tentatio*. The word *tentatio* (Ger. *Anfechtung*) goes beyond the idea of enticing or seducing into sin found in the English word *temptation* and is more broadly described as "all the doubts, turmoil, pang, tremor, pains, despair, desolation, and desperation which invade the spirit of man."[43] Given the reality of these spiritual assaults and afflictions, the Christian life starts by putting aside reliance on human reason in the midst of trials and seeking instead God's wisdom. Thus, life begins with praying to God for the gift of the Holy Spirit, who as "the real teacher of the Scriptures" guides us in understanding them.[44] Prayer for the Spirit's gratuitous descent in our lives (*oratio*) leads us to meditation on God's Word (*meditatio*).

Lest the student become "like untimely fruit which falls to the ground before it is half ripe," the good theologian moves beyond meditating only "in [his] own

---

[38]Luther, "Baptismal Booklet," 11, *BC*, p. 373. Luther uses a similar expression later in the rite, as the sign of the cross is made thrice on the baptized: "I adjure you, you unclean spirit, in the name of the Father (+) and of the Son (+) and of the Holy Spirit (+), that you come out of and depart from this servant of Jesus Christ, N. Amen." Luther, "Baptismal Booklet," 15, *BC*, p. 374.

[39]Luther, "Baptismal Booklet," 19-22, *BC*, pp. 374-75.

[40]Luther, "Baptismal Booklet," 5, *BC*, p. 372.

[41]Luther, "Baptismal Booklet," 6.

[42]Martin Luther, *Preface to the Wittenberg Edition of Luther's German Writings*, *LW* 34:285.

[43]Roland H. Bainton, *Here I Stand* (Nashville: Abingdon, 1952), 42.

[44]Luther, *Preface to the Wittenberg Edition*, *LW* 34:285-86.

heart" and only on occasion "once or twice."[45] Humility and reliance on God are found in receiving the Spirit-breathed Word each new day. Because humility also does not seek the Spirit in one's inner heart first but rather in "the external Word" that comes graciously from outside of us, Luther teaches that meditation should similarly be done "outwardly" or publicly by writing, preaching, singing, hearing, and speaking God's Word.[46] One becomes a strong and disciplined theologian not primarily in the privacy of one's own soul's dealings with God (though there is a time for personal faith), but in the company of fellow theologians who share reliance on God's wisdom through their corporate prayers and study of God's Word. Theologians are made in the open as they gather together for worship and care for one another amid life's struggles and afflictions.

Prayer and the Word bring us back to the place of *tentatio* or *Anfechtung* in the theologian's formation. As we said before, *Anfechtung* includes spiritual assaults and afflictions that come in various ways on God's children. Just as Scripture can see God's testing and Satan's temptation as two sides of the same coin in the life of the believer, Luther sees "spiritual attacks" simultaneously as the work of God and the devil (though with the evil creature ultimately remaining under the Creator). Common to the sufferings of *tentatio* is the experience of one's faith being tested and one's need for strength and resilience in moments of doubt. Concerning *tentatio*, Luther writes:

> This is the touchstone which teaches you not only to know and understand, but also to experience how right, how true, how sweet, how lovely, how mighty, how comforting God's Word is, wisdom beyond all wisdom. Thus you see how David . . . complains so often about all kinds of enemies, arrogant princes or tyrants, false spirits and factions, whom he must tolerate because he meditates, that is, because he is occupied with God's Word. . . . For as soon as God's Word takes root and grows in you, the devil will harry you, and will make a real doctor of you, and by his assaults will teach you to seek and love God's Word.[47]

Luther's threefold evangelical adaptation of medieval monastic spirituality takes on a cyclical rhythm in the shaping of the theologian. On the one hand, the psalmist suffers spiritual afflictions "because he is occupied with God's Word," meditating on it at all times. Such prayer and meditation incite the devil

[45]Luther, *Preface to the Wittenberg Edition*, *LW* 34:286.
[46]Luther, *Preface to the Wittenberg Edition*, *LW* 34:286.
[47]Luther, *Preface to the Wittenberg Edition*, *LW* 34:286-87.

to harass God's saints, seeking to drive them away from trust in God and his Word. On the other hand, the psalmist's experience of *tentatio* leads him to run to God for help in prayer and find sweet comfort in his Word over and over again. In that humble dependence on God through prayer and the Word, the believer becomes, over time in the school of the Holy Spirit, "a real doctor" of theology.[48]

Since God remains above the devil at all times in Luther's biblical cosmology, the Creator, in his hidden will, can use the evil creature as a teacher of theology to draw us to his commands and promises, while also thwarting the devil's purposes.[49] During the entire life of God's saints, Satan teaches the saints well when he disputes Scripture with them in the midst of their trials and objects to their faith in Christ.[50] God's children should be assured that, although their spiritual trials are real and must not be taken lightly, God nevertheless uses these afflictions and struggles to make them resilient and faithful theologians.

In a little treatise entitled *Comfort When Facing Grave Temptations* (1521), Luther speaks realistically about life trials while also encouraging the saints in their struggles. On the realistic side, he notes that "trials are not rare among the godly," as the psalms of lament demonstrate, and that one should not "insist on deliverance from these trials" but rather "endure the hand of God in this and all suffering."[51] Although these statements may sound defeatist and fatalistic to modern ears, one should note that Luther works in the context of a theocentric view of life in which God works out all things in the world in accordance with his purposes. However, because such purposes are often hidden from us, and there is nothing to gain by peeking into God's inscrutable mind to discover them, one

---

[48]For a reflection on Luther's *Anfechtung* for students of theology (particularly, at seminaries), see John W. Kleinig, "*Oratio, Meditatio, Tentatio*: What Makes a Theologian?," *Concordia Theological Quarterly* 66, no. 3 (2002): 255-67.

[49]See Leopoldo A. Sánchez M., *Pneumatología: El Espíritu Santo y la espiritualidad de la iglesia* (St. Louis: Concordia, 2005), 55-60.

[50]"I didn't learn my theology all at once. I had to ponder over it ever more deeply, and my spiritual trials [Lat. *tentationes*, Ger. *Anfechtungen*] were of help to me in this, for one does not learn anything without practice. This is what the spiritualists and sects lack. They don't have the right adversary, the devil. He would teach them well. . . . For when Satan disputes with me whether God is gracious to me, I dare not quote the passage, 'He who loves God will inherit the kingdom of God,' because Satan will at once object, 'But you have not loved God!' Nor can I oppose this on the ground that I am a diligent reader [of the Scriptures] and a preacher. The shoe doesn't fit. I should say, rather, that Jesus Christ died for me and should cite the article [of the Creed] concerning forgiveness of sin. That will do it!" Martin Luther, *Theology Is Not Quickly Learned, Fall, 1532*, *LW* 54:50-51.

[51]Martin Luther, *Comfort When Facing Grave Temptations*, *LW* 42:183-84.

must never "presume to deal directly with God" when suffering but instead turn to God revealed in mercy through Christ the mediator.[52] Therefore, without denying God in his hiddenness, Luther ultimately directs the sufferer, more encouragingly, to God's gracious promises in the Word, prayer, and the community of saints for comfort.

The worst a person facing grave trial can do is to go at it alone, as it were, relying on his or her own strength rather than on God's care through his promises and saints. When facing trials and afflictions, therefore, a Christian must never "rely on himself, nor must he be guided by his own feelings," but "cling" to God's words and "direct all the thoughts and feelings of his heart to them."[53] Although one should not "insist on deliverance," one must still ask God for deliverance, following the pattern of Christ's prayer at the garden of Gethsemane (Lk 22:42).[54] The need for prayer also follows from God's command to pray and the Father's promise that he hears his children and gives the Holy Spirit to those who ask him (Mt 21:22; Mk 11:24; Lk 11:9-13).[55]

Even in times of lament, the Christian still praises God with his or her lips when under assault since "the evil of gloom cannot be driven away by sadness and lamentation and anxiety, but by praising God, which makes the heart glad."[56] Not to be confused with an empty or temporary feeling of happiness, the gladness of the heart the psalmist speaks of is one grounded in the final hope of God's deliverance, which comes in his time and not ours. Although trials "hurt" and thus should not be sugarcoated or romanticized, they can also be "the very best sign of God's grace and love for man" in that they move those under great distress to prayer and the Word.[57] We see, once again, the cycle of *oratio*, *meditatio*, and *tentatio* that shapes Luther's view of the Christian life.

Last but not least, Luther includes the comfort of knowing that God blesses his suffering children with the company of supportive saints. He cites a section of Psalm 142, where the psalmist prays, "The righteous will gather around me," which Luther interprets as a prayer for saints who will "offer thanks with me

---

[52]Luther, *Comfort*, *LW* 42:186.
[53]Luther, *Comfort*, *LW* 42:183.
[54]Luther, *Comfort*, *LW* 42:183.
[55]Luther, *Comfort*, *LW* 42:186.
[56]Luther, *Comfort*, *LW* 42:183.
[57]Luther, *Comfort*, *LW* 42:183-84.

and for me" in the midst of tribulations.[58] In an earlier and lengthier treatise from 1519 on the significance of the Lord's Supper for spiritual communion among the saints—a source we will return to in the next chapter—Luther explains further how Christians serve one another as a source of strength in the midst of adversity.

> Whoever is in despair, distressed by a sin-stricken conscience or terrified by death or carrying some other burden upon his heart, if he would be rid of them all, let him go joyfully to the sacrament of the altar and lay down his woe in the midst of the community [of saints] and seek help from the entire company of the spiritual body.[59]

When we become one with Christ by partaking of his body in the Supper, we become one spiritual body or fellowship of saints who share in each other's joys and afflictions. In the mutual solidarity of Christ's saints amid tribulations, Holy Communion at the Lord's altar assures me that "my misfortune is shared with Christ and the saints, because I have a sure sign of their love toward me."[60] Communion is thus "a sacrament of love," which effects in us a spiritual life characterized by advocacy, work, and prayer on behalf of one another, and which drives the evil spirit away.[61] When we have to fight and stand firm, we do not do it alone but together.

Joined to Christ in his mystical body, Christians share in Christ's *tentatio* or affliction precisely by sharing in each other's tribulations. Such fellowship of love should not be construed as a "misery loves company" necessary evil, but rather as a gift and blessing through which God gives weary pilgrims strength and encouragement in difficult times.

## FACING ONE'S DEMONS: SPIRITUAL PRACTICES AND ISSUES IN THE CHRISTIAN LIFE

During his elementary school days, our son became absolutely convinced that he was seeing strange dark and moving shadows in his bedroom. Such experiences caused him no little fear, not to mention anxiety and stress, and he continually talked about them. It bothered him. As an "enlightened" parent with a critical Western mind, my temptation was to explain away our son's

---

[58] Luther, *Comfort*, *LW* 42:185.

[59] Martin Luther, *The Blessed Sacrament of the Holy and True Body of Christ, and the Brotherhoods*, *LW* 35:53.

[60] Luther, *Blessed Sacrament*, *LW* 35:54.

[61] Luther, *Blessed Sacrament*, *LW* 35:54.

sense of things, hoping for a more rational—and shall we say, less "dramatic"—approach to his experiences. Perhaps the reflection of outside lights at the right angle, the whistling of winds and moving trees near the windows, and the slow screeching sounds of wooden floors in the old house combined to make the young boy's wild imagination take off into a dreamland full of strange creatures.

In the preface to his *Screwtape Letters*, C. S. Lewis famously warned against two errors commonly seen among people when dealing with devils: "One is to disbelieve in their existence. The other is to believe, and to feel an excessive and unhealthy interest in them."[62] Who knows! Perhaps our son's concern about the devils was, in its own way, an excessive one. The problem was his, not ours. Or was it? Any further attempts on my part at making sense of the situation or avoiding it altogether came to a standstill the day our son came into the kitchen after dinner, looked at mom and me straight in the face, and told us, "I am afraid of the devil!" At that moment, no wiggle room remained for us to maneuver our way out of this one. We were facing a spiritual battle.

Although Christians in the West formally hold to the existence of Satan and demons, such belief does not always play itself out very pragmatically in their lives. That was the case with me when it came to our son's claims. That attitude stopped when the boy spoke plainly that day after dinner. I had become C. S. Lewis's materialist, the term he used to call those who either formally or practically acted as if the devils did not really exist. Our Western minds had inadvertently demythologized and exorcised the devil from our modern world.[63] If others made too much of the devil, we made too little of it.

***Vigilance and security.*** What our son helped us realize in his struggles through the wilderness was that he did not want an explanation but affirmation and solidarity. To use Luther's language, our son was asking us to acknowledge his *tentatio* or *Anfechtung* moment—his fear and anxiety, his solitude and sense that God had abandoned him—and then share his burden with him. He

[62]C. S. Lewis, *The Screwtape Letters* (New York: HarperOne, 2001), ix.

[63]"Demythologization has exorcised the devil from the world, but in a different way than we read in the New Testament: not by driving him out but by denying his existence. No one, I imagine, has ever been so delighted at being demythologized as the devil, if it is true—as has been said—that Satan's greatest cunning is to make people believe he does not exist (Charles Baudelaire)." Raniero Cantalamessa, *The Holy Spirit in the Life of Jesus: The Mystery of Christ's Baptism*, trans. Alan Neame (Collegeville, MN: Liturgical Press, 1994), 27-28.

was inviting us to walk in the scary wilderness with him. I went with him to his room at bedtime and we prayed Psalm 91 together, focusing on God's sure promises for the distressed: "You will not fear the terror of the night . . . no evil shall be allowed to befall you. . . . For he will command his angels concerning you to guard you in all your ways" (vv. 5, 10, 11). He hung a copy of the psalmist's words on his bed's headboard. Since all Christians are made theologians by the Holy Spirit in the deserts of life, where assaults and afflictions abound, our son showed signs already in his young age of the theologian's need for vigilance in the company of fellow pilgrims and the thirst for security in the desert: the need to face one's demons without sugarcoating the struggle; the sense that one should not face trials alone, but in the fellowship of saints; the path of reliance on God through prayer and the Word, even as one experiences the absence of God. In short, the realization that biblical temptation is not—as Bonhoeffer once noted—an opportunity for spiritual heroes to show off their strength, but rather to acknowledge the loss of their powers and their experience of solitude and God's abandonment so that in the midst of their struggles they can find their strength and shield in Christ alone.[64] These are invaluable lessons to embrace as we learn to be vigilant in our walk through the deserts of life.

If the renewal model of the Christian life deals with the need for finding one's identity in God and for right relations before God and others in the face of the problem of guilt and the power of sins in life, the dramatic model deals with the need for security in the face of spiritual assaults. In the famous hymn of the Reformation, "A Mighty Fortress Is Our God," Luther draws inspiration from Psalm 46 to depict the Christian life as a battle between God and the devil for the lives of the saints. The hymn gives an example of how an artistic medium brings hearers into the story of the Holy Spirit's forming of Christ's saints in the wilderness. The image of a fortress or castle especially evokes a sense of safety in God. The ongoing resolution to the tense drama between good and evil lies in Jesus Christ, who "fights for us" and "must win the battle" (verse 2), and in whose name the world's prince is overcome (verse 3, "one word can overturn him").[65] In that battle, God remains our "castle" (or fortress) and "weapon"

[64]Dietrich Bonhoeffer, *Creation and Fall; Temptation: Two Biblical Studies*, 1st Touchtone ed. (New York: Simon & Schuster, 1997), 111-12, 143-44.

[65]Martin Luther, "Our God He Is a Castle Strong," *LW* 53:285.

(verse 1).[66] Because God's word stands and he "is with us, at our right hand, with the gifts of his spirit," we remain heirs of the kingdom even if everything in life is taken away from us (verse 4).[67]

***Spiritual discernment.*** Vigilance comes through prayer and the study of the Word, but also through spiritual discernment in light of the Word. One form of such discernment is the unmasking of idols—those created things that become our objects of trust at any particular time or season of life and get in the way of trust in God. A theologian asks, "What are the deserts of my life where I am tempted to follow after idols? What are those attitudes, ways of thinking or speaking, behaviors, relationships, or places that make me more likely to be seduced into the snares of the evil one, either by falling into sinful desires or habits or by losing hope in God amid difficult situations?" The dramatic model of sanctification reminds us that everyone struggles with his or her idols, that everyone has some desert where his or her spiritual Achilles' heel is most vulnerable to attack and most in need of the Spirit's strength.

We should not overspiritualize this type of discernment. If the old Spanish saying *Más sabe el diablo por viejo que por diablo* (roughly translated, "the devil is wiser for being old than for being devil") rings true, then, there is something to be said for our gathered experience of the devil's assaults over the years. A certain maturity in holiness comes simply from the accumulated wisdom of living in the desert over time, that is, from the honest knowledge of one's spiritual weaknesses and vulnerabilities, learning hard lessons from past falls, and becoming ever more vigilant as a result of those experiences. From this angle, retreat in the midst of the desert, where the spiritual battle takes place, is a time of struggle that can lead to a reality check about one's own spiritual condition and strengthen faith in God.

> Retreat is not an escape into unreality, but the very opposite. It is a time for facing the truth and for coming to grips with the real situation in the retreatant's life. It can be a time for conversion. Consequently, a period of struggle may be necessary before the retreatant can enter into the peace of God, and experience inner "rest" in harmony with God's will.[68]

---

[66]Luther, "Our God," *LW* 53:284.

[67]Luther, "Our God," *LW* 53:285.

[68]John Townroe, "Retreat," in *The Study of Spirituality*, ed. Cheslyn Jones, Geoffrey Wainwright, and Edward Yarnold (New York: Oxford University Press, 1986), 580.

Bonhoeffer offers a way to discern one's spiritual condition in light of God's Word by reflecting on our sharing in Christ's temptations in the desert.[69] Like Christ, his disciples are led into the desert by the same Spirit and face three types of temptations. Bonhoeffer calls them temptations of the flesh, spiritual temptations, and complete temptation. Because the author equates the third one with the temptation to commit the sin against the Holy Spirit, he acknowledges its possibility but focuses on the other two types in our lives.[70] In doing so, he offers us a window into the need for discerning our spiritual condition amid various types of adversity and seeing how they unmask those vulnerabilities that would lead us to follow after idols rather than live in prayer and under God's commands and promises.

As Satan tempted Jesus "in the weakness of his flesh" to be afraid of his suffering and to rely on bread rather than God's Word, we too are tempted toward "desire" for created things in a way that "we seek all our joy in the creature" and are filled with "forgetfulness of God."[71] Desire in and of itself is a divine gift, but it becomes a problem when it replaces God and leads to an unhealthy bondage to created things. The solution to this particular idolatry of desire does not lie in some heroic combat with or attack against the devil, but in submitting to the Word of God, which commands us to flee *from* forms of sinful desire that we are in bondage to and *toward* Christ in whose strength against temptation we find joy in God once again.[72] Rather than sticking around to test one's strength in combat, there are times when one must simply retreat from places, situations, thoughts, or words that are too close for comfort and will almost certainly lead to sinful desire. Although the promise that God "will not let you be tempted beyond your ability"

---

[69]Luther's preaching on the significance of Christ's life in the desert for the saints remains Bonhoeffer's greatest inspiration. For two examples of Luther's preaching on the temptation account, see Martin Luther, "First Sunday in Lent (Invocavit)," in *Sermons on Gospel Texts for Epiphany, Lent, and Easter*, ed. John Nicolas Lenker, vol. 1.2 of *The Complete Sermons of Martin Luther* (Grand Rapids: Baker Books, 2000), 133-47; and "Invocavit Sunday—First Sunday in Lent (1934)," in *Sermons on Gospel Texts for Advent, Christmas, New Year's Day, Epiphany, Lent, Holy Week, and Other Occasions*, ed. Eugene F. Klug, vol. 5 of *The Complete Sermons of Martin Luther* (Grand Rapids: Baker Books, 2000), 312-20.

[70]Bonhoeffer, *Creation and Fall*, 120-21, 142.

[71]Bonhoeffer, *Creation and Fall*, 119, 132. "It makes no difference whether it is sexual desire, or ambition, or vanity, or desire for revenge, or love of fame and power, or greed for money, or, finally, that strange desire for the beauty of the world, of nature. Joy in God is in course of being extinguished in us and we seek all our joy in the creature. . . . Satan does not here fill us with hatred of God, but with forgetfulness of God." Bonhoeffer, *Creation and Fall*, 132.

[72]Bonhoeffer, *Creation and Fall*, 133.

still stands (1 Cor 10:13), the command that one must not test God also applies (Mt 4:7; Lk 4:12; Deut 6:16). It is unwise to appeal to God's protection, but then flirt with danger.

Many saints also undergo temptations of the body that Bonhoeffer calls "suffering," which include challenging conditions such as poverty and sickness as well as persecution for Christ's sake. A key point the author makes about the former type of suffering is that, unlike the temptation of desire which leads one to forgetfulness of God, "the heat of affliction easily leads him into conflict with God," questioning why bad things happen to God's children.[73] The author's advice is not to focus on the strength of one's goodness, piety, or righteousness in order to defend God when suffering occurs, pretending to make a tough experience supposedly palatable. As to suffering for Christ's sake, which is a type of righteous and to some extent voluntary suffering for a just cause, Bonhoeffer warns that it could lead to apostasy because, when times get tough, the believer is tempted to back away from Christ altogether in order to minimize suffering and maximize happiness.[74] The more difficult move in all these circumstances is simply to find joy in communion with Christ, who suffered patiently without receiving an answer from God in his worst hour ("My God, my God, why have you forsaken me?"). One does not fight as much as stand one's ground. One does not go on the offensive as much as endure.

Bonhoeffer also speaks of spiritual temptations. In the same way Satan tempted Jesus' faith to "demand a sign from God" above God's Word as proof of God's faithfulness, power, or love, we too are seduced by the devil to deal with God apart from his Word by dismissing either his commands or promises.[75] Consider that Jesus does not have to prove his sonship to the devil by asking God to do something great. Jesus already lives under God's word and will as his beloved and obedient Son. Jesus already knows himself to be loved by his Father and undertakes his messianic mission in faithfulness to his will.

What about us? Putting aside God's commands, his children fall into bondage to "spiritual pride" (Lat. *securitas*) and put to test the seriousness of God's wrath against sin (that is, against transgressing God's shalt nots and

---

[73]Bonhoeffer, *Creation and Fall*, 134.
[74]Bonhoeffer, *Creation and Fall*, 137.
[75]Bonhoeffer, *Creation and Fall*, 119, 140.

shalts).[76] By avoiding God's promises, on the other hand, God's children fall into bondage to "spiritual despair" (Lat. *desperatio*) and thus put to test the seriousness of God's unconditional mercy in Christ.[77] Both spiritual pride and despair comprise "the one sin of tempting God."[78] The ongoing solution to spiritual pride lies neither in appeals to one's goodness to appease God's wrath (that is, justification by works) nor in appeals to one's freedom from God's wrath as license to sin (the problem of antinomianism).[79] Moreover, the solution to spiritual despair lies neither in attempts to do saintly things to make up for sins God supposedly cannot forgive nor in giving up on God's forgiveness in hopelessness by drawing away from listening to his promises.[80] Rather, those who are tempted spiritually cling to Christ's suffering of God's wrath and absence in our place and therefore find safety in Christ's own trust in God and his Word.

In a recurring theme in his reflections on temptation, Bonhoeffer observes that because we share in Christ's temptations, we also share in his victory over them. There is a sense in which, due to our being Christ's mystical body today, "every temptation which happens now is the temptation of Jesus Christ in his members."[81] Therefore, "the Christ in us is tempted—in which case Satan is bound to fall."[82] Unmasking idols such as sinful desire, appeals to piety to rationalize suffering, spiritual pride, or spiritual despair in our lives helps us see our need for Christ's help and strength in his victory over all forms of temptation. Since Satan falls when we are tempted in Christ the Victor, we can thus pray as he taught us, "Lead us not into temptation," with the full confidence that God hears us in our worst hour.[83] We are never tempted alone, but with Christ and his Spirit as our companions, protectors, and intercessors.

***Discipline, accountability, support.*** In conjunction with the Word, prayer, and spiritual discernment, vigilance can include salutary forms of external or corporal discipline. As Luther once put it, citing an old hermit's advice to a youth who complained about having sinful lusts: "You cannot prevent the birds from flying

[76]Bonhoeffer, *Creation and Fall*, 139-40.
[77]Bonhoeffer, *Creation and Fall*, 140-42.
[78]Bonhoeffer, *Creation and Fall*, 139.
[79]Bonhoeffer, *Creation and Fall*, 140.
[80]Bonhoeffer, *Creation and Fall*, 140-41.
[81]Bonhoeffer, *Creation and Fall*, 122.
[82]Bonhoeffer, *Creation and Fall*, 115.
[83]Bonhoeffer, *Creation and Fall*, 144.

over your head. But let them only fly and do not let them build nests in the hair of your head."[84] Although temptations cannot be avoided, and the devil is thus always roaming around like a lion looking for someone to devour (1 Pet 5:8), one must nevertheless not put himself in situations that would make him an easy prey. Once a person recognizes those deserts in life that make her more vulnerable to various types of temptation—and they are different for everybody—then strategies for resistance in some cases, or resilience in others, can be adopted at either personal or communal levels.

If the desert is bondage to harmful desire, then, flight from seduction might include certain habits that could make one less likely to give in too easily. If the problem is overeating, the habit of fasting might be helpful; if the idol is love of money, scheduling volunteer opportunities to assist or partner with those who have less; if addiction to pornography, setting boundaries for access to media. The possibilities are as endless as the temptations we face, and each person must see what works best for him or her. The language of battle or retreat strategy tends to work well in these contexts.

However, there are also deserts where the issue is not lustful desire for created things, but suffering ills such as poverty, sickness, and other chronic conditions—especially when such suffering is unexplainable and one feels abandoned by God and stigmatized by others. In those settings, one often struggles with loneliness, doubts about God, hopelessness, and the fear of rejection and death. When thinking of these types of suffering and the experiences that often accompany them the image of battle might not be the most appropriate. One might argue about the possibility of battling against causes of poverty by seeking to eliminate them. But how does one, for instance, eliminate or battle against an incurable condition like certain forms of cancer or depression?[85] A more apt image in these contexts might be that of a defender in a soccer match who does not go on the offensive or on the attack during the game, but rather stands firm

[84]Martin Luther, *Lectures on Genesis: Chapters 31–37*, *LW* 6:133.

[85]For a theo-memoir on dealing with incurable cancer, see Deanna A. Thompson, *Hoping for More: Having Cancer, Talking Faith, and Accepting Grace* (Eugene, OR: Cascade, 2012); for a deeper theological exploration of what it means to live with a serious illness and how to offer support in these situations, see Deanna A. Thompson, *Glimpsing Resurrection: Cancer, Trauma, and Ministry* (Louisville: Westminster John Knox, 2018); for a theology of suffering grounded in experiences of chronic and recurring depression, see Jessica Coblentz, "Sisters in the Wilderness: Toward A Theology of Depression with Delores Williams," in *An Unexpected Wilderness: Seeking God on a Changing Planet*, ed. Colleen Carpenter (Maryknoll, NY: Orbis, 2016), 193-203.

and resilient against attacks from the opposition with the ongoing help of a supportive team.

Dealing with forms of illness that are simply recurrent, chronic, or at times incurable requires a more relational approach to spiritual discipline—one where the caring presence, encouragement, consolation, and strength of fellow pilgrims dealing with similar issues are displayed and nurtured. Accountability and support groups can embody life in the desert in a more communal way, becoming environments where those tempted or tested in their sufferings become empathetic companions and face struggles together as a team. Such groups are themselves a form of discipline to withstand spiritual assaults and afflictions that, while replacing neither prayer nor the Word, do offer safe spaces for sharing each other's fears and even little victories.[86]

Not being alone in the desert, the saints keep in check their habitual forms of bondage to sinful desire through accountability or volunteer groups. The deserts of spiritual pride and despair might best be dealt with in the context of prayer and Bible study groups. In support groups, the saints can also find encouraging spaces to keep their solitude in check when facing other types of struggles such as suffering for Christ's sake or from incurable diseases or conditions, preventing solitude from slipping into hopelessness, bitterness, and hate of God.

Whatever form the desert journey takes today, this chapter has given us a realistic picture of sanctification in the midst of life struggles. Images of the dramatic model from Scripture and theologians past and present remind us that we share such afflictions with others who have come before us but also a powerful God who is able to turn the devil's attacks into times of testing that produce resilient people in the face of adversity. These voices also assure us that the Holy Spirit walks in the dangerous wilderness with those who suffer the evil spirit's assaults and afflictions then and now, leading those under attack to prayer, the Word of God, and the community of saints for comfort, protection,

---

[86]Because group prayer offers a space for "petitions, words of encouragement and praise," it functions not only as a way to face struggles personally but to do so together and experience "what it means to belong to a body, where, 'If one member suffers, all suffer together; if one member is honoured, all rejoice together' (1 Cor 12:26)." John Gunstone, "Group Prayer," in Jones, Wainwright, and Yarnold, *The Study of Spirituality*, 571. The communal dimension of support groups, in which members share each other's sufferings and joys has an affinity with the idea of "happy exchanges" under the sacrificial model covered in the next chapter.

and guidance. My hope is that our short journey with others in their desert experiences across time can equip pastors and church leaders with additional tools for teaching and caring for others in a world where vigilance and security are much needed.

# 5

# SHARING LIFE TOGETHER

## THE SACRIFICIAL MODEL

Depicting the Christian life as a sharing in Christ's humility, the *sacrificial* model describes life in the Spirit as an offering to God in thanksgiving for his gifts and for the sake of serving neighbors. Sculpting the form of Christ, the servant, in the saints, the Spirit conforms us to Christ in his humiliation or kenosis through discipleship and witness in the world. By focusing on the shaping of minds after Christ's servant attitude, this model can assist pastors and others in fostering among persons a disposition toward generosity and partnership and the practice of "happy exchanges" where they share in each other's burdens and joys.

The sacrificial model focuses on the need for purpose, significance, or meaning in life, giving sanctification a neighbor-oriented trajectory. It tackles problems such as individualism and the importance of community through a renewed appreciation for vocation and calling in life. In its vision of the economy of the Spirit, the model avoids romantic and utilitarian views of neighbors that portray their condition in life as a means for the needy (romantic) or those who help them to get closer to God (utilitarian). The model also steers away from paternalistic and dependent notions of exchange, which do not embrace the unique contributions and gifts of all people, including neighbors in need, to our life together.

## BIBLICAL PICTURES: THE MIND OF CHRIST, DISCIPLES AND WITNESSES, LIVES SHARED

At the Jordan, the Spirit descends onto Jesus (Mk 1:10). From heaven, the Father's voice brings his "beloved Son" into his mission as Yahweh's suffering servant (Mk 1:11, "with you I am well pleased"; cf. Is 42:1). This means Jesus' servanthood unto death defines his messiahship and sonship. It might not appear to be so at first, given all the manifestations of his lordship. The "Son of Man" proclaims his authority to forgive sins (Mk 2:10) and calls himself Lord of the Sabbath (2:28). The disciples see Jesus display his power over creation in calming the storm and walking on water (4:35-41; 6:45-52), driving out an unclean spirit (5:1-20), healing people from various diseases (5:25-34; 6:53-56; 7:24-37), raising the dead (5:21-24, 35-43), and feeding thousands (6:30-44; 8:1-10). The disciples get so used to such an awesome picture of Jesus that they struggle to hear his Passion predictions.

Even though Peter, who speaks for the other disciples, confesses Jesus as the Christ (Mk 8:29), he later rebukes Jesus in private for teaching that "the Son of Man must suffer many things and be rejected . . . and be killed, and after three days rise again" (Mk 8:31-32). A suffering servant is not the kind of messiah Peter wants. At the Mount of Transfiguration, Peter, James, and John behold the radiance of Jesus and hope to stay with him in the realm of glory (9:1-6), but the voice from the cloud—the same one heard at the baptism—reminds them to "listen to him" (9:7), an appeal to take to heart his Passion prediction (see v. 12). When Jesus foretells his coming death and resurrection again (9:30-31), the disciples "did not understand" (v. 32). After his third Passion prediction (10:32-34), on the way to Jerusalem, two of his disciples still ask Jesus to have places of honor by him: "Grant us to sit, one at your right hand and one at your left, in your glory" (v. 37). The disciples expected Jesus to show his sonship by means of his power and glory, not by means of his suffering and death.

Seated at God's right hand, an indication of his kingship over all things, Christ is the Lord of David—his kingdom greater than David's (Mk 12:35-37). At the end of the age, "in those days" (13:24), people "will see the Son of Man coming in clouds with great power and glory" (v. 26) to gather God's "elect" from the nations (v. 27; cf. Mk 8:38; 14:61-62). Yet the Gospel writer wants to draw attention to a deeper truth, namely, that the Son of Man and Messiah reveals his divine sonship most fully not through his great power but through his loving self-giving unto death for others on the cross. At the end of Mark's Gospel, it is not Jesus' disciples but a Roman centurion who confesses Jesus' sonship as Jesus hangs on the cross: "Truly this man was the Son of God!" (Mk 15:39).[1]

By displaying his power through service and sacrifice, Jesus shows his followers the true meaning of discipleship. After his first Passion prediction, Jesus laid out what is at stake for his disciples: "If anyone would come after me, let him deny himself and take up his cross and follow me" (Mk 8:34). Later on, after hearing his disciples argue about who was the greatest among them, Jesus teaches them that "if anyone would be first, he must be last of all and servant of all" (9:35). After foretelling his death for a third time and seeing how his disciples were indignant at Zebedee's sons' misplaced request to sit at his left and right hand, Jesus explains to all that discipleship is not about exercising authority through power. Asking to sit at Jesus' right hand would have meant a desire to share in his divinity by partaking of his great might. Indeed, Jesus will have his disciples share in his life, but only as he displays it through service, so that "whoever would be great among you must be your servant" (10:43). Disciples reflect in their own lives the identity of the Son of Man, who "came not to be served but to serve, and to give his life as a ransom for many" (v. 45).

A way in which disciples share in Christ's service is through martyrdom, their witness unto death. Quite a literal conformity to Christ in his death can be seen in Luke's striking description of the ministry and death of Stephen. One of seven deacons chosen by the apostles to take care of widows, Stephen is described as "a man full of faith and of the Holy Spirit" (Acts 6:5, cf. v. 3, "full of the Spirit and of wisdom"). As an evangelist, Stephen is "full of grace and power" (v. 8), and finds opposition to his message because his detractors "could not withstand the wisdom and the Spirit with which he was speaking" (v. 10). After his proclamation to the council and the high priest, and facing his impending stoning from an angry crowd, Stephen appears as a type of Christ, or more precisely, Stephen's life in the Spirit takes the form of Christ's own sacrificial life. Like Jesus, Stephen is "full of the Holy Spirit" (Acts 7:55; cf. Lk 4:1). As he was being stoned, Stephen cried out to the Lord Jesus, "Receive my spirit" (Acts 7:59)—words similar to those spoken by Jesus to his Father as he hung on the cross (Lk 23:46; cf. Ps 31:5). Stephen's

[1]Referring to the significance of the centurion's confession toward the end of Mark's Gospel, Matera notes that "none of the human characters of the narrative recognize Jesus as the Son of God until he has died. . . . Jesus' death, then, paradoxically reveals his divine sonship. Because of Jesus' death, disciples begin to understand that divine sonship exercises its power in weakness." Frank J. Matera, *New Testament Christology* (Louisville, KY: Westminster John Knox, 1999), 25.

Christlike life is a cruciform one. Finally, like his Lord, Stephen asks that his enemies be forgiven before he died: "Lord, do not hold this sin against them" (Acts 7:60; cf. Lk 23:34).

Bearing witness to Christ's words entails a sacrificial way of life. Such witness is a form of Spirit-led sharing in Christ's identity as the anointed servant-prophet. Like their master Christ, his servants will be hated and persecuted by the world for keeping his words (Jn 15:18-20). However, upon the Son's return to his Father, the disciples will not be left as orphans in a world hostile to him (Jn 14:18-19). Since the Father will send the Paraclete, the Spirit of truth, in his name to teach and remind them of Christ's words, they should not be troubled or afraid as they bear witness to him (Jn 14:25-27; 15:26-27). Dwelling in the disciples as their comforter, the Holy Spirit will be their defender or defense lawyer—the forensic sense of the title "Paraclete"—when the world acts as a judge against them for their belief in the Son, his fulfillment of righteousness by returning to the Father, and his overcoming of the prince of the world (Jn 16:7-11).[2]

When Paul speaks of "participation in the Spirit" (Phil 2:1), he also associates such life with the unity of the church where each member is "of the same mind" (v. 2)—a mind shaped after the likeness of Christ's humility and servanthood (vv. 3-5, 7). Though Christ was "in the form of God" (v. 6), he humbled himself "by taking the form of a servant, being born in the likeness of men" (v. 7). Christians are thus called to "have this mind among yourselves, which is yours in Christ Jesus" (v. 5), taking on the form of his servanthood and sacrificial obedience for the sake of others, doing "nothing from selfish ambition or conceit" and looking "to the interests of others" in the community (vv. 3-4).

The image of sacrifice is often used to describe the Christian life. Paul refers to his own life and work as a "drink offering" that is being poured out on "the sacrificial offering" of the Gentiles' faith (Phil 2:17). Both the Gentiles and their apostle are offerings pleasing to God. The apostle boasts in the grace given to him to be a minister of the gospel, "so that the offering of the Gentiles may be acceptable, sanctified by the Holy Spirit" (Rom 15:16). Since Christ, "by the power of the Spirit of God," has made fruitful Paul's ministry by bringing the Gentiles to the obedience of faith, the apostle is proud of what Christ has accomplished through

[2]On the forensic sense of Paraclete, see Felix Porsch, *El Espíritu Santo, defensor de los creyentes: La actividad del Espíritu según el evangelio de san Juan*, trans. Severiano Talavero Tovar (Salamanca: Secretariado Trinitario, 1983), 78-89.

him (vv. 17-20). The Holy Spirit sanctifies people through the gospel, making them "a living sacrifice, holy and acceptable to God," and renewing their mind to discern God's good and perfect will (Rom 12:1-2). Through various gifts and virtues, members of the one body exercise their "spiritual worship" (v. 1) and serve one another. Among many other works, they learn to "contribute to the needs of the saints" (v. 13).

Sharing stands out as an expression of sacrificial service in the community of saints. Life in the Spirit brings about a partaking in its fellowship, which binds the members of Christ's body in faith and love. They are called to "bear one another's burdens" (Gal 6:2; Col 3:13). They gather around the teaching of the apostles and the breaking of the bread and share all things in common (Acts 2:42-44). They externalize their spiritual unity in a mutual sharing of the community's material possessions "as any had need" (v. 45). Since the believers "were of one heart and soul," they also "had everything in common" (Acts 4:32), so that "there was not a needy person among them" (v. 34). Christians are called to "share what you have, for such sacrifices are pleasing to God" (Heb 13:16). Moreover, each member of the body uses his or her gifts "for the common good" (1 Cor 12:7) and for "building up the church" (1 Cor 14:12). Because "in one Spirit" all the members were "baptized into one body" (1 Cor 12:13), they become a communion marked by the supreme gift of love (1 Cor 13:1-13). Therefore, they share in each other's sufferings and joys (1 Cor 12:26).

There are internal and external aspects to the sacrificial identity of Jesus' disciples. Being holy has implications for life together as God's people, but also for life in the world as we become witnesses of Christ before others. As God's "elect," Christians live "in the sanctification of the Spirit" (1 Pet 1:1-2), and they are called to be holy (v. 16), loving one another (v. 22) in the community of faith. God's children are "being built up as a spiritual house, to be a holy priesthood, to offer spiritual sacrifices acceptable to God through Jesus Christ" (1 Pet 2:5). They are also called to live as a "holy nation" (v. 9) of exiles and sojourners in the world (1:17; 2:11), not being conformed to the ways of the world (1:14), so that others might see their "good deeds and glorify God" (2:12).

Because being holy in the world includes not being conformed to the pattern of this world, it also implies living in the world without retaliating against those who ridicule and marginalize us. When persecuted for their faith, the saints are called to act in a Christlike manner by not committing acts of vengeance against their enemies (1 Pet 2:20; cf. 3:9, 17). By not reviling those who revile them, especially the authorities of the world who might treat them unjustly, Christians take on the form of "servants of God" (2:16) and undergo a suffering that reflects their Lord's unjust destiny at the hands of the authorities. Like their Lord, Christians are called to endure without sinning against their enemies, "because Christ also suffered for you, leaving you an example, so that you might follow in his steps" (2:21). Offering spiritual sacrifices to God includes endurance in suffering for the sake of obedience to Jesus, his gospel, and cross-shaped way of life. It is the way of nonviolence. Such cruciform holiness becomes a form of life in the Spirit, since "the Spirit of glory and of God rests" on those who, though unjustly, share in Christ's sufferings now so that they might also share in his glory at the last day (4:14).

## CATECHETICAL IMAGES: MARTYRS, STEWARDS, AND BLESSED EXCHANGERS

What does the Spirit's work of making us living sacrifices entail? To the Scriptures, we now add images from church fathers that offer some answers to this question. Cyril of Jerusalem, John Chrysostom, and Basil of Caesarea reflect on various dimensions of sacrificial living—the last two theologians contributing significant thinking on the stewardship of resources. Martin Luther's reflections on spiritual communion and his image of life together as a "blessed exchange" share an affinity with the early Fathers' vision of stewardship not as a way of distributing or accumulating things for self but as a life of communal sharing. However, unlike certain monastic visions of material poverty as a favorable condition before God, Luther's teaching on justification grounds Christian identity before God not in a human condition but in God's gift in Christ. This move allows Luther to make good works not the basis of justification but its outworking in love. We will see how the Reformer's distinction between the two kinds of righteousness offers a promising way to distinguish and relate properly one's identity before God and one's purpose in the world through a meaningful life of service and sacrifice before others.

***Cyril of Jerusalem: Encouraging whisper, portrait of paradise, martyr's witness.*** On the site of Golgotha in Jerusalem, the place of Jesus' crucifixion, Cyril delivered his catechetical lectures to catechumens toward the beginning of his pastoral ministry. As bishop of Jerusalem, he was removed from his episcopal seat and exiled three times for confessing Christ's divinity.[3] Not unfamiliar with suffering for Christ's sake, Cyril reflects early in his career on the Spirit's role in the lives of persecuted Christians and martyrs. As the church's comforter and intercessor, the Spirit consoles and encourages those who, in the midst of torments and hardships, do not know how to pray or testify to Christ before others (see Rom 8:26-28; Lk 12:11-12).

The Holy Spirit "softly whispers" to the one who is dishonored for Christ's sake: "What is now befalling thee is a small matter, the reward will be great. Suffer a little while, and thou shalt be with Angels for ever."[4] Like an artist who unveils a beautiful painting, the Spirit shows the one who suffers unjustly before earthly judges a portrait of "the kingdom of heaven; He gives him a glimpse of the paradise of delight."[5] Since no one can confess Jesus as Lord except by the Holy Spirit (1 Cor 12:3), the Spirit alone empowers martyrs to bear witness to Christ in the world, and even to give their lives for Christ's sake.[6]

***John Chrysostom: Sharing, stealing, and stewardship.*** In his homilies on the parable of Lazarus and the rich man, Chrysostom reflects on the spiritual virtue of sharing with others the gifts God has entrusted to us. The preacher is careful not to equate the rich man's wickedness with his possession of wealth per se, but rather with his failure to use his possessions according to God's command. The issue is not the use, but the abuse of wealth and possessions.[7] In particular, he interprets God's commandment against stealing in such a way that "not only the theft of others' goods but also the failure to share one's own goods with others is theft and swindle and defraudation."[8] The rich man does not sin mainly by commission but by omission.

By failing "to share his own" goods with the needy, the rich man showed not only his lack of pity and mercy for the poor, but his inability to see that "our money

---

[3]Cirilo de Jerusalén, *El Espíritu Santo (Catequesis XVI–XVII)*, trans. Carmelo Granado (Madrid: Editorial Ciudad Nueva, 1998), 7-13.

[4]Cyril of Jerusalem, *Catechetical Lecture* 16.20 (*NPNF*[2] 7:120).

[5]Cyril of Jerusalem, *Catechetical Lecture* 16.20 (*NPNF*[2] 7:120).

[6]Cyril of Jerusalem, *Catechetical Lecture* 16.21 (*NPNF*[2] 7:120-21).

[7]"They often indeed cause our destruction, when we use them improperly. Wealth will be good for its possessor if he does not spend it only on luxury, or on strong drink and harmful pleasures; if he enjoys luxury in moderation and distributes the rest to the stomachs of the poor, then wealth is a good thing." John Chrysostom, *On Wealth and Poverty*, trans. Catharine P. Roth (Crestwood, NY: St. Vladimir's Seminary Press, 1984), 137.

[8]Chrysostom, *On Wealth and Poverty*, 49.

is the Lord's, however we may have gathered it."[9] Such a man is no different than the people of Israel whom the prophet Malachi denounced for stealing from both the Lord and the poor by using the money otherwise designated for tithes to store more treasures in their houses.[10] Chrysostom shows how a life of self-indulgence does not only negatively affect our worship of God but also our service to his vulnerable creatures: "Since you have not given the accustomed offerings . . . you have stolen the goods of the poor."[11] Self-indulgence gets in the way of sacrificial giving and makes sharing impossible.

Since everything we have belongs to the Lord, the use of one's possessions becomes a matter of faithful stewardship. Those whom God has allowed to have more wealth should not waste it on unnecessary things, but rather "distribute to those in need."[12] The preacher shows no interest in proposing a specific social program for wealth distribution, but simply reminds his hearers that, like the rich man, each one of them is but a "steward of the money" and "his own goods are not his own."[13] The issue is whether one will be a faithful or unfaithful steward of what belongs to God in the first place. Even though Chrysostom says nothing concerning the value of private property, he does exhort us to "use our goods sparingly, as belonging to others," by not spending "beyond our needs" or "for our needs only."[14] Being a good steward of God's resources means taking care not only of one's own needs but also those of others—not only a personally but a socially responsible vision of stewardship.

As the end met by the rich man in the parable suggests, those who have been entrusted with more affluence in this life will have to give an account of their spending upon their death and, if found unfaithful stewards, will meet God's harsh judgment.[15] Bringing to mind the final judgment scene in Matthew 25, the Antiochene homilist suggests that those who refuse to assist Christ in "the least of these" will be judged.[16] Conversely, the person who displays the "attitude" of a faithful steward "by nourishing Christ in poverty here" will receive

[9]Chrysostom, *On Wealth and Poverty*, 49.

[10]Chrysostom cites Malachi 3:8-10: "The earth has brought forth her increase, and you have not brought forth your tithes; but the theft of the poor is in your houses." *On Wealth and Poverty*, 49.

[11]Chrysostom, *On Wealth and Poverty*, 49.

[12]Chrysostom, *On Wealth and Poverty*, 50.

[13]Chrysostom, *On Wealth and Poverty*, 50.

[14]Chrysostom, *On Wealth and Poverty*, 50.

[15]Chrysostom, *On Wealth and Poverty*, 50.

[16]Chrysostom, *On Wealth and Poverty*, 51.

"great profit hereafter."[17] The spiritual virtue of those to whom much has been given lies in their capacity to embody a certain austerity, simplicity, and practical asceticism in everyday life that makes room for sharing God's abundance given to them with those neighbors in want whom God has placed before them.

***Basil of Caesarea: Simplicity, dealing with surpluses, generous saints.*** In a series of homilies on stewardship and sharing, Basil lays out a vision for nurturing a life of simplicity that would prevent God's people from becoming attached to their possessions and allow them to share their abundance with others.[18] In his homily *To the Rich*, Basil reflects on the grieving of the young rich man who went away after Jesus told him to sell all his possessions, give them to the poor, and follow him as his disciple if he wanted to have treasure in heaven (Mt 19:21-22). The young man's sadness showed he was "darkened by the passion of avarice . . . bound to the enjoyment of this present life" instead of the joy of eternal life and "the consolation of the many" in need of assistance.[19]

Sadness over losing material possessions arises from not realizing that the rich have merely "received wealth as a stewardship" from God and thus cannot lose "what is not really theirs" to begin with.[20] Here Basil echoes Chrysostom's sentiments on stewardship. The young man's grieving reveals an attachment to things of this world that leads to a lack of satisfaction with using "the things you already have" and shows how we "suffer constantly from the pains of acquisition."[21] Simplicity of life means being content with and making use of what God has already given us instead of accumulating or consuming more things for ourselves that we do not need. That way of life allows us to have more things to share with others whose need is greater than ours.

In his homily "I Will Tear Down My Barns," Basil warns against becoming like another rich man who, unsatisfied with what sufficed to care for his needs, decided to build bigger barns in order to store more grain for himself (Lk 12:16-21).[22]

---

[17]Chrysostom, *On Wealth and Poverty*, 55.

[18]Basil of Caesarea, *On Social Justice*, trans. C. Paul Schroeder (Crestwood, NY: St. Vladimir's Seminary Press, 2009). This work contains translations of his homilies "To the Rich" (based on Mt 19:16-22), "I Will Tear Down My Barns" (based on Lk 12:16-21), "In Time of Famine and Drought" (based on Amos 3:8), and "Against Those Who Lend at Interest" (based on LXX Ps 14:5).

[19]Basil of Caesarea, *On Social Justice*, 42-43.

[20]Basil of Caesarea, *On Social Justice*, 46-47.

[21]Basil of Caesarea, *On Social Justice*, 50.

[22]"Who are the greedy? Those who are not satisfied with what suffices for their own needs. Who are the robbers? Those who take for themselves what rightfully belongs to everyone. And you, are you not

His words raise the issue of what to do with surpluses, of having more than one needs to live. Like the rich young man who approached Jesus in Matthew 19, this man also forgot his fundamental identity as a receiver of God's beneficence, and thus as "a minister of God's goodness."[23] In receiving from the Creator more things than others who have less, the richer person has also received from God "the reward of benevolence and faithful stewardship."[24] Basil's economic vision assumes that rather than storing things up greedily for the benefit of a few people, goods must circulate constantly so that they reach as many people as possible.[25]

Using powerful, convicting images, Basil calls to repentance all who, like the rich man desiring bigger barns, are unwilling to share their abundance with others. They know their money better than their neighbor: "You recognize the inscription on the face of a coin, and can tell the counterfeit from the genuine, but you completely ignore your brothers and sisters in their time of need."[26] Rather than building more barns to store their surpluses for self-gain, the preacher exhorts his hearers: "If you want storehouses, you have them in the stomachs of the poor."[27] Preaching "In Time of Famine and Drought," the bishop takes such times of duress as an opportunity to call people to repentance, noting that "we are threatened with righteous judgment" on account of our sins: "This is why God does not open his hand: because we have closed up our hearts toward our brothers and sisters. This is why the fields are arid: because love has dried up."[28] Taking his hearers back to Eden, the homilist calls them to "undo the primal sin by sharing your food. Just as Adam transmitted sin by eating wrongfully, so we wipe away the treacherous food when we remedy the need and hunger of our brothers and sisters."[29] Moving beyond the call to repentance, the preacher begins to paint a picture for his hearers

---

greedy? Are you not a robber? The things you received in trust as a stewardship, have you not appropriated them for yourself?" Basil of Caesarea, *On Social Justice*, 69.

[23]Basil of Caesarea, *On Social Justice*, 61.

[24]Basil of Caesarea, *On Social Justice*, 69.

[25]In his introduction to Basil's work, Schroeder notes that "Basil's ethic of sustainability is based upon an economic philosophy that might be described as a 'limited resource paradigm.' He believes that God has provided enough food, land, and usable materials to satisfy the needs of all; these resources, however, are limited commodities, and must therefore be shared out equitably. In Basil's view, a healthy economic system requires that resources remain in constant circulation, rather than being stored up or accumulated in large amounts for the benefit of a few individuals." *On Social Justice*, 27.

[26]Basil of Caesarea, *On Social Justice*, 64.

[27]Basil of Caesarea, *On Social Justice*, 68.

[28]Basil of Caesarea, *On Social Justice*, 76.

[29]Basil of Caesarea, *On Social Justice*, 86.

of what a new creation looks like, a window into an eschatological form of life where the sins of avarice, greed, or misanthropy no longer have a place in our human relationships.

In his homily on Luke 12, Basil lifts up the example of Joseph in the Old Testament, who "in his philanthropic proclamation" and "with generous voice," opened the grain storehouses of Egypt and surrounding lands (including Israel) to the hungry during the seven years of famine (see Gen 41:53-57).[30] The bishop also calls his people to imitate the fruitfulness of the earth, sharing their abundant yield with others. Just as the earth "does not nurture fruit for its own enjoyment, but for your benefit," so also "whatever fruit of good works you bring forth" must be for the benefit of your neighbor.[31] In the homily given during the drought, Basil adds to Joseph another saint to imitate, one who, significantly, was not rich but poor. The story of the widow of Zarephath, who gave to Elijah from her lack, shows a generosity of spirit grounded in faith in God and his provision (1 Kings 17:8-16).[32] The widow's sacrificial generosity flowing from her modest flour vessel, which was in the end filled by God, embodies the inexhaustible mercy of God toward those who, though poor in things, become rich in faith and love. In contrast to the aforementioned rich men in the Gospel narratives, this woman has not sought enjoyment in earthly treasures but has stored up treasures in heaven. Her works show her blessed righteousness.

In contrast to the life of simplicity and sharing embodied by the saints, Basil paints a negative picture of habits that promote an economy based on accumulating greater profit. Although it would be anachronistic to read too much into Basil from the perspective of modern economic systems, his sermon "Against Those Who Lend at Interest" offers a critique of predatory lending that is as fresh today as it was back in his own day. The main problem he sees with the practice lies in the harm it does to both the lender and the debtor: "The one rushes like a hound to the hunt while the other quails like quarry at the pursuit. Poverty robs him of his courage. Both have the sums at their fingertips, since the one

---

[30]Basil of Caesarea, *On Social Justice*, 62.

[31]Basil of Caesarea, *On Social Justice*, 62. "The earth was welcoming all to its richness: it germinated the crops deep in the furrows, produced large clusters of grapes on the vine, made the olive tree bend under a vast quantity of fruit, and offered every delicious variety of the fruit tree. But the rich man was unwelcoming and unfruitful; he did not even possess as yet, and already he begrudged the needy." Basil of Caesarea, *On Social Justice*, 66-67.

[32]Basil of Caesarea, *On Social Justice*, 83-84.

rejoices at the increasing interest, while the other groans at the additional misfortune."[33] The practice tends toward making the lender greedier in his pursuit of gain and thus more likely to turn away from the treasures of heaven. It also brings shame and worry on the debtor, as well as a lack of incentive to work and further lack upon failure to pay. The bishop does not offer economic "recommendations as if laying down a law," but he does stress that "anything is preferable to borrowing" for the reasons stated above.[34] Indeed, one could argue the merits of lending and borrowing today. Yet Basil's greater advice to strive for simplicity and moderation in life, to assess the consequences of profit and debt schemes for one's material and spiritual well-being, and to invest in relationships that foster sustainable arrangements promoting mutually beneficial partnerships remains salutary even now.

What then is the alternative community to an unhealthy set of economic relationships? In keeping with his monastic background, Basil held in high esteem the example of life in community displayed in Acts 2: "Let us zealously imitate the early Christian community, where everything was held in common—life, soul, concord, a common table, indivisible kinship—while unfeigned love constituted many bodies as one and joined many souls into a single harmonious whole."[35] This is not only an idealized community for an elite band of monks in the desert.[36] We find a practical example of his vision of the monastic life as a public instrument of service in Caesarea's *Basiliad*, an institution he established—in part using his own inheritance and partly through the beneficence of the emperor and others—to take care of the poor and the sick.[37] It has been said, however, that "the *Basiliad* is not primarily a new kind of charitable institution, but rather a new set of relationships, a new social order that both anticipates and participates in the creation of 'a new heaven and new earth where justice dwells.'"[38] In that sense, the *Basiliad* represented a voluntary, contextual embodiment of what it looks like to live a life of simplicity, where no earthly riches are stored up for long for the gain of a few people—a community where resources are distributed

[33]Basil of Caesarea, *On Social Justice*, 92.
[34]Basil of Caesarea, *On Social Justice*, 96.
[35]Basil of Caesarea, *On Social Justice*, 86.
[36]Silanes notes the desire among church fathers and monastic communities to live according to the pattern of the church in Acts 2. See Nereo Silanes, *La Santísima Trinidad, programa social del cristianismo: Principios bíblico-teológicos* (Salamanca: Secretariado Trinitario, 1991), 29-36, 43-45.
[37]For a discussion of the *Basiliad*, see Schroeder's introduction to Basil's homilies, *On Social Justice*, 33-38.
[38]Basil of Caesarea, *On Social Justice*, 38.

to all as equitably as needed, and therefore no one suffers from lack or need. The bishop put his money and effort where his mouth was, practicing what he preached among his people.

***Martin Luther: Communion, exchanging profits and costs, two kinds of righteousness.*** What does fellowship in the Spirit look like? Mining the implications for the Christian life of a theology of the Lord's Supper, *The Blessed Sacrament of the Holy and True Body of Christ, and the Brotherhoods* (1519) offers Luther's vision of what the fellowship of the saints, which is the spiritual "significance or effect" of the sacrament, entails for life together.[39] Using the analogy of citizens who as members of a city enter a social contract to share in the community's profits and costs, Luther speaks of the spiritual body of Christ (i.e., the church) as the city of God in which any member "must be willing to share . . . the cost as well as the profit" of citizenship.[40] United to Christ's body in the Lord's Supper, the believer is also united to the members of Christ's mystical body, sharing in all their burdens and joys (1 Cor 12:25-26). Consequently, "whoever does him [the believer] a kindness does it to Christ and all his saints."[41] The church is not a bunch of self-reliant individuals who at their own discretion do certain things on occasion to help out, but an interdependent community where each member becomes a representative of Christ to the other in good and bad times.

When Luther speaks of the spiritual meaning of Communion, he highlights its ongoing use as "a sacrament of love," that is, a sign to foster an interdependent form of life.[42] "As love and support are given you" richly by Christ through or in his generous saints, so also "you in turn must render love and support to Christ in his needy ones."[43] In this intercommunion of love, there are no unilateral exchanges where only one gives and the other receives, but rather multilateral and reciprocal exchanges where sharing goes both ways at various times. Luther is especially critical of the "self-seeking person" who "would gladly share in the profits but not in the costs" of fellowship.[44] In receiving and giving, the saints bear

---

[39]*LW* 35:50.

[40]Luther, *The Blessed Sacrament*, *LW* 35:52-53.

[41]Luther, *The Blessed Sacrament*, *LW* 35:52.

[42]Luther, *The Blessed Sacrament*, *LW* 35:54.

[43]Luther, *The Blessed Sacrament*, *LW* 35:54. "This fellowship is twofold: on the one hand we partake of Christ and all saints; on the other hand we permit all Christians to be partakers of us, in whatever way they and we are able." Luther, *The Blessed Sacrament*, *LW* 35:67.

[44]Luther, *The Blessed Sacrament*, *LW* 35:57. "They will not help the poor, put up with sinners, care for the sorrowing, suffer with the suffering, intercede for others, defend the truth, and at the risk of [their own]

each other's burdens (Gal 6:2) as they "fight, work, pray, and . . . have heartfelt sympathy" for one another in times of persecution for Christ's sake, when the innocent suffer unjustly, and when all kinds of bodily and spiritual afflictions affect them.[45]

There is simply no end to the number of situations in which Christ comes to us in his generous and needy saints. In Luther's day, the idea that the sacrament was a humanly mediated work performed to obtain satisfaction before God for sins got in the way of seeing Communion as a source of comfort before God and a sign of fellowship among God's saints.[46] Spending energy on works of satisfaction obfuscated not only the benefits of Christ's once-for-all sacrifice offered in the sacrament, but also took energy away from the daily use of the sacrament to foster true fellowship where saints become living sacrifices to each other as they share all things in common. Luther looks with fondness to early church practices linked to the celebration of Communion, which he no longer sees in the church of his day—that time when saints "gathered food and material goods in the church, and there distributed among those who were in need."[47]

Luther uses the language of "gracious exchange" not only to describe justification—namely, Christ's giving us his righteousness in exchange for our unrighteousness—but also to describe the effects of Christ's justification in the sanctified life as the "blending of our sins and suffering with the righteousness of Christ and his saints."[48] By virtue of their becoming one body of Christ, the saints lose their individual form and take on the form of each other in their needs. In doing so, the saints reflect the attitude and take on the form of their Lord who himself took on their form, both in becoming one of us in his incarnation and in his becoming our servant unto death in order to save us.

---

life, property, and honor seek the betterment of the church and of all Christians." Luther, *The Blessed Sacrament*, *LW* 35:57.

[45]Luther, *The Blessed Sacrament*, *LW* 35:57; cf. 35:56. "Then do not doubt that you have what the sacrament signifies, that is, be certain that Christ and all his saints are coming to you with all their virtues, sufferings, and mercies, to live, work, suffer, and die with you, and that they desire to be wholly yours, having all things in common with you." Luther, *The Blessed Sacrament*, *LW* 35:61.

[46]Cf. Luther, *The Blessed Sacrament*, *LW* 35:55-56.

[47]Luther, *The Blessed Sacrament*, *LW* 35:57. "Christians cared for one another, supported one another, sympathized with one another, bore one another's burdens and affliction. This has all disappeared, and now there remain only the masses and the many who receive this sacrament without in the least understanding or practicing what it signifies." Luther, *The Blessed Sacrament*, *LW* 35:57.

[48]Luther, *The Blessed Sacrament*, *LW* 35:60.

> Christ with all saints, by his love, takes upon himself our form [Phil. 2:7], fights with us against sin, death, and all evil. This enkindles in us such love that we take on his form, rely upon his righteousness, life, and blessedness. And through the interchange of his blessings and our misfortunes, we become one loaf, one bread, one body, one drink, and have all things in common. . . . Again through the same love, we are to be changed and to make the infirmities of other Christians our own; we are to take upon ourselves their form and their necessity, and all the good that is within our power we are to make theirs, that they may profit from it. . . . In this way we are changed into one another and are made into a community by love.[49]

A passage rich in its description of the Christian life as a taking on of the form of Christ in his saints, Luther's extension of the notion of "gracious exchange" to our life together paints a decidedly neighbor-oriented picture of sanctification as christoformation. The proper use of Communion engenders Christlike sacrificial love, which "grows daily and so changes a person that he is made one with all others."[50]

Our spiritual fellowship entails a transmutation of love in which I exchange my grief for my neighbor's joy on a gloomy day. On a day where hurtful things have been said or done, my neighbor exchanges his pardon for my sin. On a day full of struggles when prayers are most needed, I exchange my inability to call upon God for my neighbor's intercession. Another day, when it is hard to make ends meet, my neighbor exchanges his abundance for my need; and later, when my neighbor struggles with loneliness, I exchange his or her lack with an abundant measure of companionship and solidarity. Such is the economy of the Spirit of Christ among us.

Luther frames the Christian life in terms of identity and purpose. Summarizing Paul's argument in the *Lectures on Galatians* (1535), for instance, Luther speaks to the human creature's twofold being in the world by drawing a distinction between two kinds of righteousness.[51] The first kind of righteousness deals with our

---

[49]Luther, *The Blessed Sacrament*, *LW* 35:58.

[50]Luther, *The Blessed Sacrament*, *LW* 35:58.

[51]"This is our theology, by which we teach a precise distinction between these two kinds of righteousness, the active and the passive, so that morality and faith, works and grace, secular society and religion may not be confused. Both are necessary, but both must be kept within their limits." Martin Luther, *Lectures on Galatians, Chapters 1–4*, *LW* 26:7. For a treatment of the significance of Luther's distinction for theological anthropology, see Robert Kolb and Charles P. Arand, *The Genius of Luther's Theology: A Wittenberg Way of Thinking for the Contemporary Church* (Grand Rapids: Baker Academic, 2008), 21-128; for a constructive proposal on the use of Luther's distinction to promote a virtue ethics, particularly in response

identity before God, and it is called *passive* because it is received through faith in the merits of Christ and thus it is not earned through our performance of the works of the law.[52] According to this passive righteousness, we are made a new creation by bearing the image of the heavenly Christ (1 Cor 15:49), "who is a new man in a new world, where there is no Law, no sin, no conscience, no death, but perfect joy, righteousness, grace, peace, life, salvation, and glory."[53] Since our identity before God is grounded in his gift of Christ to us, the passive righteousness of faith also directs us to receive Christ as our "wisdom, righteousness, sanctification, and redemption from God" (1 Cor 1:30).[54] In this realm of life in the Spirit, one notes how sanctification is defined christologically as God's gift of Christ himself on our behalf and eschatologically as the new creature's bearing of the Spirit-formed image of the risen Christ. This identity of faith is secured because it looks to Christ alone for the assurance of righteousness before God.

The second kind of righteousness deals with our horizontal relationship to neighbors, and it is called *active* because it is carried out by all Christians on behalf of others through works of the law done in the context of their callings or vocations in life. Active righteousness, which deals with the purpose of life in the world, can be seen from two angles. Seen negatively from the perspective of the sinful corruption of Adam (that is, the flesh) that still holds on to the Christian in this life, the righteousness of the law functions in such a way that it restrains the flesh from sin to some degree and accuses us of falling short of God's grace on account of our imperfect works.[55] For this reason, the distinction between the

---

to the problem of antinomianism, see Joel D. Biermann, *A Case for Character: Towards a Lutheran Virtue Ethics* (Minneapolis: Fortress, 2014).

[52]Luther, *Lectures on Galatians*, *LW* 26:4-5. "In other words, this is the righteousness of Christ and of the Holy Spirit, which we do not perform but receive, which we do not have but accept, when God the Father grants it to us through Jesus Christ. As the earth itself does not produce rain and is unable to acquire it by its own strength, worship, and power but receives it only by a heavenly gift from above, so this heavenly righteousness is given to us by God without our work or merit." Luther, *Lectures on Galatians*, *LW* 26:6.

[53]Luther, *Lectures on Galatians*, *LW* 26:8.

[54]Luther, *Lectures on Galatians*, *LW* 26:8.

[55]For Luther, the law is good and necessary because God commanded it, but it cannot save or make the sinner righteous before God. "For although the Law is the best of all things in the world, it still cannot bring peace to a terrified conscience but makes it even sadder and drives it to despair." Luther, *Lectures on Galatians*, *LW* 26:5. "Works and the performance of the Law must be demanded in the world as though there were no promise or grace. This is because of the stubborn, proud, and hardhearted, before whose eyes nothing must be set except the Law, in order that they may be terrified and humbled. For the Law was given to terrify and kill the stubborn and to exercise the old man." Luther, *Lectures on Galatians*, *LW* 26:6.

two kinds of righteousness remains, so that the Christian does not lose Christ and "fall into a trust in his own works" by placing himself "under the Law and not under grace"—a move that ends up making Christ "no longer a Savior" but a "lawgiver."[56]

Yet seen positively from the perspective of our identity as a new creation in Christ, Luther describes how both kinds of righteousness interact in the Christian's life. He does so by showing how the righteousness of good works the Spirit does in and through us richly flows from the righteousness of faith the Spirit does for us through the gospel. Luther employs the language of fertility to describe the bounty of good works that faith produces.

> When I have this righteousness within me, I descend from heaven like the rain that makes the earth fertile. That is, I come forth into another kingdom, and I perform good works whenever the opportunity arises. If I am a minister of the Word, I preach, I comfort the saddened, I administer the sacraments. If I am a father, I rule my household and family, I train my children in piety and honesty. If I am a magistrate, I perform the office which I have received by divine command. If I am a servant, I faithfully tend to my master's affairs.[57]

For Luther, vocations such as the ones named above are the created means through which Christians bear fruit for others. These God-given callings are not possessed by members of a seemingly more spiritual elite, such as those in monastic orders, but rather to every single Christian in the world. Through those callings, God gives Christians a purpose in creation and channels their efforts toward serving many neighbors who depend on them. A Christian becomes a "mask" of God in the world through which the Creator showers people with blessings, thereby serving as a representative of God in his work of sustaining and protecting life.[58] The sanctified life is thus lived out through our activities in the mundane and secular sphere of quotidian life. Life in the Spirit becomes quite earthy, concerned with the daily stewardship of our gifts and resources to care for neighbors God has entrusted to us.

---

[56]Luther, *Lectures on Galatians*, *LW* 26:9, 11.

[57]Luther, *Lectures on Galatians*, *LW* 26:11-12.

[58]"Instead of coming in uncovered majesty when he gives a gift to man, God places a mask before his face. He clothes himself in the form of an ordinary man who performs his work on earth. Human beings are to work, 'everyone according to his vocation and office,' through this they serve as masks of God, behind which he can conceal himself when he would scatter his gifts." Gustaf Wingren, *Luther on Vocation*, trans. Carl C. Rasmussen (Philadelphia: Muhlenberg, 1958), 138.

## HAPPY EXCHANGES: SPIRITUAL PRACTICES AND ISSUES IN THE CHRISTIAN LIFE

An apocryphal story tells that, upon their death, two righteous people meet blessed St. Peter at the gates of heaven.[59] "Dear brother, why should I let you into the presence of almighty God?" the apostle asked the first person. Feeling fairly confident in his righteousness, the man put out a bag full of works he brought with him to heaven and pointing at it answered, "I humbly present before God the fruits of my labors, which God worked in and through me, in the hopes that I might be found worthy of eternal life."

After listening with interest to the man's retort, St. Peter said nothing, and immediately addressed the second traveler. "And what about you, dear sister? Why should I let you into heaven, into the presence of our heavenly Father? Did you too bring a bag of good works with you?" asked Peter. A little surprised by the question, the woman nevertheless went ahead and responded, "Oh my! A bag of works? I did not realize I had to bring my righteousness and deeds to God in heaven. Here I only cling to Christ's righteousness on my behalf. So I left my bag of labors on earth with my neighbors who needed them."

Heirs of the Protestant Reformation will find the story especially meaningful. The tale of these two righteous pilgrims illustrates that, although God does work in and through us, our standing before God is secure on account of Christ's righteousness alone and does not depend on our personal righteousness or its fruits.[60] This assertion about our relationship to a gracious God, however, should not render our good works useless or make us negligent in our duties toward others. Having been made righteous before God, we are now free to live righteously or justly in the world. The purpose of our righteous deeds is now reoriented away from efforts to attain personal salvation and toward the loving care of a multitude of neighbors God has gifted us with in our lives.

---

[59]I have adapted the story from my colleague Robert Kolb's version, which I first heard in a class we taught together at seminary.

[60]McGee has argued that the search for personal significance follows from the human need for self-worth or self-esteem, and in particular that a person's desire to meet standards to feel good about himself can only be quenched by God through his work of justification. See Robert S. McGee, *The Search for Significance*, 2nd ed. (Houston: Rapha, 1990), 23-30, 43-62. McGee deals with other human needs such as approval from others, being loved even when we fail, and freedom from hopelessness and shame, which God addresses respectively through reconciliation, propitiation, and regeneration; *The Search for Significance*, 63-116. As a whole, the author's work bears an affinity with our renewal model of the sanctified life (see chapter one) in which human identity before God is grounded not in the sanctifying righteousness of the believer but in the righteousness of Christ alone.

***Neighbor-oriented spirituality.*** If the renewal model of the Christian life deals with the recurrent guilt and power of sin through a sharing in Christ's death and resurrection, and the dramatic one deals with vigilance amid the devil's attacks through participation in Christ's life of prayer and meditation on the Word, the sacrificial model defines holiness as a sharing in the form of Christ's servanthood in the world. In the Spirit's shaping of the saints after Christ's humility, disciples become living sacrifices, who in thanksgiving to God for his gifts, spread the pleasing aroma of Christ in the world through their witness and works. Sanctified by the Spirit, disciples of Christ are set apart from the world in order to shine the light of Christ in the world. As "the temple of the living God" in the world, God's people are called to have neither "partnership . . . with lawlessness" nor "fellowship . . . with darkness" (2 Cor 6:14-16). The apostle exhorts them to bring holiness to its proper end, "to completion in the fear of God," by cleansing themselves "from every defilement of body and spirit" (2 Cor 7:1). They move in the tension between not being of the world by being kept "from the evil one," and yet being sanctified in God's truth and Word by being "sent into the world" to be Christ's witnesses in the world (Jn 17:14-20).

Given its strong orientation toward the centrifugal or social dimension of holiness, the sacrificial model sees the sanctified life primarily in terms of neighbors and their needs. Over against the potential danger of an individualistic view of sanctification that is overly concerned with personal holiness, a neighbor-oriented angle on life in the Spirit allows us to make others the goal or aim of the sanctified life. By locating holiness talk in a social trajectory, the saints find their purpose in the world by serving and sharing their lives with others. This raises a dilemma: Who is my neighbor and what are my duties toward him or her?

The law of love excludes no one, as the story of the good Samaritan reminds us (Lk 10:29-37). Therefore, everybody is my neighbor, yet I cannot realistically serve everybody. We are not super-spiritual Atlases who carry the weight of the world's needs on our shoulders. If everyone is my neighbor, then, nobody is my neighbor! Love becomes an ideal, and not an incarnate reality. Without excluding neighbors we can serve as opportunities arise (and there are plenty of those instances), we can still acknowledge that certain neighbors in closer proximity to us do require our attention, wisdom, energies, and interaction more immediately, regularly, and intensely.

"Love your neighbor as yourself" sums up the second part or table of the Decalogue, which describes *what* we ought to do and not do to love our fellow human beings. But the Law does not yet tell us *how* to put that great commandment into practice in the context of a concrete neighbor's life. For this we need the Spirit of Christ, who moves us from the *what* to the *how* of the Law of God, from hearing the command as a universal call to applying it for a particular neighbor in his or her specific situation. And the Spirit shapes us to embody the law of love in a most unassuming and earthy way, namely, through the exercise of our daily vocations or callings in life.[61] Through vocations, the law of love is actually fulfilled and applied in a focused way so that our energies are spent on serving neighbors we have been especially called to look after and advocate for.[62] In that sense, vocation becomes a liberating gift, and the whole world and its needs are no longer on our shoulders. We can thus give thanks to God for our vocations, but also for those of countless others around the world serving people whom, given our creaturely limitations, we would otherwise never be able to reach and probably would never meet.

Whether a mother cares for her daughter, a farmer feeds the hungry, a lawyer defends the accused, a nurse heals the sick, a teacher forms the next generation of leaders, a city official governs on behalf of his or her constituents, or a pastor teaches the Word of God, these people are all fulfilling the law of love. By obeying God's command in the context of their callings, they are offering a spiritual service to God on behalf of neighbors and spreading the aroma of Christ in a hurting world. Since we have many callings in our life, and thus wear various hats and juggle many responsibilities at the same time, we are likely already filled with plenty of things to do to serve many people. Beyond

---

[61] It is in this context of obedience to God's law through vocation that Luther writes concerning believers, "They have the Holy Spirit and esteem highly those truly spiritual and wonderful works: Baptism, the Eucharist, absolution, *constant attendance in one's calling, and obedience to parents and superiors*" (italics mine). Luther, *Lectures on Genesis: Chapters 21–25*, *LW* 4:142.

[62] "We serve the neighbors we have been called to serve first. When the opportunity arises and the means are available, we also gladly serve as many neighbors as possible for the sake of love with the strength God provides for the task. But vocation gives us a focus that allows us to give specific neighbors the attention, assistance, companionship, or partnership they need. This makes love not an ideal, but the real thing—an incarnational love. Such a limit or boundary imposed on our creaturely capacity for work on behalf of suffering neighbors reminds us that we are not Christ (or 'saviors' of the world) but his servants, and that the fruits of our labor are not ultimately ours but God's." Leopoldo A. Sánchez M., "The Human Face of Justice: Reclaiming the Neighbor in Law, Vocation, and Justice Talk," *Concordia Journal* 39, no. 2 (2013): 126.

embodying the law of God in our ordinary vocational lives, there is no need to seek after more special or holy things to do.[63] Godliness and holiness talk, therefore, does not direct us to the exceptional and impressive feats of spiritual heroes, but is embodied in seemingly ordinary, unimportant, and quotidian acts and duties of faithful servants all over the world.[64] A neighbor-oriented spirituality highlights countless, yet often unrecognized, ways in which the Spirit of God works in cooperation with his people to care for and preserve the lives and well-being of many.

If the renewal model fosters confession and absolution, as well as practices of reconciliation; and the dramatic model encourages the use of the Word of God, prayer, and external forms of discipline such as practices of accountability in the midst of spiritual struggles; the sacrificial model promotes spiritual growth through a deeper knowledge of neighbors and their needs. There is a certain depth and maturity that comes with spending time listening to and learning from those whom God has gifted us with so that we can be of the greatest assistance to them. Neighbors are not static entities, but persons with complex lives whose needs change over time. A mother might express her love for her son early on by changing his diapers, helping him dress, or breastfeeding him. Later in his elementary school years, she might find herself reading and learning everything she can about ADHD so that she can best help her child succeed in tasks others might take for granted. Throughout various stages of her son's adulthood, she might show her love by assisting him with some college tuition, offering advice here and there as he prepares for marriage or his first job, or taking care of the

[63]"It seems to me that we shall have our hands full to keep these commandments, practice gentleness, patience, love toward enemies, chastity, kindness, etc., and all that is involved in doing so. But such works are not important or impressive in the eyes of the world. They are not uncommon and showy, reserved to certain special times, places, rites, and ceremonies, but are common, everyday domestic duties of one neighbor to another, with nothing glamorous about them." Luther, "Ten Commandments," *LC* I 313, *BC*, p. 428. "Just concentrate upon them [the commandments] and test yourself thoroughly; do your very best, and you will surely find so much to do that you will neither seek nor pay attention to any other works or other kind of holiness." Luther, "Ten Commandments," *LC* I 318, *BC*, p. 429. "If God wants to do something extraordinary through you, he will call you and will point out opportunities. Avail yourself of them. If this does not happen, let everyone nevertheless rejoice that he is in a divine calling when he assumes and performs these ordinary duties of this life." Luther, *Lectures on Genesis: Chapters 15–20*, *LW* 3:321.

[64]In his description of Luther's view of vocation as "a mysticism of ordinary life," Veith rightly notes, "If he sometimes minimizes human beings as radically sinful and limited, in his doctrine of vocation, he exalts human beings to a startling degree. In the doctrine of vocation, spirituality is brought down to earth to transfigure our practical, everyday life." Gene Edward Veith, *The Spirituality of the Cross* (St. Louis: Concordia, 1999), 71-72.

grandchildren. Although the vocation of mother remains the same, its shape depends on the changing needs of her son over time. Vocations take on the shape of neighbors as they go through the various seasons of life.

By taking its shape from the neighbor, vocation becomes a selfless act, a cross-shaped calling from God to share in Christ's self-giving to us in the Spirit. Vocation stands as a cruciform way of life in the Spirit, a dying to one's attempts to earn God's justification through works, and a taking on oneself of the neighbor's needs and burdens.[65] We speak of a spirituality of descent and kenosis, grounded in Christ's incarnation and humiliation, where disciples do not seek a higher spirituality somewhere up there in the heavens, but rather come down to earth and get their hands dirty in the messiness of life to share in its sufferings and joys with others.[66]

***Avoiding romantic and utilitarian views of the neighbor.*** So who is my neighbor? The way we think about neighbors in need will influence the manner in which we approach the sanctified life. Two errors ought to be avoided. We call the first error a romantic view of people in need, which portrays their lack of possessions as a desirable status or higher form of spiritual existence—indeed, a more sanctified life! The second error may be called a utilitarian view, which sees people in need as a means to a greater end such as the spiritual benefit or growth of the person offering assistance—say, a means to someone else's sanctification! These ways of thinking about neighbors end up distorting not only our theology of sanctification, but also our view of justification, as well as our actions toward and relationships with others.

Consider the difference between Basil's and Pseudo-Basil's approach in their homilies on the young rich man (Mt 19), whose love of things did not allow him to give his possessions to the poor and seek after heavenly treasure by following Jesus. For Basil, the story reveals the sin of avarice and misanthropy in all of us and the

---

[65]"The neighbor is relentless because he is our burden and cross, in a good sense. Vocation becomes the God-established cross that by leading us to serve our neighbors prevents us from designing our own crosses as a means to become holy and seek God's favor. The neighbor teaches us what it means to act as a Christian, as one formed by the Spirit of Christ to live under the cross through the daily sacrifices and prayers made for others." Sánchez, "The Human Face of Justice," 129.

[66]"Vocation is earthly, just as shockingly earthly as the humanity of Christ, apparently so void of all divinity. In the crucifixion of Christ the divine nature was only hidden, not absent; it was present in the lowly form of love for robbers and soldiers. Similarly, God conceals His work of love to men in cross-marked vocation, which is really of benefit to the neighbor. In Christ's victory on the cross, which looks so poor—love's victory in lowliness—God is hidden; therefore, the resurrection takes place on the third day." Wingren, *Luther on Vocation*, 57.

need for all Christians without distinction to practice a certain monasticism of everyday life through simplicity in their stewardship of God's gifts and philanthropy in their dealings with neighbors in need. However, for Pseudo-Basil, the words of Jesus are directed at those who practice the monastic life of perfection by divesting themselves of possessions. A significant shift occurs, and a two-tiered approach to spirituality that distinguishes between the common life and the monastic life is built around the text.

In the pseudo-Basilian homily "On Mercy and Justice," the writer speaks first of Jesus' "perfect followers" who have taken on themselves "the entire and complete fulfillment of mercy" by taking a vow of poverty to focus on "service to others by means of word and spirit."[67] Then, the writer distinguishes this group from "the rest," who are generous in the use of their possessions "as imitators of the kindness of God, showing mercy and giving and sharing."[68] Such a reading of the text gives the impression that perfection in sanctification is synonymous with material poverty. Another important shift occurs in the homily. Significantly, the writer identifies "the least of these" in Matthew 25 with those joining the monastic ranks, so that those who eagerly minister to these "holy people" or "poor" disciples, and thus "feed soldiers of Christ" acquire treasures in heaven by sharing their temporal possessions with them.[69] Acquiring a voluntary state of poverty, the monastic poor offer the rich and others a means to heaven: "The disciples' poverty, as the world considers it, is an opportunity for you to acquire true wealth."[70] Pseudo-Basil's reading of the text from Matthew lends itself to the idea that the state of poverty is not only an ideal form of the sanctified life, but also a means for others to become sanctified.

Interpretations of the story of the young rich man similar to those in Pseudo-Basil became influential over time. In Luther's day, for instance, people typically assumed that taking a monastic vow of poverty and giving alms to the poor were works that went as far as earning someone the forgiveness of sins.[71] A number of

[67]This homily is included in Basil of Caesarea, *On Social Justice*, 107.

[68]Basil of Caesarea, *On Social Justice*, 107.

[69]Basil of Caesarea, *On Social Justice*, 107-8.

[70]Basil of Caesarea, *On Social Justice*, 107.

[71]The following section draws from Leopoldo A. Sánchez M., "'The Poor You Will Always Have with You': A Biblical View of People in Need," in *A People Called to Love: Christian Charity in North American Society*, ed. Kent Burreson, 2012, http://concordiatheology.org/wp-content/uploads/2012/09/Sanchez-essay1.pdf; on medieval approaches to the theology of poverty, see Carter Lindberg, *Beyond Charity: Reformation Initiatives for the Poor* (Minneapolis: Fortress, 1993), esp. 22-33. "It was pretended that monastic vows

problems arose as a result of this view. First, monastic self-renunciation idealized poverty as the most favorable state in the eyes of God.[72] The Gospel's story of the rich young man who asked Jesus what he must do to be saved was "overworked by the medieval clergy" to teach that renouncing one's possessions and giving them to the poor earned God's grace.[73] Therefore, folks saw poverty as the most elevated spiritual condition one could obtain in this life, and the poor in particular as being the closest to God.[74] Second, the practice of almsgiving achieved the status of a divine means for the richer to be saved and secured the ongoing intercession of the poor on their behalf.[75] In short, almsgiving justified the existence of the poor as an indispensable step on the road to personal salvation before God. Popular biblical passages used in support of this view came from apocryphal books like Tobit, where "almsgiving saves from death and purges away every sin," and Sirach (Ecclesiasticus) where we hear that "almsgiving atones for sin."[76] Poverty and charity became a means of justification.

---

would be equal to baptism, and that through monastic life one could earn forgiveness of sin and justification before God. . . . In this way monastic vows were praised more highly than baptism." *CA* XXVII 11-13, *BC*, p. 82.

[72]"It was also said that one could obtain more merit through the monastic life than through all other walks of life, which had been ordered by God, such as the office of pastor or preacher, the office of ruler, prince, lord, and the like." *CA* XXVII 13, *BC*, p. 82 (or being a "farmer" or an "artisan," *Ap* XXVII 37, *BC*, p. 238); cf. *CA* XXVII 16-17, *BC*, p. 84.

[73]Mk 10:17-21; see Lindberg, *Beyond Charity*, 27; Melanchthon argues against the prevailing interpretation of the parallel passage (esp. Mt 19.21) by appealing to the spiritual sense of poverty: "The poverty of the gospel [Matt. 5:3] does not consist in the abandonment of property, but in the absence of greed and of trust in riches. . . . Perfection consists in what Christ says next: 'Follow me.' This sets forth the example of obedience in a calling." *Ap* XXVII 45-49, *BC*, p. 285. In other words, the "poor in spirit" are those who trust in God and serve their neighbor.

[74]For example, the monastic vow of poverty became an aspect of "Christian perfection" that led to righteousness before God. This way of thinking obscured the evangelical meaning of "true perfection and true service of God," which is to fear God, trust that he is gracious to us because of Christ, pray to and expect help from him in every need and in all afflictions, and do good works according to our callings in life. *CA* XXVII 44-50, *BC*, p. 88; cf. *Ap* XXVII 27, *BC*, p. 282; in the contemporary scene, we should note that liberation theology's "preferential option for the poor" at times led some to see the poor as "amoral and somehow closest to God" because of their material poverty, and yet this subtle "romanticism was offset by an equally strong emphasis on the *concientización* of the poor as the agents of their own destiny and liberation." See Leopoldo A. Sánchez M., "The Struggle to Express Our Hope," *LOGIA* 19, no. 1 (2010): 30. *Concientización* may be translated as critical "consciousness" or "awareness."

[75]Typically, the church received the alms of the rich presumably on behalf of the poor. In Luther's day, testaments, charters, buying and selling of indulgences, leaving money behind for the poor to participate in one's funeral, and masses for the dead assumed that the poor—also the saints—could intercede for the dead (especially, the rich). See Lindberg, *Beyond Charity*, 27-33.

[76]Tob 12:9; cf. 4:10; and Sir 3:30; see Lindberg, *Beyond Charity*, 27; in contrast to the prevailing late-medieval reading, Melanchthon interprets Tobit's statement on almsgiving not as a work that reconciles

When the needy are idealized as examples of holiness on account of their material condition in life, or when they are seen as a means to a philanthropist's own holiness or spiritual benefit, the end result is a confusion between the two kinds of righteousness and a flawed view of active righteousness. First, righteousness or justification before God is no longer brought about through the power of the gospel and received by faith, but earned by one's status in this life (in this case, lack of possessions) or the performance of good works on behalf of another (in this case, sharing possessions with the needy). Luther's teaching on justification by faith apart from works turned such views upside down. By leaving the matter of one's salvation in God's gracious hands, people could be freed from an obsessive preoccupation with their own spiritual merits and instead focus their efforts toward serving others in everyday worldly matters like embarking on vigorous initiatives to assist those in need. Indeed, Luther's teaching on justification ushered in a monumental shift in spirituality from the "I" to the "thou," from self-service to self-giving. Carter Lindberg describes the Reformer's contribution as follows:

> If salvation is by grace alone, poverty no longer serves anyone. The poor no longer possess any special sanctity; they are sinners like their wealthier compatriots. With faith, not charity, as the locus for the relationship to God, attention could be focused on this-worldly problems and their causes. Because salvation was no longer understood to be the goal of life but rather the foundation of life, human energy and reason were liberated to this-worldly concerns.[77]

Second, romantic and utilitarian views of the needy led to an inadequate approach to active righteousness and, therefore, a flawed view of Christian holiness or sanctification as it is lived out in the world. Today, one hears among people in church attitudes toward the needy similar to those in Luther's day.[78] On the one hand, North American Christians, as a reaction to their own

---

us before God but as a fruit of love that results from faith in a gracious God on account of Christ. *Ap* XXVII, *BC*, p. 163.

[77]Lindberg, *Beyond Charity*, 165.

[78]For my initial explorations of contemporary expressions of romantic and utilitarian views of people in need among Christians going to or returning from short-term mission trips, see Leopoldo A. Sánchez M., "Pedagogy for Working among the Poor: Something to Talk about before Going on Your Next Short-Term Mission Trip," *Missio Apostolica* 16, no. 1 (2008): 80-84; for an in-depth discussion of the dangers and blessings of short-term mission trips from the perspective of poverty-alleviation, see Steve Corbett and Brian Fikkert, *When Helping Hurts: How to Alleviate Poverty Without Hurting the Poor . . . and Yourself*, 2nd ed. (Chicago: Moody, 2012), 151-67.

materialist and consumerist excesses, may praise or look up to the poor for their lack of attachment to material things and presumably wish they could live simpler lives like them. By making this move, however, they romanticize the needy and, therefore, take too lightly the harsh reality of poverty and the church's need for an ongoing commitment to work with needy neighbors to improve their situation.

On the other hand, Christians may be motivated to help the poor on special occasions or through special projects, but on the condition that they hear the gospel in some way. Even though sharing the good news is the task of every Christian as the opportunity arises, this all-or-nothing way of thinking makes it sound as if ordinary works done to take care of our neighbors' temporal needs are only justifiable as a bait to convert people rather than simply because God has commanded them. Others may talk about how much their own faith has grown as a result of these special experiences or projects, and then no longer commit to further acts of solidarity toward and with the needy. Perhaps inadvertently, the focus still shifts from the neighbor as the proper end of our love to the potential benefits working among the poor might bring to the benefactor. One can easily fall into a what's-in-it-for-me attitude. Even well-meaning Christians can see and use the neighbor as a means to their own spiritual growth (or the potential growth of their church). The Spirit of Christ moves us to make the poor themselves the primary object of our works of love.

***From generosity to partnership.*** The way we think about needy neighbors shapes how we conceive our relationship to them. If we think of neighbors mainly as passive recipients of God's generosity, then, our model of dealing rightly with them will focus on their need for aid and on their donors or helpers as God's instruments of mercy to them. Although moments of crisis such as major disasters often render people completely at the mercy of God and generous folks, a sustained emphasis on the passive-receptive character of the needy leads to unilateral relations that create paternalism on the side of the donor and dependency on the side of those whom we are trying to help.[79] Indeed, an aid-based approach can assist neighbors with their immediate needs, but it can also inadvertently create a

---

[79]Sánchez, "The Human Face of Justice," 121. "Mercy without justice degenerates into dependency and self-entitlement, preserving the power of the giver over the receiver. Justice without mercy is cold and impersonal, more concerned about rights than relationships." Robert D. Lupton, *Toxic Charity: How Churches and Charities Hurt Those They Help (And How to Reverse It)* (New York: HarperOne, 2011), 41.

lack of ongoing concern for engaging these neighbors more directly to deal with underlying systemic causes leading to their situation. As Robert Lupton notes, in harmful models of generosity "doing *for* rather than doing *with* those in need is the norm. Add to it the combination of patronizing pity and unintended superiority, and charity becomes toxic."[80] Therefore, a need arises for a way of life that moves beyond unilateral, short-term generous or charitable outreach to the needy toward working in long-term partnership with them.

In their book *When Helping Hurts*, Steve Corbett and Brian Fikkert argue that "when North Americans *do* attempt to alleviate poverty, the methods used often do considerable harm to both the materially poor and the materially non-poor."[81] Such methods can exacerbate the former's sense of shame and inferiority, which perpetuates the idea that their condition is inevitable, or feed the latter's "god" or "superiority" complex, which makes them feel like their possessions are their own doing and they have been chosen to make decisions on behalf of those who have less.[82] The authors move along a spectrum for dealing with poverty-alleviation that does not linger forever in "relief" intervention from giver to receiver, but allows us to discern when it is time to move in the direction of "rehabilitation" by working with others in their own recovery, and finally toward "development" through ongoing two-way partnerships.[83] Although the authors avoid the idea that either a North American Christian or a church may perfectly embody helping without hurting (there are no perfect good works anyway), they do offer a certain vision of what such a life of serving and sharing may aspire to.

As a starting point, those who want to help will not only ask neighbors what they need, but also what they can contribute. A move toward asset-based partnerships will assess the neighbor's capacity, identifying personal skills and community resources, while fostering problem-solving through local participation of stakeholders and nurturing interdependent relationships that will lead to cooperation among local individuals and institutions.[84] Based on his experience in development,

---

[80]Lupton, *Toxic Charity*, 35.

[81]Corbett and Fikkert, *When Helping Hurts*, 27.

[82]Corbett and Fikkert, *When Helping Hurts*, 61-62. Both the poor's shame and the non-poor's "god complex" are examples, not only of the brokenness of creation, but also of a "poverty of being" often promoted in inadequate poverty-alleviation efforts.

[83]Corbett and Fikkert, *When Helping Hurts*, 99-108.

[84]Corbett and Fikkert, *When Helping Hurts*, 119-22.

Lupton offers a number of principles under his "Oath for Compassionate Service" that seek to avoid paternalism and dependency. They include the following:

- Never do for the poor what they have (or could have) the capacity to do for themselves.
- Limit one-way giving to emergency situations.
- Strive to empower the poor through employment, lending, and investing, using grants sparingly to reinforce achievements.
- Subordinate self-interests to the needs of those being served.
- Listen closely to those you seek to help, especially to what is not being said—unspoken feelings may contain essential clues to effective service.[85]

These authors offer us a vision analogous to the interconnected character of the church's spiritual fellowship, where the saints share all things in common—not only their needs but also their gifts. In happy exchanges, persons neither act like self-made individuals who feel good about their generosity at the expense of partnerships with others, nor lose their individual initiative and gifts by becoming dependent on others.[86] Through their daily vocations and callings, the saints extend this interdependent view of life to their dealings with a broad array of neighbors in the world, engaging in a multitude of exchanges where we become both receivers and givers and thus share in the benefits and costs of living in community.

By practicing such blessed exchanges among themselves, the saints become little Christs (anointed ones) to one another, living sacrifices pregnant with the fragrance of their Spirit-anointing. The church becomes a gym where the saints vigorously practice these exchanges, so that they might also spread the aroma of Christ in the world as they meet new neighbors. As receivers of the fruit and gifts of the Spirit and as givers of their own Spirit-filled lives for the sake of others, the saints embody a certain Christlikeness. As the Father's obedient Son, Jesus received from him the fullness of the Spirit and all its gifts for his mission. In his humiliation and kenosis, the Son was thus the recipient of the Father's generosity

[85]Lupton, *Toxic Charity*, 8-9.

[86]"Unlike capitalist and socialist systems of exchange, the economy of the Spirit in the world seeks neither to maximize profits for gain nor to stifle the creative stewardship of resources." Leopoldo A. Sánchez M., "Sculpting Christ in Us: Public Faces of the Spirit in God's World," in *Third Article Theology*, ed. Myk Habets (Minneapolis: Fortress, 2016), 314.

of Spirit. Yet far from modeling an unhealthy dependency on the Spirit, the Son and the Spirit work together as inseparable companions to fulfill the Father's plan of salvation. The incarnate Son fulfills a mission unique to his person as the Father's Spirit-anointed servant by giving his life sacrificially for us on the cross. He offers that life to the Father in the Spirit, making the Father a recipient of his life on our behalf. Upon his glorification, seated at the Father's right hand, the Son also gives us the fruits of his redemptive work, including the gift of his Spirit. In short, when seen from a Spirit-oriented angle, the Son is both receiver and giver of divine generosity. And so are the adopted sons and daughters.

# WELCOMING THE STRANGER

## THE HOSPITALITY MODEL

In this chapter, we look at the *hospitality* model of sanctification. Seeing the Christian life as a reaching out to the "other," this model describes life in the Spirit as a loving disposition toward marginalized and vulnerable neighbors. In this model, the Spirit conforms us to Christ in his own marginality and in his mission to and through marginal characters. By drawing attention to aspects of Jesus' mission in which he brings God's kingdom to outcasts and strangers, this model can assist us in fostering among people a heart for welcoming outsiders. The model deals with issues such as shame and exclusion as well as the need for belonging and embrace, focusing on embodying God's concern for forgotten neighbors.

### BIBLICAL PICTURES: SOLIDARITY, BORDERLANDS, STRANGERS

Yahweh reaches out to a marginal group, delivering a little flock from slavery to a powerful nation. They are a people holy to the Lord, chosen by him not because of their great size and might, "for you were the fewest of all peoples," but purely out of love (Deut 7:6-8). In the last days, the one Lord who delivered his elect in the exodus will also extend his mercy beyond Israel through a new exodus, revealing his saving arm to the nations (Is 49:6; 52:4-7, 10; see also 45:22-23). Throughout Israel's history, Yahweh also shows his compassion for neighbors often abused, forgotten, or excluded from the community such as widows, orphans, and the poor (Zech 7:10; Jer 22:3). Furthermore, since Yahweh saved his people when they were aliens in a foreign country, he calls his people to remember the strangers in their midst (Lev 19:34; Deut 10:18; see also Ex 22:21; 23:9).[1] There is a special place in God's heart for marginalized neighbors even outside the community of his own people.

Jesus takes the form of Yahweh's servant by dying on the cross, giving "his life as a ransom for many" (Mk 10:45), so that those who are under sin's bondage might be healed (Phil 2:6-8; Is 53:5; cf. Mt 8:14-17). Through his servant's self-giving unto death, Yahweh reveals his salvation to the nations in a new eschatological exodus (see Is 40–55). As the exalted servant, for instance, Jesus manifests his lordship over all creation and receives universal worship (Phil 2:9-11; see also Is 45:23). Jesus' servanthood does not only have implications for the doctrines of salvation and God. It also shapes the way his disciples live, as we pointed out in our sacrificial model of the sanctified life.

Becoming like us in the mystery of his incarnation, Christ embodies a form of solidarity with marginal neighbors. Praising the poor Macedonian Christians for their generous giving to their needy brothers and sisters in Jerusalem, Paul encourages the church in Corinth to contribute out of their abundance to assist the poor. In doing so, they follow not only the example of the Macedonians, but that of Jesus himself: "For you know the grace of our Lord Jesus Christ, that though he was rich, yet for your sake he became poor, so that you by his poverty might become rich" (2 Cor 8:9). Christ became poor by sharing in our human nature so that we might become abundantly rich by sharing in his divine generosity.

Jesus knows what it is like to be a vulnerable outsider. Raised in Nazareth of Galilee, Jesus was a marginalized Jew. After receiving Philip's news about the arrival of the Messiah, Nathanael asked, "Can anything good come out of Nazareth?" (Jn 1:46). Philip encouraged him to "come and see" (v. 46). Jerusalem was seen as the center of Jewish wisdom and power. It was the place of wise teachers who claimed to speak for God, and the site of the temple, God's dwelling place. By Jerusalem standards, Galileans lived too close to unclean Gentiles with strange customs and accents. It was in Jerusalem that Peter's accent gave him away as a follower of Jesus (Mt 26:73, "for your accent betrays you"). But how could the

---

[1]For a biblically informed approach to immigration from a Hispanic perspective, see M. Daniel Carroll R., *Christians at the Border: Immigration, the Church, and the Bible*, 2nd ed. (Grand Rapids: Brazos, 2013).

Messiah come from Galilee, such a lowly and unattractive place? Jesus was not the right kind of Jew to be the Messiah. Jesus had an accent! Mexican-American theologian Virgilio Elizondo uses the term "Galilee principle" to highlight this dynamic at work in the ministry of Jesus and his disciples, namely, that "*what humans reject, God chooses as his very own.*"[2] Surprisingly, Jesus calls his disciples and does his ministry out of the borderlands of Galilee, and from Galilee hands over his authority to the church to make disciples of all nations by baptizing and teaching (Mt 28:16-20). The disciples share in their Lord's own marginality, and God surprises us by using the lowly as instruments of his salvation. Elizondo's Galilean principle is the Gospels' version of Paul's teaching on the wisdom of the cross, according to which "the foolishness of God is wiser than men, and the weakness of God is stronger than men" (1 Cor 1:25).

Mirroring Yahweh's heart for marginalized neighbors, Jesus extends God's compassion to outsiders, bringing them into the kingdom. On one occasion, he restores the life of an outcast who was marginalized twice, a Samaritan leper, bringing him into his Father's kingdom (Lk 17:11-19). Jesus walks along a border despised by many, the shady region between Samaria and Galilee.[3] Borderlands are often in the outskirts, in places where rejected folks make their dwelling. Can God work out his salvation from such a place? Where no one else dares to walk, Jesus shows up and brings the kingdom of God to the unclean and rejected. There, ten unclean lepers cried out to Jesus for mercy, were healed, and ultimately restored to their communities. In the story, only the most unlikely character, a Samaritan leper, praised God for his healing and returned to give thanks to Jesus. Samaritans were considered enemies of God's people, unworthy to receive God's blessings. Yet this "foreigner," alone among all the cleansed lepers, is brought into the kingdom by faith. The story shows how Jesus reaches out to those on the margins of church and society, bringing healing and restoring their lives with neighbors and before God.

In Matthew's picture of the last judgment (Mt 25:31-46), Jesus' self-identification with "the least of these my brothers" (v. 40) in their most basic human needs serves as another example of his embodiment of Yahweh's love for

---

[2]Virgilio Elizondo, *Galilean Journey: The Mexican-American Promise* (Maryknoll, NY: Orbis, 1983), 91. He cites 1 Cor 1:28.

[3]For a homily on Luke 17:11-19 from the perspective of God's inclusion of the marginalized into his kingdom, see Leopoldo A. Sánchez M., "Along the Border," in *Sermons from the Latino/a Pulpit*, ed. Elieser Valentín (Eugene, OR: Wipf & Stock, 2017), 48-64.

the lowly and despised. Matthew frames Jesus' teaching on "the Son of Man" in the context of a representative Christology, according to which "whoever receives you receives me, and whoever receives me receives him who sent me" (Mt 10:40). He who receives the Son receives the Father, and he who receives the disciples receives the Son. The disciples act in the name of, under the "authority" of (Mt 28:18), or as an extension of their Lord in the world. Like their Lord, they are either rejected or welcomed.

Will the nations receive Jesus in his representatives (that is, his "brothers") and, in so doing, welcome Jesus into their lives? By feeding the hungry, giving drink to the thirsty, clothing the naked, welcoming the stranger, and visiting the sick and those in prison, these righteous or blessed ones "did it to me [Jesus]" (Mt 25:34-45). Their place in the kingdom of life has already been prepared for them, their works of love follow them, and so the King welcomes them into their inheritance at the last day. But those who "did not minister to you [Jesus]" or "did not do it to me [Jesus]" through acts of care and compassion on behalf of "the least of these my brothers" are not welcomed into the kingdom ("depart from me," v. 41; cf. Mt 7:23; and "go away," Mt 25:46). Apart from Christ, their lawlessness and unrighteousness follow them, and their destiny is hopeless and bleak, namely, "the eternal fire prepared for the devil and his angels" (Mt 25:41; cf. 18:8) or "eternal punishment" (Mt 25:46). The way of the kingdom of life is sweeter. Those who belong to the King cannot do other than extend the hand of welcome and care for "the least of these."

In one of Paul's exhortations to holiness, we hear similar language applied more broadly to Christians' dealings with their enemies: "If your enemy is hungry, feed him; if he is thirsty, give him something to drink; for by doing so you will heap burning coals on his head" (Rom 12:20; cf. Prov 25:21-22). Heaping burning coals stood as a sign of generosity toward the needy, which was often reciprocated with regret over past grievances and a renewed spirit of friendship. In a show of solidarity, Christians also "remember those who are in prison, as though in prison with them, and those who are mistreated, since you also are in the body" (Heb 13:3). Such solidarity assumes a certain identification with suffering as a shared human experience, but also a Christlike disposition to love the unlovable.

As a marginal community of disciples in the world, the church is called to embody her Lord's own concern for outcasts. His disciples are called to identify with those who are excluded from God's blessings. We see the church's outward move toward outcasts in the mystery of Pentecost. The Spirit of the ascended Christ pushes the church out of her comfort zone in Jerusalem toward neighbors who were in some way or another excluded from the blessings of the kingdom (see Acts 1:8; 8:1). Neglected Greek-speaking Jewish widows (Acts 6:1-6), despised Samaritans with an intertwined history of mixed religion and mixed race (8:4-25), a God-fearing Ethiopian eunuch without full access to the temple (8:26-39), and the unclean and uncircumcised Gentiles at the house of Cornelius (Acts 10) are notable examples of people from communities considered unworthy to become full members of God's kingdom. Nevertheless, through the Word of God, baptism for the forgiveness of sins, and the gift of the Holy Spirit (Acts 2:38), the excluded are brought into the family of God. Through the preaching of good news, outcasts receive the hand of welcome and become brothers and sisters in Christ by the power of the Holy Spirit.

Early Christians remembered the poor among them. They assisted the hungry, "every one according to his ability" (Acts 11:29), and even "beyond their means" (2 Cor 8:3). At times they gave so much of what they possessed that "there was not a needy person among them" (Acts 4:34; see also 2:44-45). The pillars of the church in Jerusalem asked Paul and Barnabas to "remember the poor" (Gal 2:10). Paul took this request to heart by giving churches instructions on a collection for the saints in Jerusalem—an undertaking that characterized much of his apostolate (1 Cor 16:1-4; cf. Rom 15:25-28; 2 Cor 8–9). Like their proclamation of the good news to outsiders, the early Christians' concern for the needy extended beyond the confines of their own churches. Calling the saints in Galatia to "do good to everyone," Paul shows that the church works "especially" though not exclusively for those "of the household of faith" (Gal 6:10). As part of their "spiritual worship" (Rom 12:1), Paul exhorts the church in Rome to "contribute to the needs of the saints and seek to show hospitality" to strangers (v. 13) and to "not be haughty, but associate with the lowly" (v. 16).

In a similar vein, the author of Hebrews reminds Christians to "show hospitality to strangers, for thereby some have entertained angels unawares" (Heb 13:2). Recalling times of old when God himself visited his people in the form of unexpected guests (see Gen 18:1-21), Christians are called to adopt Abraham's readiness to embrace and serve unexpected strangers. We see again that life in the Spirit or holiness includes loving the unlovable, embracing the excluded, and bringing into the community of life all those who are outcast and yearn for compassion and belonging.

## CATECHETICAL IMAGES: ABRAHAM'S HOSPITALITY, CHRIST IN THE STRANGER

In Scripture, hospitality is a gift of the Spirit. Both Chrysostom and Luther present Abraham as a prominent biblical model of hospitality. They highlight the unmerited character of the divine hospitality embodied by the patriarch. Both authors also reflect on Christ's and his disciples' identity as marginalized strangers in the world, and both remind us of God's love for the "least of these" and other vulnerable neighbors like exiles or migrants. Their teachings paint a picture of the church as a welcoming community in the world.

***John Chrysostom: Theater masks, Abraham's example, shipwreck rescue.*** In one of his memorable sermons on the parable of Lazarus and the rich man, John Chrysostom draws the minds of his hearers to the contrasting character of these men and the ends met by both in the afterlife. Transporting his audience to the world of the theater, the preacher shows that appearances can be deceiving when we judge people by their acting persona and not by their true disposition. Although the rich man wears the mask of luxury and wealth before the public in this life, he is the poorest of men before God due to his "great poverty of virtue," his inhospitable heart toward the poor.[4] By contrast, Lazarus wears the mask of poverty and chronic illness in the theater of everyday life, yet he "lives in righteousness and piety" and thus is the most virtuous and richest of men before God.[5]

When the masks come off, at the moment of death, the true nature and destiny of both men is revealed. The rich man ends up in torment; the poor man is carried to Abraham's bosom (Lk 16:22-23). The preacher draws attention to the fact that the rich man sees Lazarus with Abraham, the patriarch who showed hospitality to the three visitors at Mamre (Gen 18:1-8; cf. Heb 13:2), and suggests that such a sight was meant to "convict him of his inhospitality."[6] Using the story

---

[4]John Chrysostom, *On Wealth and Poverty*, trans. Catharine P. Roth (Crestwood, NY: St. Vladimir's Seminary Press, 1984), 47. In a collection of excerpts on hospitality from the early church, Oden includes several sections of Chrysostom's writings; see Amy G. Oden, ed., *And You Welcomed Me: A Sourcebook on Hospitality in Early Christianity* (Nashville: Abingdon, 2001), 39, 42-43, 60-66, 91-92, 103-5, 110, 114-16, 137, 160-63, 206, 246-49, 286-90.

[5]Chrysostom, *On Wealth and Poverty*, 48.

[6]Chrysostom, *On Wealth and Poverty*, 50; cf. 117.

as a mirror to warn hearers of their own inhospitable ways, the preacher contrasts Abraham's eagerness to run out of his tent door to meet and bring complete strangers into his house with the rich man's cold apathy toward the poor man at his gate whom he passed by every single day.[7] Will we be like Abraham or the rich man?

Chrysostom goes on to show how Abraham did not extend the hand of hospitality to the three strangers because of their moral virtue but merely because of their need. Here the preacher adds another layer of depth to his message, inviting hearers to discern why Christians should be eager to practice hospitality at all.

> You also, when you receive someone, famous and illustrious, if you show great eagerness, have done nothing remarkable, for the virtue of the guest often forces even the inhospitable person to show great good will. It is great and remarkable, however, when we receive anyone who happens by, even outcasts and worthless people, with great good will.[8]

Christian philanthropy does not operate on a quid pro quo basis. The beauty of hospitality lies in its entirely unmerited character, and therefore reflects not only the divine will but the character of God whose mercy reaches out to the unworthy apart from their merits.[9] Unremarkable love embraces what is remarkable; remarkable love embraces what is unremarkable.

Hospitality among marginalized neighbors reflects the character of God's providence, who sends the rain over the just and the unjust alike (Mt 5:45). The preacher reminds hearers that "the almsgiver is a harbor for those in necessity . . . whether they are bad or good."[10] In the same way, neighbors who have experienced "the shipwreck of poverty" in their lives should not be judged or examined as to their good deeds, but should be rescued from their misfortune and brought to safe harbor.[11] Blessed Abraham becomes an example worthy of imitation since "he did not meddle or interfere with those who passed by," inquiring about or judging their manner of life, but simply received them in their

---

[7]Chrysostom, *On Wealth and Poverty*, 50-51.

[8]Chrysostom, *On Wealth and Poverty*, 51.

[9]"Need alone is the poor man's worthiness. . . . We show mercy on him not because of his virtue but because of his misfortune, in order that we ourselves, unworthy as we are, may enjoy His philanthropy. For if we were going to investigate the worthiness of our fellow servants, and inquire exactly, God will do the same for us." Chrysostom, *On Wealth and Poverty*, 53.

[10]Chrysostom, *On Wealth and Poverty*, 52.

[11]Chrysostom, *On Wealth and Poverty*, 52.

need.[12] The question is not whether marginality comes about through personal or social causes, but whether shipwrecked persons are rescued and brought to safe harbor.

Since Christians are not judges of character but vessels of philanthropy, they practice hospitality by unlocking the door of their hearts and welcoming sojourners in their need.[13] In doing so, they also embody God's heart for "the least of these" and welcome Christ himself when entertaining strangers who seem "small and insignificant" in the eyes of the world.[14] By contrasting the rich man's lack of hospitality with Lazarus's marginality and position with Abraham, the preacher convicts hearers of their self-righteousness toward those often deemed unworthy of care in this life, grounds hospitality in the divine will and heart, and offers the example of Abraham as an embodiment of God's unconditional hospitality for strangers.

***Martin Luther: Exiles' plight, church as refuge, stranger Christ, love of the cross.*** In his *Lectures on Genesis*, Luther draws on the tradition of lifting up Abraham as a saintly example of hospitality.[15] In his commentary on Genesis 18, Luther notes that the patriarch learned to practice generosity toward strangers from the exile of the church in the world and his own experience as an exile. The first lesson comes from Adam, whom Satan deceives in Paradise away from God's word in order to drive him out of Eden as "a stranger and an exile."[16] As in the first Eden, the devil continues to stir up trouble everywhere God's Word is preached and takes hold among his people. Every time Satan was unable to darken the hearts of God's people or take the Word away from them, "he raged against their possessions, drove them out of their homes, and vexed them in exile by whatever means he could."[17] Adam the exile becomes a type of the persecuted church in the world. After Adam, all humans become suffering exiles in the world, looking for a lasting home in Paradise.

---

[12]Chrysostom, *On Wealth and Poverty*, 53.

[13]Citing Job 31:32, Chrysostom writes, "For he [Job] also accurately imitated the generosity of his ancestor [Abraham], and because of this he said, 'My door was open to every corner.' It was not open to one and closed to another, but simply was unlocked for everyone." Chrysostom, *On Wealth and Poverty*, 53.

[14]Chrysostom, *On Wealth and Poverty*, 51-52.

[15]Luther, *Lectures on Genesis: Chapters 15–20*, *LW* 3:176-200; parts of this section on Luther's teaching concerning Abraham's hospitality are taken from a fuller treatment in Leopoldo A. Sánchez M., "The Church is the House of Abraham: Reflections on Martin Luther's Teaching on Hospitality Toward Exiles," *Concordia Journal* 44, no. 1 (2018): 23-39.

[16]Luther, *Lectures on Genesis: Chapters 15–20*, *LW* 3:179; cf. 3:184.

[17]Luther, *Lectures on Genesis: Chapters 15–20*, *LW* 3:179.

Luther highlights the harsh reality of religious persecution inflicted on Christians in his day and speaks to the role of the church as a refuge for them in the present.

> The church can and must not be indifferent to these difficulties of the brethren. By God's command and by the instruction of the forefathers it is constrained to practice works of mercy, to feed the hungry and the thirsty, *to receive exiles hospitably*, to comfort prisoners, and to visit the sick.[18]

Luther assumes that Abraham is extending hospitality to strangers who had no safe haven in surrounding cities such as Sodom and thus sought refuge in the house of the God of Abraham.[19] Therefore, for Luther, Abraham's generosity falls primarily under the church's "necessary duties toward godly brethren," and teaches us that "if we want to be Christian" we must "let our homes be open to exiles, and let us assist and refresh them."[20] The church in exile becomes a church for exiles.

The second lesson about hospitality comes to Abraham from Christ himself in proleptic form or by anticipation. Luther sees "the least" of Matthew 25 (v. 40) as a reference to Christians "afflicted by spiritual persecution,"[21] and therefore to "teachers and hearers of the Word" to whom a special "brotherly love" must be extended as "those who are of the household of faith" (Gal 6:10).[22] As one who lives by faith in God's promises, Abraham already lives out his faith in a Christlike way by treating the visiting strangers at Mamre as if they were the Lord himself.

> But just as he unknowingly receives the Lord Himself in a hospitable manner, so we, too, when we show some kindness to the least in the kingdom of God, receive Christ Himself in a hospitable manner when He comes to us in the persons of His poor.[23]

The respect and reverence, as well as the eagerness and joy, with which Abraham receives the strangers in his household and shares his gifts of drink and food with them shows how the patriarch sees in them the face of God. Notwithstanding the trinitarian interpretation of the text, of which the commentator is

---

[18]Luther, *Lectures on Genesis: Chapters 15–20*, *LW* 3:180 (italics mine).

[19]"Abraham thought that these three men had been driven from their homes because of their confession of the Word, and he saw that there would be no room for them in Sodom or in the neighboring places." Luther, *Lectures on Genesis: Chapters 15–20*, *LW* 3:187.

[20]Luther, *Lectures on Genesis: Chapters 15–20*, *LW* 3:180.

[21]Luther, *Lectures on Genesis: Chapters 15–20*, *LW* 3:184.

[22]Luther, *Lectures on Genesis: Chapters 15–20*, *LW* 3:185.

[23]Luther, *Lectures on Genesis: Chapters 15–20*, *LW* 3:184.

aware, Luther instead chooses to draw attention to Abraham's bowing down before the strangers and his calling them "my Lord" as a sign of respect for the God who visits us in the poor and distressed stranger.[24] By making this move, Luther interprets the text in the framework of a representative Christology as found in Matthew 25 according to which the one who receives God's messengers receives God himself (cf. Jn 13:20).[25]

Even though the church is still not a Paradise for the oppressed, it remains a haven, and thus heaven-like, because there Christ himself is met and served in and through his poor and exiled saints. For this reason, Luther argues that, as far as Abraham is concerned, "it seems to him that he is all but in heaven; for guests like these have happened along, and he has been considered worthy of receiving them."[26] Abraham saw the guests not only as needy "human beings," but also as strangers sent by "the Lord, whom he is worshipping in the persons of these guests" through his acts of hospitality.[27] The practice of Christian hospitality thus treats those in whom God dwells with the greatest honor possible, since being in their presence amounts to dealing with God himself. Such an attitude defines and shapes "the church, which acknowledges that it is the servant of the servants of God and—since God dwells in His saints—unworthy of so great an honor that it should give lodging to God in the persons of the brethren."[28] Summing up the meaning of the text, Luther writes:

> This is the historical meaning of this passage and an outstanding praise of hospitality, in order that we may be sure that God Himself is in our home, is being fed at our house, is lying down and resting as often as some pious brother in exile because of the Gospel comes to us and is received hospitably by us.[29]

---

[24]Luther, *Lectures on Genesis: Chapters 15–20*, *LW* 3:184-86. "All these details are recorded by Moses for the purpose of stressing that glorious faith of Abraham, whose undoubting conscience persuaded him that he had the God of heaven and earth as a guest. Not indeed that he recognized God as he recognized Him later on, but he is sure that God is coming to him in his brethren." Luther, *Lectures on Genesis: Chapters 15–20*, *LW* 3:196.

[25]"Moreover, the historical meaning shows that Abraham performed services of love toward the brethren and those who shared doctrine and faith with him. Christ, too, teaches us to do this when He says (John 13:20): 'He who receives you receives Me; but he who receives Me receives Him who sent Me.' A great and wonderful statement indeed, provided that you ponder it carefully! Abraham did not have this promise so clearly. Yet how eagerly he invites the strangers, and how generously he treats them!" Luther, *Lectures on Genesis: Chapters 15–20*, *LW* 3:186.

[26]Luther, *Lectures on Genesis: Chapters 15–20*, *LW* 3:186.

[27]Luther, *Lectures on Genesis: Chapters 15–20*, *LW* 3:188.

[28]Luther, *Lectures on Genesis: Chapters 15–20*, *LW* 3:188.

[29]Luther, *Lectures on Genesis: Chapters 15–20*, *LW* 3:189.

Since identity and action go together, Abraham becomes not only "a father of faith and of believers," but also "a father of good works . . . a most beautiful example of love, gentleness, kindness, and all virtues."[30] Here Luther has in mind primarily "brotherly love" among believers. Yet he also teaches that the love of God in Christ extends beyond the boundaries of the church. Although the "Christian charity" that flows from faith among spiritual brothers and sisters may be seen as "greater than that general kindness which is extended even to strangers and enemies when they are in need of our aid," hospitality still extends to others for at least three reasons.[31]

First and most obviously, believers are not the only ones "who experience misfortune" in this world, and thus our compassion toward them falls under God's command to love the neighbor.[32] Second, God in his providence extends his goodness to all creation. Through acts of mercy, Christians especially serve as an extension of the Father's work in the world. By doing so, they follow the words of Christ in the Sermon on the Mount, where he "exhorts us with the example of the Heavenly Father to show kindness also to our enemies."[33] Correspondingly, we note, for instance, that in the context of Christendom in his day, Luther appealed to the role of the state in providing refuge to believers who were suffering religious persecution.[34] But he also acknowledged that Christians should practice and advocate at some level for generosity "toward those who are strangers in the state, provided that they are not manifestly evil. . . . Even though he is not suffering because of the Word but is in distress in other respects, he should not be disregarded by us."[35] God's love in Christ pours over into the world from the church.

Third, and no less significant, is the argument that Christians show hospitality to strangers because the church is, at heart, an exiled community in the world. Since Abraham "lived in exile after his departure from Ur of the Chaldeans,

---

[30]Luther, *Lectures on Genesis: Chapters 15–20*, *LW* 3:185; cf. 3:190.

[31]Luther, *Lectures on Genesis: Chapters 15–20*, *LW* 3:189.

[32]Luther, *Lectures on Genesis: Chapters 15–20*, *LW* 3:185.

[33]Luther, *Lectures on Genesis: Chapters 15–20*, *LW* 3:185.

[34]"Satan rages and through the pope, the bishops, and tyrannical princes fills the entire world with poor people and exiles who roam about in misery, thirst, hunger, and are oppressed in various ways. Hence there should be some Lot, there should be an Abraham, and there should be some little domain of a godly prince in which there can be room for such people; for where there is no house, there can be no hospitality." Luther, *Lectures on Genesis: Chapters 15–20*, *LW* 3:179.

[35]Luther, *Lectures on Genesis: Chapters 15–20*, *LW* 3:183-84.

wandered through the land of Canaan, and did not live in one definite place," he represents the pilgrim church, which has no final resting place to call her own in this world.[36] As a sojourner in exile, Abraham "endured the rigors of the weather in the open country and under the sky; he was often troubled by hunger, often by thirst."[37] The hardships the patriarch suffered as an exile "enabled him to learn to be gentle, kind, and generous toward exiles."[38] Like Abraham, the church has a unique opportunity to stand in solidarity with people who find no place of their own to call home due to either religious persecution or other misfortunes of life. For this reason, when compared to the lack of hospitality one often finds in the world and its leaders, the church acts as a home of Abraham in the world.[39]

Luther does not refer in this commentary to his own experience as a persecuted Christian and displaced person in his own homeland, but he is still clearly aware of the plight of exiles passing through German lands. He notes how his prince, Elector John Frederick the Magnanimous, welcomed exiles fleeing for refuge and safety.[40] For various reasons, he also shows his frustration with different sectors of society—"nobles, the burghers, and the peasants"—that he feels are not assisting the churches enough in their outreach efforts toward exiles.[41] In the end, Luther is not merely interested in admonishing a few groups. Instead, he calls to repentance all Christians who, acting according to the flesh, fail to act generously toward strangers.[42] When God's people look at strangers through "physical eyes," they do not see God or Christ as a "truly present Guest" in these persons; therefore, like Abraham, they "must have inner eyes of faith."[43] Hospitality is the fruit of faith in Christ leading to acts of loving Christ in the stranger.

---

[36]Luther, *Lectures on Genesis: Chapters 15–20*, *LW* 3:180.

[37]Luther, *Lectures on Genesis: Chapters 15–20*, *LW* 3:180.

[38]Luther, *Lectures on Genesis: Chapters 15–20*, *LW* 3:180.

[39]Luther, *Lectures on Genesis: Chapters 15–20*, *LW* 3:188.

[40]Luther, *Lectures on Genesis: Chapters 15–20*, *LW* 3:182.

[41]Luther, *Lectures on Genesis: Chapters 15–20*, *LW* 3:182.

[42]"Today nobody gives anything." Luther, *Lectures on Genesis: Chapters 15–20*, *LW* 3:182. "Since we do not have this faith, we are not at all like Abraham, and we are very slow in performing these services of love. But if we were convinced by an unquestioning conscience that when we receive some brother or someone exiled because of the Word or otherwise in distress, we are receiving God Himself and that on the Last Day we shall have the Son of God Himself to bear witness to the service, we, too, would surely rejoice over the arrival of guests and would not think that we were being burdened." Luther, *Lectures on Genesis: Chapters 15–20*, *LW* 3:195-96.

[43]Luther, *Lectures on Genesis: Chapters 15–20*, *LW* 3:196. "The fact that we are slow to do these services and are either displeased or grumble when brethren arrive—these are signs of a faith which, if not altogether

Seeing with the right eyes makes all the difference. Reasons abound for turning the other way when encountering strangers, exiles, refugees, and immigrants in our midst. Luther acknowledges the presence of "impostors and idle beggars . . . who abuse the generosity of the godly."[44] Like some widows in Paul's day (see 1 Tim 5:16), Luther similarly notes how some people, including some who seek help "under the pretense of being exiles in distress," have become "an unfair burden which is imposed on the churches."[45] In spite of such situations, abuse does not remove the church's responsibility to attend to the need of the desperate and vulnerable, exercising a measure of common sense discernment even as she maintains a Christlike attitude in her dealings with neighbors.

> If we are deceived now and then, well and good. In spite of this our good will is demonstrated to God, and the kind act which is lost on an evil and ungrateful person is not lost on Christ, in whose name we are generous. Hence just as we should not intentionally and knowingly support the idleness of slothful people, so, when we have been deceived, we should not give up this eagerness to do good to others. Christ heals ten lepers, and He knew that only one would be grateful (Luke 17:11-19). This will also be our lot, and we should not on this account give up our eagerness to confer benefits on others.[46]

A fundamental problem getting in the way of our eagerness to welcome the "other" is that the stranger's "physical appearance is a hindrance to us."[47] Strangers do not look lovely and desirable by worldly standards, yet Christ comes to us in his poor saints, and God calls us to care for the undesirable. In the last theological thesis of his *Heidelberg Disputation* (1518), Luther expands on the type of love that is at work when the church sees the vulnerable neighbor with the eyes of faith and according to the wisdom of the Spirit. Thesis twenty-eight draws a contrast between two types of love: "The love of God does not find, but creates, that which is pleasing to it. The love of man comes into being through that which is pleasing to it."[48] This contrast corresponds to the *Disputation*'s earlier and fundamental distinction

---

dead, is nevertheless asleep and very lazy." Luther, *Lectures on Genesis: Chapters 15–20, LW* 3:196. "This faith is the chief thing, but the flesh hampers it in us in various ways. Like an intervening wall, it obstructs our eyes and prevents us from recognizing God in our brethren, as Abraham did, and from worshiping Him so dutifully." Luther, *Lectures on Genesis: Chapters 15–20, LW* 3:199.

[44]Luther, *Lectures on Genesis: Chapters 15–20, LW* 3:188-89.

[45]Luther, *Lectures on Genesis: Chapters 15–20, LW* 3:182.

[46]Luther, *Lectures on Genesis: Chapters 15–20, LW* 3:183.

[47]Luther, *Lectures on Genesis: Chapters 15–20, LW* 3:196.

[48]Luther, *Heidelberg Disputation, LW* 31:41.

between two types of theologians, namely, the theologian of glory and the theologian of the cross.[49] Luther does not use the term "theologian" as a narrow reference to a "professional" theologian or church worker, but as a broad designation for any person who interprets the world theologically and operates according to such a way of seeing the world. Everyone, in this sense, is already a theologian. The more important question is what kind of person or theologian one thinks, acts, and *loves* like—a theologian of glory or a theologian of the cross.

The theological theses can be divided into four parts, dealing with the impossibility of humans to perform works of the law to earn righteousness before God (theses one through twelve), the inability of free will to avoid sin (theses thirteen through eighteen), the two kinds of theologians and how they approach the knowledge of God (theses nineteen through twenty-four), and finally the contrast between human love and the love of God for and in humans (theses twenty-five through twenty-eight).[50] Correspondingly, theologians of glory put their final trust in the beauty of their works (law), right choices (free will), and knowledge of God through what they see in creation.[51] When used to establish one's worthiness to be loved by God, such gifts from God that are good in themselves (that is, our works, will, and reason) nevertheless become "mortal sins" or "evil" in that they will drive us to self-pleasing love and thus away from God's unmerited and unconditional love in Christ.[52] Theologians of the cross, on the other hand, put their final trust in God's works, will, and reason as revealed in the crucified Christ—a move that appears "evil" in the eyes of the world but is ultimately "good" for us.[53] This

---

[49]The contrast between two types of theologians comes through especially in theses 19–21. Luther, *Heidelberg Disputation*, *LW* 31:40.

[50]For this categorization of the theological theses, see Gerhard O. Forde, *On Being a Theologian of the Cross: Reflections on Luther's Heidelberg Disputation, 1518* (Grand Rapids: Eerdmans, 1997), 21-22.

[51]In critiquing human attempts to know God through what is seen in creation, Luther has in mind the speculative theology of the scholastics. Yet the critique is aimed broadly at human attempts to justify God or justify oneself before God on the basis of a rational explanation of "the invisible things of God" (thesis 22)—that is, divine attributes such as "wisdom, glory, power"—through human logic and thus apart from God's self-revelation in Christ and faith in him. The problem lies in making too much of natural theology, so that it replaces Christian or redemptive revelation. For Luther's explanation of thesis 22, see Luther, *Heidelberg Disputation*, *LW* 31:53-54.

[52]"Although the works of man always seem attractive and good, they are nevertheless likely to be mortal sins" (thesis 3). Luther, *Heidelberg Disputation*, *LW* 31:39. "A theologian of glory calls evil good and good evil" (thesis 21). Luther, *Heidelberg Disputation*, *LW* 31:40.

[53]"Although the works of God always seem unattractive and appear evil, they are nevertheless really eternal merits" (thesis 4). Luther, *Heidelberg Disputation*, *LW* 31:39. In his explanation of thesis 21, Luther notes that "the friends of the cross say that the cross is good and [human] works are evil, for through the cross

radical trust in God makes the theologian of the cross receptive to God's radical love in Christ.

Gerhard Forde sees the structure of the theses as "a great arch stretching between two pillars," moving the reader or hearer "from the law of God to the love of God through the cross."[54] Going through the cross amounts to being conformed to Christ in his death and resurrection, or moving a person from being a theologian of glory to becoming a theologian of the cross. This means dying to our human attempts to earn the love of God—even if only in part—in order to be raised anew as a humble receiver of God's lavish love in Christ. If we interpret the whole *Disputation* from the lens of the last thesis dealing with the two types of love, we can then reflect on the ways human love, which naturally looks for "that which is pleasing to it," must be put to death in us, so that the love of God "which does not find, but creates, that which is pleasing to it" might shape us to love that which is not naturally attractive to us. In his explanation to thesis twenty-eight, Luther defines "the love of the cross":

> Rather than seeking its own good, the love of God flows forth and bestows good. Therefore sinners are attractive because they are loved; they are not loved because they are attractive. For this reason the love of man avoids sinners and evil persons. Thus Christ says: "For I came not to call the righteous, but sinners" [Matt. 9:13]. This is the love of the cross, born of the cross, which turns in the direction where it does not find good which it may enjoy, but where it may confer good upon the bad and needy person. "It is more blessed to give than to receive" [Acts 20:35], says the Apostle.[55]

Since thesis twenty-eight speaks of the love of God in and through the saints, it deals with the sanctified life. Being made a certain kind of person through death and resurrection, theologians of the cross embody or image in their lives the type of divine love they have received in Christ. Luther calls such embodiment "the love of the cross, born of the cross." Just as God did not love us because we were good but rather made us good by his love, so also God's people do not love neighbors because they are attractive or beautiful but rather confer on them God's spiritual and material blessings to restore them as God's beautiful creation. At this point,

---

works are destroyed and the old Adam, who is especially edified by works, is crucified." Luther, *Heidelberg Disputation*, *LW* 31:53.

[54]Forde, *On Being a Theologian*, 21.

[55]Luther, *Heidelberg Disputation*, *LW* 31:57.

our renewal, sacrificial, and hospitality models of sanctification coalesce into one reality. Faith receives and bestows God's love, born of the cross, to undesirable neighbors at the margins, whether sinners, those weak in faith, enemies, the poor, the sick, the needy, exiles, refugees, and other vulnerable neighbors. Such sacrificial and welcoming love, which loves the unlovable, flows through those who walk the way of the cross, dying to self in order to make room for the least attractive neighbors among us.

## CROSSING BORDERS: SPIRITUAL PRACTICES AND ISSUES IN THE CHRISTIAN LIFE[56]

As humans created by God for communion, we crave belonging and acceptance. All of us share a common need for friendship, for being included, and thus value welcoming and being welcomed. Hospitality is the practice or ritual that speaks to those aspirations of the human family. But we also experience alienation, isolation, betrayal, and hostility. And at times, unfortunately, we practice such values too, thus showing the dark, sinful side of the human race, the worst in us. We feel connected to others through friendship and the hand of welcome, but also feel marginalized from others when rejected and excluded.

These experiences are common to all humans, but there are certain groups of people whose lives bring a higher degree of awareness to them. Immigrants are one of such groups. They experience hospitality and marginality, welcome and hostility, and have to navigate discourses about who belongs and who does not. Are they in or out? When I first came to the United States as an immigrant, I experienced signs of hospitality. For two years, I lived with a family of farmers in Iowa who welcomed me with open arms in a new country. They took care of this stranger in their midst. Over time, I became one of them, as it were. When they asked me to partake in the regular family rituals of toilet and pigsty cleaning with the rest of the children, I realized right away that I had become a member of the family! I belonged.

Many teachers and students at the local high school often went out of their way to make me feel included as a valued member of the learning community. Above all, it was by partaking in the rituals of weekly concert, marching, jazz, and pep

---

[56]With the exception of my engagement with Alfaro's and Snavely's works, this section is a revised version of Leopoldo A. Sánchez M., "Can Anything Good Come Out of ___________. Come and See! Faithful Witness in Marginality and Hospitality," *Concordia Journal* 41, no. 2 (2015): 111-23.

band rehearsals and performances that I experienced a very strong sense of acceptance in a strange land. We created music together, which required listening to one another. We needed each other's contributions in order to make music. Hospitality blessed both host and guest. To be honest, I also experienced subtle and crass signs of hostility and alienation in the community. I was often reminded that I was not entirely or fully in, that I was a stranger after all, a foreigner, an alien. I was reminded that I had an accent and, in the worst cases, was the object of discriminatory jokes and remarks against me or about people who talked and looked like me. I was not one of them. I felt like an outsider.

Experiences of hospitality and marginality, stories about who belongs and who does not, words about who is in and who is out. Experiences immigrants typically go through. As the church meets neighbors in these spaces of hospitality and marginality and listens to their hopes and struggles, what can she learn from their life stories? And then how can the Christian story deepen or illuminate these experiences with the embracing gospel of God's love in Christ?

***The experience of* mestizaje.** To answer those questions, might it not be especially helpful to hear from theologians whose life experiences in the world have made them especially aware of the pain of exclusion and the gift of a welcoming community? What about exploring some insights from theologians who are themselves immigrants, members of ethnic or linguistic minorities, or who have lived and worked among such neighbors on a regular basis? By focusing on their experiences of exclusion and welcome, we can learn broader lessons about the human condition that apply to persons beyond members of a particular group and begin to ask how the Christian story speaks to such experiences.

In his book *Models of Contextual Theology*, Stephen Bevans offers six different ways to think through the relationship between the church and the world. One of such ways is what he terms the transcendental model, which starts with "the authenticity of the subject who is trying to express his or her experience as a person of faith and a person in a particular context."[57] In this model, "the best person to do theology within a particular context is the subject of that context as such."[58] Beginning with particular life experiences, theologians then reflect on what these mean in light of the Scriptures and their theological tradition. Broader lessons are then drawn for others, both for the saints in the church and neighbors in the world.

[57]Stephen B. Bevans, *Models of Contextual Theology*, rev. ed. (Maryknoll, NY: Orbis, 2002), 106.

[58]Bevans, *Models of Contextual Theology*, 106.

The model moves from the particular to the general, from the individual or communal to that which humans share in common.[59]

Using this approach, we can posit that the experiences of hospitality and marginality among particular individuals or communities in which the theologian lives and works have a broader significance beyond their immediate context. Such events speak beyond the individuals or communities originally involved and transcend, at some level, the situation in which such experiences first arose. Bevans suggests a horticultural or garden image to sum up what the transcendental model entails. As he puts it, "A person can be inspired to work in his garden because of the example—or lack thereof—from others working in their own gardens."[60] Applying this insight, we may argue that Christians can learn much about interacting with people in the world who are marginalized and crave belonging when they see and hear from brothers and sisters who have those aspirations and needs on a consistent basis, when they live and work most closely among them, or when they themselves come from those communities.

Take for instance the Hispanic experience of *mestizaje*, that is, the coming together of races and cultures as a result of the conquest and colonization of the Americas. Justo González, Protestant Hispanic historian and theologian, has reflected on what such an experience of Hispanic origins—one that is not without its fair share of violence—means not only for Hispanics but also for the church at large today. Although unique to Hispanics, González argues that the colonial experience of *mestizaje* transcends Hispanic culture. It has implications for others. If so, we have an example of Bevans's transcendental model at work.[61]

González has argued that being a Hispanic or *mestizo* Christian is an ambivalent reality, a bittersweet event.[62] Bittersweet because *mestizaje* resulted from a

---

[59]According to Bevans, this model holds "that while every person is truly historically and culturally conditioned in terms of the content of thought, the human mind nevertheless operates in identical ways in all cultures and at all periods of history. . . . No matter where one knows or when one knows, one begins to process in experience, organizes this experience by means of concepts, judges the truth or falsity of one's conceptual understanding in judgment, and integrates the knowledge arrived at in judgment by means of a decision." Bevans, *Models of Contextual Theology*, 107.

[60]Bevans, *Models of Contextual Theology*, 108.

[61]Bevans includes González under this model, highlighting his proposal to deepen major themes in the Christian tradition by looking at them through Hispanic eyes. Bevans, *Models of Contextual Theology*, 113-16. Bevans focuses on Justo L. González, *Mañana: Christian Theology from a Hispanic Perspective* (Nashville: Abingdon, 1990).

[62]See González, "Yesterday," in *Under the Cross of Christ—Yesterday, Today, and Forever: Reflections on Lutheran Hispanic Ministry in the United States* (St. Louis: Concordia Seminary Publications, 2004), 23-46.

violent evangelization, in which the cross and the sword went hand in hand. In other words, *mestizaje* comes from a painful experience of hostility and shame, an experience of marginality. Yet being a *mestizo* is also and ultimately, under the sign of the cross, a sweet event. A new creation still came about in spite of violence and death. Life out of death. By his mysterious design, God brought together into one a new people, extending his mercy to outsiders, transforming their shame into the joy of being brought into the family of God, an experience of divine embrace to be celebrated. God's inclusion in his kingdom breaks into *fiesta*.[63] In the new creation, outsiders are invited to have fellowship with the Lord and partake of his meal.

González's hymn "De los cuatro rincones del mundo" (Eng. "From the Four Corners of the Earth") sums up well what the theologian sees as the broader implications of the experience of *mestizaje* for the church's identity and hope. The first stanza reads:

> From the four corners of the earth
> Flow the blood in these veins
> Of these peoples who sing their pains,
> Of these peoples who speak their faith;
> Unwitting blood brought from Spain,
> Noble blood of the suffering native,
> Strong blood of the oppressed slave,
> All blood surely bought on the cross.[64]

Through song, González reimagines the Hispanic experience of *mestizaje*, the coming together of the blood from many continents to form a new people, as a sign in creation of the church catholic that is gathered from "the four corners of the earth." One notes how, for the hymnist, the Hispanic experience of *mestizaje* deepens the church's understanding of her own identity as a catholic or universal church, which in turn reminds her to live according to her identity as a global church of many languages and cultures. The church learns that she herself is *mestizo*.[65] She is neither monocultural nor monolingual.

---

[63]González's reflections on *mestizaje* are shaped significantly by Mexican-American theologian Virgilio Elizondo. For example, see Elizondo, *Galilean Journey*, 115-25.

[64]Justo L. González, "De los cuatro rincones del mundo," in *Libro de liturgia y cántico* (Minneapolis: Augsburg Fortress, 1998), 450 (translation mine).

[65]The Hispanic experience of *mestizaje* also reminds the church of her intercultural identity in the world. Beyond inclusion, intercultural exchange leads to collaboration with others. It moves beyond

At the end of the stanza, note how the church's understanding of her catholicity or *mestizo* identity in turn illuminates the Hispanic experience of *mestizaje*, making it clear to people who experience hostility and shame from others because of their mixed skin color, ethnicity, accent, or language that the gospel is for all nations, all ethnic and language groups. We see how the gospel also deepens the experience of *mestizaje*, giving it a fresh meaning in light of the cross. Christ shed his blood to redeem all blood. Another stanza from González's hymn reads:

> From the four corners of the earth,
> From the flowery fields of Cuba,
> From Asia and the coast of Africa,
> From Borinquen, Quisqueya, and Aztlán:
> To this blessed hour has brought us
> Heaven's mysterious divine design,
> Which all brought together into one destiny
> And from all one reign will create.[66]

In this stanza, the author sings about the experience of God's inclusion of the *mestizo*—again, a sign of the church catholic—into his reign. By "Heaven's mysterious divine design," God brings about the *mestizo* people from the blood of many nations and lands. They do not only share a common destiny of pain and alienation, but also, in light of the Christ whose blood redeems all blood, a common hope of being invited and welcomed into God's family. Reflecting on the hybrid or mixed identity of the Mexican-American, who is neither Mexican enough for the Mexicans nor North American enough for the North Americans, Elizondo has noted that the *mestizo* experience of belonging neither here nor there in the world allows them to have a special place in their heart for neighbors who are ignored or rejected.[67] Similarly, in his Galilean ministry, Jesus chooses excluded Galileans as his disciples, showing his self-identification with, mercy toward, and giving of new life

---

multicultural discourses, in which there is merely an awareness of otherness but no meaningful engagement with the "other." It sets the stage for creating a community of "happy exchanges" (see our sacrificial model in chapter five). For a reflection on Hispanic identity in light of *mestizaje*, see Leopoldo A. Sánchez M., "Hispanic Is Not What You Think: Reimagining Hispanic Identity, Implications for an Increasingly Global Church," *Concordia Journal* 42, no. 3 (2016): 223-35.

[66]González, "De los cuatro rincones del mundo" (translation mine).

[67]Elizondo, *Galilean Journey*, 100-102; for a Hispanic American exploration of "otherness" from the perspective of exile, see Fernando F. Segovia, "In the World but Not of It: Exile as Locus for a Theology of the Diaspora," in *Hispanic/Latino Theology: Challenge and Promise*, ed. Ada María Isasi-Díaz and Fernando F. Segovia (Minneapolis: Fortress, 1996), esp. 212-17.

in God's kingdom to "sinners" rejected by the world. In González's hymn, we see how the gospel deepens the experience of *mestizaje* in light of the cross and the hope of the new creation, going as far as calling such a human experience a "blessed hour." Sweetness out of bitterness.

***The Spirit of Christ working at and from the margins.*** In recent years, US theologians have explicitly formulated a Spirit Christology that addresses the situation of neighbors at the margins of church and society. In his published dissertation, *Divino Compañero*, Sammy Alfaro argues that a Spirit Christology provides a more apt framework than a Logos Christology for making sense of the five-fold gospel Pentecostal description of Jesus as Savior, Sanctifier, Baptizer, Healer, and Soon-Coming King. Drawing mainly from early Pentecostal authors, Alfaro shows the decisive influence of the Spirit in the fulfillment of Jesus' past work of atonement for our sins, as well as in the effecting of his saving work by sanctifying the regenerated from evil, empowering of the church for a holistic mission (inclusive of healing), and preparing the church to meet Christ the King at the last day.[68]

As a Hispanic immigrant to the US and church planter in a southwestern bilingual Hispanic church, Alfaro brings his Spirit Christology into conversation with Latin American and US Hispanic Christologies, which explore how the story of Jesus addresses the situation of people marginalized due to socio-economic, racial-ethnic (*mestizo*), and gender status.[69] Inspired by the devotional spirituality of *coritos* (canticles) and hymns learned in his tradition, Alfaro argues that the image of Jesus as the *Divino Compañero* (Eng. "Divine Companion") who walks with his people in the midst of their suffering, poverty, and marginality best captures the experience of US Hispanic Pentecostals.[70] Alfaro's contribution lies not only in showing how the pneumatic dimension of Jesus' mission better articulates his own tradition's Christology, but also in imbuing it with a more socially conscious dimension that speaks to US racial-ethnic minority and minoritized churches and communities. In doing so, Alfaro invigorates christological reflections from the Latin American and US Hispanic world with a much needed pneumatological element.

---

[68]Sammy Alfaro, *Divino Companero: Toward a Hispanic Pentecostal Christology* (Eugene, OR: Pickwick, 2010), 28-46.

[69]Alfaro, *Divino Compañero*, 94-114.

[70]Alfaro, *Divino Compañero*, 128-47.

Adopting a similar concern for the ethical implications of Jesus' life and mission for outcasts, Andréa Snavely's published dissertation, *Life in the Spirit*, offers the first attempt to bring into conversation Stanley Hauerwas's post-Constantinian critique of the church with my approach to Spirit Christology. Although the post-Constantinian calling of the church to repentance for being too comfortable in its accommodation to worldly values remains helpful, he argues that only a Spirit Christology, which fosters living in the Spirit of Jesus today, offers the energy to transform the American church into a countercultural community that adopts the ways of nonviolence, contentment and sharing, and racial reconciliation and unity.[71]

Critical of what he sees as his own Pentecostal tradition's progressive accommodation to American values, Snavely argues that even though the early Pentecostals did not articulate theologically their experience of sonship as one of conformity to Jesus' life in the Spirit, they nevertheless mirrored in their lives a Christlike commitment to kingdom values.[72] In his final reflections, the author sums up the kind of cruciform life the Spirit of Christ seeks to engender in the North American church today.

> As the lives of the early twentieth-century Pentecostals demonstrate, the indwelling of the Spirit is the reason people live like Jesus lived; by loving and trusting God by living non-violently, by being content with God's provisions and sharing with those in need, and by being content with how one has been created by God so as to love people of other ethnicities and cultures.[73]

Snavely's third description of life in the Spirit of Jesus as one where racial and ethnic boundaries are broken down most closely resembles a hospitality model where outcasts are welcomed into Christ's body. Life in the Spirit for Jesus meant not only that he loved people who were "despised and shamed" by political and religious society, but that by identifying himself "with the despised, he became the most despised among them since there was no greater shame and despising by [sic] which culture inflicted than crucifying a person on the cross."[74] A cruciform Spirit Christology shows that Jesus was despised precisely because he was born of Mary by the power of the Spirit as an outsider, and through his mission as God's

---

[71]Andréa Snavely, *Life in the Spirit* (Eugene, OR: Pickwick, 2015), 1-70, 154-93.
[72]Snavely, *Life in the Spirit*, 154-61.
[73]Snavely, *Life in the Spirit*, 193.
[74]Snavely, *Life in the Spirit*, 185.

Spirit-anointed servant unto death on a cross he proclaimed God's kingdom to outcasts.[75] By becoming "the most radically 'other' of humanity" in the Spirit before God and for our sake, Jesus takes the place of sinners but also brings about a new ethnic society where the "other" at the margins who is most despised and unlike us is loved into God's kingdom.[76] Life in the Spirit is cruciform in that it made Christ the radically other in his death for our salvation, but also in that it leads the saints to be the radically other in the world by welcoming the other into the fellowship of Christ where not the righteous but sinners are welcomed, where the unlovable are loved.

***The need to belong.*** The renewal model of the sanctified life addresses our need for reconciliation, as well as problems such as fatalism and perfectionism, through a life of daily repentance. The dramatic model deals with our need for security, vigilance, and resilience in the midst of life's struggles through reliance on the Word, prayer, and disciplines of accountability and support. The sacrificial model offers purpose in a world full of neighbors in need through a life of simplicity, sharing, and service. The hospitality model addresses the need for belonging and acceptance through practices of hospitality in marginal places. It involves a habitual disposition to love the unlovable and the inclusion of outcasts into God's family and mission.

At the beginning of this chapter, we read biblical stories through marginal eyes: Jesus the Galilean and his Galilean disciples, Jesus walking along the despised border between Samaria and Galilee, and Philip's work among Greek-speaking Jewish widows, Samaritans, and an Ethiopian eunuch. How can these biblical narratives shape our witness? First, we recognize that neighbors out there can connect at some level with these stories. They have felt welcomed and unwelcomed. Who are those neighbors in our neck of the woods? Who are the Galileans, lepers, Samaritans, or Greek-speaking Jewish widows in our churches and communities? Christians who work among immigrants, minorities, the sick and dying, the lonely, or other marginal groups, can use these stories to connect with them. They provide some common ground for listening and learning about the struggles and needs of neighbors. They provide a common human story, as it were, to engage those who

---

[75]Snavely, *Life in the Spirit*, 185.

[76]Snavely, *Life in the Spirit*, 186-87; for an important Pentecostal theological interpretation of Pentecost as the revelation of the Spirit's radical hospitality toward the other and its implications for justice, economics, and cultural transformation, see Daniela C. Augustine, *Pentecost, Hospitality, and Transfiguration: Toward a Spirit-inspired Vision of Social Transformation* (Cleveland, TN: CPT Press, 2012).

feel lonely or rejected. But these biblical stories also complement those experiences of marginality with the light and hope of God's grace in Christ, providing a new perspective on life for the outsiders in our midst. They are not just common stories, but truly new stories when seen through the cross. What they offer, therefore, is a surprising view of God's gracious disposition toward and work through marginal characters.

The biblical stories shared above function as stories of God's justification in and through Christ. They remind us of what Oswald Bayer once called "the ontological significance of justification," which means that every single human being seeks to be justified by someone, and therefore justify his or her own life in this world.[77] As Bayer puts it: "It is not true that judgment is an addition to being. What I am, I am in my judgment about myself, intertwined with the judgment made of me by others."[78] Even the claim that I do not need to be justified by anyone is itself yet another attempt at justification. Ultimately, neither reason nor works, neither theodicy nor praxis, can justify us, but only God's unconditional word of justification in Christ.[79] In general, this universal need for justification arises from our need to belong, be accepted, included, and assured our lives are worth living before God and others.

In our reading of biblical narratives through marginal eyes, we are reminded that people are not received into God's kingdom and family because of their language, culture, ethnicity, place of origin, or any other condition in life. Humanity is not justified by these things, but only through faith in Christ. Without saying the word "justification" once, all these stories of God's welcoming inclusion of marginal characters into his kingdom of life through Christ teach us that humans are not deemed worthy or unworthy of divine grace on the basis of their pedigree, but on the basis of God's mercy in Christ. This realization radically shapes how we live the sanctified life among and interact with people who are outcasts, leading us to embrace the apostolic teaching on hospitality with new vigor.

What are other marginal spaces where we can learn from and in turn illumine experiences of hostility and hospitality today with the message of God's sure sign of justification in Christ? To name a few relatively recent groups in our collective memory, I think of religious minorities being persecuted around the

---

[77]Oswald Bayer, *Living by Faith: Justification and Sanctification*, trans. Geoffrey W. Bromiley (Grand Rapids: Eerdmans, 2003), xi-xiv.

[78]Bayer, *Living by Faith*, 4.

[79]Bayer, *Living by Faith*, 9-25.

world, who are experiencing the care and hospitality of humanitarian agencies and Christian groups. I think of unaccompanied minors along the US-Mexico border, including Christians, who are in many cases fleeing persecution in their own homelands and are caught in the middle of a heated national debate on immigration law and reform that, though important, seems to go nowhere and often vilifies these minors. And yet these folks, as well as other refugees and immigrants, are still experiencing, in many cases, the hospitality of people in the US through social agencies such as Catholic Charities USA, Lutheran Immigration and Refugee Service, and World Relief, working in partnership with individuals and congregations nationwide.[80] I think of places like Ferguson, Missouri, where we have seen both signs of hostility and hospitality, alienation and community, including an outpouring of Christian support for marginal neighbors through prayer, donations, advocacy, and community dialogue. These responses of solidarity in listening and then speaking and acting become, in the light of Christ, a mirror that reflects his self-identification with persons deemed unlovable and an invitation to them to taste and see his salvation and love.

[80]For theological reflections on immigration, see M. Daniel Carroll R. and Leopoldo A. Sánchez M., eds., *Immigrant Neighbors Among Us: Immigration Across Theological Traditions* (Eugene, OR: Pickwick, 2015). The book includes a selected bibliography.

7

# WORK, PRAY, AND REST

## THE DEVOTIONAL MODEL

In this chapter, we explore the *devotional* model of sanctification. Approaching the Christian life as an expression of devotion to the Creator, this model depicts life in the Spirit as a rhythm of movement and repose, work and rest. In this model, the Spirit conforms us to Christ in his life of prayer and obedience to the Father. By directing us to reflect on God's created intent for his creatures, reflected most fully in a human life by his Son, this model can assist pastors and others in promoting among people a life of work, prayer, rest, and play. The model deals with issues such as the need for balance and rhythm in life, avoiding the dangers of burnout and idleness, and inviting persons to stand still and rejoice in God's gifts of creation and salvation in a busy world.

### BIBLICAL PICTURES: CREATED FOR RHYTHM, FREED IN CHRIST, DELIGHTED IN GOD'S WORKS

Already on the first day of creation, God establishes a rhythm to life on earth. There is darkness and light, evening and morning, night and day (Gen 1:4-5). Later, when God creates male and female in his image and likeness (vv. 26-27), their lives are already framed in the context of this daily cycle. In each God-given day, there is therefore a time for motion and activity, and a time for stillness and repose. Resting in God, humans reflect the Creator in whose image they were made, for even the Lord God who made the heavens and the earth "rested on the seventh day from all his work that he had done" (Gen 2:2). Just as God blessed his work (Gen 1:22, 28) and called all of it "very good" (v. 31), God also blessed the day of rest and "made it holy" (Gen 2:3). Humans reflect the image and likeness of God in their stewardship of the earth (Gen 1:26-31), which in God's own design also includes a time for rest and renewal.

Life in the garden is life in communion with the Creator. When God breathed into the man "the breath of life," he created humans for fellowship with him (Gen 2:7). The garden becomes the place of God's presence, and therefore the place of worship where God addresses the man through his word and he responds to it (Gen 3:8). Even before the fall into sin and the breaking of this blissful fellowship with their Creator, man and woman were made for prayer, for conversation with the Lord God—even if such talk turned awkward after disobeying God's word (Gen 3:8-13). In the Garden of Eden, God speaks his commands to Adam, who hears God's "you may . . ." and "you shall not . . ." (2:16-17). God also speaks his blessings to Adam, providing him not only with life (v. 7) but also with rest (vv. 3, 21), a garden to work and keep (v. 15), and "a helper fit for him" taken from his rib as he lay in a "deep sleep" (vv. 18, 20-21). As creatures living under God's evening and morning, man and woman were made to be devoted to God from the very beginning—working and resting, listening and praying in the garden God fashioned for them by speaking his words of life.

Since the fall into sin, humans have attempted to subvert their own creaturely identity as people devoted to the Creator by transgressing the rhythm of life he established for their own good. For instance, work is experienced differently now than in that first garden. Working the ground outside Eden (Gen 3:23) is no longer bliss but pain, thorns and thistles, and sweat (3:17-19)—indeed, a sort of preamble to death. You toil and then you die! (v. 19).

With this sober picture of Genesis 3 in the background, the author of Ecclesiastes reminds his readers that a person can either make too little of work, failing to "take pleasure in all his toil" and see it as "God's gift to man" (Eccles 3:13; see also Eccles 2:24-25; 3:22; 8:15). Or one can make too much of work, giving in to "despair over all the toil of my labors" for fear that someone else might enjoy its fruits who did not work for it (Eccles 2:20-21) or out of "envy of his neighbor" (4:4), so that "his heart does not rest" (2:23; see also 4:12) and he ends up depriving himself of any joy or pleasure (4:8). Lest work become a replacement for wisdom, a sort of idol replacing the Creator, and given the reality of our eventual return to the dust (3:20-22), man is reminded that when death comes he "shall take nothing for his toil that he may carry away in his hand" (5:15). Although there is a place for work under God's blessing for his creatures, neither the business of humans in their labors nor the lack of sleep that often accompanies these anxious endeavors can replace the work of God who alone does all things according to a higher wisdom (8:15-17). In the end, the Preacher teaches us that wisdom lies in reorienting the busy creature toward the Creator, calling people to fear God and fulfill his commandments, which are "the whole duty of man" (12:13). True wisdom lies in the worship of God: "The fear of the Lord is the beginning of knowledge; fools despise wisdom and instruction" (Prov 1:7).

Keeping the day of rest went beyond the required cessation of rest, that literal respite without which life is impossible. It was also a day of spiritual resting and refreshment in God, and thus a time of prayer. The psalmist mirrors the Creator by resting from his labors in order to behold the greatness of his magnificent works (Ps 92:5; see also Gen 2:1-3). Remembering that the Sabbath became an occasion for the creature's worship of the Creator, the psalmist sings praises in thanksgiving for God's goodness in the rhythm of each day (Ps 92:1). Accordingly, the psalmist thanks the Lord for his "steadfast love in the morning" and his "faithfulness by night" (v. 2). The day of rest becomes a time to cease focusing on one's works in order to behold, sing, and rejoice in "the works of your hands" (v. 4), in the gift of God's creation. As a tangible way to embody the command to rest, the people of Israel celebrated a sabbatical year every seven years in which the land itself was allowed to rest (Ex 23:10-11). All creation praises the works of God (Ps 104:24-30; Ps 148).

In light of the exodus experience, the observance of the Sabbath also served as an occasion for Israel to remember and thank the Lord for his salvation (Deut 5:12-15). God commanded his chosen people to keep the Sabbath as a sign of his everlasting covenant with them, "that you may know that I, the Lord, sanctify you" (Ex 31:12-13, 16-17). Israel declared the Lord's favor over his people in other sabbatical cycles. Every seven years, creditors were to forgive debtors their debts and slaves were freed (Deut 15:1-2; Ex 21:1-3). Moreover, every fifty years, after the completion of seven cycles of sabbatical years, a great Jubilee Year was celebrated for a similar purpose (Lev 25:8-22). On the Day of Atonement, the sound of the trumpet announced the Lord's favor throughout the land (v. 9). Since no work was done on the Day of Atonement, the people could take time to focus on God's work of reconciliation with his fallen creation through the cleansing of their sins. A sinful people were blessed to rest in God's deliverance from their sins and rejoice in his forgiveness. Israel's sabbatical cycles stood as an ongoing invitation to worship, to behold and praise God for his mighty works of creation and redemption.

God created us for worship, for a life devoted to him and our neighbor. By working and by resting both literally and spiritually, humans express their love for God and his gift of creation. After the fall, such human devotion to the Creator wavers, upsetting the rhythm of life established by God and placing humanity in a restless state. Summed up in the love of God and neighbor, God's good law served as a way to teach humans again the way of wisdom and true worship, but it did not possess the power to bring about in humans such a life of devotion (Gal 3:10-12; Ps 119). Yet God did not choose the way of the law as the means of justifying humans before his presence, since even before the law was given to Moses, God had already established a covenant with Abraham whereby "the righteous shall live by faith" (Gal 3:7-9, 11).

Instead, in the mystery of the incarnation, God "sent forth his Son, born of a woman, born under the law, to redeem those who were under the law" (Gal 4:4-5). Through his death on a tree, Christ "redeemed us from the curse of the law," thus putting to rest all restless human attempts of justification before God through the works of the law and bestowing on us his Spirit to make us children of God through faith in him (3:13-14). Through baptism into Christ, humans are no longer slaves to the law, but are adopted as free sons and daughters of God (3:23–4:7). Paradoxically, having been freed from the law, the adopted children are now free to use their freedom in Christ to fulfill the law of love ("the law of Christ," Gal 6:2) by serving one another according to the fruit of the Spirit (Gal 5:13-25). By walking in the Spirit, they embody their faith in the world as devoted children of the Father. Their faith in Christ and the gift of the Spirit received through faith (Gal 3:2, 5) shape their Christlike character in their works and relationships.

Born under the law, Jesus fulfills it even unto death for our redemption, giving us rest from the law as a means to salvation before God. At the same time, Jesus embodies the law in his life as an example of love that we might grow in our devotion to God and neighbor. Jesus observes regularly the Sabbath as a day of spiritual rest, attending synagogue where God's Word is read and heard, and prayers are raised to God (see Lk 4:16). Prayer is part of the rhythm of Jesus' whole life (Lk 3:21; 4:42; 6:12; 9:18, 28-29; 11:1-13; 22:39-46; 23:34, 46). Jesus "rejoiced in the Holy Spirit," thanking and praising the Father for revealing his good news to the disciples (10:21). Jesus also keeps busy doing his Father's business throughout his life and mission. Yet he does not let his work get in the way of his time with the Father. At times, he withdraws from the needy crowds in order to pray (5:15-16).

Over against a legalistic approach to the day of rest that included a cessation of labor that prevented assisting neighbors in need, Jesus criticized the hypocrisy of his critics and proclaimed himself "lord of the Sabbath" (Lk 6:5; Mk 2:28). Rest had become an idol, driving people away from God's command to love their neighbor. Jesus unveils this idolatry and reorients the day of rest toward devotion to God in his merciful acts. In the midst of a Sabbath day, for instance, Jesus goes against the harsh letter of the Sabbath upheld by traditionalists in his day by doing the work of healing, and thus freeing a woman from her bondage to sickness and Satan (Lk 13:10-17; see also 6:1-11; 14:1-6). In an ironic twist, Jesus' healing of the woman actually leads her and the people to fulfill the true spirit of the Sabbath, since the woman "glorified God" and the people "rejoiced" in the work of God (Lk 13:13, 17; cf. 18:43).

As Lord of the Sabbath, Jesus embodies God's favor toward neighbors in bondage to sin, death, and Satan, freeing them to worship God. In doing so, Jesus uses the day of rest to carry out the Father's life-giving work (Jn 5:1-17), pointing us to himself as rest for weary souls (Mt 11:25-30). Because of their sin and rebellion against God in the desert, a disobedient Israel could never enter God's rest (Heb 3:7-19). Through faith in Christ, God's promise of rest stands for those who believe, and they can look forward to entering that final rest in God's presence at the last day (Heb 4:1-11). In that final "Sabbath rest for the people of God," the believer will reflect most fully the Creator's own resting on the seventh day by resting "from his works as God did from his" (Heb 4:9-10; see also Rev 14:13). In the meantime, Jesus teaches his disciples that "the Sabbath was made for man, not man for the Sabbath" (Mk 2:27) and calls them to embody their faith in him by sharing the Father's mercy for his weary and restless creatures (Mt 12:7-8).

Prayer and work. These aspects of a human life, designed by God, come to fulfillment in the mystery of the Son's incarnation. For the Son, life in the Spirit involves a life of divine wisdom, the human embodiment of full devotion to God and neighbor even unto death. Such devotion makes Jesus' whole human life a holy act of worship, a life marked by prayer and obedience to the Father on behalf of weary humans in a restless world. Jesus' life in the Spirit allows neither work nor rest to become idols that get in the way of the love of God and neighbor by reorienting all labor, prayer, and respite to the proper worship of God.

Walking by the Spirit, Christians live by faith in Christ and are no longer slaves to the law, yet are eager to fulfill the law of Christ without neglecting that rest which praises and give thanks to God for all things. Living according to the rhythm of a life of activity and respite brings God's people a delight that invites them to rejoice in God's creation in manifold ways. We see a glimpse of this joy in the psalmist's celebration of God's deeds through dance and music: "Let them praise his name with dancing, making melody to him with tambourine and lyre!" (Ps 149:3). Rejoicing through song, they reflect God's own delight in his works of creation (Ps 104:31-34). Dancing to the sound of music, they image the Father's celebration of his prodigal children's return home (Lk 15). Being still in the Lord, marveling at his providence and grace, Christians can also delight in and celebrate God's creation through play. Through an array of leisurely activities, hobbies, and other pastimes that afford them the opportunity to explore that creative space between work and rest, Christians reclaim their joy in God's creation and trust in God's ultimate care of the world.

## CATECHETICAL IMAGES: SOLITUDE AS WORSHIP, SPIRITUAL IDLENESS, BLESSED WORK, AND RESTING IN GOD

In this section, we focus on Basil's reflections on solitude or retreat as the proper setting for the worship of God and on Chrysostom's and Luther's reflections on the spiritual meaning of the day of rest. Prior to his rise to the episcopacy, Basil spent time in solitude as a monk. In a letter to his friend Gregory, Basil reflects on the benefits of spiritual retreat for shaping saints to become devoted to God not only in the solitude of a monastery but in the way they carry out their duties in the world. For Chrysostom the preacher, true sabbath takes place when God's saints are moved from spiritual idleness to devotion to God and neighbor. In continuity with these early church voices, Luther notes how resting in God includes setting time aside for the Word. Even though the Reformer sees labor as part of God's created intent for humanity, he also includes literal rest in his understanding of worship as an act of faith that places all cares in God's hands even while we sleep. All authors address forms of idolatry that get in the way of true devotion to God, which includes responsible stewardship of the created gifts of work and rest.

***Basil of Caesarea: Solitude as Christlike self-denial, quiet as the start of sanctification, and the artist's imitation of a devotional life.*** In a letter to his friend Gregory, Basil draws lessons from his brief experience in monastic solitude near Pontus (modern day Niksar, Turkey) for the church's life of devotion to God. Seeing the monastic life as one example of Christlike self-denial that prepares the mind for a quiet receptivity to God's truth and doctrine, Basil speaks to the benefits of retreat in shaping a habitual life of devotion in prayer, study of Scripture, singing of hymns, and labor. In so doing, the monk in retreat, who would one day become a bishop in the public eye, paints a compelling picture of life in the Holy Spirit as a sanctification process of being continually receptive to the remembrance of God's truth and drawn to the imitation of God's saints and their virtues in the world.

Beginning his letter by admitting his own lack of appreciation for the gift of solitude, Basil moves on to describe his retreat experience as a way of dying with Christ, a way "to keep close to the footprints of Him who has led the way to salvation."[1] Citing Jesus' words in Matthew 16:24 ("If anyone would come after me, let him deny himself and take up his cross and follow me"), Basil presents the monastic life as an example of a cruciform life, a form of self-denial that prepares the way for devotion to God. Because the mind is too often "distracted by a thousand worldly cares" that make it difficult for the heart to "be able to clearly apprehend the truth" and "readily receive every impress of divine doctrine," the saints "must strive after a quiet mind."[2] Basil is not arguing against Christians' responsibility for daily tasks, especially in married and family life, but warning against "the day's anxieties" that take over the mind so as to stifle the worship of God.[3] As a form of death to the anxieties of the world, or the idolatrous attachment

[1]Basil of Caesarea, *Letter II* 1 (*NPNF*[2] 8:110).

[2]Basil of Caesarea, *Letter II* 2 (*NPNF*[2] 8:110).

[3]Basil uses terms like "frenzied cravings," "rebellious impulses," and "hopeless attachments" to describe a life of anxious attachment to everyday tasks that leads to detachment from devotion to God in prayer and the Word (Basil of Caesarea, *Letter II* 1 [*NPNF*[2] 8:110].). In the broader context of Basil's letter, one notes that the problem does not lie in the care of the world through one's given tasks, but in worldly care about such tasks. The issue is not fulfilling one's daily tasks, but an idolatrous conception of work.

to the busyness of the world, the quietness of solitude forms the mind and heart for a receptive spirituality.

Solitude "stills our passions" in order to make us still in God through habituation in "pious exercises" or spiritual disciplines that "nourish the soul with divine thoughts."[4] In light of the cruciform context in which Basil lays out his receptive spirituality, dying to one's idolatrous attachment to the world makes room for the worship of God through practices such as prayer, work, singing of hymns and spiritual songs, and the study of Scripture.[5] For the monk, "quiet . . . is the first step in our sanctification," because it leads the wondering mind away from focusing on self through attachment to the world "to the contemplation of God."[6] The point of detachment is to make room for faith. However, far from thinking of the contemplation of God as a neglect of one's duties in the world, Basil notes that the purpose of detachment from worldly cares and anxieties lies in forming the person to grow and flourish in all kinds of spiritual virtues that will "properly enable the good man to discharge all the duties of life."[7] To have true devotion toward God is to leave the world in order to return to the world and engage it rightly.

Basil argues that "the study of inspired Scripture is the chief way of finding our duty, for in it we find both instruction about conduct and the lives of blessed men."[8] The true worship of God makes room for receptive faith to grasp God's truth and doctrine, but also to imitate his saints' virtues or ways of self-denial in the world for the sake of love. Through meditation on Scripture, the saints are brought into the narratives and lives of the saints of old and are thus invited to receive these "images of godly living, for the imitation of their works."[9] Basil likens the way of imitation of the saints to the work of a painter who diligently seeks to capture in his own artistic expression the features of the model he is replicating.

> Thus, generally, as painters, when they are painting from other pictures, constantly look at the model, and do their best to transfer its lineaments to their own work, so

---

[4]Basil of Caesarea, *Letter II* 2 (*NPNF*[2] 8:110).

[5]Basil of Caesarea, *Letter II* 2-3 (*NPNF*[2] 8:110-11).

[6]Basil of Caesarea, *Letter II* 2 (*NPNF*[2] 8:111).

[7]Basil of Caesarea, *Letter II* 2 (*NPNF*[2] 8:111).

[8]Basil of Caesarea, *Letter II* 3 (*NPNF*[2] 8:111).

[9]Basil of Caesarea, *Letter II* 3 (*NPNF*[2] 8:111). For example, saints learn endurance from Job amid great adversity and meekness and from Moses amid criticisms against him.

> too must he who is desirous of rendering himself perfect in all branches of excellency, keep his eyes turned to the lives of the saints as though to living and moving statues, and make their virtue his own by imitation.[10]

In the same way as the study of Scripture focuses distracted minds on God's truth and doctrine, as well as on the imitation of the lives and virtues of the saints, prayers "after reading [Scripture] . . . find the soul . . . more vigorously stirred by love towards God."[11] Through the Word and prayer, "the worshipper flees from all things and retreats to God."[12] Prayer and the Word in the solitude of the perilous wilderness appears in the dramatic model of sanctification as part of the cycle of life in the Spirit that the saints depend on amid the attacks of the devil. Basil's description of solitude adds an additional but complementary dimension, namely, the notion of a life devoted to God that moves the worshiper from unhealthy attachment to the world to virtuous living in the world. The worship of God, which begins with self-denial and is internalized by the soul's receiving of God's Word and praying to God, is also externalized in the ways the worshiper honors God through his body. Thus, a measured manner of speech, modesty of dress, and moderation in eating are all seen as forms of virtue that honor and give glory to God.[13] Whereas cruciformity runs through the renewal and sacrificial models of sanctification, respectively, as a dying to self in order to be raised through the forgiveness of sin and a dying to self to make room for needy neighbors, the devotional model highlights a dying to self in order to make room for devotion to God.

Basil's pneumatology is subtle, implicit throughout his letter. His reflections invite us to ask *who* shapes the Christlike life of self-denial, of quiet and receptive solitude, he speaks of. The answer comes indirectly in a reference to God's indwelling of the saints as his temple. Prayers informed by Scripture focus the mind on God through "memory" or "recollection," but such remembrance of God "in

---

[10]Basil of Caesarea, *Letter II* 3 (*NPNF*[2] 8:111).

[11]Basil of Caesarea, *Letter II* 3 (*NPNF*[2] 8:111).

[12]Basil of Caesarea, *Letter II* 3 (*NPNF*[2] 8:111).

[13]Basil of Caesarea, *Letter II* 5-6 (*NPNF*[2] 8:111-12). For instance, concerning eating, Basil observes: "One ought not to eat with any exhibition of savage gluttony, but in everything that concerns our pleasures to maintain moderation, quiet, and self-control; and, all through, not to let the mind forget to think of God, but to make even the nature of our food, and the constitution of the body that takes it, a ground and means for offering Him the glory, bethinking us how the various kinds of food, suitable to the needs of our bodies, are due to the provision of the great Steward of the Universe." Basil of Caesarea, *Letter II* 5-6 (*NPNF*[2] 8:112).

self" is established by "God's indwelling" in the saints.[14] By God's indwelling "we become God's temple . . . when the worshipper flees from all things and retreats to God . . . and passes his time in the pursuits that lead to virtue."[15] Together with Basil's description of "a quiet mind" as one that is able "to apprehend the truth," his comments make implicit use of the Johannine portrayal of the third person as the "Spirit of truth," the Paraclete who dwells in the disciples to teach them and bring to remembrance in them the words of Jesus (see Jn 14:16-17, 26). By describing God's saints as his "temple" and spiritual virtues in language akin to aspects of the fruit of the Spirit (for example, patience, gentleness, self-control), Basil also makes implicit use of Pauline teaching on the indwelling Spirit's leading role in the saints' glorifying of God in their bodies and their crucifying of the desires of the flesh (see 1 Cor 6:19-20; Gal 5:22-24).

***John Chrysostom: Idleness and leisure, sleep and beds, food and nourishment.*** In his first sermon on the parable of the rich man and Lazarus, Chrysostom denounces the former's life of self-indulgence and luxury. The fundamental problem with such life lies in the spiritual "idleness" it reveals and fosters—an idleness that orients the creature toward self and away from proper devotion to God and neighbor. The Antiochene preacher likens the self-indulgent man in the parable, and those who follow in his footsteps, to the rich and powerful who ignored or trampled on the poor in the days of the Old Testament prophet Amos. Because of their injustice and unrighteousness, the Lord spoke through Amos, denouncing the feasts, assemblies, burnt offerings, and songs of the people of Israel (Amos 5:21-25). Chrysostom calls their practices "false sabbaths" (Amos 8:5) because they set themselves against the Sabbath's true purpose, namely, "that they may remove themselves from worldly cares and devote all their leisure to spiritual concerns."[16] Paradoxically, their lack of actual work (or idleness) on a Sabbath reveals a deeper spiritual idleness in the things of God, a neglect in living as children of the covenant and fulfilling God's commandments.

Leisure lies not in enjoying an extravagant lifestyle at the expense of faith and love, but in devoting oneself to "spiritual work" or "spiritual matters, such as self-control, kindness, and hearing the divine Scriptures."[17] Fulfilling

---

[14]Basil of Caesarea, *Letter II* 4 (*NPNF*$^2$ 8:111).

[15]Basil of Caesarea, *Letter II* 4 (*NPNF*$^2$ 8:111).

[16]John Chrysostom, *On Wealth and Poverty*, trans. Catharine P. Roth (Crestwood, NY: St. Vladimir's Seminary Press, 1984), 23.

[17]Chrysostom, *On Wealth and Poverty*, 23.

the Sabbath amounts to living according to the fruit of the Spirit. Breaking the Sabbath or practicing "false sabbaths," on the other hand, leads to making God's created gifts into idols by indulging in them while neglecting God's own suffering creatures.[18] A life of "unnecessary luxury" in the public eye manifests an internal forgetfulness of the heart that keeps a person away from attending to the necessary needs of hurting neighbors, as well as to the life of prayer and thanksgiving.[19] The idolatry of self replaces the virtue of true devotion.

To get at the horizontal problem of lack of devotion through neglect of the poor, the golden-mouthed preacher uses the image of a bed. Drawing his hearers' attention to Amos's denunciation of the powerful who "sleep upon beds of ivory, and live delicately on their couches" while others around them suffer (see Amos 6:4-6), Chrysostom asks whether "the beauty of the bed" amounts to a "sweeter or more pleasant" pleasure, or rather "a more onerous and burdensome" experience.[20] God's gift of sleep, which brings humans peaceful rest in the world, can also become a restless accuser of the conscience.

> For when you consider that, while you sleep on a bed of ivory, someone else does not enjoy even sufficient bread, will your conscience not condemn you, and rise up against you to denounce this inequity?[21]

Yet a bed can also give us a window into a beautiful life of repentance, for even a rich and powerful king like David "adorned" his bed "with tears and confessions."[22] Rather than being distracted with the restlessness of the world around him or using his "time of leisure" to rest idly like powerful people who care little for God

---

[18]The powerful showed their spiritual idleness by "gorging themselves, getting drunk, stuffing themselves, feasting luxuriously, for this reason the prophet condemned them. For when he said, 'Woe . . . to you who are approaching the evil day,' and added, 'and adopting false sabbaths,' he showed by his next words how their sabbaths were false. How did they make their sabbaths false? By working wickedness, feasting, drinking, and doing a multitude of shameful and grievous deeds." Chrysostom, *On Wealth and Poverty*, 23-24.

[19]Chrysostom, *On Wealth and Poverty*, 26-27.

[20]Chrysostom, *On Wealth and Poverty*, 24.

[21]Chrysostom, *On Wealth and Poverty*, 24. "But if we lie on silver beds, not only will we not gain any pleasure, but besides we will endure distress. For when you consider that in the most extreme cold, in the middle of the night, when you are sleeping on a bed, the poor man has thrown himself a pile of straw by the door of the bath-house, wrapping the stalks around him, shivering, stiff with cold, pinched with hunger—even if you are the stoniest of all men, I am sure that you will condemn yourself for providing for yourself unnecessary luxury while not allowing him even what is necessary." Chrysostom, *On Wealth and Poverty*, 25-26.

[22]Chrysostom, *On Wealth and Poverty*, 25.

or others, the king showed that he "loved God in his soul" by his "confession, prayers, and tears."[23]

Calling his hearers to "make a bed like this for yourself," the preacher invites us to keep the true Sabbath by resting in God's Word.[24] To do so is to seek a life beyond filling one's belly with food by making room also for the spiritual sustenance that God alone provides. Christ himself offers us an example of hungering after "divine sayings" in his feeding of the crowds, since he not only "satisfied their need" but also "led them to spiritual nourishment."[25]

To underscore God's designed intent for created life on earth, Chrysostom takes his audience back to the Garden of Eden before the fall: "At the beginning life was not made for eating, but eating for life. But we, as if we had come into the world for this purpose, spend everything for eating."[26] By making problematic the notion that life is reduced to spending and consumption, the preacher portrays self-indulgence as a form of life at odds with God's will for his creatures, and therefore, with one's own creaturely identity. The rich man's neglect of Lazarus becomes, in a sense, a form of inhumanity, a corrupted image of the full life for which humans were originally made. Through the negative example of the rich man, Chrysostom urges the saints to fulfill the divine purpose for which they were designed in the Garden of Eden by hearing God's Word, praying, and working on behalf of God's creatures.

***Martin Luther: Created for work and rest, trusting God's Word in a restless world.*** In his *Lectures on Genesis*, Luther lays out the foundations of a theology of creation that attends to the significance of work and rest in God's plan for his creatures. Luther distinguishes God's resting on the seventh day after establishing the original creation (Gen 2:2) from his continuous work in the care and preservation of creation until the end of time: "He has, therefore, ceased to establish; but He has not ceased to govern."[27] God does not only continuously preserve his creation, but will finally transform it from its corrupted state: "And on the Last Day there will be a far greater change and a renewal of the entire creation,

[23]Chrysostom, *On Wealth and Poverty*, 25.

[24]Chrysostom, *On Wealth and Poverty*, 25. Jacob's resting on the rock in Genesis 28 signifies his resting on the vision of Christ, the spiritual Rock (cf. 1 Cor 10:4).

[25]Chrysostom, *On Wealth and Poverty*, 27.

[26]Chrysostom, *On Wealth and Poverty*, 28.

[27]Martin Luther, *Lectures on Genesis: Chapters 1–5*, *LW* 1:7. Following Augustine, Luther states that Christ's words, "My Father is working until now, and I am working" (Jn 5:17), refer to God's continuous "management of the creatures, not to the act of creating." Luther, *Lectures on Hebrews*, *LW* 29:161 (cf. *LW* 1:74).

which, as Paul says (Rom 8:20), is now subjected to futility because of sin."[28] As a creative act of God, the virgin birth and incarnation, which Luther sees as the event ushering in the fulfillment of God's promise in Genesis 3:15, stands as the turning point in God's renewal of his good, yet fallen, creation through the Son's crushing defeat of Satan, sin, and death.[29]

Luther speaks of rest and work in the framework of creation and new creation, noting especially the harshness of life in its present brokenness where God's promises sustain us along a laborious journey toward our final rest in God at the end of the present age. As part of the original creation, God established the Garden of Eden and placed humans in it to work it and guard it (Gen 2:15). Had it not been for the earth's disfigurement after the fall, Adam "would have tilled the earth . . . in play and with the greatest delight."[30] Work and play go together in Paradise. Since work is now also linked to God's curse on the ground, it is experienced not only as joy but also as God's punishment against us on account of Adam's sin.[31] All the woes, stresses, and abuses associated with work remind us we are no longer in Eden, and it is at times easy to see work itself as a curse. Yet work precedes the fall as God's good will and command for us, since "man was created not for leisure but for work, even in the state of innocence."[32] Though laborious and toilsome, God's human creatures continue to do their divinely appointed work through various stations, offices, and callings at home, the state, and the church.[33]

Even in its condition as difficult or inconvenient labor, work remains a divine mandate and blessing. In his *Notes on Ecclesiastes* (1526), Luther observes that the Preacher's assessment of labor as "vanity" is not directed at the works that "God

---

[28]Luther, *Lectures on Genesis: Chapters 1–5, LW* 1:77.

[29]Luther, *Lectures on Genesis: Chapters 1–5, LW* 1:79; cf. 1:188-98.

[30]Luther, *Lectures on Genesis: Chapters 1–5, LW* 1:102.

[31]Luther, *Lectures on Genesis: Chapters 1–5, LW* 1:103. "Therefore whenever we see thorns and thistles, weeds and other plants of that kind in a field and in the garden, we are reminded of sin and of the wrath of God as though by special signs. Not only in the churches, therefore, do we hear ourselves charged with sin. All the fields, yes, almost the entire creation is full of such sermons, reminding us of our sin and of God's wrath, which has been aroused by our sin." Luther, *Lectures on Genesis: Chapters 1–5, LW* 1:209.

[32]In this context, "leisure" is used negatively as a synonym for idleness. Luther, *Lectures on Genesis: Chapters 1–5, LW* 1:103. Luther often associates idleness with the special works of members of monastic orders, who, at times, left their ordinary callings in the household to adopt so-called holier works not commanded by God. Luther also associates idleness with ecclesial officers who use their positions to acquire wealth and power, but do little to advance the work of proclaiming the Gospel. See Luther, *Lectures on Genesis: Chapters 1–5, LW* 1:213-14.

[33]Luther, *Lectures on Genesis: Chapters 1–5, LW* 1:212. Adam held all three stations since he "supported his family, ruled it, and trained it in godliness; he was father, king, and priest." Luther, *Lectures on Genesis: Chapters 1–5, LW* 1:213-14.

Himself works in us or has commanded us to work" in our vocations and callings, but rather to those self-made plans humans conceive and design apart from God's counsel.[34] Therefore, the problem lies not in our labors per se, but in the "vain anxieties" that accompany our toil.[35] Such anxieties come from a lack of trust in the Creator's present and future provision and get in the way of our present enjoyment of God's gifts of creation. Because God provides through our labors, our work can be seen as a divine blessing, and one can find joy in life despite its difficulties. When trust in God's provision replaces the restless heart's worries, it is possible to say with the eyes of faith and the Holy Spirit that man "has joy in his toil here, and here in the midst of evils he enters into Paradise."[36] Luther praises work without romanticizing it.

Humans were created for work, but also for sabbath. While God commands work for humanity's sake, God sanctifies the Sabbath for himself as a time and space for humans to worship him.

> He did not sanctify for Himself the heaven, the earth, or any other creature; but the seventh day He did sanctify for Himself. This has the special purpose of making us understand that the seventh day in particular should be devoted to divine worship. For "holy" is that which has been set aside for God and has been removed from all secular uses. Hence to sanctify means to set aside for sacred purposes, or for the worship of God.[37]

Luther paints a picture of what sanctified rest would have looked like in the Garden of Eden. There Adam praised God, gave thanks, made sacrifices, prayed, and conversed with others about the Creator's kindness and goodness.[38] In light of the saints' entrance into God's rest through their resurrection from the dead in a restored creation, Luther concludes that, before the fall, Adam must have enjoyed immortality in the blissful presence of God.[39] After the fall, "the Sabbath command

[34]"Nor is he speaking about the labor of man's hands, which was commanded by God in Gen. 3:19, 'In toil shall you eat bread,' but he is speaking about our striving and planning, by which we try to accomplish what we please." Luther, *Notes on Ecclesiastes*, *LW* 15:14.

[35]Luther, *Notes on Ecclesiastes*, *LW* 15:93. "For God has commanded the work, but forbidden the anxiety." Luther, *Notes on Ecclesiastes*, *LW* 15:70. "The labor must be present, but the burdensome and troublesome anxieties must not. One must tire his body with labor, but one's heart must be free of anxiety and be content with what is in the present." Luther, *Notes on Ecclesiastes*, *LW* 15:150.

[36]Luther, *Notes on Ecclesiastes*, *LW* 15:93.

[37]Luther, *Lectures on Genesis: Chapters 1–5*, *LW* 1:79.

[38]Luther, *Lectures on Genesis: Chapters 1–5*, *LW* 1:79-80; cf. 1:82.

[39]Luther, *Lectures on Genesis: Chapters 1–5*, *LW* 1:80.

remains for the church," and "it denotes that spiritual life is to be restored to us through Christ."[40] Such "spiritual life" amounts to the Holy Spirit's work of making alive, which is his special office since the beginning when he hovered over the first waters.[41]

Keeping the day of rest anticipates our human end and fulfills our purpose as God's creatures, since "man was especially created for the knowledge and worship of God."[42] Since humans come to know God by hearing and responding to his Word, as in the Garden of Eden, keeping the Sabbath holy has always meant setting time aside for the preaching and hearing of God's Word.[43] Resting in God by hearing his Word entails living by and rejoicing in his promises, including those dealing with the reversal of Adam's death through participation in Christ's immortality.[44] When we occupy ourselves with God's Word, "we, like Adam in Paradise, become citizens of heaven," getting a glimpse of past life in the first Eden and anticipating our future life in a new Eden.[45]

Although keeping the Sabbath included refraining from hard labor and taking time for physical rest, "so that both human beings and animals might be refreshed and not be exhausted by constant labor," Christ criticized a narrow reading of the command and pointed toward its final devotional aim in the worship of God.[46] For Luther, "a Christian interpretation" of the third commandment includes the need for workers to "retire for a day to rest and be refreshed," as well as for God's people "to hear and discuss God's Word and then to offer praise, song, and prayer to God."[47] This latter interpretation of the Sabbath concerns the "spiritual man," who rests when he "occupies himself with faith and the Word."[48] For Luther, the term "spiritual man" does not refer to a higher nature inherent in humans that somehow

---

[40]Luther, *Lectures on Genesis: Chapters 1–5, LW* 1:80.

[41]"As a hen broods her eggs, keeping them warm in order to hatch her chicks, and, as it were, to bring them to life through heat, so Scripture says that the Holy Spirit brooded, as it were, on the waters to bring to life those substances which were to be quickened and adorned. For it is the office of the Holy Spirit to make alive." Luther, *Lectures on Genesis: Chapters 1–5, LW* 1:9.

[42]Luther, *Lectures on Genesis: Chapters 1–5, LW* 1:80.

[43]"This is what the Sabbath, or the rest of God, means, on which God speaks with us through His Word and we, in turn, speak with Him through prayer and faith." Luther, *Lectures on Genesis: Chapters 1–5, LW* 1:81. "This is the real purpose of the seventh day: that the Word of God be preached and heard." Luther, *Lectures on Genesis: Chapters 1–5, LW* 1:81.

[44]Luther, *Lectures on Genesis: Chapters 1–5, LW* 1:81.

[45]Luther, *Lectures on Genesis: Chapters 1–5, LW* 1:82.

[46]Luther, "The Ten Commandments," *LC* 80, *BC*, p. 396.

[47]Luther, "Ten Commandments," *LC* 83-84, *BC*, p. 396.

[48]Luther, *Lectures on Hebrews, LW* 29:162.

transcends the body, but rather to the whole person (body and spirit) under the influence of the Holy Spirit as a new creature in Christ.[49]

For the new creature in whom God's Spirit rests, keeping the day of rest holy involves not only hearing God's Word, but also keeping it or living according to it—in other words, "devoting it [the Sabbath] to holy words, holy works, and holy living."[50] Because God's holy Word "makes everything holy," it alone sanctifies our rest and work by the power of the Spirit.[51] Holiness of life, which is included in the worship to God, comes as a result of God's sanctifying Word: "By it [the Word] all the saints have themselves been made holy."[52] There is, therefore, no greater worship in the Spirit than faith and the fruits of faith.

To worship God is to trust God and his promises. Taking time to rejoice in God's gifts, including food, play, and sleep, are ultimately signs of faith in the God who will fulfill his promises. Therefore, Christians must care about their work, but not be anxious about it or force what it will accomplish, since God alone brings about fruit in his time. In a sermon from 1522, Luther applies this teaching to the preaching task: "We should preach the Word, but the results must be left solely to God's good pleasure."[53] Speaking of the power of the Word in gaining hearts for the gospel against the abuses of the papacy of his day, Luther notes how the Reformers did not constrain anyone to believe by force, but simply proclaimed the Word and left the rest to God.

> Take myself as an example. I opposed indulgences and all the papists, but never with force. I simply taught, preached, and wrote God's Word; otherwise I did nothing. And while I slept [cf. Mark 4:26-29], or drank Wittenberg beer with my friends Philip and Amsdorf, the Word so greatly weakened the papacy that no prince or emperor ever inflicted such losses upon it. I did nothing; the Word did everything.[54]

---

[49]On Luther's use of "the antithesis *caro-spiritus*" (i.e., flesh-spirit), Prenter has shown that it corresponds to the old creature (Lat. *vetus homo*) and the new creature (Lat. *novus homo*), and furthermore argues "that the contrast *caro-spiritus* is not anthropological, so that *spiritus* means the most noble part of man, the source of his idealistic striving for God and the spiritual realities, and *caro* the sensual nature, by which man attaches himself to all the base, the outward and corruptible. No, this contrast is a theological one: *spiritus* is the whole of man, if it is dominated by the Spirit of God; and *caro* is the whole of man, if it lacks the Spirit of God." Regin Prenter, *Spiritus Creator: Luther's Concept of the Holy Spirit*, trans. John M. Jensen (Philadelphia: Muhlenberg, 1953), 5.

[50]Luther, "Ten Commandments," *LC* 87, *BC*, p. 398.

[51]Luther, "Ten Commandments," *LC* 91-92, *BC*, p. 399.

[52]Luther, "Ten Commandments," *LC* 92.

[53]Luther, *The Second Sermon, March 10, 1522, Monday After Invocavit*, *LW* 51:76.

[54]Luther, *Second Sermon*, *LW* 51:77.

In this seemingly mundane picture of Luther sleeping without a care in the world, and of his drinking the local beer with friends Philip Melanchthon (1497–1560) and Nicholas von Amsdorf (1483–1565) amid difficult times, we see the spiritual and literal senses of the Sabbath come together. Taking time to delight in God's gifts of food and drink, friendship and fellowship, and sleep flows from a trust in the Creator who made heaven and earth and thus is able to fulfill his promises. A life of devotion to God prevents us from falling prey to the idolatry of work.

## A BALANCING ACT: SPIRITUAL PRACTICES AND ISSUES IN THE CHRISTIAN LIFE

In elementary school, I disliked music classes and could not wait to stop playing what sounded to me then like a squeaky and annoying recorder. That all changed in middle school when three or four high school teachers introduced us to the world and sounds of musical instruments we had never heard or heard of before. At that moment, I fell in love with music. Early on, my parents did everything in their power to embark me on a career in music. Music became serious business, a discipline, even a school after regular school—in short, music became work! My delight in it diminished. After several years of hard labors in the conservatory, training under the pressure to become one of the best future musicians of my country's symphony orchestra, I crashed and burned. To my music teachers' dismay, I took a much needed and long rest from music. I never returned to the conservatory.

Even though I always sought to excel in musical activities well into my college years, took private instruction on my main instrument, and even flirted at times with the idea of making a career and vocation out of music, I never seriously entertained music as a full-time profession again. A career path as a teacher of theology became my main work (in the sense of livelihood), responsibility, and vocation in the church. After spending a significant amount of time learning about, growing in, and perfecting my main craft as a theologian, I decided to take up music again not as another job or profession but as a serious hobby, auditioning for a community orchestra at about the same time I started my first job as a full-time professor of theology. To build my chops, I complemented my orchestra practices with private double bass instructions. I started to rejoice once again in the gift of music and feel I have become a more mature player now than I ever was in my younger years.

While I delight in God's gift of music by playing an instrument in the company of fellow musicians, the orchestra requires mental and physical engagement. Hours of study, practice, and performance. Even so, to me it never feels like my everyday work. Like play is supposed to be, my time with music functions as a space to delight in God's gift of music with others for its own sake. While play does not have to serve an ulterior purpose, I have also seen how the time set aside for music often functions as a type of rest that energizes me for the labors that await me in other vocations in life at seminary, church, and home.

Returning to music as a serious hobby has brought balance into my life, a creative space between movement and repose—quite literally, a rhythm between daily work and rest. Of course, I rejoice also in my primary church vocation and in various opportunities to rest without having some agenda behind it. Yet music as play has given me a special space for *fiesta*, by which I mean a space for celebrating God's creation in the midst of the restlessness of life. Music has allowed me to embrace my identity as a person made for work, rest, and even play. As a new creature in Christ, the Spirit shapes us continually to live in such a way that our God-given vocations in life are carried out without giving up either our time with the Father in prayer and the Word or our delight in the Father's created gifts. In the devotional model of the sanctified life, growth in holiness is not measured as much as acknowledged and celebrated in the daily rhythm of labor, repose, and delight in God's created gifts.

***Embracing our creatureliness.*** In the catechetical flow of the Creed, the Father creates, the Son redeems, and the Holy Spirit sanctifies. Even though all three persons of the Trinity do all these works in the world indivisibly and thus in unity (Lat. *opera ad extra indivisa sunt*), the creedal arrangement still appropriates or assigns a special work to each of the persons. To the uninitiated, however, the impression can be given that the Holy Spirit only acts after the other two persons have done their respective works. Basil offers a tighter way to describe the unity of the three while retaining their distinction. In the descending pattern of the triune God's action in the world, the Father works all things through the Son in the Spirit. In other words, the Holy Spirit perfects or brings to fulfillment what God the Father brings about through his Son. This pattern applies to creation and new creation.

When we pair Genesis 1 and John 1 in a theological interpretation of Scripture, we see a trinitarian pattern in which God the Father creates and re-creates through the preexistent and incarnate Word (Gk. *logos*, Heb. *dabar*), on whom the Holy Spirit (Gk. *pneuma*, Heb. *ruaḥ*) rests (Jn 1:1-3, 14, 33; cf. Gen 1:1-3; Ps 33:6). The Spirit's resting on the incarnate Son, which at the waters of the Jordan announces the coming of a new creation ushering in a new birth into the kingdom of God (cf. Jn 1:33; 3:5-8), echoes the Spirit's hovering over the waters in the original creation (Gen 1:2). Early church theologians saw Christ's breathing of the Spirit on the church after his resurrection as the beginning of this new creation. The Spirit-breath, which made Adam a spiritual being in Paradise, but which he lost after the fall, returns to dwell in humans definitively through the glorified Son who gives the Holy Spirit (see Jn 20:22; cf. Gen 2:7). In this confluence of images, which highlights the Holy Spirit's identity as "the Lord and Giver of Life" (Nicene Creed), the Father brings his creation to fulfillment through the Son on whom the Spirit rests and from whom it is poured out to others.

The Spirit is from the beginning and, therefore, first and foremost the Creator Spirit. This means that the Spirit does not only create Adam and Eve, but also the space they inhabit and the created framework in which they live in communion with God and the rest of the creatures. As Bonhoeffer observes in his biblical study of the creation account in Genesis, God created the gift of the day (Gen 1:4-5) before anything else (including humans) and in so doing established "the great rhythm, the natural dialectic of creation."[55] By setting up the day (and night), with its inherent movement of evening and morning, the Creator has framed our lives within the natural rhythm of "repose and movement."[56] Bonhoeffer highlights how determinative this rhythm remains for life on earth, and how it points to God's continuous "giving and taking" in our lives.[57] There is, in other words, a certain repetition in the cycle of repose and movement that opens our eyes to God's daily gifts to his creation.

God's gift of the day precedes us, and so does its cycle of repose and movement. Yet God's creatures often rebel against the power of God's day by failing to submit to it.

> The day is the first finished work of God. In the beginning God created the day. The day bears all other things, and the world lives amid the changes of the day. The day

[55]Dietrich Bonhoeffer, *Creation and Fall; Temptation: Two Biblical Studies*, 1st Touchtone ed. (New York: Simon & Schuster, 1997), 29.
[56]Bonhoeffer, *Creation and Fall*, 29.
[57]Bonhoeffer, *Creation and Fall*, 29.

> possesses its own being, form, and power. . . . For us the creatureliness and miraculousness of the day has completely disappeared. We have deprived the day of its power. We no longer allow ourselves to be determined by the day. We count and compute it, we do not allow the day to give to us. Thus we do not live it.[58]

We fail to submit to the day and its rhythm when we make our work into an idol and cannot or will not find time for rest. Work becomes an idol when it transgresses the gift of God's day by trying to transcend it. But we cannot transcend this law of creation: "And there was evening and there was morning, the first day" (Gen 1:5). Lack of sleep makes us cranky and unproductive for a reason. We were made not only for movement, but also for repose. Lack of rest signals a rebellion against the day, which amounts to a denial of one's creatureliness. Taking the time to sleep, on the other hand, reminds us that the world does not ultimately depend on us in order to run, because—as the famous African American spiritual goes—"He's got the whole wide world in his hands!" How then can we embrace our creatureliness again? By learning to submit to the day as God's good gift for us. Which means learning to rejoice once again in being the creature God has made us to be.

***Spiritual rest.*** What is spiritual rest? It is the rest that the Holy Spirit makes room for in our lives. In the monastic tradition of the Benedictines, the rhythm of the day and the call to embrace it is summed up in the motto "pray and work!" (Lat. *ora et labora*). Such activities describe life in Paradise, where Adam conversed with God and worked in the Garden. But they also describe the life of Christ, the new Adam, who lived in our place the life Adam could not live by becoming the human fulfillment of God's plans for his human creatures. In his human obedience, the divine Son humbly prays to his Father and does the work the Father has given him in the Spirit. The Spirit also shapes this life in others. By its indwelling in the adopted sons (and daughters), the Spirit of the Son fulfills God's intent for their lives by making them new creatures who express their sonship (and daughterhood) both in their conversation with God (prayer) and stewardship of God's creation (work).

Reflecting on Christ's anointing into his threefold office as king, prophet, and priest, Raniero Cantalamessa argues that the Spirit who anointed Christ to fight against Satan, proclaim the Word, and pray to the Father also anoints Christians so

---

[58]Bonhoeffer, *Creation and Fall*, 28.

that they mirror the life of their Lord.[59] Drawing from his Catholic tradition, the author highlights Heribert Mühlen's definition of the church as "the continuation in history of the anointing of Christ with the Holy Spirit" and draws what he calls the moral implications of such anointing.[60] In the vein of the monastic tradition, Cantalamessa, a Capuchin priest, draws attention to Luke's picture of Jesus as a man of prayer who, though occupied in his Father's business, is not afraid to leave the crowds to go to the mountain and spend time with him in prayer (Lk 5:15-16).[61] Jesus is portrayed as a man who embodies the rhythm of *ora et labora.*

> Jesus like any other devout Israelite observed the thrice-daily fixed prayer times: at sunrise, in the afternoon during the Temple sacrifice, and at night before going to bed. If then, to all this we add the thirty years of silence, work, and prayer at Nazareth, the overall picture of Jesus that emerges is of a contemplative who every so often goes over into action, rather than of a man of action who every so often allows himself periods of contemplation.[62]

Jesus is not only the faithful Son, committed to his Father's mission for our sake. He is also a man of prayer, the Son who is always in deep communion with his Father. In Luke's Gospel, we see how Jesus' praying precedes every major moment of his life and mission—the Spirit's descent on him in baptism, his choosing of the disciples, his transfiguration, teaching his disciples how to pray, and his Gethsemane experience (Lk 3:21-22; 6:12-13; 9:28-29; 11:1; 22:41).[63] By taking the form of the servant, Jesus submits his life to the Father in the Spirit. In his life of obedience unto death, prayer prepares Jesus for his Spirit-anointed mission and is his way to seek guidance and strength from the Father to fulfill his work. Indeed, Jesus' own self-giving unto death is his final prayer to God (see Heb 9:14).[64]

---

[59]Raniero Cantalamessa, *The Holy Spirit in the Life of Jesus: The Mystery of Christ's Baptism*, trans. Alan Neame (Collegeville, MN: Liturgical Press, 1994), 20-63. Cantalamessa's treatment of the church's Christ-like identity under his kingly and prophetic offices bears an affinity, respectively, with our dramatic (chapter four) and sacrificial (chapter five) models of the sanctified life.

[60]Cantalamessa, *Holy Spirit in the Life of Jesus*, 16-17. For a fuller treatment of Mühlen's conception of the church as one person (i.e., the Holy Spirit) in many persons (i.e., Christ and Christians), see *Una Mystica Persona: Die Kirche als das Mysterium der Identität des Heiligen Geistes in Christus und die Christen: Eine Person in vielen Personen*, 2nd ed. (Munich: Schöning, 1967), 196-200; for a brief summary of Mühlen's approach in English, see Congar, *I Believe in the Holy Spirit*, 1:22-25.

[61]Cantalamessa, *The Holy Spirit in the Life of Jesus*, 51.

[62]Cantalamessa, *The Holy Spirit in the Life of Jesus*, 52.

[63]Cantalamessa, *The Holy Spirit in the Life of Jesus*, 52.

[64]"The priestly unction unfolds in Jesus' life, in his prayer life, but it culminates in his sacrifice on the cross." Cantalamessa, *The Holy Spirit in the Life of Jesus*, 54.

Cantalamessa reminds pastors that, following in the footsteps of the apostles, they should set time aside for devoting themselves "to prayer and to the ministry of the word" (Acts 6:4). He suggests that such apostolic arrangement establishes "a basic principle for the Church: that a pastor may delegate everything, or nearly everything, to other people round about him, but not prayer!"[65] While the people of Israel worked hard to defeat the Amalekites, it is Moses' intercession for them on the mountain, the place where he prays to God with arms raised, that assures them of their victory (see Ex 17:8-16).[66] The implications for the church are clear: One cannot set out for work, or have the strength to do it, without the guidance and power of the Spirit. Yet we often act as if the church is a business more than a house of prayer, a busy and stressful place more than an oasis to find rest in God.[67] When meetings are going nowhere, we do not take time to pray, and we forget to "place our trust back in God, not in ourselves."[68]

Today the crowds also come to us, asking for our help. They come to us not only in person, but also via countless phone, email, and social media messages. There is, of course, a time and place to serve them. There is a time to be responsible stewards of the garden God has given us to care for and watch over. But we were also created to rest in God and, like Jesus did in the Spirit, go to the mountain to dialogue with the Father. No prayer without work, but also no work without prayer. Cantalamessa exhorts us to pray ceaselessly in the Spirit by finding our mountain, as it were, getting rid of as many distractions as possible and striving ideally for "a fixed time set apart for prayer, perhaps in some deserted place, like Jesus."[69] As we learn to embrace our creatureliness daily, the rhythm of activity and repose, Cantalamessa offers us a way to submit to the power of the day—as Bonhoeffer puts it—by reclaiming our need for spiritual rest, our need to attend to meaningful vocation and nurturing relationships without neglecting our relationship with God.

***Making room for fiesta.*** In his treatise on the history of Sunday, Justo González shows how the Day of the Lord only became an official time set aside for

---

[65]Cantalamessa, *The Holy Spirit in the Life of Jesus*, 55.

[66]Cantalamessa, *The Holy Spirit in the Life of Jesus*, 56.

[67]Cantalamessa, *The Holy Spirit in the Life of Jesus*, 57.

[68]Cantalamessa, *The Holy Spirit in the Life of Jesus*, 62. "When discussions get bogged down and no progress is made, our faith makes us bold to say, 'Friends, let us take a short break and see what light the Lord is willing to throw on our problem!'" Cantalamessa, *The Holy Spirit in the Life of Jesus*, 62.

[69]Cantalamessa, *The Holy Spirit in the Life of Jesus*, 58-59.

physical rest under Emperor Constantine's edict (AD 321), a practice that continued to be enforced throughout the medieval period and progressively had the effect of making Sunday function like a Christian Sabbath.[70] Under the influence of the majority of the monastic orders in the Middle Ages, the ideal purpose of rest on Sunday was not leisure but dedication to prayer and meditation, although in reality folks did engage in plenty of leisurely activities (some of them prohibited by the church) such as going to the theater, listening to musicians, dancing, and at times doing licentious acts.[71] The Jewish Sabbath had traditionally been a time to rest from work in order to make room for prayer and the Word, including the remembrance of God's covenant with his people. When Sunday became the day in Christendom associated with the cessation of labor and devotion to God, the question arose as to what Christians should make of the traditional Sabbath.

Drawing on the theological distinction between the moral and ceremonial fulfillment of the Sabbath, González notes that the majority of the Protestant reformers held the duty under God's moral law (commandment) to set aside a day for resting and attending to the things of God (Sunday or otherwise).[72] They also taught that the ceremonial laws concerning the Jewish Sabbath no longer applied to Christians, but that the intention of the Sabbath had been fulfilled with the coming of Christ and the church's rest in him. González shows that, in addition to the preaching and teaching of the Word, many of the Reformers were also concerned under the moral use with the need for giving a day of rest to servants and all workers.[73]

As González tracks the history of Sunday, he argues that after Constantine the church lost an important dimension of Sunday as the day of the Lord's resurrection ushering in a new creation. In the practice of the early church, the seventh day remained the day of rest, and both Jewish and Gentile Christians kept it as they were able, but Sunday was seen as the first day of creation in which all things were made new on account of Christ's resurrection from the dead (see 2 Cor 5:17).[74] Linked to

[70]Justo González, *Breve historia del domingo: Descubre el gozo de la celebración del día del Señor* (El Paso: Editorial Mundo Hispano, 2016), 60-66, 73-77, 89-90, 111-15, 125-26.

[71]González, *Breve historia del domingo*, 115-18.

[72]González mentions, in particular, Thomas Aquinas's use of the distinction. See González, *Breve historia del domingo*, 121-25; cf. 146.

[73]González, *Breve historia del domingo*, 146.

[74]González, *Breve historia del domingo*, 41, 44-45.

the Passover redemption of Israel from death, the celebration of the Lord's Supper was not a sad occasion but a celebration of Christ as the victorious Passover Lamb by whose blood we are freed from death.[75] In a similar vein, Easter Sunday, the church's foremost feast in the liturgical year (even before Christmas), was the ideal time for the celebration of baptisms where catechumens died and rose with Christ from the dead.[76] It is telling that the pre-Constantinian emphasis on the Day of the Lord as the day of Christ's resurrection and the first day of the new creation is barely mentioned by the time we get to the Reformation period. González believes that, in addition to the Empire's legislation of Sunday as a day of rest, the medieval period's focus on the Mass as a sacrifice gave the Eucharist a more somber tone.[77] The overall effect is a minimization of the joy of Sunday as a resurrection day.

The question remains for us: Where did the *fiesta* go? The celebration of Sunday as the first day of the new creation was identified by some early church theologians as the eighth day, that day of resurrection hope when we will rest eternally in Christ.[78] Indeed, Scripture and liturgy portray Christian death as a falling asleep in Christ and the day of our resurrection as an awakening from sleep to life (e.g., Is 26:19; Dan 12:2; see also Jn 5:28-29; 11:11; Rom 13:11; 1 Cor 15:20-22; Eph 5:14; 1 Thess 4:14-17). In these images, we see that the overall tone of Sunday—and more broadly, the day of rest in its spiritual sense—is one of proclaiming hope. How do we live the rest of the week—indeed, our whole lives—in light of that hopeful joy?

One way is to make room for *fiesta*. By the term *fiesta* we mean to evoke neither a licentious party where immorality and abuses are rampant nor a stereotypical view of Latino/a life which racializes Hispanics as fun and uncontrollable as opposed to wise and sober. We mean instead a time to celebrate God's gifts and revel in the beauty of his creation in the midst of a society that often sucks the life out of workers (including church workers!) and leaves little room for rest and recreation. There are, of course, many ways to draw joy from God's created gifts. Surely, church festivals, special family events, or national holidays offer spaces for enjoyment. Perhaps, we can speak of finding a place for play in our lives. Play is neither rest nor work, yet is related to both.[79] Oftentimes, avocations, pastimes, or

[75]González, *Breve historia del domingo*, 40-41.

[76]González, *Breve historia del domingo*, 44.

[77]González, *Breve historia del domingo*, 95-109, 125-26.

[78]González, *Breve historia del domingo*, 45-48.

[79]As Schumacher rightly puts it, "not everything in life is easily labeled as 'work' or 'rest.' There is, in fact, a whole spectrum of human activity that lies between the labor of our livelihood (work) and passive

hobbies that take us out of our daily labor routines (particularly, those linked to our livelihood) for a time involve much effort and require the full engagement of our senses. Amateur pursuits like playing sports, singing, gardening, reading and writing, or working at the shop on some project require honing one's skill and craft over time. Yet these occasions for play feed mind, body, and spirit in creative and constructive ways. Although play in this context is not literal rest, many find refreshment in such activities. Play becomes like an oasis in the desert. Play also allows the mind and body to rest from other responsibilities and activities that await us throughout the week. In this sense, play functions paradoxically as a sort of restful activity that can also energize us to focus on other tasks ahead.

Finding a place for play in our lives reminds us that it is salutary to stand still before God amid the busyness of life and behold his creation. Making room for *fiesta* allows us to embrace our creatureliness by rejoicing in and making use of God's created gifts simply because they are beautiful and wonderful even in the midst of a world so full of pain and suffering. Such a playful attitude, as it were, comes through in the hope of Zechariah who gives us a glimpse of a restored Zion, the new creation where "the streets of the city shall be full of boys and girls playing in its streets" (Zech 8:5).

relaxation (rest). . . . 'Play' is work we do for the sheer pleasure of it. It is not intended to be confused with idleness or mere pastimes or entertainment. Hobbies, avocation, and amateur pursuits often demand intense labor, practiced skill, and long hours or even years of accumulated knowledge." William W. Schumacher, "Faithful Witness in Work and Rest," *Concordia Journal* 41, no. 2 (2015): 145.

# 8

# I WANT TO TELL THE STORY

## NORTH AMERICAN SPIRITUALITY *and the* MODELS

Acknowledging that spirituality is too broad a category, a distinctively Christian contribution must look at its own theological sources and spiritual traditions to address adequately the spiritual or religious concerns of neighbors in North America. In this chapter, we will test the usefulness of a Spirit Christology and the models of sanctification it yields for dealing with the perceived spiritual needs, struggles, and hopes of North American neighbors. To do so, we will hear from these neighbors as they express their attitudes toward religion and spirituality. We might find that their voices sound familiar, perhaps like those of people we know in our own churches, families, workplaces, and neighborhoods. Hearing their thoughts and cries, we will ask how our proposal on the sanctified life can assist us in engaging and interacting with their interests in, questions about, or yearnings for a meaningful life.

What are sociologists of religion, demographers, generational gurus, and church writers saying about the state of spirituality in North America, including the spiritual condition of Christians themselves and other neighbors? By taking a bird's-eye view of various themes in this growing literature, we will take time to hear from various sectors of the population. The big picture includes Christians with various levels of commitment to their denominations or congregations, people who might consider themselves spiritual but not religious, and those who choose what they find most helpful about different forms of spirituality and religion. This chapter assumes that pastors and other church leaders first need to listen to the spiritual struggles and concerns of the people under their care and other neighbors in their midst before they are able to understand their spiritual conditions, address issues or problems in their lives, and engage or interpret their stories through the Christian story.

Notwithstanding the particularities of different groups, we will show that there are some predominant spiritual stories that come across in the research. These comprise the desire for nurturing relationships, security in a broken world, purpose in life, a socially active faith that makes a difference in the world, community and interdependence, hospitality and belonging, reaching out to vulnerable neighbors and strangers, and a healthy lifestyle or rhythm that finds a proper balance between work and rest. We will also show ways in which a Spirit Christology and our models-based approach to the sanctified life can interact with these neighbors' stories. What might Christians learn about their own spiritual condition by engaging in conversation with neighbors facing similar spiritual struggles and hopes? How might Christians theologically relate the common experiences they share with others to the Christian story, particularly as that story bears witness to Jesus Christ, the bearer and giver of the Spirit of God? These are some of the questions we bring to the table as we explore ways in which the stories of life in the Spirit in each of our models open a space for engaging North Americans through dialogue about the spiritual life, attraction to such life by modeling or embodying it, and invitation to the same through participation in the spiritual vision of life portrayed in the Christian story.

## SEARCHING FOR A COHERENT STORY

Sociologist of religion Robert Wuthnow has argued that baby boomers (born about 1946–1964) represent the shift in the American religious landscape from a dwelling-oriented to a seeking-oriented spirituality.[1] Humans desire both dwelling and seeking. They are drawn to fixed sacred spaces for stability, as well as more fluid journeys in life where change is expected or needed.[2] Yet a shift has

[1]"In brief, I argue that a traditional spirituality of inhabiting sacred places has given way to a new spirituality of seeking—that people have been losing faith in a metaphysic that can make them feel at home in the universe and that they increasingly negotiate among competing glimpses of the sacred, seeking partial knowledge and practical wisdom." Robert Wuthnow, *After Heaven: Spirituality in America Since the 1950s* (Berkeley: University of California Press, 1998), 3.

[2]Wuthnow, *After Heaven*, 4-6.

occurred in which Americans no longer find religious identity primarily or only by membership in a religious organization or institution, but more so "by the search for connections with various organizations, groups, and disciplines, all the while feeling marginal to any particular group or place."[3] Far from reshaping America as a hopelessly secular nation, this shift does not reveal a move away from spirituality but toward different ways of approaching the sacred.[4] Accordingly, in his study of the baby-boom generation, W. C. Roof observes that the American religious landscape "is characterized not so much by a loss of faith as a qualitative shift from unquestioned belief to a more open, questing mood . . . a search for certainty, but also the hope for a more authentic, intrinsically satisfying life."[5] The question is not whether people are still religious or spiritual, but what kind of religiosity or spirituality is at work in their lives.

***Dwellers, seekers, and tinkerers.*** For Wuthnow, neither a spirituality of dwelling nor one of seeking is sufficient in and of itself to address the spiritual yearnings of North Americans. Dwellers find an anchor in their association with a stable group or organization and its accompanying traditions and stories, but such dependency may create an "idolization" of structures[6] and is "not likely to generate deep introspection about one's identity."[7] If a dwelling-oriented spirituality is perhaps too comfortably stable for its own good, a seeker-oriented one suffers from being "too fluid" to provide a community that can foster maturity and commitment[8] and offer "coherence to individual biographies."[9] The former type of spirituality is too communal and organizational to be personally appropriated, and the latter type too loosey-goosey to earn our commitment and promote discipline.[10] This impasse leads Wuthnow to propose a "practice-oriented" spirituality that focuses on the ongoing formation of the individual in becoming a more integrated and mature type of person.

---

[3]Wuthnow, *After Heaven*, 7.

[4]Wuthnow, *After Heaven*, 10.

[5]Wade Clark Roof, *Spiritual Marketplace: Baby Boomers and the Remaking of American Religion* (Princeton, NJ: Princeton University Press, 1999), 9-10.

[6]Wuthnow, *After Heaven*, 15.

[7]Wuthnow, *After Heaven*, 188.

[8]Wuthnow, *After Heaven*, 16.

[9]Wuthnow, *After Heaven*, 188.

[10]"Neither of these views is adequate: spirituality is not just communal or else trivial. It can also be quite serious, practiced deliberatively by individuals. . . . To say that spirituality is practiced means that people engage intentionally in activities that deepen their relationship to the sacred." Wuthnow, *After Heaven*, 169.

In a similar vein, W. C. Roof offers the phrase "reflexive spirituality" to describe a dominant feature of post–World War II American culture and religion. In distinction from assumed adherence to institutionalized forms of religion, reflexivity is defined as "a more intentional, self-directed approach to cultivating spiritual sensitivity and religion consciousness"[11] or as a type of spirituality that "reorients notions about religious and spiritual strength, away from custom, institution, or doctrinal formulation toward greater focus on the inner life and its cultivation."[12] Despite the general distrust of institutions and the high value placed on individual freedom among North Americans, Roof does not dismiss the potential role of religion and religious institutions in fostering or "cultivating the interior life. The challenge is to become religious 'from within,' to start with a personal commitment in search of a religious center."[13] While the metaphor of America as a religious marketplace where people make spiritual choices that fit them may put too much weight on supply and demand in spiritual identity and formation,[14] Roof's argument for nurturing a person in a reflective way of life around a coherent center suggests a place for the role of formation and growth in the spiritual life centered on a meaningful story.[15]

Recommending a spirituality that addresses the human need for dwelling and seeking while moving beyond these goals as ends in themselves, Wuthnow calls his third alternative a "practice-oriented" spirituality. Religious organizations can provide for such needs by giving their people "both roots and wings—roots to ground them solidly in the traditions of their particular faith, wings to explore their own talents and the mysteries of the sacred."[16] To promote this type of spiritual life, religious leaders cannot act simply as gatekeepers of the tradition or providers of services to consumers: "In this view, clergy must serve as models of spirituality, rather than as guardians or shopkeepers."[17] The goal lies in "shaping

---

[11]Roof, *Spiritual Marketplace*, 12.

[12]Roof, *Spiritual Marketplace*, 310.

[13]Roof, *Spiritual Marketplace*, 310; see also 308-9.

[14]See Robert Wuthnow, *After the Baby Boomers: How Twenty- and Thirty-Somethings Are Shaping the Future of American Religion* (Princeton, NJ: Princeton University Press, 2007), 16.

[15]"Agency, or the role of the individual actively engaging and creating an ongoing personal religious narrative in relation to the symbolic resources available, is set forth as crucial to our understanding of contemporary spiritual quests." Roof, *Spiritual Marketplace*, 12. Roof observes that "individuals and small groups will turn to traditions as resources yet exercise freedom in making religious choices and in modes of spiritual cultivation." Roof, *Spiritual Marketplace*, 309.

[16]Wuthnow, *After Heaven*, 17.

[17]Wuthnow, *After Heaven*, 17.

the person" or habituating people in intentional spiritual practices (e.g., prayer, meditation, discernment, worship) on a regular basis, so that they "can exercise wisdom when new situations necessitate making difficult judgments, . . . knowing how to relate the practice responsibly to one's other obligations and areas of life."[18] Sustained formation in spiritual practices nurtures integrated persons who engage in "*deep reflection* about who one is" and "results in a core narrative that provides coherence to their practice over time."[19]

Wuthnow's call for a spirituality of "sustained commitment, without which no life can have coherence" involves the work of institutions as facilitators of people's involvement in (and growth through) spiritual practices, but also, paradoxically, promotes the formation of persons with "the moral fortitude to participate in them [institutions] without expecting to receive too much from them."[20] Over time, such formation ideally produces a mature person with firm roots in a tradition and relative freedom to appropriate the tradition meaningfully at a personal level. In his later study on young adults from the post-baby-boom generation (often known as Generation Xers; born about 1965–1980), Wuthnow found out that, somewhat like the seeker in their parents, they approached religion and spirituality resourcefully as "tinkerers," namely, those who put "together a life from whatever skills, ideas, and resources . . . are readily at hand."[21] Yet post-boomers also reported a desire "to become more serious about their spiritual life if they are to grow in it and mature," showing a move from mere seeking and tinkering to ongoing spiritual practice.[22] The research shows that religious leaders' embodiment of a spirituality centered around a coherent story with corresponding devotional practices seems to offer a compelling way to invite and habituate others into the spiritual life.

***Moralistic therapeutic deists.*** In contrast to the aforementioned studies, Christian Smith and Melinda Lundquist Denton conclude that very few

---

[18]Wuthnow, *After Heaven*, 184.

[19]Wuthnow, *After Heaven*, 186.

[20]Wuthnow, *After Heaven*, 198.

[21]Wuthnow, *After the Baby Boomers*, 13.

[22]Wuthnow, *After the Baby Boomers*, 127. Among young people who are "religiously uninvolved" (about fifty-five percent of twenty-one-to-forty-five-year-olds), Wuthnow notes that "sixty percent . . . say spiritual growth is at least fairly important to them, 30 percent say it is very or extremely important to them, 29 percent say they have devoted at least a fair amount of effort to their spiritual life in the past year, 25 percent say their interest in spirituality has been increasing, and 25 percent say they meditate once a week or more." *After the Baby Boomers*, 134.

American teenagers of the millennial generation (born about 1981–2001) "appear *themselves* to be active spiritual seekers who think of themselves as spiritual but not religious and actually incorporate spiritual practices of other faiths into their own lives."[23] Most teens identified themselves as Christians and, of the remaining ones, those who identified as "nonreligious" were often "nominal Christians."[24] More commonly, thirteen-to-seventeen-year-olds typically did not rebel against their parents' religions (or religious institutions) but adopted them as their default practice—evidence that parents remain "the single most important social influence on the religious and spiritual lives of adolescents."[25] In a follow-up study of eighteen-to-twenty-three-year-olds, Christian Smith and Patricia Snell concluded that these "emerging adults tend to report that they are quite like their parents and somewhat like their close friends when it comes to religion," but also noted that "the importance and practice of religion generally declines between the ages of 13-17 and 18-23."[26] This suggests that there is another side to the story.

It is one thing to say that American young people are religious, it is another to ask what kind of religion they practice. They are generally "inarticulate and confused" about what they believe, what their religious traditions teach, or how these things are important for their everyday lives.[27] Still, American youth's attitudes toward spirituality reveal a dominant narrative that Smith and Denton refer to as Moralistic Therapeutic Deism (MTD).[28] According to this popular view, "God wants people to be good . . . to each other," and "the central goal of life is to be happy and to feel good about oneself." God gets involved in our lives only when we need him to help us, and "good people go to heaven when they die."[29]

---

[23]Christian Smith and Melinda Lundquist Denton, *Soul Searching: The Religious and Spiritual Lives of American Teenagers* (New York: Oxford University Press, 2005), 115; see also 27.

[24]Smith and Denton, *Soul Searching*, 260.

[25]Smith and Denton, *Soul Searching*, 261; see also 28, 56, 115-17.

[26]Christian Smith and Patricia Snell, *Souls in Transition: The Religious and Spiritual Lives of Emerging Adults* (New York: Oxford University Press, 2009), 142.

[27]Smith and Denton, *Soul Searching*, 27; see also 262. The authors argue that "the net result, in any case, is that most religious teenagers' opinions and views—one can hardly call them worldviews—are vague, limited, and often quite at variance with the actual teachings of their own religion. . . . This suggests that a strong, visible, salient, or intentional faith is not operating in the foreground of most teenagers' lives." *Soul Searching*, 134. "Most religious communities' central problem is not teen rebellion but teenagers' benign 'whateverism.'" *Soul Searching*, 266. Smith and Snell observe that, five years later, the same youth were "lacking in conviction or direction to even know what to do with their prized sovereignty. Emerging adults are determined to be free. But they do not know what is worth doing with their freedom." *Souls in Transition*, 294.

[28]Smith and Denton, *Soul Searching*, 118-71.

[29]Smith and Denton, *Soul Searching*, 162-63.

Upon entering emergent adulthood, these young people continue to hold to the basic tenets of MTD, even if it becomes a bit more diluted or complex due to less dependence on parents and accumulated real-life experiences and difficulties.[30] Given the overwhelming influence of MTD among youth, the authors wonder if "a significant part of Christianity in the United States is actually only tenuously Christian in any sense that is seriously connected to the actual historical Christian tradition."[31] For instance, if the goal of life is feeling happy and doing what makes me feel happy, how does that square with the Christian call to live according to what makes God happy (say, God's Word) or make sacrifices to attend to others' needs? An interesting paradox is at work in these emergent adults. They default to the religion of their parents who gave them MTD, and yet they pull away from this watered-down parental religion, because it does not seem to deal adequately with the sufferings and crosses life brings on them. At least a number of emergent adults seem to yearn for more of a meat-and-potatoes spirituality. Given the rise of MTD, we see the need for a compelling spiritual story with the capacity to invite North American neighbors to a devotionally deeper and more generous form of life in the world—in short, a Christlike life.

## MOVING FROM THE THERAPEUTIC TOWARD A CRUCIFORM STORY

We can interact with the aforementioned studies, bringing insights from the sociology of religion into conversation with theology. Wuthnow reminds us of the role of religion and spirituality in the formation of a worldview, a coherent story that makes sense of life in relation to the sacred and that influences behavior. As a framework that is deeply rooted in Scripture and finds expression in Christian traditions, Spirit Christology offers us not only a legitimate trinitarian narrative of divine action in relation to human persons but also a coherent trajectory for describing the spiritual life. Following Irenaeus and others, a Spirit Christology functions as an overarching narrative that moves from God's sending of the Creator Spirit on the human race to the grieved Spirit's departure from sinful humanity and then to the sanctifying Spirit's return to humanity through Jesus Christ as the definitive receiver, bearer, and giver of God's Spirit. While not the only overarching biblical story with a thematic center and movement, a Spirit Christology does lend

[30]Smith and Snell, *Souls in Transition*, 154-56.
[31]Smith and Denton, *Soul Searching*, 171.

itself uniquely to questions about the relationship between God's Spirit and the human spirit.

***Forming spiritually mature persons.*** Key to the story of the Son's receiving and giving of the Spirit to humanity is the Spirit's inseparable union to the Son's flesh—not only in his birth, but also in his anointing unto death. Whereas the Gnostics see "Spirit" (or the spiritual element in Christ) departing from the Son before his passion, Irenaeus posits an incarnational view of the Son and of the Holy Spirit in his humanity with an orientation toward the cross and resurrection.[32] It is a paschal view of life in the Spirit that gives spirituality an earthy, sober, and cruciform trajectory. In Irenaeus's view, because the Word has truly assumed human suffering, he can ask his followers to take up their cross and follow him.[33] This is a spirituality shaped not by flight from the world, but by solidarity with the human race, faithfulness to God, anointing for a sacrificial mission as Yahweh's servant, and life in the hope of the resurrection. It is a spiritually mature life worth sacrificing for—not for the faint of heart, as it were.

Wuthnow points to a need among North Americans for a spirituality that moves beyond mere institutional membership and consumer gratification toward lifelong formation in spiritual practices. Similarly, Roof speaks of the need for personal reflexivity and cultivation of the inner life around a coherent center or story. Due to its emphasis on the Spirit's continuous sculpting of persons after the likeness of Christ, a Spirit Christology affords us an entry point into the biblical story precisely through human participation in the kind of life the Spirit of Christ is able to engender and nurture in people. Otherwise stated, a Spirit Christology offers a living story with the potential to move people interested in spirituality into forms of life and accompanying habits that foster sustained and mature faithfulness to God and commitment to love of neighbor. A Spirit-oriented account of the sanctified life has the capacity to move Wuthnow's

[32]"For the [Gnostic] Ophites, Jesus is only the Son of God between his baptism and his Passion. [Jesus is] united to the [spiritual] Christ who descends on him at the Jordan, and is abandoned by him on the eve of his Passion. After that time, Jesus is no longer the Son of God, not even after being revived." Antonio Orbe, "El Espíritu en el bautismo de Jesús (en torno a San Ireneo)," *Gregorianum* 76, no. 4 (1995): 668 (translation mine).

[33]"[Christ] condemns Peter for his vulgar biases against the Passion of the Christ, whom he had just confessed as the living Son of God. The Christ, according to the Savior himself, had to pass through the Passion and the Cross. Not only does Irenaeus point to the suffering of Jesus. After this follows the exhortation to the disciples to carry the Cross and follow him unto death. What sense would such an exhortation make if—as the heretics declare—Christ himself were the first one to forsake the Cross and fly to heaven before his Passion?" Orbe, "El Espíritu en el bautismo de Jesús," 694 (translation mine).

dwellers and seekers into deep conversations about spiritual maturity and practices that are defined by neither blind loyalty to organizations nor the desire for quick fixes, but by ongoing fidelity to Christ's sacrificial way of being in the Spirit in the world.

Smith and Denton noted that the majority of American youth has adapted MTD as the go-to narrative to make sense of their lives. Yet they question whether the type of therapeutic life fostered by this story is "Christian" in any historic sense.

> Moralistic Therapeutic Deism is . . . about providing therapeutic benefits to its adherents. This is not a religion of repentance from sin, of keeping the Sabbath, of living as a servant of a sovereign divine, of steadfastly saying one's prayers, of faithfully observing high holy days, of building character through suffering, of basking in God's love and grace, of spending oneself in gratitude and love for the cause of social justice.[34]

As Kenda Creasy Dean has aptly put it in her summary of Smith and Denton, what teenagers are lacking is a "theological language with which to express their faith or interpret their experience of the world."[35] She argues that, in contrast to MTD, a Christian community can foster faith and spiritual maturity by teaching and modeling "governing theology," emphasizing those aspects of the Christian story that can "speak to God's personal and powerful nature, the interpersonal and spiritual significance of the faith community, the centrality of Christian vocation, and the hope that the world is ultimately in good hands."[36] This formative teaching and modeling depends on "the power of the Holy Spirit," who "empowers the church to resist and overwhelm self-focused spiritualities with the self-giving love of Jesus Christ."[37]

***The Spirit and the cross.*** A Spirit Christology highlights aspects of the Christian story that can lead to the cultivation of a spiritual life oriented away from self and toward God and neighbor. If one considers the trajectory of a Spirit Christology in the Gospels, one sees its cruciform orientation toward the paschal mystery. Contrary to popular notions of Spirit-anointing as a means to financial

---

[34]Smith and Denton, *Soul Searching*, 163-64.

[35]Kenda Creasy Dean, *Almost Christian: What the Faith of Our Teenagers Is Telling the American Church* (New York: Oxford University Press, 2010), 18.

[36]Dean, *Almost Christian*, 194.

[37]Dean, *Almost Christian*, 194.

success in prosperity gospel contexts, God's anointing of Jesus with the Spirit actually marks and makes him the suffering servant.[38] Life in the Spirit is challenging. For Jesus, it means a life of vocation and sacrifice for others in faithfulness to God's mission in the world. If the goal of a spiritual life is feeling happy and acquiring abundant temporal blessings, then Jesus' life in the Spirit is a resounding failure.[39]

The Christian life mirrors Christ's own life in the Spirit, a life under the cross in which Jesus faced struggles of all kinds. Jesus is anointed to die, offering his holy life to God through the eternal Spirit for us. Jesus is led by the Spirit into the desert to be tempted by the devil, is persecuted and rejected like the prophets, and prays to his Father in the intense agony of the garden of Gethsemane as his hour draws near. Jesus' boundary-crossing ministry of welcoming "sinners" who are outsiders into God's kingdom gets him in trouble on several occasions. He teaches his disciples to take up their cross and follow him and to learn from him not by being served but by serving others. Life in the Spirit of Christ means sacrificing self to make room for God and neighbor. As Jesus carries out his difficult vocation, living under God's Word, he also rejoices in the Spirit even in the midst of his sufferings and prays to his Father in both good and bad times. He is also raised from the dead by the Father according to the Spirit. Christians surely share in Christ's glory, but also in his sufferings. They are not promised a fleeting happiness, but the joy of the Spirit, which remains even in tough times. They do not live by sight, but by faith in God's promises in the hope of God's deliverance. They do not live for self-gratification but for others.

A Spirit Christology can offer the type of alternative narrative that moves people from the therapeutic to the paschal, from a focus on meeting subjective needs to an embrace of Jesus' cruciform life—in short, to a devotionally deeper and more generous way of life. Smith and Denton suggest that religious leaders must challenge young people in articulating a story that is not morally indifferent or morally equivalent to whatever is out there but grounded in a tradition that yields habitual practices and makes a difference in people's lives.[40] Dean finds in

---

[38]Leopoldo A. Sánchez M., "A Missionary Theology of the Holy Spirit," *Missio Apostolica* 14, no. 1 (2006): 29, 38-40.

[39]"One could say that the Spirit is given to Jesus more in view of his lack of success than of his success. . . . The mission of servant, accepted by Jesus at his baptism, passes by way of rejection, failure, and defeat." Raniero Cantalamessa, *The Holy Spirit in the Life of Jesus: The Mystery of Christ's Baptism*, trans. Alan Neame (Collegeville, MN: Liturgical Press, 1994), 40.

[40]Smith and Denton, *Soul Searching*, 267-69. "The language, and therefore experience, of Trinity, holiness, sin, grace, justification, sanctification, church, Eucharist, and heaven and hell appear, among most

God's grace and Spirit the energy for moving teenagers from "the cult of nice" to suffering love:

> Imitating Christ makes people lay down their wallets, their reputations, their lives for the sake of others, which is why parents rightly fear it for their children. The cult of nice is so much safer; God is friendly and predictable, offering little and asking less.[41]

Given its cruciform orientation, a Spirit Christology offers a story with the potential to invite youth to ask deeper and tougher questions about the spiritual life not considered by MTD. Such questions might deal with the challenges and joys of fulfilling a vocation in life, the role of struggle and suffering in building character, the means of strengthening trust and hope in a personal God through devotional habits, or ways of fostering solidarity toward underserved neighbors and communities—all issues addressed in various ways by our models of sanctification.

***Describing spiritual journeys.*** People are more likely to become anchored to a story that gives meaning, purpose, and energy to their lives and to their relationship to God and the rest of the world. Wuthnow notes how coherent and compelling stories provide a framework for people to describe their spiritual journey, its beginnings and purpose, including its high and low points. "They develop a story about their spiritual journey, and this story provides a way for them to understand their origins, how they have changed, the role that crisis events or significant others have played in their lives, and where they think they are headed."[42]

Yielding a plurality of models of the sanctified life, a Spirit Christology paints for us a rich tapestry of portrayals of God's work in Christ and his saints by the Spirit. Each of these models offers distinct yet often related and simultaneous narratives and images that help us articulate our spiritual journeys (their corresponding purposes and struggles or crisis moments) and foster spiritual

---

Christian teenagers in the United States at the very least, to be supplanted by the language of happiness, niceness, and an earned heavenly reward. . . . Christianity is actively being colonized and displaced by a quite different religious faith." Smith and Denton, *Soul Searching*, 171. "The Triune God espoused by Christianity is both personal and powerful, qualities associated with moral influence. . . . The call to discipleship invokes a morally significant universe in which actions have consequences for others, and a hopeful future—because God has designed it—is worth investing in." Dean, *Almost Christian*, 79.

[41]Dean, *Almost Christian*, 40.

[42]Dean, *Almost Christian*, 40.

disciplines.[43] Consider, for instance, how the renewal model frames life as a journey of death leading to resurrection, the dramatic one as a wilderness pilgrimage, and the sacrificial one as a life of service and communal sharing. The hospitality model paints the Christian journey as a move from the center to the margins, a posture of welcome toward the forgotten and excluded "other," and a vision of shared life in God's kingdom with the unlovable of our day. In the devotional model, God's people rediscover and embrace their creatureliness as they journey toward final communion with God in paradise, a new heaven and earth, where humans talk with and praise their Creator. In that pilgrimage, we learn to live according to God's designed rhythm of movement and repose, work and rest.

Each of these spiritual walks through life has its lows and highs, its times of suffering and hope. There is a cruciform orientation to life in the Spirit. Humans face a struggle, crisis, or conflict before they experience a resolution, transformation, or newness of life by the power of the Spirit. For example, in the renewal model, the pain of sins is met with the sweetness of pardon. In the dramatic model, the disappointment of falling trapped under Satan's seductions leads to increased dependence on God's Word and prayer. Under the sacrificial model, an unfulfilling search for significance focused on self-fulfillment or having more things gives way to a review of life's priorities that finds sharing one's gifts and lives with others rewarding. Experiences of marginality lead to solidarity with vulnerable neighbors (hospitality). A restless body and mind receives the gifts of leisure with family and friends and time with God (devotional).

Certain disciplines or practices correspond with each description of the spiritual journey: confession and absolution under the renewal model, prayer for the Spirit's deliverance from evil in the dramatic model, and engaging in "happy exchanges" where each other's strengths and gifts contribute to each other's

---

[43]Bryant suggests that the Christian journey begins with repentance, moves to a concern for strengthening faith, and then focuses on maturity in love. Yet he also notes that "spiritual development is no steady, regular advance, but is punctuated by crises in which growth appears to have come to a stop for a time; old battles have to be refought and old experiences relived at a deeper level." See Christopher Bryant, "The Nature of Spiritual Development," in *The Study of Spirituality*, ed. Cheslyn Jones, Geoffrey Wainwright, and Edward Yarnold (New York: Oxford University Press, 1986), 566. Although our models-based approach does include the notion of crisis moments, it also sees various experiences along the journey in more simultaneous (rather than linear) terms. For a non-linear theological account of human development as "a circumambulation of the human spirit around the center, who is the One triune God," see James E. Loder, *The Logic of the Spirit: Human Development in Theological Perspective* (San Francisco: Jossey-Bass, 1998), 74; see also 75-77, 339-42.

weaknesses and needs in an intercommunion of love (sacrificial model). Cross- and intercultural exchanges with neighbors different from us often come from a recognition of our own marginality and a welcoming spirit (hospitality). Restoring balance to life in the face of spiritual or literal idleness and weariness includes an appreciation for cultivating the garden God has given us through our labors and vocations and for honoring the day of rest through reception of God's Word, prayer, sleep, and play (devotional).

All these practices assume an opposite, life-denying way of being that the Spirit has to move humans out of, so that the Spirit can shape the mind of Christ in them. The Spirit moves the sinner from guilt to forgiveness, from vulnerability to vigilance and resistance, and from self-centeredness (or conversely, the loss of self) to a communion that embodies a diversity of gifts (and burdens). The Spirit moves humans from the shame of marginality and exclusion to the joy of belonging in God's kingdom and reaching out to others in the margins who have yet to experience such divine embrace. The Spirit also moves weary souls from the restlessness of the idolatry of work and spiritual idleness to an embrace of their creatureliness through devotion to God in the healthy rhythm of activity, rest, and play.

## HEARING THE SPIRITUAL NEEDS AND HOPES OF NORTH AMERICANS

What do North Americans need and hope for when it comes to spirituality? Answers vary depending on the study and its questions, the groups or generations interviewed, and the interpretations of the data. Yet there are recurring themes in the literature. People yearn for purpose and meaning, belonging and community, right relations with family and peers, reaching out to marginal neighbors, meaningful work and causes, and the proper balance between work and other important aspects of life. As we saw above, North Americans hope for these ways of life even as they struggle with the negative and sinful impulses in them that work against considering and embodying such a vision of a spiritual life.

***On Nones and millennials.*** A feature of religious life among emergent adults in North America is their pragmatic interest in religion and even religious institutions as a means of moral transformation and social change.[44] In short, the research shows how religiously affiliated and unaffiliated North Americans agree on

[44]Smith and Snell, *Souls in Transition*, 291-92.

the centripetal value of churches in building community and the centrifugal benefit they offer to society in reaching out to needy and vulnerable neighbors. Paradoxically, this moral interest in religion remains as emergent adults are becoming less interested in spirituality as a belief system grounded in a scriptural narrative and an accompanying commitment to a religious institution (either through membership or regular attendance).[45]

Most of the religiously unaffiliated (or "Nones") in North America believe "that churches and other religious institutions benefit society by strengthening community bonds and aiding the poor," though they also "think that religious organizations are too concerned with money and power, too focused on rules and too involved in politics."[46] Regardless of whether they believe in God, pray, or attend religious services (and many of them still do), many Nones appeal to Jesus' teaching on the good Samaritan as an influential example of a "care ethics" grounded in radical love toward outsiders.[47]

Given the high value placed on religion as a "social asset" across age groups and generations, congregations often serve as communities that nurture values of caregiving and volunteering, which in turn "may also be a reason to continue participating in a congregation."[48] Young adults' preferences in church selection likely have to do more with "a sense of community" than the size of a congregation.[49] Among Nones, their sense and practice of relationality shows in their being "socially cosmopolitan in their embrace of all manner of difference, rather than narrowly communitarian or tribal."[50] Among the unaffiliated, those who are theists embody a spirituality of "immanent transcendence," in which God acts in everyday life events such as the encouragement of family and friends in difficult times, "rather than in either a mystical bridging of divine and human worlds or a promised eternal hereafter."[51] On the other hand, "non-believing Nones" have

[45]Smith and Snell, *Souls in Transition*, 286-87, 291.

[46]Pew Research Center, "'Nones' on the Rise," October 9, 2012, www.pewforum.org/2012/10/09/nones-on-the-rise, p. 10; see also 23, 58-60. Similar trends were reported subsequently in Pew Research Center, "U.S. Public Becoming Less Religious," November 3, 2015, www.pewforum.org/2015/11/03/u-s-public-becoming-less-religious, pp. 30-31, 92-96; see also Elizabeth Drescher, *Choosing Our Religion: The Spiritual Lives of America's Nones* (New York: Oxford University Press, 2016), 9, 182-217.

[47]Drescher, *Choosing Our Religion*, 203-8.

[48]Wuthnow, *After the Baby Boomers*, 229.

[49]Wuthnow, *After the Baby Boomers*, 223.

[50]Drescher, *Choosing Our Religion*, 249.

[51]Drescher, *Choosing Our Religion*, 248.

adopted "non-theistic practices of self-transcendence . . . in an 'immanent frame'" that focus on "compassionate, ethical action."[52]

Similarly, in their study of young Christian millennials, David Kinnaman and Aly Hawkins show that they are not only "self-centered," but also "very communal and peer-oriented."[53] They crave belonging to a lively community that makes a difference in the world. Because their "participatory mindset" is based on the idea that "everyone has the right to belong," they look with suspicion at "spiritual communities that feel like insider-only clubs."[54] Their unprecedented global interconnectedness has made them "keenly aware of economic and social disparities" worldwide.[55] For many young millennial Christians, their "focus on social justice" has been linked to their belief that "evangelism must be connected to actions on behalf of others."[56] Their organic view of faith and justice drives their special concern for excluded neighbors, whom they believe the church has at times forgotten.

> Passionate, mission-driven exiles seem to share the conviction that the North American church has somehow lost its heart for the very kinds of people Jesus sought out during his earthly ministry—the oppressed, the poor, and the physically, emotionally, and socially crippled.[57]

In his work on understanding and reaching out to the Nones, James Emery White suggests that, although belonging to a community is important to the religiously unaffiliated for affirmation, having a cause to live by or advocate for drives their need "for attraction."[58] The logical priority given to community over cause, or vice versa, depends on the audience with whom one shares the Christian story. Whereas an Acts 2 model of missions assumes a biblically literate audience, an Acts 17 model best addresses the situation of North Americans like the Nones who are increasingly less familiar with biblical narratives.

---

[52]Drescher, *Choosing Our Religion*, 248.

[53]David Kinnaman and Aly Hawkins, *You Lost Me: Why Young Christians Are Leaving Church . . . and Rethinking Faith* (Grand Rapids: Baker Books, 2011), 77.

[54]Kinnaman and Hawkins, *You Lost Me*, 174.

[55]Kinnaman and Hawkins, *You Lost Me*, 171.

[56]Kinnaman and Hawkins, *You Lost Me*, 177.

[57]Kinnaman and Hawkins, *You Lost Me*, 178-79.

[58]James Emery White, *The Rise of the Nones: Understanding and Reaching the Religiously Unaffiliated* (Grand Rapids: Baker Books, 2014), 143.

> In Acts 2, you have Peter before the God-fearing Jews of Jerusalem. . . . Peter was able to speak to a group of people who were already monotheists, already buying into the Old Testament Scriptures, and already believing in a coming Messiah. Now move to Acts 17:22-31. Paul is on Mars Hill speaking to the philosophers and spiritual theorists of Athens. This was a spiritual marketplace where truth was relative, worldviews and gods littered the landscape, and the average person didn't know Abraham from an apricot. . . . They didn't have any knowledge of the Christian faith to start with. Like today.[59]

In Acts 2, Peter proclaims the word, hearers are baptized in the name of Jesus Christ, and the Holy Spirit makes them one in the apostolic community, from which they go out into the world as witnesses of Christ. We see a movement from a proclamation event (that is, preaching) to the formation of a community that in turn nurtures a cause to live by. Community around the Word precedes and guides cause. White claims that, unlike other groups in the past, Nones typically do not come into the church through "proclamation-oriented" events such as "revivals, crusades, or door-to-door visitation."[60] Instead, they are more likely to consider church through a process that begins with attraction to a common cause and then to being part of a community, and such engagement in turn leads to the proclamation and hearing of Christ and his way of life as the fulfillment of God's plan for creation and humanity.

In Acts 17, Paul first engages a skeptical and biblically illiterate audience with one of their familiar cultural-religious symbols, then moves on to the story of God's work in the creation of the world and the human family while appealing to their poets' acknowledgment of a common origin that transcends them, and eventually arrives at a proclamation of Christ's resurrection as the fulfillment of the Creator's plan for the human race.[61] One could argue that the audience in Acts 17 is still a religious one, like a sizeable number of North American Nones, who though religiously unaffiliated are still religious or spiritual at some level and, moreover, have some Christian background.[62] Having said that, White's comments

---

[59]White, *Rise of the Nones*, 65-66.

[60]White, *Rise of the Nones*, 101.

[61]"Process models are needed in Acts 17, Mars Hill, *nones*/skeptical contexts. . . . The presentation of Christ must remain central to our thinking, to be sure. . . . But is that where we start? On Mars Hill, the spiritual illiteracy was so deep that Paul had to begin with cultural touchstones, lead into creation, and work his way forward. It took him a while to get to Christ." White, *Rise of the Nones*, 101.

[62]Drescher's study of North American Nones addresses, for the most part, the situation of people with some Christian background who are nevertheless not affiliated. Drescher, *Choosing our Religion*, 16-17, 82.

about the Christian illiteracy of Nones (with or without some Christian background) still hold. Furthermore, White raises the question of what constitutes a proper starting point for communicating life in Christ when dealing with hearers with little or no knowledge of the Christian story. White's thoughts suggest that not dialogue about the spiritual life alone but also embodiment of such a life by God's people, mainly in service and hospitality, has the potential for attracting neighbors to a more fulfilling life in a world full of suffering.

Indeed, the attraction of living for a cause points to another spiritual need and hope, namely, the search for a meaningful life. Among reasons for dropping out of church, Kinnaman and Hawkins found that "few young Christians can coherently connect their faith with their gifts, abilities, and passions" and, therefore, struggle to have "a sense of calling."[63] Channeling what a person has to offer through a cause, vocation, or calling contributes toward his or her personal integration and fosters a sense of being a contributor in a world filled with needy neighbors. Kinnaman and Hawkins find it "heartbreaking" and "a modern tragedy" that "next-generation Christians have no idea that their faith connects to their life's work, . . . no clear vision for a life of meaning."[64] The authors suggest that when young adults struggle with their faith in college, "many times it is because the Christian community has not provided a sufficiently strong set of relationships, sense of purpose, or whole-life coaching."[65] In addition to adhering to a creed, belonging to a community of faith, and having a hope to live by, Dean argues, a "consequential faith" among highly devoted Christian teenagers includes a clear sense of purpose, call, or mission in the world.[66] In contrast to the diluted Christianity of

---

Given the predominant Christian background of her survey sample, Drescher's observation that "becoming None does not erase or overwrite whatever came before it" is worth remembering. *Choosing our Religion*, 88. I often use the terms "religion" and "spirituality" interchangeably throughout this book. Yet I agree with Drescher that, among Nones, the word "religion" functions negatively. It "carries historical, ideological, and political baggage" associated with institutional structures complicit in violence, hypocritical and judgmental leaders, and the tendency "to overwrite self-identity . . . to compromise personal integrity and authenticity." Drescher, *Choosing our Religion*, 45-46.

[63]Kinnaman and Hawkins, *You Lost Me*, 92.

[64]Kinnaman and Hawkins, *You Lost Me*, 207. "One of the recurring themes in our research with young exiles is the idea that Christianity does not have much, if anything, to say about their chosen profession or field. The ways career and calling connect to faith and church community seem to be missing pieces in the puzzle for many young exiles." Kinnaman and Hawkins, *You Lost Me*, 78. The authors define "young exiles" as people who "want to inform and transform the 'foreign' culture that surrounds them, rather than withdrawing from it." Kinnaman and Hawkins, *You Lost Me*, 76-77.

[65]Kinnaman and Hawkins, *You Lost Me*, 141.

[66]Dean, *Almost Christian*, 22, 42, 75-76. The "devoted" (8% of American youth) appear as a religious type in the 2003–2005 National Study of Youth and Religion in the United States. Dean, *Almost Christian*, 40-41.

MTD, for instance, she notes that "highly devoted Christian teenagers did not think about their actions or their futures simply in terms of what *they* wanted. They considered themselves morally bound to contribute to God's purpose in the world."[67] This research seems to support an assumption in our argument, namely, that when God's people grasp more deeply and habitually what life in the Spirit of Christ entails in their own lives, they are also in a better position to guide others in their spiritual journeys—indeed, to dialogue, attract, and invite others into the spiritual life they know, embody, and delight in.

***Generational struggles.*** Another lens for understanding and interpreting the spiritual landscape in North America lies in the comparative study of generations. In his study of generational intelligence among North Americans, Shaw and Kolbaba look at the different spiritual strengths and temptations of Traditionalists (born before 1945), baby boomers, Generation Xers, and millennials.[68] Against the tendency of people from one generation critiquing those of another, the authors argue that each generation has its gifts and vulnerabilities that foster and stunt spiritual growth, respectively.[69] The authors' description of generational struggles as "temptations" bears an affinity with our dramatic model of the sanctified life, in which believers struggle with their vulnerabilities and are tempted to live in ways that honor neither God nor neighbor.

Although Traditionalists give financially out of duty so that their generosity often comes without too many strings attached, they nevertheless struggle with reaching a proper balance between a leisurely life and lack of purpose in their retirement years.[70] With the boomers, a shift occurs from loyalty to a religious group found among Traditionalists to a focus on the experience of a personal relationship with God; yet the boomers' time to search for spiritual meaning arguably became too self-centered, and the primary role of religion became therapeutic (namely, to make people feel good about themselves).[71] They prepare the way for the formation of moralistic therapeutic deists!

---

[67]Dean, *Almost Christian*, 76.

[68]Haydn Shaw and Ginger Kolbaba, *Generational IQ: Christianity Isn't Dying, Millennials Aren't the Problem, and the Future Is Bright* (Carol Stream, IL: Tyndale House, 2015).

[69]Shaw and Kolbaba, *Generational IQ*, 19-20.

[70]Shaw and Kolbaba, *Generational IQ*, 32-40. Shaw and Kolbaba critically suggest that "God didn't give Traditionalists—or any of us—more life, more money, and more health for our quality of life alone. God gave it to get his work done in the world." *Generational IQ*, 40.

[71]Shaw and Kolbaba, *Generational IQ*, 49-56. "If society valued self-expression, self-exploration, and personal satisfaction, there was little to keep Boomers from becoming self-centered. Boomers . . . became

Due in part to the experience of seeing higher divorce rates among their boomer parents, Gen Xers value long-term and stable relationships by making family and play time with their children a higher priority than work.[72] They are more likely to sacrifice work for family than family for work. In contrast to their predecessors' therapeutic "search for self-fulfillment," Gen Xers reclaimed the importance of community and Christ's concern for the disadvantaged.[73] By focusing on meaningful work, millennials began to channel their energies toward making an immediate impact in an unpredictable and flawed world.[74] They assume no one is perfect, but still demand authenticity and loyalty in relationships.[75] While Gen Xers and millennials share a more realistic (and at times cynical or negative) view of the world than their predecessors, as well as an interest in communal life and social causes, they seem to hold slightly different views on the value of work. If Gen Xers view work as a necessary means of survival, millennials approach it as a means of creative expression for a worthy cause.[76]

The same spiritual yearnings mean different things, depending on the generation in view. Take the desire for meaning or purpose in life. It can include searching for self-fulfillment among boomers, reclaiming devotion to family among Gen Xers, or finding a cause that makes a difference in the world among millennials. Another is the need for balance in life, exemplified in the tension that often exists between work or vocation and other important aspects of life. We see an attempt at resolving this tension in the priority Traditionalists give to leisurely activities over participation in God's mission during their retirement. We also see

---

*hyper*individualistic. This hyperindividualism has led to two temptations that Boomers (and the rest of us) face: a focus on self and church hopping." Shaw and Kolbaba, *Generational IQ*, 51. Shaw and Kolbaba implicitly suggest that, with their hyperindividualism and "overconfidence in psychology," the boomers laid out the foundation for the millennials' adherence to MTD: "The major goal of religion is to make you *be* good, and the major benefit God provides is to make you *feel* good. Millennials told Smith that God wants you to feel good about yourself, and he is there to comfort you—like a cross between a loving uncle who is almost never angry no matter what you do and a therapist who helps you feel better about yourself. The Boomers, like Homer Simpson, had lost faith that Jesus' 'well-meaning rules' still 'work in real life.' So they latched on to psychology and the therapeutic techniques. This overconfidence in psychology and the therapeutic is the spiritual vulnerability that allowed Christianity to be hacked until it became about us rather than God. In the 'feel good' mentality, God serves us rather than us serving God." *Generational IQ*, 110-11.

[72]Shaw and Kolbaba, *Generational IQ*, 68-71.

[73]Shaw and Kolbaba, *Generational IQ*, 70-71.

[74]Shaw and Kolbaba, *Generational IQ*, 87-88.

[75]Shaw and Kolbaba, *Generational IQ*, 88-89.

[76]Shaw and Kolbaba, *Generational IQ*, 87.

the human search for balance in the high valuing of family bonding among Gen Xers, and, on the other hand, in the renewed emphasis on work as a creative means of self-expression among millennials.

Another dominant theme is the cry for building community and belonging in a highly individualistic and utilitarian culture. Traditionalists feel they belong when they are members of an institution to which they are bound by duty. Boomers sense belonging when they experience a personal relationship with God and others. Gen Xers find acceptance in strong family and friend networks. Millennials know they belong when they work in teams as advocates for a worthy cause. Finally, all generations have a place for reaching out to vulnerable neighbors, and they see the church and religious institutions as helpful channels of humanitarian assistance or advocacy for those who cannot speak for themselves. Of course, their rationale or means of involvement in social causes might be different depending on their generational worldviews.

***What about the Global South factor? A US Hispanic angle.*** As one considers often-cited voices in the field of the sociology of religion and the way church writers interact with their findings, one notes a significant gap. How do the aforementioned spiritual characteristics of North Americans square with the situation of racial-ethnic minorities and the children of Global South immigrants to the US? In White's study on the Nones, he rightly observes that the rise of the religiously unaffiliated is "only an American phenomenon, not a global one."[77] Moreover, he notes that the rise of the unaffiliated is mostly a white phenomenon.[78] Although made in passing, these comments express a certain tension in studies on groups such as US Hispanics, who, as bearers of a cultural hybridity or *mestizaje* that includes a coming together and mixing of at least two different cultural worlds, can exhibit spiritual characteristics similar to both the rest of the North American population and the Global South communities from where their parents or ancestors claim their geographical or spiritual origins.

For instance, Jenkins argues that, unlike the rest of the industrialized nations in Europe where Christianity is decreasing, the US will experience significant

---

[77]White, *Rise of the Nones*, 18.

[78]"Of all *nones*, 71 percent are white, 11 percent are Hispanic, 9 percent are black, and 4 percent are Asian. If you narrow the pool to just agnostics and atheists, the group is even whiter: 82 percent." White, *Rise of the Nones*, 22.

Christian growth by 2050 and thus remain essentially a Christian country.[79] Those Christians, however, will reflect the changing demographics of the nation, including the growth of its Hispanic population.[80] Due in part to "the continuing Christian influx from Africa, Asia, and above all, Latin America" as a result of global migration, Christianity's center of gravity in the US will reflect Christianity's global shift from the north to the south.[81] From this angle, some of the characteristics of Global South Christianity, such as its focus on God's direct intervention in everyday affairs; prayers for healing; spiritual battle with demonic forces; concern for the poor, the exiles, or the persecuted; and strongly inculturated forms of worship are present in some shape among US Hispanics.[82] Rather than imagining the US as an increasingly secular, agnostic, and atheistic nation, Jenkins asserts that the "secularization model . . . works wonderfully well in Western Europe, where Christian loyalties and Christian numbers really are in decline, but woefully badly in the United States, where Christian churches continue to grow and flourish in the world's most advanced economy."[83] The Hispanic presence and growth in the nation shows that the Global South has already been a major part of the religious history of North America.

An important Pew study on Latino/a religion found that "for the great majority of Latinos . . . God is an active force in everyday life. Most Latinos pray every day, most have a religious object in their home and most attend a religious service at least once a month."[84] While there is similarity between Hispanics and non-Hispanic Christians on the frequency and practice of various religious beliefs, "Latinos appear to be different . . . in the intensity of their beliefs . . . [and are] somewhat more likely than non-Hispanics to say that religion is very important in their lives."[85] Hispanic Evangelicals are more likely than their non-Anglo

[79]Demographics show that the Christian population of the US will grow from 270 million in 2025 to 350 million in 2050. See Philip Jenkins, *The Next Christendom: The Coming of Global Christianity*, 3rd ed. (New York: Oxford University Press, 2011), 113; see also 131-33.

[80]White, *Rise of the Nones*, 125-30.

[81]White, *Rise of the Nones*, 133. "A United States with 100 million Latinos is very likely to have a far more Southern religious complexion than anything we can imagine at present." *Rise of the Nones*, 264.

[82]For selections of Jenkins's descriptions of Global South Christianity, see *Next Christendom*, 7-10, 98-100, 134-70, 269-76.

[83]Philip Jenkins, *The New Faces of Christianity: Believing the Bible in the Global South* (New York: Oxford University Press, 2006), 188.

[84]Pew Research Center, "Changing Faiths," April 25, 2007, www.pewforum.org/2007/04/25/changing-faiths-latinos-and-the-transformation-of-american-religion-2, p. 3.

[85]Pew Research Center, "Changing Faiths," 15-16.

counterparts to "participate in prayer groups and share their faith with others."[86] The study also shows that, similar to the explosive growth of Pentecostal and Charismatic churches in the Global South, "renewalist Christianity, which places special emphasis on God's ongoing, day-to-day intervention in human affairs through the person of the Holy Spirit, is having a major impact on Hispanic Christianity."[87] On this aspect of religious practice, Hispanic Protestants and Catholics alike are more likely than their non-Hispanic counterparts to describe themselves as "charismatic or pentecostal Christians."[88] Furthermore, Latino Catholics are more likely than other Catholics to have experienced or witnessed an exorcism or divine healing.[89]

Despite the influential element of assimilation to mainstream US culture, Hispanic worship still shares the Global South's focus on an inculturated congregational life that accounts for a people's language and cultural background, as well as pastoral leadership coming from the people's group.[90] Furthermore, similar to Christians in the Global South, Hispanic religiosity shares a concern for addressing, either through advocacy or action, the plight of the poor and the socially disadvantaged: "More than half say churches and other houses of worship should address the social and political questions of the day."[91] More recently, the trend among Hispanics and non-Hispanics has been for the church and religious institutions to stay out of politics, although a sizable share of Hispanics still assert that the church should speak out on social and political issues.[92]

---

[86]Pew Research Center, "Changing Faiths," 17.

[87]Pew Research Center, "Changing Faiths," 3. "Renewalists believe that the power of the Holy Spirit is manifested through such supernatural phenomena as speaking in tongues, miraculous healings and prophetic utterances and revelations." Pew Research Center, "Changing Faiths," 27. A more recent study confirms these findings. See Pew Research Center, "The Shifting Religious Identity of Latinos," May 7, 2014, www.pewforum.org/2014/05/07/the-shifting-religious-identity-of-latinos-in-the-united-states, pp. 93-109.

[88]Pew Research Center, "Changing Faiths," 27; see also 30-32.

[89]Pew Research Center, "Changing Faiths," 27-28, 34-35; cf. Pew Research Center, "Shifting Religious Identity of Latinos," 110-16.

[90]"While the prevalence of Hispanic-oriented worship is higher among the foreign born, with 77% saying they attend churches with those characteristics, the phenomenon is also widespread among the native born, with 48% saying they attend ethnic churches." Pew Research Center, "Changing Faiths," 4. A more recent Pew report basically confirms these findings, although it also notes a somewhat smaller share of Hispanics attending churches with "ethnic characteristics." See Pew Research Center, "Shifting Religious Identity of Latinos," 75-84.

[91]Pew Research Center, "Changing Faiths," 4.

[92]Pew Research Center, "Shifting Religious Identity of Latinos," 123-24.

The Pew study also highlights the role of personal encounter with God in religious conversions (mostly from Catholicism to another religion): "By an overwhelming majority (82%), Hispanics cite the desire for a more direct, personal experience with God as the main reason for adopting a new faith."[93] Significantly, at the time of the study, "almost one-in-five (18%) Latinos said they had either converted from one religion to another or to no religion at all."[94] More recent Pew studies have drawn attention to the increasing number of Nones among Latino/as, with fifteen percent of younger Hispanics claiming to be "nothing in particular."[95] Yet even religiously unaffiliated Hispanics with a "medium level of religious commitment" are a bit more religious than their non-Hispanic counterparts.[96] As a whole, these studies remind us of the complexity and hybridity of the spiritual life of North Americans such as Hispanics, giving us a slightly different perspective to compare our data on general trends to particular groups and individuals who may or may not fit the demographics in every situation.

As Aponte argues, the conception and practice of what is *santo*—that is, sacred or holy—among Latino/as is comprehensive and includes "perspectives on traditional religion, life interpretation and explanations (sense-making), healing, health, wholeness, understandings of existence and the future, and balancing relationships at all levels of existence."[97] Within that diversity, there are common spiritual needs and hopes embodied in varieties of Latino/a spirituality (a certain shared *latinidad*), including the "*importance of community and family and the shared experience of assigned identity in the United States.*"[98] For example, the elaborate celebration of the *quinceañera* (fifteenth-year-old girl), a popular rite of passage into womanhood in many US Hispanic settings, or the remembrance of the departed on the Day of the Dead (Sp. *día de los muertos*) festivities (particularly among Mexican Americans) "contribute to contextualizing the sense of community and connection among Latinos and Latinas."[99]

---

[93]Pew Research Center, "Changing Faiths," 3; see also 42-43.

[94]Pew Research Center, "Changing Faiths," 40.

[95]Pew Research Center, "Shifting Religious Identity of Latinos," 29.

[96]Pew Research Center, "Shifting Religious Identity of Latinos," 60.

[97]Edwin David Aponte, *¡Santo! Varieties of Latino/a Spirituality* (Maryknoll, NY: Orbis, 2012), 10; see also 51-55.

[98]Aponte, *¡Santo!*, 76; see also 74-77. For a more in-depth woman's perspective, see Michelle A. González, *Embracing Latina Spirituality: A Woman's Perspective* (Cincinnati: St. Anthony Messenger Press, 2009).

[99]Aponte, *¡Santo!*, 97; see also 86-87, 95-96.

Because Latino/a spirituality transcends the mainstream US dichotomy between the sacred and the secular, it incorporates everyday life (Sp. *lo cotidiano*) into its practice of spirituality.[100] At some point, many Hispanics have received spiritual *consejo* (advice) or a *bendición* (blessing) from *abuela* (grandma).[101] These are practices that not only bring spirituality into the noninstitutional setting of family life, but also highlight the public role of mentors in fostering spiritual, bodily, and relational health and wholeness. Sacred spaces such as temples, family altars, and places of pilgrimage function as "places of quiet contemplation, of prayer and meditation, or places where persons withdraw to recharge . . . locations where there is a feeling of safety and protection."[102] Among Hispanics, the family altar and places of mourning such as cemeteries often foster a sense of belonging to a larger community, but also provide a place to remember and pass on family stories to other generations.[103] Building on the work of Nanko-Fernández and others, Aponte highlights the role of a "Spanglish spirituality"—that is, the ethnic-racial, cultural-linguistic mixing between two or more worlds—among Latino/as in fostering "daily border crossings" or intercultural exchanges between different people groups.[104] We have here a move away from static monocultural visions of North American life toward a more dynamic engagement with the "other."

A cursory reading of the varieties of Latino/a spirituality in North America reveals an affinity between the needs and hopes of this growing sector of the population and our models of the sanctified life. Consider how sacred spaces offer security and refreshment, a coming together of our dramatic and devotional models. Or consider how *quinceañeras*, family altars, and life in Spanglish can foster community, belonging, and right relations across generations and cultures—a portrayal of life that brings together aspects of our sacrificial, hospitality, and renewal models. At the same time, the study of a particular group allows us to reflect theologically on the actual lived experience of neighbors, and thus to remind systematic theology of the specific contexts and people it interacts with and of its pastoral or practical function.

---

[100] Aponte, *¡Santo!*, 100.

[101] Aponte, *¡Santo!*, 107-9.

[102] Aponte, *¡Santo!*, 117.

[103] Aponte, *¡Santo!*, 124-26, 130-32.

[104] Aponte, *¡Santo!*, 134; see also 133-47. See Carmen Nanko-Fernández, *Theologizing en Espanglish: Context, Community, and Ministry* (Maryknoll, NY: Orbis, 2010).

## I WANT TO TELL THE STORY: THE CRY OF THE HUMAN SPIRIT AND THE HOLY SPIRIT'S WORK

When we speak of the human spirit in theological terms, we speak more specifically of the human person as both created in the image of God (Lat. *imago Dei*) and corrupted by sin. Humans are a paradox. Made as God's good creatures for communion with God, and yet sinful creatures, separated from God. Religious and open to transcendence, yet idolatrous and turned in on themselves. Deeply gifted, yet deeply flawed. Accordingly, Luther described the Christian as being simultaneously saint and sinner (Lat. *simul iustus et peccator*), or in pneumatological terms, as being both killed in the flesh (Lat. *caro*) as a sinner and made alive as a spiritual person (or spirit, Lat. *spiritus*) by the Holy Spirit. A number of early church theologians such as Irenaeus, Cyril of Jerusalem, and Basil, spoke of this paradox of human existence through the story of the life-giving Spirit's coming to the human race (via the first Adam) in the first creation, its departing from the race of Adam on account of sin, and finally its returning to the human race in the fullness of time through Christ, the second or last Adam, the firstfruits of a new creation.

Behind this telling of the story of the human spirit lies a Christological interpretation of the Genesis account according to which Christ, the last Adam, becomes a life-giving spirit through his resurrection from the dead and opens the way for the bestowal of life to the dead race of Adam through his breathing of the Spirit on others (cf. Gen 2:7; 1 Cor 15:45; Jn 20:22).[105] The eschatological contrast between the first Adam (signifying the old creation, and thus our death) and the last Adam (signifying the new creation, and thus new life in Christ) can be restated in pneumatological terms. Christ bears the fullness of the Spirit to live the life Adam cannot live in full communion with God and to die in our place the death Adam cannot escape. Through the breathing of the gift of the Spirit, the risen Christ gives to the race of Adam the life Adam cannot live, raising us from the dead after his image and likeness as the last Adam, and thus restoring us to fellowship with God. In anthropological terms, we can state our human predicament

[105]Concerning Christ's identity as "life giving spirit" in 1 Cor 15:45, Fee argues that "Christ is not *the* Spirit; rather, in a play on the Genesis text, Paul says that Christ through his resurrection assumed his new existence in the spiritual realm, the realm of course that for the believer is the ultimate sphere of the Spirit." Gordon D. Fee, *God's Empowering Presence: The Holy Spirit in the Letters of Paul* (Peabody, MA: Hendrickson, 1994), 267. Montague sees the text as an indication that "the risen body of Jesus possessed the Spirit in a way to give it to whoever contacts the risen Lord through faith and sacrament . . . it is his body which becomes the seat and the source of the Spirit." George T. Montague, *Holy Spirit: Growth of a Biblical Tradition* (Peabody, MA: Hendrickson, 1976), 142.

as follows: The human spirit is dead. The Holy Spirit must bring the dead back to life.

***The cry of the human spirit and the Holy Spirit.*** In *The Logic of the Spirit*, James E. Loder argues that even though theories of human development deal with "issues of purpose and meaning," they do so "insufficiently" and thus require a theological perspective.[106] The problem lies in the paradox of the human spirit, which on the one hand "will always point beyond itself" to a wisdom that transcends it, and on the other hand, cannot set itself "free *from* its proclivity to self-inflation, self-doubt, self-absorption, and self-destruction . . . to participate in the Spirit of God and to know the mind of God."[107] Beginning with St. Paul's teaching on the self-knowledge of the human spirit, which nevertheless cannot know God unless it has the mind of Christ by receiving God's Spirit (1 Cor 2:10-16), the author posits a "Christomorphic" understanding of the relationship between the human spirit and the Holy Spirit.[108] By delving into the depths of human self-knowledge, theories of human development uncover, in various ways, the human struggle for survival from non-being. But they do not offer a lasting solution to the threat of death.

> The ego's aim is adaptation to its physical, social, and cultural environment so as to maximize satisfaction and ensure survival. . . . When the human spirit finds its ground in the Divine Spirit, then its aim is disclosed as . . . personal union with the presence and purposes of God. Subsequently, the human spirit . . . will seek to bring all ego competencies into line with those purposes, even if it means counteradaptive behavior and suffering in place of satisfaction and survival.[109]

Instead of avoiding the inevitability of death, to which we are heading already from the moment of birth as we move along the axis of human development, the point is to face death head-on. By conforming us to Christ's death, the Holy Spirit breaks into our contingent lives to bring us out of death into Christ's life.[110] Loder draws from Regin Prenter's *Spiritus Creator*, a classic work on the pneumatology

[106]Loder, *Logic of the Spirit*, xiii.

[107]Loder, *Logic of the Spirit*, 10.

[108]Loder, *Logic of the Spirit*, 41. In his second chapter (17-43), the author uses various terms to refer to this christomorphic spirit-Spirit relationship, such as "analogy of spirit" (Lat. *analogia spiritus*, 35), "bipolar relational unity between two spirits" (36), and "'I-not I-but Christ' identity" (36).

[109]Loder, *Logic of the Spirit*, 72-73.

[110]"Recognizing that human beings begin to die the moment they are born, the higher order of reality revealed in the life, death, and resurrection of Jesus Christ includes the ego's development, but only in light of its incipient potentiality for new being in him. Thus, the spiritual axis not only exposes the suppression

of Luther, to describe the Holy Spirit's transformational work of conforming sinners to Christ's death and resurrection by mortification (being convicted of sin) and illumination (receiving the alien righteousness of Christ), respectively.[111] Through God's judgment against the sinner, the Spirit brings the human spirit into a conflict with God from which only the Spirit itself can bring him or her out alive. Through the proclamation of the gospel, the Spirit communicates Christ's alien righteousness to the sinner, establishing a new identity for him or her in Christ. In the language of development, "the ego can release its defensive patterns . . . and allow the 'ego-alien righteousness' of Christ to bestow the Gospel, and to establish for the person a higher order of meaning and purpose."[112] By conforming us to Jesus Christ in his death and resurrection, the Holy Spirit establishes a new identity in us. Loder speaks in Pauline terms of the process whereby the human spirit receives such an identity. It is an "I–Not I–but Christ" experience.[113] A Spirit-led move has thus taken place from the "I" to the "Not I" and finally to the "but Christ," so that our death is swallowed up in Christ's death and our life is taken up in Christ.

Although Prenter does not share Loder's high view of differentiated affinity between the human spirit and the Holy Spirit, both authors attribute to the Holy Spirit alone the work of shaping the human person after the pattern of Christ's death and resurrection.[114] For Prenter, such christoformation involves inner conflict, namely, the sinner's experience of guilt before God and his or her death under God's wrath.[115] Yet this "alien work" (Lat. *opus alienum*)

---

of death, which is so prevalent in studies of ego development, but also makes death a dominant theme as the human spirit seeks union with God and God's purpose." Loder, *Logic of the Spirit*, 73.

[111]Loder, *Logic of the Spirit*, 114-16.

[112]Loder, *Logic of the Spirit*, 116.

[113]Loder, *Logic of the Spirit*, 36, 120, 145-46.

[114]Prenter notes Luther's opposition to the idea that "God's Spirit and the spirit of man are spirit, that there in man's own spirit is an urge toward the spiritual, and that it is the task of grace to sublimate this urge and guide it to its high goal." Regin Prenter, *Spiritus Creator: Luther's Concept of the Holy Spirit*, trans. John M. Jensen (Philadelphia: Muhlenberg, 1953), 23. There are at least two reasons for Luther's opposition to the analogy of spirit-to-Spirit in scholastic theology. First, the anthropology at work divides the person "into a lower, sensually directed stratum and a higher stratum directed toward the spiritual realities of our nature" (*Spiritus Creator*, 22), which diverts attention away from the Spirit's work of conforming "the whole man" (Lat. *totus homo*) to Christ (see 5-6, 26). Second, the theology of grace at work is not monergistic and therefore gives the impression that the Holy Spirit is not the sole subject of vivification but an "aid" (though a critical one in offering grace) to human natural (or supernatural) striving for spiritual things (10, 18-21). There is an accompanying fear of salvation by works, in which persons "striving by the constant aid of grace, reach upward on the meritorious ladder toward . . . the enjoyment of God" (21).

[115]See Prenter, *Spiritus Creator*, 14-15.

of the Spirit against the "flesh" (Lat. *caro*)—that is, the whole person (Lat. *totus homo*) as sinner or without the Spirit—leads to its "proper work" (Lat. *opus proprium*), which is to make the sinner alive in Christ.[116] The experience of "inner conflict" (Luther's *tentatio* or *Anfechtung*) brings home our distance from God, but also our need for God's deliverance from guilt and death. The Spirit uses the inner conflict to turn the old creature into "spirit" (Lat. *spiritus*) or a spiritual person, which means that the person is freed from guilt and becomes a new creation under the Holy Spirit's influence. The Spirit puts to death in order to make alive.

From the perspective of human development, Loder sees such conflict as essential to make persons aware of their distance from and need for God as the starting point for dealing with (instead of avoiding) deep-seated life struggles. Although experiencing the absence of God in the midst of life struggles is not pleasant, it does awaken persons to a recognition of the truth about their situation and opens the door for trust, perseverance, healing, forgiveness, and reconciliation with God and others.[117] In contrast to Erikson's negative diagnosis of young man Luther's *Anfechtungen* as a form of "psychopathology" to deal with psychological guilt, Loder argues that Luther's struggles with both the absence and nearness of God are "an expression of his spiritual life."[118] In other words, his life reveals not a defense mechanism of the ego, but a cruciform life in the Spirit.

A Spirit Christology shows how Christ's own life in the Spirit is shaped by the cross. On the cross, Christ experiences his *Anfechtung* in the Spirit. Becoming a sinner for us, the sinless Christ undergoes God's judgment against sinners. In this act of solidarity, Christ does not avoid death but faces it head-on for us. Raised by the Father in the eschatological realm of the Spirit, Christ becomes an incarnate life-giving spirit and thus the firstfruits of our resurrection. Loder and Prenter lay out the way the Spirit incorporates us to Christ's life in the Spirit in a way that brings together our descriptions of the sanctified life under the renewal and dramatic models. Through the word of judgment and conviction, the Holy Spirit makes the human spirit aware of its struggle with sin, death, and the devil, and thus of its separation from God. Through the word of forgiveness and promise, the

---

[116]Prenter, *Spiritus Creator*, 16.

[117]Loder offers the story of Helen's transformation as a case study. See Loder, *Logic of the Spirit*, 46-55.

[118]Loder, *Logic of the Spirit*, 246.

Holy Spirit brings the human spirit near to God, and it can now face life—not only in the hereafter, but even now—without the fear of death.

Through the cyclical event of proclamation, the Spirit's work of killing and making alive effectively leads to a continual recognition of our grieving of the Spirit and an ongoing prayer (*epiclesis*) for the gracious return of the Spirit into our lives. The grand story of the Holy Spirit's departure and return that Irenaeus and others described as a sweeping account of salvation history is now effectively carried out in the Spirit's descent through the sacramental Word in baptismal initiation and the spoken Word in preaching, teaching, and spiritual care. We become participants of the Spirit of Christ in the story. The life that flows from the Spirit's work is also Christlike. Having the mind of Christ, we are made partakers of the things of God, and we receive the wisdom of the Spirit to walk by the Spirit. We do so according to the fruit of the Spirit, which is the life Christ lives in and through us—or put in pneumatological terms, the life of Christ that the Spirit forms in us.

As we have argued, such life looks like Christ's own life in the Spirit and involves such forms of being and becoming described under our models. The sculptor Spirit molds us after the likeness of Christ in his death and resurrection (renewal model), in his struggle and conflict with the devil (dramatic), in his sacrificial witness and life sharing with the literal poor and the poor in spirit (sacrifice), in his self-identification with and embrace of marginalized and unlovable neighbors into God's kingdom (hospitality), and in his devotion to the Father in prayer and to the world in labor for its healing (devotional).

***Dialogue, modeling, and invitation.*** How do we tell the story of God's work in and through Christ by the Spirit in a way that connects with neighbors who hunger for a spiritual life? What forms might such engagement take? Through dialogue, modeling, and invitation, we can hear our neighbors' stories and share our own spiritual journeys with them. Each form of engagement offers a different entry point into conversations about our perceived spiritual needs and hopes.

*The way of dialogue*. In *dialogue*, the saints listen to and learn from neighbors with struggles and aspirations similar to theirs. Such sharing creates a space for trust and relationship building, but also for revisiting or rethinking one's identity in light of a compelling narrative. In dialogue, one interprets theologically what one hears and says in the interest of better understanding, communication, and even action. Consider our hospitality model of the sanctified life and its capacity to speak to persons craving for belonging. After years of working in the Lutheran Church in the US, a denominational family with German immigrant roots, I still get some puzzling looks when people learn that I am a Latino Lutheran. Is that even possible? Aren't Latinos supposed to be Catholic? How exactly does an immigrant with a strange accent and different traditions become a Lutheran? They are really asking, can "they" become one of "us"? Reactions range from disbelief to curiosity to fear, and often take place in changing neighborhoods where the church is surrounded by strangers with similar accents and traditions—people who speak and look like me! As I listen generously to their concerns, I hear their worries of losing their sense of religious and cultural identity, their customs and traditions being replaced by those of newcomers, and their powerlessness to engage the unknown with wisdom and grace.

As a way to prepare fearful folks for similar encounters with their "other" neighbors, I often share with them how, upon arriving in America, their own German-speaking Lutheran forefathers and foremothers were often met with similar suspicion and reservations by the English-speaking locals. If one reads old newspapers speaking of the newbies in town, the locals also anxiously wondered about their strange accents and odd customs. Do they speak the right way? Do they have the right religion? Can "they" be one of "us"? Are they in or out? In short, do they belong? Typically, as people in churches listen to this immigrant stranger engage them in conversation through a little peek into history, they begin to tap into an immigrant past they had long forgotten or not thought much about. They see not only how such remembrance honors the life and sacrifices of their ancestors and unveils the cloud of suspicion their predecessors at times were under, but also how they share with them a common desire for acceptance. Hearing each other out, with a little help from the past, we learn together that, though quite different from each other, we share fears of becoming marginalized and a common hunger for hospitality.

We can go even further back in history and make the same point by appealing to Scripture's compelling narratives of hospitality, stories of outsiders who are included in God's kingdom through faith in Jesus. Dialoguing with neighbors undergoing experiences of marginality can remind a church too comfortable in the world's ways of speaking about "others" of her own Galilean identity—that is to say, her own marginality in and rejection by the world. What is the church but a little Galilean community of disciples under the lordship of a rejected

Galilean Jesus! A people who like their Lord speak with strange accents and dance to odd drumbeats in a world hostile to the gospel message. Strangers remind us who we are as God's people! Outsiders who do not belong in the eyes of the world.

Yet these are also strangers who, like the Samaritan leper, are brought into God's kingdom by faith in the Galilean Jesus, the one who dared to walk along the despised border between Samaria and Galilee for their sake (Lk 17:11-19). Stories of marginality and hospitality help us to revisit and rethink our identity in light of God's Word. Strangers among us with strange accents and customs serve as a sign of the catholicity or universality of the church. Such a powerful reminder can in turn lead folks to a deeper appreciation for God's justification and acceptance in Christ of the Galileans and Samaritans in our midst apart from their performance and pedigree, and therefore to a greater disposition to love the unlovable among us and extend the hand of welcome to outsiders. Through dialogue, themes and narratives from a model of sanctification can foster understanding about common spiritual needs and address them in a winsome and constructive way leading to self-reflection and action.

Another story illustrates how the gift of dialogue can engage the spiritual concerns of neighbors seeking vocational and family health. Years ago, I had the opportunity to see my father, now a retired Panama Canal occupational health and safety officer, offer company workers a workshop on safety in the workplace. After years away from the church, my father had recently become an active lay catechist in his local parish. He began to see not only his personal life but his own vocation in the workplace through the eyes of his revitalized faith. Although the company line appeared to stress how safety training was critical to increase efficiency and productivity in the workplace, my father brought to the table a more spiritual dimension. He approached his educational task by arguing that the most important reason for safety was to promote the workers' health and well-being, so that they could be there for their families as long as possible.

During one of his talks, he told the tragic story of an underwater repairman who did not make it out of his last job alive. He cemented in the attendees' minds the eerie picture of the man's car parked by itself in the large empty lot, still waiting for its driver to take it back home. Sadly, the man was never to return to his car again or, more devastatingly, to his family. Suddenly, workers who were otherwise not very thrilled to partake in the assigned rituals of job training, resonated with the spiritual dimension of the presenter's argument, that is, his pitch for the preservation of a healthy lifestyle in one's vocation for the sake of the well-being of the family. Moving beyond the normal utilitarian reasons for safety training struck a powerful chord with the workers. They felt appreciated as people whose lives and loved ones mattered.

Needless to say, in a materialistic and consumerist society bent on profits and efficiency, the workers craved a more humanizing approach to life. As the workshop went on, they wanted to know more about the vision of the spiritual life that drove my father's moral compass. By indirectly denouncing a utilitarian view of workers and announcing a more humane way of seeing work, the speaker went against the grain, the status quo, and opened a safe space for conversations about the need for a healthy vocational balance in life. In his own way, my father was engaging colleagues in self-reflection about the need for balancing work and family in the context of a concern for the health of the human person as God's creature. I remember my father sprinkling theological language into his argument, making passing references to God's care for his creatures at various points. In so doing, he was offering a devotional framework, a compelling story, for addressing a deep spiritual yearning of the workers that, in their estimation, had been long neglected.

*The way of modeling or embodiment.* Another way to encounter the neighbor is through *modeling*. Shaped by the Spirit after the likeness of Christ, the saints live according to the fruit of the Spirit. They embody life in the Spirit in a way that can often be naturally and even unassumingly attractive to others. In the words of St. Francis of Assisi's famous prayer, the saints become Christ's instruments of God's peace, love, pardon, faith, hope, light, and joy on earth:

> Make me an instrument of your peace: where there is hatred, let me bring your love; where there is injury, your pardon; where there is doubt, faith in you; where there is despair, your hope; where there is darkness, your light; where there is sadness, joy in you.[119]

Christ's disciples are set apart from the world as a holy people in order to be a light to the world. To the tune of the African American spiritual, they sing, "This little light of mine, I'm gonna let it shine!" Embodying a lived witness in our

[119]Adapted from the Spanish version, "Hazme un Instrumento de Tu Paz," in *Oramos Cantando, We Pray in Song* (Chicago: GIA Publications, 2013), 663. Translation mine.

relationships can make a lasting impression on people peeking every so often into the life of the church, looking at times for positive role models who can speak compelling truths and live by what they preach—role models they might not always see in the world. Christ's blessed disciples live by his words: "Let your light shine before others, so that they may see your good works and give glory to your Father who is in heaven" (Mt 5:16). And so the blessed ones of the Beatitudes are a blessing to others. Not a perfect but a faithful witness in word and deed can go a long way in our world today and set the stage for further engagement with the spiritually curious and hungry person.

Consider our sacrificial model of the sanctified life and its capacity to address the human need for community. As a fellowship sharing joys and burdens, the saints embody a sacrificial form of life that is attractive to many in a highly individualistic and utilitarian society. Holiness of life is, of course, tricky business. Admittedly, the institutional church and her scandals have shed light on the dark side of human nature, often posing as religious piety. Religious institutions are not easily trusted in our current climate. Christians can acknowledge their failures and sins. There is no perfect sanctification, and the saints especially can be upfront about their struggles. Avoiding a triumphalistic view of holiness that raises the bar too high, they can share not only their joys and victories with others, but also (and perhaps even more importantly in our cynical and narcissistic age) their burdens, failures, and transgressions.

Interestingly, Gen Xers and millennials actually expect no perfection from religious leaders, but they do expect and appreciate sacrifice and authenticity from them and their flocks. When the saints engage in "happy exchanges" with one another, they openly acknowledge their vulnerability and brokenness, as well as their need for mutual support and intercession. The church comes across not as a group of self-made individuals and spiritual superheroes, but as an interdependent family with its spiritual highs and lows where all sufferings and joys are shared in common. Sharing life through thick and thin becomes an attractive example of an authentic community at work that displays a generosity of spirit—a model of the spiritual life that, with the Spirit's intervention, leads neighbors to say, "Look at how they love each other!" (see Jn 13:35). In their suffering love for one another, God's living sacrifices spread the aroma of Christ in the world in the hope of eventually drawing people hungry for community into the eucharistic table where saints gather in the fellowship of the Spirit with their Lord.

As a young seminarian, I was once tasked by a congregation in a small Midwest town to canvass the neighborhood by visiting residents with Spanish last names. The congregation had expressed an interest in reaching out to their Hispanic neighbors, but had never had the know-how, time, or courage to engage them in any significant way—even though these neighbors had already been living among them for many years. After knocking on doors for weeks and talking to lots of folks, a common theme began to surface in a number of exchanges. A middle-aged Mexican man summarized it well: "We have always been here. We know that church. But they don't help us. They don't talk to us. They don't care about us."

After further conversation, I realized that the man's feelings about the congregation focused on what he perceived to be a disconnect between the church's faith in a loving Christ and her modeling or embodiment of Christ's love in the community. Perhaps the man was too quick to judge, but perceptions can be revealing. What struck me was that the man knew the church had an important spiritual message to share, but on account of her apparent lack of interest in neighbors like him, he was not sure he could trust her message. It is as if the man were saying, "If I can't trust you with the little things of mercy, how can I trust you with the big spiritual questions?" The man expected and wished the church to model, in "happy exchanges" with Hispanic neighbors, the love of God in Christ she proclaimed. The man craved for community and for the church to embody it in the Hispanic community too. His was a call for the church to extend the life shared together among her faithful to others yearning for meaningful relationships. Our story reminds us how sanctification, while not the cause or energy of justification, can still serve as an entry point into the spiritual life among neighbors who long for genuine people who, though by no means perfect, seek to model by the power of the Spirit a trustworthy message and way of life in a world filled with empty voices who talk the talk but do not walk the walk.

Another story of modeling comes to mind. It is the story of my longtime friendship with a self-proclaimed atheist, a former professor of mine. He did not fit the angry atheist stereotype. A very nice man and generous teacher, he was always polite about his beliefs even as he shared his convictions with others. On one occasion, I remember him questioning the notion that people could be "gifted" in some skill, because such a way of talking assumed a transcendent cause for being a certain kind of person. He preferred to say people were responsible for their own talent through hard work. Another time he spoke of love not as a metaphysical reality, but as a biological reaction and process. The message was clear: love could be explained scientifically, and thus not through a relational philosophy or a religious tradition. There are other examples of a secular humanist streak in my friend's observations, but his point was the same: Life has no ground in a spiritual reality. Life is what humans make of it.

The professor, a doctor of music, and I hit it off. I took classes from him at a later time in my life, which meant I was a doctor myself (a doctor of theology!) when we met in his classroom. He made a number of gestures in the course of our classes and conversations outside the classroom to show me and others how he honored my position in life. For instance, he once told me I could address him by his first name at any time during class. My conversations with him revealed to me that he wanted to show respect for someone who had devoted his life to the pursuit of knowledge, scholarship, and teaching. As one who walked the path of doctoral studies himself, he understood the sacrifices made and at times the modest pay that came from such a life. I was struck by his way of honoring what was in fact, from my own theological perspective, a life of devotion to God in service to others. He acknowledged me as one devoted to God, without explicitly acknowledging God's existence.

Over the years, we have spent enough time together for us to have had deep conversations about life, and especially about suffering. Losing his first wife at a young age to a terminal disease, my friend understandably had a hard time believing in the existence of a good and powerful God in the midst of such pain and tragic loss. Like many, he had a hard time with theodicy. Over lunch, he once expressed to me how he struggled with the God of the book of Job, who seemed to let an innocent man suffer for the sake of a stupid bet with the devil. "Explain that to me, Leo!" I did not try to defend God. To do so would have turned me into one of Job's friends, providing answers to questions hidden from us. Instead, I shared with him that Christians, like Job, deal with tragedy through prayer and lament, "My God, my God, why have you forsaken me?" (Ps 22:1; cf. Mt 27:46; Mk 15:34). That seemed unsatisfying, but we left it at that.

Some time passed by, and I heard the news that my friend had met a wonderful woman who would later become his wife. My wife and I were invited to their wedding, a beautiful event. Then it was baby shower time, and we were once again invited to attend. I was thrilled for him! So many blessings (from God) to be gifted with! But that was my way of thinking about reality theologically, not his. And yet, in the presence of all his friends and family, and to my complete surprise, right before mealtime he said to me, "Leo, would you please say grace?" I couldn't believe what I was hearing! My atheist friend was asking me to model devotion to God, even if he himself did not have scientific proof for his existence. Indeed, he was asking me to model a life of devotion in prayer, to live according to such Job-like devotion even if it did not make sense to him. But in doing so, he was also asking me to share such devotion with others, even those closest to him. Modeling can be a compelling way to attract others to ask deeper and difficult questions about a life of devotion in a suffering world, and perhaps even to attract them to such life itself by the power of the Spirit. Will my friend see his own life of study, scholarship, and teaching as a life of devotion to God? Will he cry out to God someday in lament amid the sufferings of life? Only the Spirit can make a crucified God attractive. Only the Spirit can attract someone to the Christlike life.

*The way of invitation.* Our models of the sanctified life do not merely comprise interesting metaphors about the spiritual life but intend to give us a window into divine realities grounded in God's ways of working in the world in and through Christ by the Spirit. Otherwise stated, our models reveal an economy of life in the Spirit that shapes hearers of God's story into spiritual persons. The aim of the Spirit's sculpting work in the world—as many church fathers remind us—is nothing less than human participation by the grace of adoption into the life of Christ for the sake of the world. Sharing our stories in light of God's story of the Spirit's work in and through Christ offers an open *invitation* for neighbors to consider seeing their own lives in light of the same story.

Let me illustrate this point with a couple of stories. The first story shows how a move toward hospitality in the context of relationship building opened the door for an invitation to set things right and experience reconciliation. Being a member of a large civic orchestra affords networking opportunities that lead to various kinds of musical associations and engagements out in the broader community. For years, I have collaborated with a talented musician and arranger who leads a combo in the city, and I have become great friends with him. When we first met, and he found out what my denominational church background was, he started telling me about how badly his mother had been treated by a pastor in my church body! Not a great way to get a conversation and gig started. He explained that, in her final years of life, she had become bitter about the church because of past hurts that were never dealt with. So she left the Lutheran church. I told him I was truly sorry to hear that and acknowledged that at times the church as a human institution has done wrong. He did not respond. I could tell he was holding a grudge, and rightfully so. For sure, I was not the pastor who had caused his mother much grief, but I was from the same church family!

Soon after that first engagement, we spoke a bit further over some food and drink. And then, he dropped the other shoe: "I told my mother I would never set foot in that church again!" I took him at his word. Over the next months, I began to offer my home for the ensemble's practices, and as part of the invitation, I would also ask everyone to arrive early for dinner. I was doing nothing more than opening my home to guests. But such hospitality did not only open doors, it opened hearts too. One summer, my church needed some organists to fill in for Sunday morning services. I knew my friend also played the organ in various churches, but I hesitated to ask him to help us. After all, this is the same man who had said to me about a year earlier, "I told my mother I would never . . ." But I went ahead and asked him anyway.

Something had happened that year. We went from being strangers to becoming friends. So next time we met, and thinking about my request, he looked at me straight in the eyes and said, "Leo, I told my mother I would never set foot in that church again." Then he paused, and not with a frown on his face but a winsome smile, he said in his own nuanced way, "But for you, Leo, I just might!" I sensed he no longer passively transferred his anger against that pastor who had mistreated his elderly mother to me. It is quite likely he never intended to make me feel bad, but I felt guilty by association anyway. Be that as it may, I still felt he no longer implicitly held my congregation or whole church body accountable for the sins of that other congregation his mother had attended. It had taken a year to hear an answer to my first, "I'm truly sorry about your mom." But my friend and I were now reconciled to one another. Hospitality invited reconciliation in. Hospitality opened the way for setting things right, which in turn has also led to my friend's opening his home for musical practices and conversations around meals. The guest became not only the host, but a gracious one.

Now on to the second story, which shows how a conversation about the struggles of life in the world led to an invitation for sharing in a Christlike life of devotion to God amid the deserts of life where the devil attacks.[120] I once heard of

[120] I have adapted the story from my colleague, John Nunes, who shared it at a symposium at Concordia Seminary.

a woman who lived in an economically depressed urban neighborhood filled with broken homes and rampant violence. Not a day went by on her way to and from work in which she did not witness some display of verbal or physical abuse or some sign of despair and hopelessness in her neighborhood—another boarded up home, another high school dropout, another family broken apart. In the middle of this crumbling neighborhood stood a gorgeous old Catholic church. Rather than leaving for the suburbs, the bishop had decided to let this church stick around the city and pitch its tent in the struggling community. The church had been built with the most beautiful marble, mosaics, and stained-glass windows anywhere. Every day, the woman would stop by the church to hear Mass and say her prayers.

One day, she overheard a man walking by the church talk about how much money could be gathered for the poor by stripping the temple of all its artifacts and selling them. Disgusted by what he saw as the opulence displayed in the church's architecture, artwork, and vestments, the man wondered if the church had neglected her mission among the least fortunate. He had seen too many churches leave his neighborhood over the years and had serious concerns about the church's ability to make sacrifices for others. After listening intently to his complaint, the poor woman shared another perspective with him. She said to her neighbor, "Sir, I see your point. There is much need in our midst and the church is far from perfect. But please do not take my church away from me! This is the only place around here where I can come and find safety and repose in an often violent and restless neighborhood." She closed with an invitation: "Sir, where do you go to seek protection and respite in this city? God knows we need these things!"

For the woman, the church had become a refuge—indeed, a mighty fortress—in a dangerous wilderness where the devil prowled around, looking for new victims to devour. The church had also become a refreshing oasis in the desert, a place to seek God's help and drink deeply from the waters of his wisdom to make it through the week. The church was the woman's place to find security in God's promises and to delight again, through the beauty of her church, in the beauty of God's creation. The church was like a little piece of heaven on earth. Although the woman acknowledged the man's concern for the poor's well-being and his expectation for the church to make sacrifices for others, her engagement with the neighbor offered a complementary perspective on the spiritual life and included an invitation to find safety and rest in God amid the attacks of the evil one and a chaotic world.

The woman embodied the life of the woman at Bethany who anointed Jesus with a very expensive perfume, even amid criticisms that she should have sold it to feed the poor (Mk 14:3-9; cf. Mt 26:6-13; Lk 7:36-50; Jn 12:1-8). She modeled the life of Mary who, unlike anxious Martha, made time to sit at Jesus' feet and listened to his teaching (Lk 10:38-42). Indeed, she embodied the life of Jesus himself who though busy at work in his Father's mission still took time to pray to him and delight in his work (Lk 5:15-16; 10:21). At the same time, the woman invited her neighbor to share in the same kind of spiritual life she was privileged to experience, to revel in the Spirit's gracious work of making persons after the likeness of Christ by drawing them into his desert journey toward God's eternal rest. Conversations about poverty and the poor and the need for security ultimately led to an invitation to live with others in devotion to God as the anchor needed for journeying through a perilous world for the sake of serving a hurting world.

To sum up, my hope in this chapter has been to take us on a journey into the lives of North American neighbors in the church and outside the church, paying particular attention to their attitudes, thoughts, and feelings about spirituality and religion. The purpose of such a journey is twofold. First of all, it is an exercise in listening attentively to their spiritual struggles, needs, and hopes, which in turn opens a space for voicing and learning from human experiences we may share in common. Second, the journey is an exercise in interpreting, discerning, and addressing such spiritual challenges and yearnings theologically, that is to say, from the perspective of a Christian spirituality grounded as a starting point in our models of life in the Spirit.

Finally, I hope this chapter has served as the beginning of a broader conversation about how a theology of sanctification or holiness that moves from concept or argument to image and story can assist missional leaders in promoting, among disciples of Christ, fruitful dialogue about, modeling or embodiment of, and invitation into the life the Spirit forms in human persons as ways of engaging neighbors with the Christian story. This angular or indirect narrative approach to missional engagement through a models-based approach to sanctification is not meant to replace the more direct approach to missions through proclamation leading to lifelong discipleship. Instead, my proposal in this chapter is rather humble, namely, to see how a theology of sanctification that does not merely talk about holiness but leads to formation or habituation in spiritual disciplines can set the stage for or serve as a preparation for the gospel. It is a proposal for thinking through and living in our communities as Christ's "light of the world" in the power of his Spirit—indeed, an exhortation and encouragement to walk by the Spirit and, as we noted before, "let your light shine before others, so that they may see your good works and give glory to your Father who is in heaven" (Mt 5:14, 16).

# CONCLUSION

What does an account of the Holy Spirit in the life of Christ contribute to our understanding and fostering of the sanctified life? I have argued that a Spirit Christology yields a multidimensional models-based theology of sanctification or holiness that finds expression in Christian traditions past and present. My investigation into the productivity of a Spirit Christology for linking theology and life produced five models of sanctification with their corresponding biblical narratives, catechetical images, spiritual practices, and practical applications to various life issues.

I began with a basic thesis: the same Spirit in whom Christ lived his life shapes the life of his disciples today. Highlighting the relative continuity of the activity of the Spirit in Christ and his saints, I laid out five models of the sanctified life:

- ***Renewal model.*** The Spirit in whom Christ died and is raised from the dead to reconcile us to God and one another shapes us to die and be raised with Christ through a life of daily repentance in which sinners draw strength to forgive one another as God has forgiven them.
- ***Dramatic model.*** The Spirit in whom Christ stands firm against the evil one in the desert and the garden shapes us to resist and be resilient amid spiritual attacks through dependence on the Word and prayer, as well as through safe spaces for mutual support with others undergoing similar struggles.
- ***Sacrificial model.*** The Spirit in whom Christ is anointed to give his life for others as God's faithful Son and suffering servant shapes us to be faithful witnesses and living sacrifices who engage in "happy exchanges" with others by sharing in their burdens and joys.

- ***Hospitality model.*** The Spirit in whom Christ brings good news and mercy across borders to marginalized neighbors in need of belonging and justification shapes us to identify with "the least of these" and love the unlovable of our day by embodying a life of hospitality that welcomes sinners and strangers into God's kingdom.
- ***Devotional model.*** The Spirit in whom Christ labors in the Father's mission, prays to him, and rejoices in his works shapes us to devote our lives to God by becoming good stewards of his created gifts through a life that honors the Creator in our work, rest, and play.

## INTERACTING CREATIVELY WITH THE MODELS

The models of life in the Spirit laid out in this book are by no means exhaustive. They are comprehensive, but not in an absolute manner. Indeed, there are many aspects of Christ's life in the Spirit such as his proclamation of the Word, prayer life, and ministry of healing that take shape in various ways in the life of his followers. Each of these aspects was partly covered but could also be treated further as part of my proposed models. For instance, the Word as a means of forgiveness that delivers from guilt and reconciles us to one another falls under the renewal model, its nature as a reliable anchor to hang on to in moments of testing belongs under the dramatic model, and its spoken proclamation in faithful witness to a world that persecutes God's prophets fits well in the sacrificial model. The hospitality model highlights the Word as an invitation to the excluded and forgotten to share in the blessings of the kingdom. In its spiritual appropriation of the day of rest, the devotional model brings out the comfort of the Word as rest for weary souls in a busy and often chaotic world.

The spiritual discipline of prayer also finds a place in all the models. Praying for enemies and for our trespasses falls under our need for renewal. Prayer as filial trust in God's protection amid temptations to give up on his commands and promises fits best under the dramatic model. So does prayer as lament and expectation of the fulfillment of God's eschatological promises of protection and deliverance in the midst of life struggles. Prayer as intercession for neighbors in need is better suited for the sacrificial model. Praying for and with vulnerable neighbors may be seen as a practice of hospitality. The devotional model makes room for prayer as part of our spiritual rest in God. When seen holistically, healing too appears in all the models in one way or another. In the renewal model, healing comes through sins forgiven and reconciliation with those whom we have hurt and who have hurt us. In the dramatic model, healing comes from driving out oppressive demonic forces from our lives and setting up boundaries that can prevent us from falling too easily into the devil's seduction. Healing also comes from being resilient against despair and hopelessness in safe spaces where people undergoing similar and ongoing adversities in life support each other. Such a communal dimension to healing can also be seen in the sacrificial and hospitality models, insofar as the former promotes sharing in our neighbors' struggles and joys and the latter fosters outreach to and welcoming of the "others" who are often excluded by our human standards from the fullness of God's life. Undoubtedly, such sharing and welcoming includes making room in our lives for those who experience physical, emotional, and mental challenges. In the devotional model, the healing of the whole person (soul and body) is in view when speaking of our need for resting in God both spiritually and literally.

Seeing how the Word, prayer, and healing interface and find coherence with our models of sanctification, one could argue that each of these aspects of Christ's life in God's saints should have received special treatment. For instance, could these three aspects of Christ's Spirit-formed life shared with us be described, respectively, as kerygmatic, priestly, and healing models in their own right?[1] This is, of course, possible, and my study opens the door for further reflection on different articulations and portrayals of life in the Spirit of Christ.

Because the models are relatively comprehensive, they allow us flexibility in how we use them in spiritual discernment, preaching, teaching, spiritual care, service, and other Christian practices. We can interact creatively with these models, and indeed we want to do so given the complexity of life itself. Models are discrete, heuristic, compartmentalized structures that mirror reality to some degree. In presentations of these models around the country, participants often

---

[1]In his Spirit Christology, for example, Raniero Cantalamessa dedicates chapters to Jesus' and the church's struggle against Satan (kingly office), preaching (prophetic office), and prayer life (priestly office). See Cantalamessa, *The Holy Spirit in the Life of Jesus*, trans. Alan Neame (Collegeville, MN: Liturgical Press, 1994), chaps. 2–4. See also Leopoldo A. Sánchez M., *Receiver, Bearer, and Giver of God's Spirit* (Eugene, OR: Pickwick, 2015), chaps. 7–9, where proclamation, prayer, and sanctification receive separate treatments. Although Ronald Rolheiser does not work out of a Spirit Christology per se, his discussion of the implications of the incarnation for the church's prayer, reconciliation and healing, guidance or discernment, community, religious experience in ordinary life, and mission offers another example of how Christology remains central in shaping an understanding of Christian spirituality. See Rolheiser, *The Holy Longing* (New York: Doubleday, 1999), 82-107.

saw themselves operating in a particular model's sphere. Some felt guilt and shame for not measuring up to God's expectations (renewal), and others felt like life was a daily struggle filled with spiritual challenges and dangers (dramatic). Some had an urge to share their gifts with others in their congregations and communities (sacrificial) or to partner with vulnerable and marginalized neighbors such as refugees as they are resettled in a new land (hospitality). Others felt they needed to set apart more time for prayer and play in the midst of very busy schedules and agendas (devotional).

The life experiences and spiritual issues described in each of these models often intersect in everyday life. To face his demons, a man struggling with habitual temptations seeks a community of accountability with others who share similar burdens, and in their mutual encouragement they become gifts to one another (dramatic and sacrificial). An urban congregation working on racial reconciliation issues also partners with social agencies to assist refugees and migrants in need (renewal and hospitality). A hard-working mother struggling with stress and anxiety at work sets time apart for much-needed rest and recreation, even though occasionally she feels guilty about spending time away from her responsibilities at home and is tempted to give up on the whole idea of resting to catch up on neglected duties (all models at work!). In ordinary life, various dimensions of our models remain operative depending on the issues we face and the ways we deal with them at any point in time.

At a workshop I gave on these models, a couple of church leaders suggested that perhaps the devotional model could offer the rhythm or most adequate worshipful framework into which all the other models operate. All aspects of life in the Spirit are lived in the context of devotion to God anyway! Life in the Spirit happens within the rhythm of rest and work often displayed in the spiritual disciplines. Sharing the models with a pastor on another occasion led him to wonder whether the renewal model actually offered the best theological framework for all the others. In all models, you have to die to something and be raised to new life! Yet other colleagues suggested to me that socially oriented models dealing with sacrificial and hospitality themes yielded the ethical or moral vision for the right communal appropriation of the other models. A life of renewal, fighting demons, and devotion sets you up not only for personal growth but for living in the Spirit with others and for the sake of others! Then and now, my reaction has been to listen attentively and learn joyfully from others' engagement with the models without stifling their critical, creative, and constructive observations. Indeed, my models-based approach not only welcomes but is meant to engender these types of conversations. It is an exercise in what US Hispanic theologians call *teología en conjunto*, that is, collaborative theology done with others and inviting others' participation in its conceptualization, contextualization, and extension.[2]

Given their intersectionality and simultaneity, models should be approached flexibly and in a contextualized way that accounts for the actual lived experiences of persons in our families, congregations, and communities. Otherwise stated, models can equip pastors and other church workers with a toolbox of biblical narratives, theological truths, and pastoral insights that must nevertheless be applied rightly to the situation of people entrusted to their care. In doing so, it is wise not to make any one model work too hard. At the same time, in moving from description to possible use in pastoral and missional practice, a models-based approach can alert church leaders to possible blind spots in their understanding of the spiritual needs and hopes of neighbors. For instance, we may ask which images of life in the Spirit are being neglected in one's theological reflection, practice of ministry, worship life, or approaches to mission and engagement in society. Which issues or problems in the Christian life are not receiving proper attention or perhaps have been misunderstood or misinterpreted as a result of such neglect? By displaying and focusing on a rich variety of aspects of the spiritual life, models can enrich our theological understanding, worship and devotional life, pastoral care, and missional engagement.

## ON THE WORK OF THE SCULPTOR SPIRIT

At the beginning of this work, I suggested that the Spirit's formation of human persons after Christ's likeness evokes in some ways the craft of a sculptor. Let me explore this image a bit further in light of the five models. First, consider how sculptors remove from or add material to the mass they are working on. In the world of sculpting, chiseling or carving are called "substractive" techniques, and casting is an "additive" one. These techniques in the sculpting process are suggestive for describing the Holy Spirit's work of shaping persons after the image of

[2]For a proposal, see Justo L. González, *Mañana: Christian Theology from a Hispanic Perspective* (Nashville: Abingdon, 1990), 28-30; for an example of the approach, see José David Rodríguez and Loida I. Martell-Otero, eds., *Teología en Conjunto: A Collaborative Hispanic Protestant Theology* (Louisville: Westminster John Knox, 1997).

Christ. Christoformation may be seen, for instance, as an additive operation akin to casting, which occurs when a sculptor pours melted material such as metal into a mold. When thinking of melting, we can imagine the Holy Spirit as an all-consuming fire that burns and refines us. Under the renewal model of the sanctified life, we can further think of the Spirit melting the old creature in us to make a new one by casting us in the mold of Christ. In doing so, the Spirit adds to the person without erasing his or her human nature, conforming it daily to Christ's death by burning its old corruption and to his resurrection by refining it into a new creature. Moreover, speaking of the Spirit's Christlike casting of the human person as an additive technique highlights the continual gratuity of its creative action in our lives, which establishes our new identity in Christ as a surprising and undeserved gift from above.

Melting mass into a mold by burning and refining it offers a compelling image of the Spirit's ongoing work in human persons. In each of the models, the Spirit must burn something away in order to refine us into mirroring Christ's love for God and neighbor. Indeed, in the sacrificial model, fire language especially evokes the image of the new creature as a living sacrifice that is pleasing to God and spreads the aroma of Christ in the world through a faithful life and witness. To bring about such a life, the Spirit burns away our selfishness and individualism and sets our hearts on fire to serve and share with others, turning self-absorbed sinners bent on themselves into generous partners who share life together.

If burning away is akin to taking away, then, the transformative fire of the Spirit in our lives becomes what sculptors call a "substractive" operation. The image of burning converges with the substractive processes of carving and chiseling, where the artist polishes the work that has already been cast into its desired form. As a new creation in Christ, we are already the Spirit's finished mold; and yet, the Spirit is not finished with us. There are rough edges, as it were, that require the Spirit's continuous intervention and care. When it comes to the sanctified life, we are a work in progress, always in need of refining, reshaping, or re-formation, until the final form of the glorified Christ is shaped in us at the end of the present age. In one of its stanzas, the medieval Pentecost hymn *Veni Sancte Spiritus* (Eng. Come, Holy Spirit) beautifully sums up the church's prayer for the Spirit's sculpting work in us: "Bend that which is inflexible, fire that which is chilled, correct what goes astray."

What are those rough edges that the Spirit continually chips away at in our lives? Each of our models suggests different areas that need chiseling. Is it an all-consuming guilt that finds it hard to believe God can forgive us, or is it a fatalistic cynicism that gives up on the possibility of setting things right with others? Then, to the tune of another famous Pentecost hymn, the *Veni Creator Spiritus* (Eng. Come, Creator Spirit), we pray for the Spirit to descend on us and transform us: "O comforter, to Thee we cry, oh heavenly gift of God Most High. . . . Oh, may Thy grace on us bestow the Father and the Son to know." Is the issue flirting with danger in the perilous desert where we are vulnerable and feeling too confident in our own powers to overcome Satan's attacks, or is it being overly anxious and self-defeating about falling into temptation in times of struggle without putting up a fight? Then, with the hymnist, we cry out, "Far from us drive the foe we dread, and grant us Thy peace instead; so shall we not, with Thee for guide, turn from the path of life aside."

At times, the Spirit might have to put a fire in our bellies to lead us out of our comfort zones and overall good life in order to carve out time for sharing our lives with forgotten, lonely, rejected, or oppressed neighbors. Then we ask the Holy Spirit, the "fount of life and the fire of love," to descend on us and move us to act: "Kindle our sense from above, and make our hearts o'erflow with love; with patience firm and virtue high the weakness of our flesh supply." Other times, the Spirit might enlighten us to spend some time away from the needy crowds to go to our mountain and commune with God in the Word and prayer—or maybe to head to the lake or river and rest from the crowds at work, spending quality time with loved ones or in solitude! If so, in the words of the *Veni Creator Spiritus*, we ask, "Come, Holy Spirit, Creator blest, and in our souls take up Thy rest, come with Thy grace and heavenly aid to fill the hearts which Thou hast made." Or to the tune of the *Veni Sancte Spiritus*, we can sing, "In labour, [be our] rest." In the language of the church's liturgy and song, we find a treasure of ways to call on the Holy Spirit in our times of spiritual weakness and restlessness.

Admittedly, the picture of the Holy Spirit as a sculptor who shapes and molds us after Christ's image emphasizes the divine agency in sanctification. God has made us his people, as a potter molds the clay (Is 64:8). The indicative of God's action comes through clearly in the metaphor. Yet as new creatures in Christ, the saints are also participants in the Spirit's sculpting work, coworkers who cooperate with yet under the Spirit in the cycle or process of sanctification. They are akin to clay that is not only hard but also made soft, like new moldable clay that the Spirit works with in order to shape it into the likeness of Christ. In sanctification, the new creature's response to the Spirit's work in and through him or her may be portrayed as a joyful yielding to the hands of the sculpting Spirit. The imperative of our response to the Spirit's action in us neither sets itself above nor is equal to the Spirit's divine agency, but remains always the fruit of the indicative reality of the Spirit's indwelling presence in us. Yet it is we who are called and exhorted to live according to such fruit under the guidance of the Spirit: "If we live by the Spirit, let us also keep in step with the Spirit" (Gal 5:25). Whereas the image of the Spirit as sculptor affirms the priority of divine grace in sanctification, the picture of the new creature as moldable clay may account better for our receptive cooperation in sanctification as the believer fights the desires of the sinful flesh and delights in the desires of the Spirit. While our book does not intend to deal with all issues raised in sanctification studies, it is clear that in a fully developed theology of holiness, both the indicative of the divine gift of sanctification and the imperative of the believer's response must be affirmed so that both moralism (neglect of the Spirit's work through the gospel) and antinomianism (neglect of the Spirit's work through the law) are, respectively, avoided.[3]

## MAKING ROOM FOR FURTHER QUESTIONS

Like the models, the number of voices chosen in my work are meant to be illustrative and evocative of the potential of a Spirit Christology as a robust trinitarian framework for describing the sanctified life in a variety of ways. In that spirit, I chose some authors, and left others behind for later research. I justified this methodological choice of the Spirit Christology of fourth century church fathers because they were among the first post-apostolic authors—Irenaeus being the exception before them—who more consciously articulated a theology of the Spirit in an incarnational trinitarian key. Moreover, by suggesting ways of connecting the Spirit in Christ to the life of the saints, these early church theologians offered key building blocks for my project. In highlighting the ways the Spirit shapes

[3]Reflecting on Ephesians 2:10, Adolf Köberle argues that the "antithesis" between "the imperative and indicative moods" of sanctification "must be maintained in Christian ethics with the utmost care. Man must be denied all credit but dare never be relieved of his full responsibility." *The Quest for Holiness*, trans. John C. Mattes (Evansville, IN: Ballast, 1999), xii.

Christ in human persons, these writers' understanding of sanctification or holiness is often quite broad and serves as an umbrella reality that includes the indwelling of the Spirit in the believers' hearts, their adopted status as children of God and their union with Christ through faith, the fruit of the Spirit in their lives and their good works, the Christlike character of their actions in relation to God and neighbor, and their deification through communion with God begun in conversion and fulfilled through their sharing in Christ's resurrection and being in the Father's presence at the last day. Because these writers placed such realities under the more foundational trinitarian mystery of the Holy Spirit's presence and activity in Christ and the saints, I spoke more broadly of the implications of a Spirit Christology for the sanctified life. While I welcome further work dealing more explicitly with how early church theologians distinguish and relate terms such as sanctification, adoption, and deification, my work shows how a Spirit Christology can bring these realities into a relatively organic, unifying, and coherent perspective that makes pneumatology the vital link between Christology and the sanctified life.[4]

Given the recent commemoration of the five-hundredth anniversary of the Reformation in 2017, it seemed appropriate to let Martin Luther's voice be heard once again. Not on the issue of justification by faith per se, but on the matter of sanctification! The saying goes that Luther had much to say about justification, but little or nothing to say about sanctification. While there are undoubtedly many contributions on the topic before and after Luther, my research shows that the Reformer had a rich theology of the sanctified life, often articulated in continuity with earlier patristic motifs. There are, of course, controversial topics raised by critics surrounding Luther and his writings, such as his harsh statements dealing with the peasant revolt and later in his life with the Jews, which might put into question for some his capacity to talk about or exemplify a sanctified life. Aside from the historical or theological reasons for such statements, here we must also remember that only Christ has the Spirit without measure,

[4]For a collection of patristic quotes, where the Spirit's work of deification (*theosis*) and sanctification are described under separate categories, see Joel C. Elowsky, ed., *We Believe in the Holy Spirit* (Downers Grove, IL: InterVarsity Press, 2009). On the other hand, consider how in Cyril of Alexandria's anthropology, for instance, these realities are organically related, since human communion with the divine nature can only occur through Christ's sanctification of his flesh and ours by his Spirit. See Joel C. Elowsky, "Bridging the Gap: Theosis in Antioch and Alexandria," in *Theosis: Deification in Christian Theology*, ed. Vladimir Kharlamov (Eugene, OR: Pickwick, 2011), 2:149-54.

and we only do so by participation and in a continual struggle where the Holy Spirit in us fights against our flesh, the devil, and a world often hostile to God's love in Christ. Luther himself recognized that no theologian—including himself—is perfect or without sin, but remains always a beggar in need of God's continuous grace.[5] In each chapter, I have attempted to read theologians and their contributions with a measure of charity, evaluating them as much as possible in light of their whole work.

Discussions continue about whether Luther taught forensic justification by faith and/or some form of *theosis*-like ontological or ontic union with Christ.[6] Our research does not delve into this question per se, but it does suggest that both justification and sanctification have a defining pneumatological component. A way forward might simply lie in appreciating the Holy Spirit's external and internal works in the believer. Externally, the Spirit justifies sinners by imputing to them Christ's alien righteousness and bringing them to faith in him. Here the Spirit points believers outside of themselves to that righteousness by which Christ lived in the Spirit in perfect love toward God and us through his fulfillment of the law and his death on the cross—what theologians call, respectively, Christ's active and passive obedience. That righteousness is forensic and effective, declaring and making the believer righteous before God on account of Christ. Internally, the indwelling Spirit sanctifies the justified by conforming their will, works, and reason to God's Word throughout their lives. This righteousness of obedience or sanctifying righteousness shapes the believer after the likeness of Christ already now and ultimately in the resurrection. While such righteousness is not perfect in this life on account of the sinful flesh, it is nevertheless worked out in the justified by the Spirit and can be described—as I have done in this book—according to various biblical narratives and catechetical images.

---

[5]Thus Luther's famous parting words—"We are beggars. That is true."—left on a note before he died, as recorded by his student Jerome Besold. See *LW* 54:476.

[6]For two different North American perspectives on the Finnish interpretation of Luther on justification, see Carl E. Braaten and Robert W. Jenson, eds., *Union with Christ: The New Finnish Interpretation of Luther* (Grand Rapids: Eerdmans, 1998), and William W. Schumacher, *Who Do I Say That You Are? Anthropology and the Theology of* Theosis *in the Finnish School of Tuomo Mannermaa* (Eugene, OR: Wipf & Stock, 2010). Cooper argues that, in addition (but not in opposition) to forensic justification by faith, the Lutheran tradition offers a theology of "Christification" grounded in the believer's mystical union with Christ, which has an affinity with early church fathers' view of *theosis* and can be described as progressive sanctification. Jordan Cooper, *Christification: A Lutheran Approach to Theosis* (Eugene, OR: Wipf & Stock, 2014).

There is no need to reduce one aspect of the Spirit's work to the other, that is to say, the juridical/forensic to the participatory/indwelling, or vice versa.[7] Both can be affirmed and spoken of as a union with Christ, respectively, by faith and in love that the Spirit effects, or as Christ's living in believers by faith to do his works through them according to his Spirit.[8] Our union with Christ by *faith* establishes our justified status before God apart from our cooperation. Here the Spirit of Christ works outside of us (Lat. *extra nos*) to reconcile us to God on account of the external righteousness of Christ alone. Our union with Christ by the Spirit's *indwelling* in our hearts displays the life of the justified in the world as the Spirit shapes or forms us to be Christlike. Here the Spirit forms Christ in us (Lat. *in nobis*) by cooperating with the justified as they mature in Christ to grow in their love for God and neighbor. In describing sanctification as either a cycle of life or process of growth that the sculptor Spirit works in and through believers, one need not shy away from the language of the believer's "cooperation" in that way of life or growth in holiness. At the same time, because of the primacy of God's justifying grace in relation to the believer, it is proper to note that "whatever cooperation the believer has is only due to the new nature that God has granted."[9] The imperative flows from the indicative.

---

[7]Similar conversations happen outside of Lutheranism. For instance, a prominent Reformed theologian warns against finding too easy an affinity between Wesley's doctrine of sanctification and Eastern *theosis*, given that "Wesley understood the work of Christ along the lines of penal substitution and the threefold office—in broad agreement with Calvin." Bruce L. McCormack, "Sanctification After Metaphysics: Karl Barth in Conversation with John Wesley's Conception of 'Christian Perfection,'" in *Sanctification: Explorations in Theology and Practice*, ed. Kelly M. Kapic (Downers Grove, IL: InterVarsity Press, 2014), 113.

[8]Brannon Ellis speaks of the "double grace" of justification and sanctification, which results from union with Christ by faith, as a common Reformed teaching. See "Covenantal Union and Communion: Union with Christ as the Covenant of Grace," in Kapic, *Sanctification*, 84-85. On the other hand, Scaer speaks of sanctification in the language of Christ's living in the justified: "The Christian or sanctified life is Christological, first of all because Christ lives in us by faith; secondly it is Christ who is doing these works in us; and thirdly these works are clearly recognizable as those which Christ alone can do and which He in fact does in us." David P. Scaer, "Sanctification in the Lutheran Confessions," *Concordia Theological Quarterly* 53, no. 3 (1989): 177. Gorman has argued, in contrast to a juridical vis-à-vis participationist distinction or paradigm, that Paul only has one soteriological model, namely, "justification by co-crucifixion, understood also as theosis—becoming like God/Christ." Michael J. Gorman, *Inhabiting the Cruciform God: Kenosis, Justification, and Theosis in Paul's Narrative Soteriology* (Grand Rapids: Eerdmans, 2009), 163. Here Gorman defines *theosis* as "transformative participation in the kenotic, cruciform character of God through the Spirit-enabled conformity to the incarnate, crucified, and resurrected/glorified Christ" (162) and sees such *theosis* as "*the center of Paul's theology*" (171).

[9]Cooper, *Christification*, 45. He cites the Lutheran scholastic dogmatician Johannes Andreas Quenstedt (1617–1688), who argued that "regenerate man cooperates with God in the work of sanctification, but not by an equal action, but in subordination and dependence on the Holy Spirit, because he does not work with native but with granted powers" (Cooper, *Christification*, 45); similarly, the *Formula of Concord*

Since my work does not deal with issues in the theology of justification but rather with the shape of the sanctified life by the indwelling of the Spirit of Christ in the saints, I understandably focused on various portrayals of the Spirit's sanctifying work in the justified. Readers are invited to add other voices to the aforementioned sources as they seek to understand and communicate to various audiences how the Spirit of God shapes the lives of people after the form of Christ's life in the Spirit. We may ask, for example, what fifth-century theologians such as Augustine, Cyril of Alexandria, and Theodore of Mopsuestia add to a discussion of the Spirit in the mystery of the incarnation and the life of the church in the world.[10] What about the implicit or explicit use of a Spirit Christology in the monastic traditions, which Luther himself at times draws from in his descriptions of the Christian life?[11] What might Protestant theologians after Luther such as Calvin, Wesley, and others add to the formulation of a theology of sanctification when read from the perspective of a Spirit Christology?[12] In-depth studies on the use of a Spirit Christology in the history of Christian thought, particularly for framing spirituality, are still needed.[13]

My interaction with contemporary voices represented a broader array of theological traditions, and these voices were chosen mostly on the basis of their contributions to the field of Spirit Christology or the sanctified life—particularly in a North American context. Further questions may be asked concerning research on spirituality and religion in contexts other than North America and whether the models are adequate to address the spiritual struggles and aspirations of those

(1577) notes that "as soon as the Holy Spirit has begun his work of rebirth and renewal in us through the Word and the holy sacraments, it is certain that on the basis of his power we can and should be *cooperating* with him, though still in great weakness. This occurs not on the basis of our fleshly, *natural powers* but on the basis of the *new powers* and gifts which the Holy Spirit initiated in us in conversion" (italics mine). *FC, SD* 65, *BC*, p. 556.

[10]For brief examples of such an investigation from a history of exegesis perspective, see Daniel A. Keating, "'For as Yet the Spirit Had Not Been Given': John 7:39 in Theodore of Mopsuestia, Augustine, and Cyril of Alexandria," in *Studia Patristica*, ed. F. Young, M. Edwards, and P. Parvis (Louvain: Peeters, 2006), 39:233-38; and Leopoldo A. Sánchez M., "The Holy Spirit and the Son's Glorification: Spirit Christology as a Theological Lens for Interpreting John 7:37-39," *Journal of Theological Interpretation* 12, no. 1 (2018): 76-89.

[11]As an example, for a collection of essays on the Christological character of Franciscan spirituality, see *Franciscan Christology: Selected Texts, Translations and Introductory Essays*, ed. Damian McElrath (St. Bonaventure, NY: Franciscan Institute Publications, 1980).

[12]A notable historic contribution to Spirit Christology in the Reformed tradition comes from John Owen, *The Holy Spirit* (Grand Rapids: Sovereign Grace, 1971).

[13]For a recent survey, see Herschel Odell Bryant, *Spirit Christology in the Christian Tradition: From the Patristic Period to the Rise of Pentecostalism in the Twentieth Century* (Cleveland, TN: CPT Press, 2014).

neighbors. As an example, and to return to my earlier discussion on interacting creatively with the models, I can imagine how in the context and worldview of Global South Christians, healing might require its own comprehensive model.[14] Perhaps such a model would weave together into a holistic narrative of restoration the concern for the proclamation of the Word to the excluded, deliverance from bondage to evil spirits, and calls for the community's work of mercy and justice among the sick and poor.

Even when sculptors work on replicas of a model, each representation of the original remains a little bit different from the other, revealing the personalized care the sculptor takes in forming each individual version of the model. In a similar way, the Holy Spirit is ultimately in charge of how people are brought into participation in the various ways Scripture speaks to their spiritual needs, struggles, and hopes. As a master sculptor, the Spirit is able to do what is needed at various times in human history to shape persons in the image of Christ. Marveling at such craft and care in the Spirit's work of formation, we boldly pray for the sculptor Spirit to come among us today and, in the words of the *Veni Sancte Spiritus*, "cleanse that which is unclean, water that which is dry, heal that which is wounded." Thankfully, the Spirit knows best when, where, and how to answer this prayer for us at this time, whether we live in the Global South or the North Atlantic. So, come, Sculptor Spirit! Come! Amen.

[14]Philip Jenkins has argued for the centrality of healing in Global South Christianity. See Jenkins, *The Next Christendom: The Coming of Global Christianity*, 3rd ed. (New York: Oxford University Press, 2011), 157-60, and *The New Faces of Christianity: Believing the Bible in the Global South* (New York: Oxford University Press, 2006), 113-24.

# APPENDIX

| Models of Sanctification | | | | | |
|---|---|---|---|---|---|
| | Renewal | Dramatic | Sacrificial | Hospitality | Devotional |
| **Description of Christian Life** | dying and being raised to new life | standing firm amid spiritual attacks | serving and sharing life with neighbors | welcoming strangers and marginalized neighbors | worshiping God through work, rest, and play |
| **Biblical Pictures** | Jesus is anointed to die; raised in the Spirit<br>baptism into Christ's death and resurrection<br>being clothed with Christ's righteousness and holiness | Jesus' life in the desert, prayer in the garden<br>gladiator in the arena<br>disciplined athlete, runner, boxer | Jesus teaches servant discipleship<br>sharing things in common<br>living sacrifices<br>spreading the aroma of Christ | Jesus works from Galilee and through Galileans<br>Jesus heals a Samaritan leper<br>Philip serves outcasts (widows, Ethiopian eunuch, Samaritans) | Jesus does his Father's work and prays to him<br>tending the garden<br>rejoicing in God's creation and salvation<br>Jesus, rest for weary souls |
| **Catechetical Images** | Spirit lost via Adam, Spirit returns via last Adam<br>Spirit as a purifying fire | Spirit pilots the church through life's tempests<br>Spirit as rain for thirsty desert pilgrims | Spirit whispers comfort to martyrs<br>stewards of God's gifts<br>Joseph shares surpluses with others | Abraham welcomes strangers<br>exiled church is a house of Abraham for other exiles | quiet or solitude as first step of holiness<br>sleep convicts the spiritually idle in their beds<br>keepers of the Sabbath use their beds for prayer |

| Models of Sanctification | | | | | |
|---|---|---|---|---|---|
| | Renewal | Dramatic | Sacrificial | Hospitality | Devotional |
| | Spirit uses baptismal waters as our tomb and exodus<br>Spirit judges via fatherly conscience<br>drowning the old sinner and raising a new creature<br>baptism as a daily garment | wounded fighters are healed with the medicine of Scripture<br>prayer and meditation amidst spiritual attacks<br>baptism as a little exorcism | widow of Zarephath shares the little she has<br>Lord's Supper as source of spiritual communion<br>practicing "happy exchanges" | Christ comes to us in strangers<br>the love of the cross turns in the direction where it does not find good | Sabbath as devotion to God's Word and a life of holy words, works, and living<br>*ora et labora* (pray and work) |
| **Issues in the Christian Life** | establishing identity as a child of God<br>dealing with guilt and shame for sins<br>need to forgive and be forgiven; reconciliation<br>avoiding fatalism and perfectionism | finding security or safety<br>vigilance in temptations, resilience in testing times<br>dealing with areas of vulnerability (Achilles' heel)<br>need for boundaries, safe spaces | meaning or purpose in life, vocation or life's calling<br>simplicity to make room for sharing<br>hunger for community, relationships<br>sharing each other's needs and gifts<br>solidarity, sustainable partnerships | welcoming disposition toward the "other"<br>need for belonging<br>need for being justified before others<br>shame and pain of exclusion<br>cross- and intercultural exchanges | achieving balance in life<br>stewardship of time (labor and rest)<br>avoiding workaholism, burnout, view of work as a curse<br>creativity and joy in play<br>spiritual retreat |
| **Work of the Holy Spirit** | kill and make alive, convict and forgive<br>reconcile sinners to one another<br>empower good works through the gospel | strengthen trust in God through the Word<br>defend and lead in our wilderness journeys<br>intercede for us when we do not know how to pray | anoint for witness in word and deed<br>form disciples to be faithful servants<br>create a healthy interdependent community | call forgotten folks from the margins to share in the kingdom<br>push people to marginal spaces to welcome "others" into the kingdom | bring people into the devotional rhythm of labor and rest<br>lead us to spiritual and literal rest<br>give joy in God's works of creation and salvation |

| Models of Sanctification | | | | | |
|---|---|---|---|---|---|
| | Renewal | Dramatic | Sacrificial | Hospitality | Devotional |
| **View of Growth** | cyclical via daily return to the cross; life of daily repentance | cyclical via dependence on prayer and the Word amid attacks<br>process via awareness of vulnerability, accountability in the desert journey | cyclical via sharing in Christ's body in order to share his life with others<br>process via greater knowledge of neighbor's needs and gifts<br>process via practicing of "happy exchanges" | process via deeper knowledge of the "other" and life at the margins<br>process via learning practices of welcome | cyclical via the rhythm of movement and repose<br>cyclical via the rhythm of prayer, study, and labor<br>process via study and/or learning a craft/hobby (play) |
| **Spiritual Disciplines** | confessing and forgiving sins<br>mutual consolation among brothers and sisters<br>practices of reconciliation with others | vigilance via prayer and meditation on the Word<br>setting limits via support groups and networks (or other external disciplines such as fasting) | vocational excellence<br>evangelical witness<br>sharing gifts and talents in community<br>sharing burdens via intercession and advocacy<br>engaging in partnerships via "happy exchanges" | practices of hospitality<br>working with marginalized persons or groups (e.g., poor, widows, orphans, refugees, ethnic minorities) | balancing work and rest<br>regular quiet time for prayer and the Word (spiritual day of rest)<br>setting aside time for play, recreation, and creative endeavors outside of regular job or vocation |

# BIBLIOGRAPHY


Alexander, Donald L., ed. *Christian Spirituality: Five Views of Sanctification*. Downers Grove, IL: InterVarsity Press, 1988.

Alfaro, Sammy. *Divino Compañero: Toward a Hispanic Pentecostal Christology*. Princeton Theological Monograph Series 147. Eugene, OR: Pickwick, 2010.

Ambrosio de Milán. *El Espíritu Santo*. Translated by Carmelo Granado. Biblioteca de patrística 41. Madrid: Editorial Ciudad Nueva, 1998.

Aponte, Edwin David. *¡Santo!: Varieties of Latino/a Spirituality*. Maryknoll, NY: Orbis, 2012.

Aquinas, Thomas. *Summa Theologiae*. London: Blackfriars. New York: McGraw-Hill, 1964–1980.

Atanasio. *Epístolas a Serapión sobre el Espíritu Santo*. Translated by Carmelo Granado. Biblioteca de patrística 71. Madrid: Editorial Ciudad Nueva, 2007.

Athanasius. *Letters to Serapion on the Holy Spirit*. In *Works on the Spirit: Athanasius the Great and Didymus the Blind*, translated with an introduction and annotations by Mark DelCogliano, Andrew Radde-Gallwitz, and Lewis Ayres, 51-137. Crestwood, NY: St. Vladimir's Seminary Press, 2011.

Augustine, Daniela C. *Pentecost, Hospitality, and Transfiguration: Toward a Spirit-inspired Vision of Social Transformation*. Cleveland, TN: CPT Press, 2012.

Aulén, Gustaf. *Christus Victor: An Historical Study of the Three Main Types of the Idea of Atonement*. Eugene, OR: Wipf & Stock, 2003.

Bainton, Roland H. *Here I Stand*. Nashville: Abingdon, 1952.

Basil. *On Social Justice*. Translated by C. Paul Schroeder. Crestwood, NY: St. Vladimir's Seminary Press, 2009.

———. *On the Holy Spirit*. Translated by David Anderson. Crestwood, NY: St. Vladimir's Seminary Press, 1980.

Bayer, Oswald. *Living by Faith: Justification and Sanctification*. Translated by Geoffrey W. Bromiley. Grand Rapids: Eerdmans, 2003.

Bevans, Stephen B. *Models of Contextual Theology*. Rev. and expanded ed. Faith and Cultures Series. Maryknoll, NY: Orbis Books, 2002.

Biermann, Joel D. *A Case for Character: Towards a Lutheran Virtue Ethics*. Minneapolis: Fortress, 2014.

Bobrinskoy, Boris. "The Indwelling of the Spirit in Christ: 'Pneumatic Christology' in the Cappadocian Fathers." *St. Vladimir's Theological Quarterly* 28, no. 1 (1984): 49-65.

Bonhoeffer, Dietrich. *Creation and Fall; Temptation: Two Biblical Studies*. 1st Touchtone ed. New York: Simon & Schuster, 1997.

Boff, Leonardo. *Come, Holy Spirit: Inner Fire, Giver of Life and Comforter of the Poor*. Maryknoll, NY: Orbis, 2015.

Braaten, Carl E., and Robert W. Jenson, eds. *Union with Christ: The New Finnish Interpretation of Luther*. Grand Rapids: Eerdmans, 1998.

Bryant, Christopher. "The Nature of Spiritual Development." In *The Study of Spirituality*, edited by Cheslyn Jones, Geoffrey Wainwright, and Edward Yarnold, 565-67. New York: Oxford University Press, 1986.

Bryant, Herschel Odell. *Spirit Christology in the Christian Tradition: From the Patristic Period to the Rise of Pentecostalism in the Twentieth Century*. Cleveland, TN: CPT Press, 2014.

Bulgakov, Sergius. *The Comforter*. Translated by Boris Jakim. Grand Rapids: Eerdmans, 2004.

Cantalamessa, Raniero. *The Holy Spirit in the Life of Jesus: The Mystery of Christ's Baptism*. Translated by Alan Neame. Collegeville, MN: Liturgical Press, 1994.

Carroll R., M. Daniel. *Christians at the Border: Immigration, the Church, and the Bible*. 2nd ed. Grand Rapids: Brazos, 2013.

Carroll R., M. Daniel, and Leopoldo A. Sánchez M., eds. *Immigrant Neighbors Among Us: Immigration Across Theological Traditions*. Eugene, OR: Pickwick, 2015.

Chan, Francis, and Danae Yankoski. *Forgotten God: Reversing Our Tragic Neglect of the Holy Spirit*. Colorado Springs: David C. Cook, 2009.

Chrysostom, John. *On Wealth and Poverty*. Translated by Catharine P. Roth. Crestwood, NY: St. Vladimir's Seminary Press, 1984.

Cirilo de Jerusalén. *El Espíritu Santo (Catequesis XVI–XVII)*. Translated by Carmelo Granado. Biblioteca de patrística 11. Madrid: Editorial Ciudad Nueva, 1998.

Coblentz, Jessica. "Sisters in the Wilderness: Toward A Theology of Depression with Delores Williams." In *An Unexpected Wilderness: Seeking God on a Changing Planet*, edited by Colleen Carpenter, 193-203. Maryknoll, NY: Orbis, 2016.

Coffey, David. *Deus Trinitas: The Doctrine of the Triune God*. New York: Oxford University Press, 1999.

———. *"Did You Receive the Holy Spirit When You Believed?" Some Basic Questions for Pneumatology*. The Père Marquette Lecture in Theology 2005. Milwaukee: Marquette University Press, 2005.

———. "Spirit Christology and the Trinity." In *Advents of the Spirit: An Introduction to the Current Study of Pneumatology*, edited by Bradford E. Hinze and D. Lyle Dabney, 315-46. Milwaukee: Marquette University Press, 2001.

Congar, Yves. *I Believe in the Holy Spirit*. Translated by David Smith. 3 vols. Milestones in Catholic Theology. New York: Crossroad, 1997.

———. *The Word and the Spirit*. Translated by David Smith. San Francisco: Harper & Row, 1986.

Cooper, Jordan. *Christification: A Lutheran Approach to Theosis*. Eugene, OR: Wipf & Stock, 2014.

Corbett, Steve, and Brian Fikkert. *When Helping Hurts: How to Alleviate Poverty Without Hurting the Poor . . . and Yourself*. 2nd ed. Chicago: Moody, 2012.

Dean, Kenda Creasy. *Almost Christian: What the Faith of Our Teenagers Is Telling the American Church*. New York: Oxford University Press, 2010.

Del Colle, Ralph. *Christ and the Spirit: Spirit-Christology in Trinitarian Perspective*. New York: Oxford University Press, 1994.

Dídimo el Ciego. *Tratado sobre el Espíritu Santo*. Translated by Carmelo Granado. Biblioteca de patrística 36. Madrid: Editorial Ciudad Nueva, 1997.

Didymus the Blind. *On the Holy Spirit*. In *Works on the Spirit: Athanasius the Great and Didymus the Blind*, translated with an introduction and annotations by Mark DelCogliano, Andrew Radde-Gallwitz, and Lewis Ayres, 143–227. Crestwood, NY: St. Vladimir's Seminary Press, 2011.

Dieter, Melvin E., ed. *Five Views on Sanctification*. Counterpoint Series, ed. Stanley N. Gundry. Grand Rapids: Zondervan, 1987.

Drescher, Elizabeth. *Choosing Our Religion: The Spiritual Lives of America's Nones*. New York: Oxford University Press, 2016.

Dulles, Avery. *Models of the Church*. Expanded Image Books ed. New York: Doubleday, 1987.

———. *Models of Revelation*. New York: Doubleday, 1983.

Dunn, James D. G. *Christology*. Vol. 1 of *The Christ and the Spirit*. Grand Rapids: Eerdmans, 1998.

———. *Jesus and the Spirit: A Study of the Religious and Charismatic Experience of Jesus and the First Christians as Reflected in the New Testament*. Grand Rapids: Eerdmans, 1975.

———. "Jesus—Flesh and Spirit: An Exposition of Romans 1:3-4." In *Christology*, 126-53. Vol. 1 of *The Christ and the Spirit*. Grand Rapids: Eerdmans, 1998.

———. *Pneumatology*. Vol. 2 of *The Christ and the Spirit*. Grand Rapids: Eerdmans, 1998.

———. "Rediscovering the Spirit (1)." In *Pneumatology*, 43-61. Vol. 2 of *The Christ and the Spirit*. Grand Rapids: Eerdmans, 1998.

———. "Rediscovering the Spirit (2)." In *Pneumatology*, 62-80. Vol. 2 of *The Christ and the Spirit*. Grand Rapids: Eerdmans, 1998.

———. "2 Corinthians 3:17 'The Lord Is the Spirit.'" In *Christology*, 115-25. Vol. 1 of *The Christ and the Spirit*. Grand Rapids: Eerdmans, 1998.

Eilers, Kent, and Kyle C. Strobel, eds. *Sanctified by Grace: A Theology of the Christian Life*. New York: Bloomsbury T&T Clark, 2014.

Elizondo, Virgilio. *Galilean Journey: The Mexican-American Promise*. Maryknoll, NY: Orbis, 1983.

Ellis, Brannon. "Covenantal Union and Communion: Union with Christ as the Covenant of Grace." In *Sanctification: Explorations in Theology and Practice*, edited by Kelly M. Kapic, 79-102. Downers Grove, IL: InterVarsity Press, 2014.

Elowsky, Joel C. "Bridging the Gap: Theosis in Antioch and Alexandria." In *Theosis: Deification in Christian Theology*. Vol. 2, edited by Vladimir Kharlamov, 146-89. Princeton Theological Monograph Series 16. Eugene, OR: Pickwick, 2011.

———, ed. *We Believe in the Holy Spirit*. Ancient Christian Doctrine Series 4. Downers Grove, IL: InterVarsity Press, 2009.

Fee, Gordon D. *God's Empowering Presence: The Holy Spirit in the Letters of Paul*. Peabody, MA: Hendrickson, 1994.

Finn, Nathan A., and Keith S. Whitfield, eds. *Spirituality for the Sent: Casting a New Vision for the Missional Church*. Downers Grove, IL: InterVarsity Press, 2017.

Forde, Gerhard O. "A Lutheran Response." In *Christian Spirituality: Five Views of Sanctification*, edited by Donald L. Alexander, 119-22. Downers Grove, IL: InterVarsity Press, 1988.

———. "The Lutheran View." In *Christian Spirituality: Five Views of Sanctification*, edited by Donald L. Alexander, 13-32. Downers Grove, IL: InterVarsity Press, 1988.

———. *On Being a Theologian of the Cross: Reflections on Luther's Heidelberg Disputation, 1518*. Grand Rapids: Eerdmans, 1997.

———. *Theology Is for Proclamation*. Minneapolis: Fortress, 1990.

González, Justo L. *Breve historia del domingo: Descubre el gozo de la celebración del día del Señor*. El Paso: Editorial Mundo Hispano, 2016.

———. *Mañana: Christian Theology from a Hispanic Perspective*. Nashville: Abingdon, 1990.

———. "Yesterday." In *Under the Cross of Christ—Yesterday, Today, and Forever: Reflections on Lutheran Hispanic Ministry in the United States*, 23-46. Concordia Seminary Publications Monograph Series 6. St. Louis: Concordia Seminary Publications, 2004.

González, Michelle A. *Embracing Latina Spirituality: A Women's Perspective*. Cincinnati: St. Anthony Messenger Press, 2009.

Gorman, Michael J. *Inhabiting the Cruciform God: Kenosis, Justification, and Theosis in Paul's Narrative Soteriology*. Grand Rapids: Eerdmans, 2009.

Granado, Carmelo. *El Espíritu Santo en la teología patrística*. Salamanca: Ediciones Sígueme, 1987.

———. "Pneumatología de San Cirilo de Jerusalén." *Estudios Eclesiásticos* 58 (1983): 421-90.

Gunstone, John. "Group Prayer." In *The Study of Spirituality*, edited by Cheslyn Jones, Geoffrey Wainwright, and Edward Yarnold, 570-72. New York: Oxford University Press, 1986.

Habets, Myk. "Prolegomenon: On Starting with the Spirit." In *Third Article Theology: A Pneumatological Dogmatics*, edited by Myk Habets, 1-19. Minneapolis: Fortress, 2016.

———. "Spirit Christology: Seeing in Stereo." *Journal of Pentecostal Theology* 11, no. 2 (2003): 199-234.

———. *The Anointed Son: A Trinitarian Spirit Christology*. Eugene, OR: Pickwick, 2010.

———, ed. *Third Article Theology: A Pneumatological Dogmatics*. Minneapolis: Fortress, 2016.

Haight, Roger. "The Case for Spirit Christology." *Theological Studies* 53 (1992): 257-87.

Hoekema, Anthony A. "The Reformed Perspective." In *Five Views on Sanctification*, edited by Melvin E. Dieter, 61-90. Counterpoint Series, ed. Stanley N. Gundry. Grand Rapids: Zondervan, 1987.

Jenkins, Philip. *The Next Christendom: The Coming of Global Christianity*. 3rd ed. New York: Oxford University Press, 2011.

———. *The New Faces of Christianity: Believing the Bible in the Global South*. New York: Oxford University Press, 2006.

Johnson, Andy. *Holiness and the* Missio Dei. Eugene, OR: Cascade, 2016.

Jones, Cheslyn, Geoffrey Wainwright, and Edward Yarnold, eds. *The Study of Spirituality*. New York: Oxford University Press, 1986.

Kapic, Kelly M. "Faith, Hope, and Love: A Theological Meditation on Suffering and Sanctification." In *Sanctification: Explorations in Theology and Practice*, edited by Kelly M. Kapic, 212-31. Downers Grove, IL: InterVarsity Press, 2014.

———, ed. *Sanctification: Explorations in Theology and Practice*. Downers Grove, IL: InterVarsity Press, 2014.

Kasper, Walter. *Jesus the Christ*. Translated by V. Green. New York: Paulist, 1976.

Keating, Daniel A. "'For as Yet the Spirit Had Not Been Given': John 7:39 in Theodore of Mopsuestia, Augustine, and Cyril of Alexandria." Vol. 39 of *Studia Patristica*, edited by F. Young, M. Edwards, and P. Parvis, 233-38. Papers presented at the Fourteenth International Conference on Patristic Studies held in Oxford 2003. Louvain: Peeters, 2006.

Kieschnick, John H. *The Best Is Yet to Come: 7 Doors of Spiritual Growth*. Friendswood, TX: Baxter, 2006.

Kinnaman, David, and Aly Hawkins. *You Lost Me: Why Young Christians Are Leaving Church . . . and Rethinking Faith*. Grand Rapids: Baker Books, 2011.

Kleinig, John W. "*Oratio, Meditatio, Tentatio*: What Makes a Theologian?" *Concordia Theological Quarterly* 66, no. 3 (2002): 255-67.

Köberle, Adolf. *The Quest for Holiness: A Biblical, Historical and Systematic Investigation*. Translated by John C. Mattes. Minneapolis: Augsburg, 1938. Reprint, Evansville, IN: Ballast, 1999.

Kolb, Robert, and Charles P. Arand. *The Genius of Luther's Theology: A Wittenberg Way of Thinking for the Contemporary Church*. Grand Rapids: Baker Academic, 2008.

Kolb, Robert, and Timothy J. Wengert, eds. *The Book of Concord: The Confessions of the Evangelical Lutheran Church*. Minneapolis: Fortress, 2000.

LaCugna, Catherine Mowry. *God for Us: The Trinity and Christian Life*. San Francisco: HarperCollins, 1991.

Ladaria, Luis F. "Cristología del Logos y cristología del Espíritu." *Gregorianum* 61 (1980): 353-60.

———. "La unción de Jesús y el don del Espíritu." *Gregorianum* 71, no. 3 (1990): 547-71.

Lampe, G. W. H. *God as Spirit*. New York: Oxford University Press, 1977.

———. "The Holy Spirit and the Person of Christ." In *Christ, Faith and History*, edited by S. W. Sykes and J. P. Clayton, 111-30. London: Cambridge University Press, 1972.

Lewis, C. S. *The Screwtape Letters*. New York: HarperOne, 2001.

*Libro de liturgia y cántico*. Minneapolis: Augsburg Fortress, 1998.

Lindberg, Carter. *Beyond Charity: Reformation Initiatives for the Poor*. Minneapolis: Fortress, 1993.

———. "Do Lutherans Shout Justification but Whisper Sanctification?" *Lutheran Quarterly* 13 (1999): 1-20

Lodahl, Michael E. *Shekinah/Spirit: Divine Presence in Jewish and Christian Religion*. Studies in Judaism and Christianity. Mahwah, NY: Paulist, 1992.

Loder, James E. *The Logic of the Spirit: Human Development in Theological Perspective*. San Francisco: Jossey-Bass, 1998.

Lupton, Robert D. *Toxic Charity: How Churches and Charities Hurt Those They Help (And How to Reverse It)*. New York: HarperOne, 2011.

Luther, Martin. "The Baptismal Booklet: Translated into German and Newly Revised." In *The Book of Concord: The Confessions of the Evangelical Lutheran Church*, edited by Robert Kolb and Timothy J. Wengert, 371-75. Minneapolis: Fortress, 2000.

———. *The Blessed Sacrament of the Holy and True Body of Christ, and the Brotherhoods*. In *Luther's Works*, edited by Helmut T. Lehmann, vol. 35. Philadelphia: Muhlenberg, 1960.

———. *Comfort When Facing Grave Temptations*. In *Luther's Works: Devotional Writings I*, edited by J. J. Pelikan, H. C. Oswald, and H. T. Lehmann, vol. 42. Philadelphia: Fortress, 1969.

———. *First Sermon at the Baptism of Bernard of Anhalt Matthew 3:1-17*. In *Luther's Works: Sermons V*, edited by C. B. Brown and translated by J. S. Bruss, vol. 58. St. Louis: Concordia, 2010.

———. "First Sunday in Lent (Invocavit)." In *Sermons on Gospel Texts for Epiphany, Lent, and Easter*. Vol. 1.2 of *The Complete Sermons of Martin Luther*, edited by John Nicolas Lenker, 133-47. Grand Rapids: Baker Books, 2000.

———. *Heidelberg Disputation*. In *Luther's Works: Career of the Reformer I*, edited by Harold J. Grimm and Helmut T. Lehmann, vol. 31. Philadelphia: Fortress, 1957.

———. "Invocavit Sunday—First Sunday in Lent (1534)." In *Sermons on Gospel Texts for Advent, Christmas, New Year's Day, Epiphany, Lent, Holy Week, and Other Occasions*. Vol. 5 of *The Complete Sermons of Martin Luther*, edited by Eugene F. Klug, 312-20. Grand Rapids: Baker Books, 2000.

———. *Lectures on Galatians, 1535, Chapters 1–4*. In *Luther's Works*, edited by J. J. Pelikan, H. C. Oswald, and H. T. Lehmann, vol. 26. St. Louis: Concordia, 1963.

———. *Lectures on Genesis: Chapters 1–5*. In *Luther's Works*, edited by J. J. Pelikan, H. C. Oswald, and H. T. Lehmann, vol. 1. St. Louis: Concordia, 1958.

———. *Lectures on Genesis: Chapters 15–20*. In *Luther's Works*, edited by J. J. Pelikan, H. C. Oswald, and H. T. Lehmann, vol. 3. St. Louis: Concordia, 1961.

———. *Lectures on Genesis: Chapters 21–25*. In *Luther's Works*, edited by J. J. Pelikan, H. C. Oswald, and H. T. Lehmann, vol. 4. St. Louis: Concordia, 1964.

———. *Lectures on Genesis: Chapters 31–37*. In *Luther's Works*, edited by J. J. Pelikan, H. C. Oswald, and H. T. Lehmann, vol. 6. St. Louis: Concordia, 1970.

———. *Lectures on Hebrews*. In *Luther's Works: Lectures on Titus, Philemon, and Hebrews*, edited by J. J. Pelikan, H. C. Oswald, and H. T. Lehmann, vol. 29. St. Louis: Concordia, 1968.

———. *Notes on Ecclesiastes*. In *Luther's works: Ecclesiastes, Song of Solomon, Last Words of David, 2 Samuel 23:1-7*, edited by J. J. Pelikan, H. C. Oswald, & H. T. Lehmann, vol. 15. St. Louis: Concordia, 1972.

———. "Our God, He Is a Castle Strong." In *Luther's Works: Liturgy and Hymns*, edited by J. J. Pelikan, H. C. Oswald, and H. T. Lehmann, vol. 53. Philadelphia: Fortress, 1965.

———. *Preface to the Wittenberg Edition of Luther's German Writings*. In *Luther's Works: Career of the Reformer IV*, edited by J. J. Pelikan, H. C. Oswald, and H. T. Lehmann, vol. 34. Philadelphia: Fortress, 1960.

———. *The Second Sermon, March 10, 1522, Monday After Invocavit*. In *Luther's Works: Sermons I*, edited by J. J. Pelikan, H. C. Oswald, and H. T. Lehmann, vol. 51. Philadelphia: Fortress, 1959.

———. *A Sermon of Dr. Martin Luther, Delivered in Halle on the Day of Christ's Epiphany, 1546. From Matthew 3 [:13-17], on the Baptism of Christ*. In *Luther's Works: Sermons V*, edited by C. B. Brown and translated by G. Paul, vol. 58. St. Louis: Concordia, 2010.

———. *Sermon on Matt. 3:13-17 at the Baptism of Bernhard von Anhalt, Preached in Dessau, April 2, 1540*. In *Luther's Works: Sermons I*, edited by J. J. Pelikan, H. C. Oswald, and H. T. Lehmann, vol. 51. Philadelphia: Fortress, 1959.

———. "Theology Is Not Quickly Learned." In *Luther's Works: Table Talk*, edited by J. J. Pelikan, H. C. Oswald, and H. T. Lehmann, vol. 54. Philadelphia: Fortress, 1967.

Matera, Frank J. *New Testament Christology*. Louisville: Westminster John Knox, 1999.

Mavis, W. Curry. *The Holy Spirit in the Christian Life*. Grand Rapids: Baker Book House, 1977.

McCormack, Bruce L. "Sanctification After Metaphysics: Karl Barth in Conversation with John Wesley's Conception of 'Christian Perfection.'" In *Sanctification: Explorations in Theology and Practice*, edited by Kelly M. Kapic, 103-23. Downers Grove, IL: InterVarsity Press, 2014.

McDonnell, Kilian. *The Baptism of Jesus in the Jordan: The Trinitarian and Cosmic Order of Salvation*. Collegeville, MN: Liturgical Press, 1996.

———. *The Other Hand of God: The Holy Spirit as the Universal Touch and Goal*. Collegeville, MN: Liturgical Press, 2003.

McElrath, Damian, ed. *Franciscan Christology: Selected Texts, Translations and Introductory Essays*. Franciscan Sources Series, ed. George Marcil, no. 1. St. Bonaventure, NY: Franciscan Institute Publications, 1980.

McGarry, Joseph. "Formed by the Spirit: A Third Article Theology of Christian Spirituality." In *Third Article Theology: A Pneumatological Dogmatics*, edited by Myk Habets, 283-96. Minneapolis: Fortress, 2016.

McGee, Robert S. *The Search for Significance*. 2nd ed. Houston: Rapha, 1990.

Moltmann, Jürgen. *The Spirit of Life: A Universal Affirmation*. Minneapolis: Fortress, 1992.

Montague, George T. *Holy Spirit: Growth of a Biblical Tradition*. Peabody, MA: Hendrickson, 1976.

Moore, Peter. "Sanctification Through Preaching: How John Chrysostom Preached for Personal Transformation." In *Sanctification: Explorations in Theology and Practice*, edited by Kelly M. Kapic, 251-68. Downers Grove, IL: InterVarsity Press, 2014.

Mühlen, Heribert. "Das Christusereignis als Tat des Heiligen Geistes." In *Mysterium Salutis*, edited by J. Feiner and M. Löhrer, vol. 3, pt. 2, 513-44. Einsiedeln: Benziger, 1969. Translated by Guillermo Aparicio and Jesús Rey under the title "El acontecimiento Cristo como acción del Espíritu Santo," 960-84 (Madrid: Cristiandad, 1992).

———. *Espíritu. Carisma. Liberación. La renovación de la fe cristiana*. Translated by Luis Artigas. 2nd ed. Salamanca: Secretariado Trinitario, 1975.

———. *Una Mystica Persona: Die Kirche als das Mysterium der Identität des Heiligen Geistes in Christus und die Christen: Eine Person in vielen Personen*. 2nd ed. Munich: Schöning, 1967.

Nanko-Fernández, Carmen. *Theologizing en Espanglish: Context, Community, and Ministry*. Maryknoll, NY: Orbis, 2010.

Nation, Philip. *Habits for Our Holiness: How the Spiritual Disciplines Grow Us Up, Draw Us Together, and Send Us Out*. Chicago: Moody, 2016.

Oden, Amy G., ed. *And You Welcomed Me: A Sourcebook on Hospitality in Early Christianity*. Nashville: Abingdon, 2001.

O'Donnell, John J. "In Him and Over Him: The Holy Spirit in the Life of Jesus." *Gregorianum* 70, no. 1 (1989): 25-45.

Oord, Thomas Jay, and Michael Lodahl. *Relational Holiness: Responding to the Call of Love*. Kansas City, MO: Beacon Hill, 2005.

*Oramos Cantando: We Pray in Song*. Chicago: GIA Publications, 2013.

Orbe, Antonio. "El Espíritu Santo en el bautismo de Jesús (en torno a san Ireneo)." *Gregorianum* 76, no. 4 (1995): 663-69.

Owen, John. *The Holy Spirit*. Grand Rapids: Sovereign Grace, 1971.

Peterson, David. *Possessed by God: A New Testament Theology of Sanctification and Holiness*. Downers Grove, IL: InterVarsity Press, 1995.

Pew Research Center. “Americans May Be Getting Less Religious, but Feelings of Spirituality Are on the Rise.” January 21, 2016. www.pewresearch.org/fact-tank/2016/01/21/americans-spirituality.

———. “Changing Faiths: Latinos and the Transformation of American Religion.” April 25, 2007. www.pewforum.org/2007/04/25/changing-faiths-latinos-and-the-transformation-of-american-religion-2.

———. “‘Nones’ on the Rise.” October 9, 2012. www.pewforum.org/2012/10/09/nones-on-the-rise.

———. “The Shifting Religious Identity of Latinos in the United States: Nearly One-in-Four Latinos Are Former Catholics.” May 7, 2014. www.pewforum.org/2014/05/07/the-shifting-religious-identity-of-latinos-in-the-united-states.

———. “U.S. Public Becoming Less Religious: Modest Drop in Overall Rates of Belief and Practice, but Religiously Affiliated Americans Are as Observant as Before.” November 3, 2015. www.pewforum.org/2015/11/03/u-s-public-becoming-less-religious.

Pinnock, Clark H. *Flame of Love: A Theology of the Holy Spirit*. Downers Grove, IL: InterVarsity Press, 1996.

Porsch, Felix. *El Espíritu Santo, defensor de los creyentes: La actividad del Espíritu según el evangelio de san Juan*. Translated by Severiano Talavero Tovar. Salamanca: Secretariado Trinitario, 1983.

Prenter, Regin. *Spiritus Creator: Luther's Concept of the Holy Spirit*. Translated by John M. Jensen. Philadelphia: Muhlenberg, 1953.

Rahner, Karl. *The Trinity*. Translated by Joseph Donceel. With an introduction, index, and glossary by Catherine Mowry LaCugna. New York: Herder and Herder, 1970. Reprint, New York: Crossroad, 1998.

Roberts, Alexander, et al., eds. *The Ante-Nicene Fathers: Translations of the Fathers down to A.D. 325*. 10 vols. The Christian Literature Publishing Company, 1885–97; Reprint, Peabody, MA: Hendrickson, 1994.

Rodríguez, José David, and Loida I. Martell-Otero, eds. *Teología en Conjunto: A Collaborative Hispanic Protestant Theology*. Louisville: Westminster John Knox, 1997.

Rogers, Eugene F., Jr. *After the Spirit: A Constructive Pneumatology from Resources Outside the Modern West*. Grand Rapids: Eerdmans, 2005.

Rolheiser, Ronald. *The Holy Longing: The Search for a Christian Spirituality*. New York: Doubleday, 1999.

Roof, Wade Clark. *Spiritual Marketplace: Baby Boomers and the Remaking of American Religion*. Princeton, NJ: Princeton University Press, 1999.

Rosato, Philip J. "Spirit Christology: Ambiguity and Promise." *Theological Studies* 38, no. 3 (1977): 423-49.

Royo Marín, Antonio. *Teología de la perfección cristiana*. Biblioteca de autores cristianos 114. Madrid: BAC, 2012.

Rusnak, Jonathan W. "Shaped by the Spirit." *LOGIA* 24, no. 3 (2015): 15-20.

Sánchez M., Leopoldo A. "Along the Border." In *Sermons from the Latino/a Pulpit*, edited by Elieser Valentín, 48-64. Eugene, OR: Wipf & Stock, 2017.

———. "Can Anything Good Come Out of ____________. Come and See!: Faithful Witness in Marginality and Hospitality." *Concordia Journal* 41, no. 2 (2015): 111-23.

———. "God Against Us and for Us: Preaching Jesus in the Spirit." *Word & World* 24, no. 2 (2003): 134-45.

———. "Hispanic Is Not What You Think: Reimagining Hispanic Identity, Implications for an Increasingly Global Church." *Concordia Journal* 42, no. 3 (2016): 223-35.

———. "The Church is the House of Abraham: Reflections on Martin Luther's Teaching on Hospitality Toward Exiles." *Concordia Journal* 44, no. 1 (2018): 23-39.

———. "The Holy Spirit and the Son's Glorification: Spirit Christology as a Theological Lens for Interpreting John 7:37-39." *Journal of Theological Interpretation* 12, no. 1 (2018): 76-89.

———. "The Holy Spirit in Christ: Pneumatological Christology as a Ground for a Christ-Centered Pneumatology." In *Propter Christum: Christ at the Center*, edited by Scott Murray et al., 343-56. St. Louis: Luther Academy, 2013.

———. "The Human Face of Justice: Reclaiming the Neighbor in Law, Vocation, and Justice Talk." *Concordia Journal* 39, no. 2 (2013): 117-32.

———. "Individualism, Indulgence, and the Mind of Christ: Making Room for the Neighbor and the Father." In *The American Mind Meets the Mind of Christ*, edited by Robert Kolb, 54-66. St. Louis: Concordia Seminary Press, 2010.

———. "Life in the Spirit of Christ: Models of Sanctification as Sacramental Pneumatology." *LOGIA* 22, no. 3 (2013): 7-14.

———. "A Missionary Theology of the Holy Spirit: The Father's Anointing of Christ and Its Implications for the Church in Mission." *Missio Apostolica* 14, no. 1 (2006): 28-40.

———. "More Promise Than Ambiguity: Pneumatological Christology as a Model for Ecumenical Engagement." In *Critical Issues in Ecclesiology: Essays in Honor of Carl E. Braaten*, edited by Alberto García and Susan K. Wood, 189-214. Grand Rapids: Eerdmans, 2011.

———. "Pedagogy for Working among the Poor: Something to Talk about before Going on Your Next Short-Term Mission Trip." *Missio Apostolica* 16, no. 1 (2008): 80-84.

———. *Pneumatología: El Espíritu Santo y la espiritualidad de la iglesia*. Biblioteca teológica Concordia. St. Louis: Concordia, 2005.

———. "Pneumatology: Key to Understanding the Trinity." In *Who Is God? In the Light of the Lutheran Confessions*, edited by John A. Maxfield, 122-42. Papers presented at the 2009 Congress on the Lutheran Confessions. St. Louis: Luther Academy, 2012.

———. "'The Poor You Will Always Have With You': A Biblical View of People in Need." In *A People Called to Love: Christian Charity in North American Society*, edited by Kent Burreson. September 2012. http://concordiatheology.org/wp-content/uploads/2012/09/Sanchez-essay1.pdf.

———. "Praying to God the Father in the Spirit: Reclaiming the Church's Participation in the Son's Prayer Life." *Concordia Journal* 32, no. 3 (2006): 274-95.

———. *Receiver, Bearer, and Giver of God's Spirit: Jesus' Life in the Spirit as a Lens for Theology and Life*. Eugene, OR: Pickwick, 2015.

———. "Sculpting Christ in Us: Public Faces of the Spirit in God's World." In *Third Article Theology: A Pneumatological Dogmatics*, edited by Myk Habets, 297-318. Minneapolis: Fortress, 2016.

———. "The Struggle to Express Our Hope." *LOGIA* 19, no. 1 (2010): 25-31.

———. *Teología de la santificación: La espiritualidad del cristiano*. Biblioteca teológica Concordia. St. Louis: Concordia, 2013.

Scaer, David P. "Sanctification in Lutheran Theology." *Concordia Theological Quarterly* 49, nos. 2–3 (1985): 181-95.

———. "Sanctification in the Lutheran Confessions." *Concordia Theological Quarterly* 53, no. 3 (1989): 165-81.

Schaaf, Philip, and Henry Wace, eds. *A Select Library of the Christian Church: Nicene and Post-Nicene Fathers*. 28 vols. in two series. 1886–1900. Reprint, Peabody, MA: Hendrickson, 1994.

Schoonenberg, P. J. A. M. "Spirit Christology and Logos Christology." *Bijdragen* 38 (1977): 350-75.

Schumacher, William W. "Faithful Witness in Work and Rest." *Concordia Journal* 41, no. 2 (2015): 136-50.

———. *Who Do I Say That You Are?: Anthropology and the Theology of* Theosis *in the Finnish School of Tuomo Mannermaa*. Eugene, OR: Wipf & Stock, 2010.

Segovia, Fernando F. "In the World but Not of It: Exile as Locus for a Theology of the Diaspora." In *Hispanic/Latino Theology: Challenge and Promise*, edited by Ada María Isasi-Díaz and Fernando F. Segovia, 195–217. Minneapolis: Fortress, 1996.

Senkbeil, Harold L. *Sanctification: Christ in Action. Evangelical Challenge and Lutheran Response*. Milwaukee: Northwestern, 1989.

Senn, Frank C., ed. *Protestant Spiritual Traditions*. New York: Paulist, 1986.

Shaw, Haydn, and Ginger Kolbaba. *Generational IQ: Christianity Isn't Dying, Millennials Aren't the Problem, and the Future Is Bright*. Carol Stream, IL: Tyndale House, 2015.

Silanes, Nereo. *La santísima Trinidad, programa social del cristianismo: Principios bíblico-teológicos*. Salamanca: Secretariado Trinitario, 1991.

Smith, Christian, and Melinda Lundquist Denton. *Soul Searching: The Religious and Spiritual Lives of American Teenagers*. New York: Oxford University Press, 2005.

Smith, Christian, and Patricia Snell. *Souls in Transition: The Religious and Spiritual Lives of Emerging Adults*. New York: Oxford University Press, 2009.

Snavely, Andréa. *Life in the Spirit: A Post-Constantinian and Trinitarian Account of the Christian Life*. Eugene, OR: Pickwick, 2015.

Sosa Siliezar, Carlos Raúl. *La condición divina de Jesús: Cristología y creación en el evangelio de Juan*. Salamanca: Ediciones Sígueme, 2016.

Surburg, Mark P. "Speaking like Paul and Luther: Pauline Exhortation and the Third Use of the Law." *LOGIA* 27, no. 2 (2018): 15-25.

Thiselton, Anthony C. *A Shorter Guide to the Holy Spirit: Bible, Doctrine, Experience*. Grand Rapids: Eerdmans, 2016.

———. *The Holy Spirit—In Biblical Teaching, Through the Centuries, and Today*. Grand Rapids: Eerdmans, 2013.

Thompson, Deanna A. *Glimpsing Resurrection: Cancer, Trauma, and Ministry*. Louisville: Westminster John Knox, 2018.

———. *Hoping for More: Having Cancer, Talking Faith, and Accepting Grace*. Eugene, OR: Cascade, 2012.

Townroe, John. "Retreat." In *The Study of Spirituality*, edited by Cheslyn Jones, Geoffrey Wainwright, and Edward Yarnold, 578-81. New York: Oxford University Press, 1986.

van der Kooi, Cornelis. "On the Identity of Jesus Christ: Spirit Christology and Logos Christology in Converse." In *Third Article Theology: A Pneumatological Dogmatics*, edited by Myk Habets, 193-206. Minneapolis: Fortress, 2016.

Veith, Gene Edward. *The Spirituality of the Cross: The Way of the First Evangelicals*. St. Louis: Concordia, 1999.

Welker, Michael. *God the Spirit*. Translated by John F. Hoffmeyer. Minneapolis: Fortress, 1994.

White, James Emery. *The Rise of the Nones: Understanding and Reaching the Religiously Unaffiliated*. Grand Rapids: Baker Books, 2014.

Wingren, Gustaf. *Luther on Vocation*. Translated by Carl C. Rasmussen. Philadelphia: Muhlenberg, 1958.

Wong, Joseph H. P. "The Holy Spirit in the Life of Jesus and of the Christian." *Gregorianum* 73 (1992): 57-95.

Wuthnow, Robert. *After Heaven: Spirituality in America Since the 1950s*. Berkeley: University of California Press, 1998.

———. *After the Baby Boomers: How Twenty- and Thirty-Somethings Are Shaping the Future of American Religion*. Princeton, NJ: Princeton University Press, 2007.

Yong, Amos. *The Spirit Poured Out on All Flesh: Pentecostalism and the Possibility of Global Theology*. Grand Rapids: Baker Academic, 2005.

# AUTHOR INDEX


Alfaro, Sammy, 164
Ambrose of Milan, 55-58, 64, 81, 97-98
Aponte, Edwin, 216-17
Aquinas. *See* Thomas
Athanasius of Alexandria, 1-2, 45, 48-51, 53-54, 62-64
Augustine of Hippo, 30, 55, 180, 246
Aulén, Gustaf, 89-90
Barth, Karl, 24-25
Basil of Caesarea, 52-53, 56, 59-61, 73-74, 123-27, 136-37, 174-78, 186, 218
Bayer, Oswald, 85, 167
Bevans, Stephen B., 160-61
Biermann, Joel D., 130
Bobrinskoy, Boris, 19, 50, 76-77
Bonhoeffer, Dietrich, 107, 109-11, 187-88, 190
Braaten, Carl E., 244
Bulgakov, Sergius, 25
Calvin, John, 245
Cantalamessa, Raniero, 106, 188-90, 203, 237
Chrysostom, John, 74-77, 98-100, 121-23, 149-51, 174, 178-80
Coffey, David, 30, 33-34
Congar, Yves, 16, 20-22
Cooper, Jordan, 244-45
Corbett, Steve, 139, 141
Cyril of Alexandria, 243, 246
Cyril of Jerusalem, xvi, 47-48, 64, 66, 72-73, 78, 96-97, 120-21, 218
Dean, Kenda Creasy, 202-4, 210-11
Del Colle, Ralph, 16, 29-38, 40
Denton, Melissa, 198-200, 202-4
Didymus the Blind, 53-56
Drescher, Elizabeth, 207-10
Dunn, James D. G., 34
Elizondo, Virgilio, 146, 162-63
Elowsky, Joel C., 243
Fee, Gordon, 218
Fikkert, Brian, 139, 141
Florovsky, Georges V., 19
Forde, Gerhard O., xv, 85, 157-58
González, Justo L., 161-64, 190-92
Gorman, Michael J., 245
Granado, Carmelo, 56-57, 72, 81, 96
Gregory of Nazianzus (Nazianzen), 50, 60, 73, 77-78, 175
Habets, Myk, 2-3
Hauerwas, Stanley, 165
Hawkins, Aly, 208, 210
Irenaeus of Lyons, 43-47, 56, 61-63, 200-201, 218, 222, 242
Jenkins, Philip, 213-14, 247
Jenson, Robert W., 24, 244
John of Damascus, 26
Kasper, Walter, 33-34, 36
Kinnaman, David, 208, 210
Kleinig, John W., 103
Köberle, Adolf, 69, 242
Kolb, Robert, 129, 132
Kolbaba, Ginger, 211-12
LaCugna, Catherine Mowry, xiii
Ladaria, Luis F., 40
Lampe, G. W. H., 16-20
Lewis, C. S., 106
Lindberg, Carter, 12, 137-39
Loder, James, 205, 219-21
Lupton, Robert D., 140-42

Luther, Martin, 12, 40, 77-81, 95-96, 100-109, 111-12, 120, 127-31, 134-35, 137-39, 151-58, 174-75, 180-85, 218, 220-21, 243-44
Matera, Frank J., 117
McDonnell, Kilian, 81
McGarry, Joseph, 6
Mersch, Émile, 30-31
Montague, George T., 218
Mühlen, Heribert, xiv, 34, 189
Nanko-Fernández, Carmen, 217
Orbe, Antonio, 44, 201
Peterson, David, 1, 5
Pieris, Aloysius, 36-37
Porsch, Felix, 118
Prenter, Regin, 184, 219-21
Pseudo-Basil, 136-37
Rahner, Karl, xiii-xiv, 31, 33
Rogers, Eugene F., 16, 23-29, 37-38, 40
Rolheiser, Ronald, 237
Roof, Wade Clark, 196-97, 201
Rosato, Philip J., 19
Sánchez M., Leopoldo A., xiv, xv-xvi, 5-6, 39-40, 44, 50, 89, 95, 103, 134, 136-40, 142, 146, 151, 159, 163, 203, 237, 246
Scaer, David P., 245
Scheeben, Matthias Joseph, 30-31
Schmemann, Alexander, 25
Schumacher, William, 192-93, 244
Segovia, Fernando F., 163
Shaw, Haydn, 211-12
Silanes, Nereo, 126
Smith, Christian, 198-200, 202-4, 206-7, 212
Snavely, Andréa, 165-66
Snell, Patricia, 199-200, 206-7
Sosa S., Carlos R., 68
Staniloae, Dumitru, 26
Surburg, Mark P., 70
Theodore of Mopsuestia, 19, 246
Thiselton, Anthony C., 1
Thomas Aquinas, 20-21, 30, 33-34, 191
Van Beeck, Franz Jozef, 36
Veith, Gene Edward, 135
Wesley, John, 245
White, James Emery, 208-10, 213-14
Wingren, Gustaf, 131, 136
Wuthnow, Robert, 195-98, 200-202, 204, 207

# SUBJECT INDEX

adoptionism, 17-22, 48, 62-63
and "anthropological maximalism," 19, 22
*Anfechtung*. See *oratio–meditatio–tentatio*
appropriation, theory of, xiii, 30-31, 186
*See also proprium* (proper work), divine persons
Arianism, 48-51, 61-65
baptism, 23, 28, 46-47, 51-53, 57, 60, 64, 67-71, 79-80, 85, 96, 138, 148, 172, 192, 222
and clothing, garment, robe, 28, 47, 70-73, 79-82, 96
and exodus, 73-74, 77-78, 82
and exorcism, 100-101
and image of God, 53, 76, 82
and little Jordan, 48, 64, 81-82
and little Pentecost, 73, 82
and new birth, 60, 68, 77, 80, 100, 187, 246
and repentance, 80-81, 88
*See also* Holy Spirit: and anointing; Jesus Christ: and anointing
causality (trinitarian), types of, 30-34
christoformation, christification, xv-xvii, 2-3, 6-11, 15, 21-22, 27-29, 33, 40-44, 48, 51-54, 58, 63-67, 71, 86, 95, 119, 127, 130, 176-77, 220-22, 232, 237-40, 244-47
and Christ's marginality and mission in the margins, 144-45, 148
and Christ's prayer and work, 169, 175-76
and Christ's temptation and testing, 90, 94-95, 102, 107
and cruciformity, 68-69, 74, 78-82, 85, 88, 94, 115-20, 128-29, 133, 136, 145, 158, 165-66, 175-76, 189, 200-205, 219-21
*See also* imitation of Christ, of God
conscience, 75-76, 82, 93, 105, 130, 154-55, 179, 250
deification. *See under* Jesus Christ; sanctification
devotion. *See* sanctification, models of: devotional
economics, economy, 124-26, 129, 142, 164, 208, 231
and debt (borrowing and lending), 125-26, 142, 171
and generosity, 115, 123-25, 127-28, 137, 140-47, 151-56, 200, 203, 211, 226, 240
and partnership, 126, 133-34, 140-43, 168, 238-40
and simplicity, 121-26, 137, 166
and surpluses, profit, 25, 122-29, 142, 225
*See also* spiritual disciplines: stewardship; sanctification: and happy exchanges; work: and stewardship
exiles, immigrants, refugees, strangers, 149-60, 164-66, 168, 214, 223, 238
Galilean identity, 91, 145-46, 163-67, 223-24
*See also* marginality
*genus habitualis, pneumatikon* (of the Spirit), 39-40
*genus maiestaticum*, 39
Gnosticism, 43-47, 61, 201
habitual grace (*gratia habitualis*), habitual gifts, 33-34, 39-40
healing, health, 10, 75, 93, 97-100, 134, 164, 195, 206, 211, 214-17, 221-25, 236-37, 247
*See also* Jesus Christ: and healings
holiness, xiv-xvi, xviii, 1, 3-6, 12, 15, 28, 40-42, 51, 59-61, 67, 71, 74, 79-81, 84-86, 93-94, 108, 120, 133-35, 139, 147-48, 184-86, 203, 226, 232, 235, 242-45, 249
*See also* Holy Spirit: and divine holiness; sanctification

Holy Spirit
and adoption, 1, 40, 45, 52-54, 60, 65, 83-84, 229, 243
alien work (*opus alienum*) and proper work (*opus proprium*) of, 85, 158, 220-21
and anointing, 1, 28, 31, 47-51, 54-58, 62-64, 68, 78, 142, 188-89, 202-3
and aroma (fragrance) of Christ, 47-48, 57-58, 133-34, 142, 226, 240
and breath (of life), xv, 51-55, 58, 68, 72, 82, 102, 170, 187, 218
and conformation, conformity to Christ (*see* christoformation, christification)
descent(s), 21, 28-29, 44-46, 48-49, 57, 61, 64, 68, 72-73, 97, 101, 116, 186, 189, 201, 222, 241
and divine holiness, xiii, 1, 5, 21, 51, 54, 59, 93-94
and *epiclesis*, 35, 100, 222
and exaltation, 49-50
and fire, 73, 82, 240-41, 249
and firstfruits, 35, 72, 83
and flesh (human nature, life), 2, 22, 27-28, 32, 44-52, 56-57, 60-64, 72, 76-78, 97, 201, 243-44
and flesh (works of), 46-47, 52, 69-71, 74, 81-84, 99, 109, 130, 155-56, 178, 184, 218, 221, 241-44, 246
and gifts, graces, charisms, fruit(s), and virtues, 4, 10, 20, 32, 35, 40, 47, 54-57, 66-67, 71-76, 81, 86, 98-99, 108, 119-23, 128-33, 137, 142, 154, 172, 175-79, 186, 205-6, 210-11, 222, 225, 238, 242-43, 246, 249-51
and image of the Son, 51
indwelling, inhabitation, 19, 23, 27, 30-33, 39, 45-51, 54-55, 63, 65, 165, 178, 242-46
and love, 27-28, 34-35, 72, 240-41, 244-45
pilot of the church, 96, 249
and rain, xvi, 97-98, 249
resting on (Christ, saints), 1, 22-29, 37-40, 46-48, 57-58, 120, 187
and resurrection, 1, 29, 35, 47-53, 60-61, 68-71, 93-94, 182, 244
as seal, 1, 27, 51, 54, 97
sculpting, xv, 115, 229, 239-42, 245-47
*Spiritus praesens*, 34-35
as teacher, Spirit of truth, 53-55, 101, 118, 175-78
and transfiguration, 19, 23-25, 29, 36
and wisdom, 53-55, 66, 99, 101-2, 108, 117, 156, 219, 222

hospitality. *See* sanctification, models of: hospitality model
idolatry, 70, 90, 94, 108-12, 170, 173-76, 179, 185, 188, 196, 206, 218
image of Christ, of God, xv-xvi, 2, 43-48, 51-54, 62, 65-67, 71-74, 93, 130, 158, 169-70, 174, 218, 241, 247
*See also* christoformation, christification
imitation of Christ, of God, 6, 19, 48, 63, 74, 137, 204
*See also* christoformation, christification; saints, imitation of
Jesus Christ
and Adam, 28, 44-47, 53, 61-62, 68, 72-73, 77-82, 93, 183, 187-88, 218
and anointing, 21-22, 28, 31, 40, 44-51, 57-58, 61-64, 68, 76, 91, 118, 143, 166, 188-89, 201-3, 235
ascension, 23, 29, 38
birth, conception, 20-21, 27, 40, 57-58, 64, 118, 165, 172, 181, 201
*Christus praesens*, 34-35
*Christus Victor*, 89
and created gifts (grace), 20, 32
death, crucifixion, 27-28, 36-37, 40, 44, 68-69, 74, 80-82, 92-94, 116-17, 120, 128, 136, 145, 157, 166, 172, 189, 192, 201, 220, 229, 244
and deification, 29, 49-51, 62
descent into hell, 96
exaltation, 39, 51, 57, 61-63, 96, 145
and exorcisms, 92, 96
and grace, 19-20, 33-34, 39-40, 49, 63-64, 70-72, 80, 97-98, 145
and healings, 19, 46, 56, 91-92, 116, 145-46, 156, 164, 173, 236-37
and holiness, sanctification, 28, 33, 39-40, 50-51, 71, 79-81
and *homoousios* (of the same substance), 20, 27, 48, 54
and Israel, 73-74, 77-78, 90-91, 144-45, 173, 189, 192
and obedience, righteousness, 20, 49, 61-63, 91, 118, 169, 174, 188-89, 244
and preaching, teaching, 46, 68, 83, 91, 118, 166, 237
resurrection, 21-29, 35-40, 49-53, 58, 69, 116, 191-92, 209, 218
temptation, 90-93, 109-11, 203
transfiguration, 19, 23, 28, 116, 189
*See also* prayer: and Jesus' life
labor. *See* work

Lord's Supper (Communion, Eucharist), 25, 28, 35, 39, 105, 127-29, 134, 192, 226
marginality, xviii, 10, 119, 144-51, 159-68, 196, 205-6, 222-24, 236-38
  *See also* sanctification, models of: hospitality model
*mestizaje*, 160-64, 213
modalism, 18, 22, 34
monastic spirituality, 96, 102, 126, 131, 137-38, 174-76, 181, 188-89, 191, 246
  and Acts 2, 126
  and Basil of Caesarea, 137, 174-75
  and Basil's *Basiliad*, 126
  and Benedictines, 188
  and Cistercian thought, 28
  and Jesus' prayer life, 189
  and Martin Luther, 96, 102, 131, 137, 181
  and Matthew 25, 137-38
  *ora et labora* (pray and work), 188-89, 250
  and Pseudo-Basil, 137
  and retreat or solitude, 174-76
  and Sunday, 191
  *See also* spirituality; vocation
*oratio–meditatio–tentatio*, 9, 90, 94-96, 101-4, 107, 133, 135, 106, 166, 205, 221, 237, 250
  *See also* temptation, testing
prayer, 3, 5-6, 9-10, 168, 226, 231, 247
  and the Christian's life, 23-24, 29, 35, 90, 95-97, 100-113, 129, 133-36, 166, 169-71, 175-80, 183, 186-88, 191, 198, 202, 205-6, 214-17, 222, 228-29, 235-41
  Flood Prayer, 77-78, 80
  and Jesus' life, 29, 90-95, 104, 173-74, 189-90, 249
  of St. Francis of Assisi, 225
  *Veni Creator Spiritus*, 241
  *Veni Sancte Spiritus*, 240-41, 247
*proprium* (proper work), divine persons, xiii, 26, 30-33, 221
  *See also* appropriation, theory of
renewal. *See* sanctification, models of: renewal model
rest, repose, xviii, 10, 169, 174-75, 180, 185-86, 195, 205-6, 236-38, 249
  eternal, 173, 181-83, 191-92, 232
  and idleness, 156, 169, 181, 193, 206
  and idolatry, 173, 206
  and leisure, 179, 191-92
  physical, 171-73, 179, 183, 188, 191
  and play, 174, 186, 192-93
  and restlessness, 172, 179, 182, 186-88, 206, 231
  and Sabbath, sabbatical cycles, 169-72, 191
  and sleep, 171, 175, 179, 184-85, 188, 192, 206
  spiritual, 188-91
  and work, 170, 173-74, 184-88, 205, 241
  and worship, 171-74, 183
  *See also* sanctification, models of: devotional model; vocation; work
Sabbath. *See* rest, repose
saints, biblical
  Abraham, 99, 148-56, 172, 209
  David, 101-2, 116, 179
  Israel, people of, 37, 73-74, 77-78, 90-91, 94, 122, 125, 144, 171-73, 178, 189-92
  Job, 98-99, 151, 176, 228-29
  Joseph, 125, 249
  Lazarus, 75, 82, 98-100, 121, 149-51, 178, 180
  Mary, mother of Jesus, 23, 27-28, 55-58, 165
  Mary, sister of Martha, 232
  Moses, 73-74, 153, 172, 176, 190
  Noah, 77-78, 82
  widow of Zarephath, 125
saints, imitation of, 125-26, 150-51, 175-77
  *See also* imitation of Christ, of God
sanctification
  and active righteousness (righteousness of the law, of obedience), 47, 69-70, 91, 98-99, 110, 118, 120, 128-34, 138-39, 147-49, 244
  and antinomianism, 111, 130, 242
  and athletic arena, 95-97, 100, 249
  and athletic race, 85-86, 93-94
  and cultural exchanges, 162-63, 206, 217, 226-27, 235
  and deification, *theosis*, 24, 29-30, 45, 49-53, 60-62, 243-45
  and desert, wilderness, 9, 90-98, 106-9, 112-14, 173, 177, 193, 203-5, 230-32, 235, 241
  and faith, xv, 4, 6, 10, 34-35, 47, 53-54, 58-61, 70-71, 77, 80-81, 93, 98-103, 108, 110, 117-19, 125, 129-31, 139-40, 146, 148, 152-62, 167, 172-78, 182-84, 190, 195-97, 202-3, 208-10, 215-16, 223-27, 243-45
  and fatalism, 67, 83-86, 103, 166, 241
  and God's law, 57, 70, 83, 86, 130-35, 157, 172-74, 188, 191, 242-44
  and garden(s), 90-97, 104, 170, 190, 206, 235
  and good works (or works of the law, of the Spirit), 12, 46, 51-52, 63, 99, 119-20, 125, 129-35, 138-41, 147-48, 152-54, 157-58, 172, 176, 182-84, 226, 233, 243-45
  and grace, xv-xvi, 1-4, 16, 19-21, 25, 29-34, 38, 40, 45-49, 52-56, 59, 64, 73-76, 80, 97-98,

104, 117-18, 129-31, 138-39, 167, 174, 202-4, 220, 229, 241-45
and happy exchanges, 79-80, 115, 120, 127-29, 142
and human cooperation or response, 4, 9, 34, 61, 70-71, 86, 135, 168, 170, 183, 241-42, 245-46
and imperative and indicative senses, 69-70, 241-42, 245
and justification (by grace, by faith), 4, 9, 12, 85, 120, 128, 132, 136-39, 167, 172, 203, 224, 227, 236, 243-46
and law (contrition) and gospel (forgiveness), 4, 12, 46, 76, 85-86, 119, 131, 139-40, 158-60, 163-64, 181, 184, 220, 242
and love, 71-72, 75, 83, 87, 105, 109, 119-20, 124-29, 133-36, 140, 144-60, 165-68, 172-80, 201-7, 224-28, 236, 240-41, 244-45
and moralism, 242
and passive righteousness (righteousness of faith, of the gospel), 70-71, 79-82, 85, 94, 98, 104, 120, 125, 128-32, 138-39, 147-49, 157, 172, 220, 244-45
and perfection, 29, 52, 78, 83, 93-94, 137-38, 141, 177, 186, 212, 231, 245
and perfectionism, 67, 83-86, 166, 226-27, 244
and preparation for the gospel, 232-33
and romantic view of neighbor, 115, 136, 138-40
and sin, 4, 12, 33, 36, 40, 47, 53, 60, 65-90, 93, 98, 100-101, 105-13, 120-21, 124-30, 133-39, 148, 157-59, 164-66, 170-73, 177, 181, 200-206, 218-21, 226, 230, 235-37, 240-44
and spiritual battle, 89, 91, 95, 100, 106-8, 112, 214
and spiritual idleness, 74-76, 99, 174, 178-79, 206
and spiritual journey, xviii, 67, 86-87, 90, 94-100, 113, 181, 195, 204-6, 211, 222, 232
and struggle, crisis, 4-6, 9, 83-84, 89-95, 98, 100-108, 112-13, 129, 135, 166, 194-95, 203-6, 210-11, 219-22, 226-29, 232, 235-38, 241, 244
and theodicy, 98-99, 138-40, 157, 167, 228
and utilitarian view of neighbor, 115, 136, 139-40
and vigilance, 9, 90, 94-97, 106-8, 111, 114, 133, 166, 206
and wisdom, 101-2, 108, 130, 133, 198, 222-23
and works- (self-) righteousness (or justification by works), 48, 111, 128, 131, 136-39, 151, 157-58, 166-67, 172, 220, 224
*See also* holiness; spiritual growth, maturity; vocation; work
sanctification, models of, xvii-xviii, 9-10, 205, 217, 222, 235-39
devotional model, 10, 169-93, 205, 217, 236-38
dramatic model, 9, 89-114, 133-35, 166, 205, 217, 221, 236-38
hospitality model, 10, 144-68, 205, 217, 236-38
renewal model, 9, 66-88, 90, 107, 132-35, 159, 166, 177, 205, 217, 221, 236-40
sacrificial model, 10, 115-43, 159, 166, 177, 205, 217, 236-40
Spirit. *See* Holy Spirit
Spirit Christology, xvi, 2-3, 8, 5-11, 15-43, 58-67, 164-66, 194-95, 200-206, 235-37, 242-43, 246
and early church building blocks, 8, 42-43, 58-65
and European complementary approach, 20-22
and European revisionary approach, 17-20
and Logos (two natures) Christology, 2, 16-18, 20-23, 30-34, 39-45, 164
and Lutheran Christology, 38-40
and marginalized neighbors, 164-66
and models-based approach to sanctification, 6-9, 40, 67, 204, 235-36
and North American historical approach, 29-38
and North American narrative approach, 23-29, 37-38
and sanctification, spirituality studies, 3-5, 8-11, 194-95, 200-206, 221
and US Pentecostal proposals, 164-66
spirit (human), 19, 218-22
spirit(s) (evil), 73, 133, 147, 151, 154, 173, 177, 181, 188, 205, 221-22, 228, 231, 235-37, 241, 244, 247
*See also* sanctification, models of: dramatic model
spiritual discipline(s), 4-5, 9, 93-94, 99, 111, 204-5, 232, 239
accountability and support groups, 90, 102, 113, 135, 166
Bible study, 66, 100-103, 113, 175-78, 247
confession and absolution, 67, 75, 82-84, 135, 179-80, 205
fasting, 66, 90, 112
hospitality, 205

prayer, 236
service, 112, 205
stewardship (of resources), 120-24, 137, 142, 177
worship, 205
spiritual growth, maturity, 5-7, 12, 47, 70-71, 85-86, 108, 135-36, 140, 186, 196-98, 201-2, 205, 211, 238, 245
spiritual needs and hopes, xvii, 10, 135, 166, 195, 206-18, 232
balance, 169, 186, 206, 211-13, 225
belonging, community, 29, 96, 104-5, 113-15, 119, 126-29, 141-49, 159-68, 196, 202, 206-13, 216-17, 222-27, 236-38
guilt, dealing with, 67, 79-80, 85-87, 107, 133, 220-21, 236-38, 241
identity, 69-71, 83-88, 107, 120, 124, 129-30, 149, 154, 162-63, 170, 180, 186, 196-97, 220-24, 240
justification, 85, 120, 167, 224
purpose, significance, 115, 120, 129-33, 183, 204, 210-12, 219-20
reconciliation, 67, 82, 86-88, 172, 229-30, 235-38
safety, security, 90, 100, 106-7, 111, 114, 155, 217, 231-32
shame, dealing with, 126, 141, 144, 162-63, 238
spirituality, xiv-xv, 3-5, 8-13, 16, 66, 194, 232, 246
and baby boomers, 195-98, 211-13
and dialogue, 36-37, 210, 222-25
dwelling-oriented, 195-97, 202
and Generation Xers, 198, 211-13, 226
and Global South, 10, 213-15, 247
and invitation, 229-32
and millennials, 3, 10, 199, 208, 211-13, 226
and modeling, embodiment, 225-29
and Moralistic Therapeutic Deism (MTD), 198-204, 211-12
neighbor-oriented, 133-36
and Nones (religiously unaffiliated), 3, 10, 206-10, 213-16
practice-oriented, 10, 82-88, 105-14, 132-43, 159-68, 185-93, 196-99, 201-6
and receptivity, 94, 158, 175-77, 242
seeking-oriented, 195-99, 202
and tinkerers, 196-98
US Hispanic, Latino/a, 10, 161-64, 192, 213-17, 227, 239
*See also* monastic spirituality
temptation, testing, 90, 94-97, 102-3, 107-13, 211, 236-38, 241
and vulnerability, 90, 95, 108-9, 112, 206, 211-12, 241
*See also* Jesus Christ: temptation
theologian, 5, 98, 101-3, 107-8, 113, 244
of the cross and of glory, 157-58
*theosis*. *See* Jesus Christ: and deification; sanctification: and deification, *theosis*
Trinity, xiii-xiv, xvi-xvii, 2, 8, 11, 15-18, 22-34, 37-39, 42-43, 48, 51-53, 57-58, 60, 63, 67, 152, 186, 200, 242-43
vocation (calling), 5-6, 24, 115, 130-31, 134-36, 142, 185-86, 202-6, 210-12, 224-25
and active righteousness, 130-31
and health, 224-25
and humanly designed spirituality, 135-36, 182
and humans as "masks of God" (Luther), 131
and Jesus' life, 136, 203
and law, 130, 134-35
and leisure, 181, 212
and meaning, 210
and neighbor-oriented spirituality, 135-36, 142
and play, 185-86
and rest, 186, 190
and spiritual maturity, 202-4
*See also* work
Word of God, xviii, 4, 7, 12, 102-4, 108-9, 148, 151, 167, 170-74, 177, 180, 183, 200, 222, 236, 244-46
and commands, xiv, 130-32, 170-73, 178, 181-83, 191, 236
and deliverance from evil, 92, 95, 101
and forgiveness, absolution, 46, 67-68, 71, 85-86, 111, 116, 148, 235-36
and preaching and teaching, 34, 54, 68, 76, 102, 109, 148, 183-84, 190-91, 209, 222, 237
and promises, xiv, 35, 69, 72-73, 81, 84-85, 90, 94-97, 103-4, 107-11, 130-32, 152, 173, 181-85, 203, 221, 231, 236
and sanctification, xv, 47, 61, 184
and spiritual rest, 172-74, 177, 180, 183, 186, 191, 206, 236, 241
and wisdom, 101-2, 117, 170-74, 231
and witness, 36, 55, 118, 133, 209, 226, 236
*See also* Jesus Christ: preaching, teaching; *oratio–meditatio–tentatio*
work, xviii, 10, 25, 63, 118, 126, 161, 169, 175, 180, 183, 186-88, 236
and anxiety, pain, 170-71, 181-84
and burnout, workaholism, 169

and divine blessing, command, gift, 170-71, 180-84
and health, 224-25
and idolatry, 170, 174-75, 185, 188, 206
and meaning in life, cause in life, 210-13
and play, 181, 186, 192-93, 212, 238
and stewardship, 10, 134, 188-90
and worship, 171-76, 189-91, 232
*See also* monastic spirituality: and *ora et labora*; rest, repose; vocation

# SCRIPTURE INDEX


**Old Testament**

**Genesis**
1, *186*
1:1-3, *187*
1:2, *187*
1:4-5, *169, 187*
1:5, *188*
1:22, *170*
1:26-31, *170*
1:28, *170*
2:1-3, *171*
2:2, *170, 180*
2:3, *170*
2:7, *52, 68, 72, 170, 187, 218*
2:15, *181*
3, *93, 170*
3:8, *170*
3:8-13, *170*
3:15, *181*
3:23, *170*
18, *151*
18:1-8, *149*
18:1-21, *148*
28, *180*
41:53-57, *125*

**Exodus**
13:21, *73*
14:22, *73*
17:8-16, *190*
21:1-3, *171*
22:21, *145*
23:9, *145*
23:10-11, *171*
31:12-13, *171*
31:16-17, *171*

**Leviticus**
19:34, *145*
25:8-22, *171*

**Deuteronomy**
5:12-15, *171*
6:13, *91*
6:16, *91, 110*
7:6-8, *144*
8:1-3, *90*
8:3, *91*
9:13-21, *91*
10:18, *145*
15:1-2, *171*
32:39, *85*

**1 Kings**
17:8-16, *125*

**Job**
4:2-6, *98*
31:32, *151*

**Psalms**
14:5, *123*
22:1, *228*
31:5, *117*
33:6, *187*
45:7, *48*
45:7-8, *57*
46, *107*
91, *107*
92:1, *171*
92:5, *171*
104:24-30, *171*
104:31-34, *174*
119, *101, 172*
142, *104*
148, *171*
149:3, *174*

**Proverbs**
1:7, *171*
25:21-22, *147*

**Ecclesiastes**
2:20-21, *170*
2:24-25, *170*
3:13, *170*
3:22, *170*
8:15, *170*

**Isaiah**
11:1, *58*
26:19, *192*
40–55, *145*
42:1, *68, 116*
45:23, *145*
49:6, *144*
52:4-7, *144*
52:10, *144*
53:5, *145*
61:1-2, *91*
64:8, *241*

**Jeremiah**
22:3, *145*

**Daniel**
12:2, *192*

**Joel**
2:28, *46*
2:28-29, *72*

**Amos**
3:8, *123*
5:21-25, *178*
6:4-6, *179*
8:5, *178*

**Zechariah**
7:10, *145*
8:5, *193*

**Malachi**
3:8-10, *122*

**Apocrypha**

**Tobit**
12:9, *138*

**Sirach**
3:30, *138*

**New Testament**

**Matthew**
4:7, *110*
5:14, *233*
5:16, *226, 233*
5:45, *150*
5:48, *83*
6:10, *95*
6:13, *95*
7:23, *147*
8:14-17, *145*
10:40, *147*
11:25-30, *173*
12:7-8, *173*
12:22-24, *91*
12:25-26, *92*
12:28, *96, 97*
16:24, *175*
19, *124, 136, 138*
19:16-22, *123*
19:21-22, *123*
21:22, *104*
22, *28*
25, *122, 137, 152, 153*
25:31-46, *146*
25:34-45, *147*
25:41, *147*
25:46, *147*
26:6-13, *232*
26:73, *145*
27:46, *228*
28:16-20, *146*
28:18, *147*
28:19, *46, 52, 60*

**Mark**
1:10, *116*
1:11, *116*
2:10, *116*
2:27, *173*
2:28, *173*
4:26-29, *184*
8:29, *116*
8:31-32, *116*
8:34, *117*
8:38, *116*
10:17-21, *138*
10:38, *68*
10:45, *145*
11:24, *104*
12:35-37, *116*
14:3-9, *232*
14:34, *92*
14:36, *92, 93*
14:61-62, *116*
15:34, *228*
15:39, *117*

**Luke**
1:35, *27, 55*
3:21, *173*
3:21-22, *68, 189*
3:22, *91*
3:23-38, *93*
4:1, *55, 56, 90, 91, 117*
4:3-7, *90*
4:8, *91*
4:12, *110*
4:13, *92*
4:14, *55, 91*
4:16, *173*
4:18, *57*
4:29, *91*
4:42, *173*
5:15-16, *189, 232*
6:5, *173*
6:12, *173*
6:12-13, *189*
6:36, *83*
7:36-50, *232*
9:18, *173*
9:28-29, *173, 189*
9:54, *83*
10:17, *92*
10:21, *232*
10:29-37, *133*
10:38-42, *232*
11:1, *189*
11:1-13, *173*
11:9-13, *104*
11:20, *92*
12, *125*
12:11-12, *55, 121*
12:16-21, *123*
12:50, *68*
13:10-17, *173*
13:13, *173*
13:17, *173*
15, *174*
16:19-31, *74*
16:22-23, *149*
17:11-19, *146, 156, 224*
22:39-46, *173*
22:40, *92*
22:41, *189*
22:42, *104*
23:34, *118, 173*
23:46, *93, 117, 173*
24:49, *96*

**John**
1, *186*
1:1-3, *187*
1:14, *187*
1:33, *57, 68, 72, 187*
1:46, *145*
3:5, *74*
3:5-8, *187*
3:34, *68*
3:34-35, *72*
4:24, *59*
5:1-17, *173*
5:17, *180*
5:28-29, *192*
7:37-39, *246*
7:39, *246*
11:11, *192*

12:1-8, *232*
13:20, *153*
13:35, *226*
14:16-17, *178*
14:18-19, *118*
14:25-27, *118*
14:26, *178*
15:18-20, *118*
15:26-27, *118*
16:7-11, *118*
16:14, *51*
17:14-20, *133*
19:34, *28*
20:22, *68, 72, 187, 218*
20:22-23, *52, 68*

**Acts**
1:8, *148*
2, *126, 208, 209*
2:16-18, *72*
2:17, *46*
2:38, *148*
2:42-44, *119*
4:31, *54*
4:32, *119*
4:34, *148*
6:1-6, *148*
6:4, *190*
6:5, *117*
6:10, *55*
7:55, *117*
7:59, *117*
7:60, *118*
8:1, *148*
10, *148*
10:37-38, *57*
11:29, *148*
17, *208, 209*
17:22-31, *209*
20:35, *158*
28:4, *98*

**Romans**
1:3-4, *34*
1:4, *21*
5:17, *70*
6, *69, 74, 80*
6:5, *69*
6:5-7, *69*
6:12-13, *69*
6:13, *69, 70*
6:19, *70*
6:22, *74*
7:5, *74*
7:25, *83*
8, *24*
8:2, *83*
8:9-10, *46, 55*
8:9-11, *83*
8:11, *1, 27*
8:13, *46*
8:15, *92, 95*
8:20, *181*
8:26-28, *121*
8:29, *2, 21, 22, 51*
11:17, *47*
12:1, *148*
12:1-2, *119*
12:20, *147*
13:11, *192*
13:14, *81*
15:16, *118*
15:25-28, *148*

**1 Corinthians**
1:24, *54*
1:25, *146*
1:28, *146*
1:30, *130*
2:10-16, *219*
6:19-20, *178*
9:24-27, *94*
10:1-13, *94*
10:2, *73*
10:4, *180*
10:13, *110*
12:3, *121*
12:7, *119*
12:8, *54*
12:13, *119*
12:25-26, *127*
12:26, *113, 119*
13:1-13, *119*
14:12, *119*
15, *46*
15:20-22, *192*
15:45, *218*
15:49, *74, 130*
15:50, *46*
15:53, *46*
16:1-4, *148*

**2 Corinthians**
2:15, *51, 58*
3:17, *34*
3:18, *2*
4:4, *2*
5:17, *69, 191*
5:21, *79*
6:14-16, *133*
7:1, *133*
8–9, *148*
8:3, *148*
8:9, *145*

**Galatians**
2:10, *148*
3:2, *172*
3:5, *172*
3:7-9, *172*
3:10-12, *172*
3:11, *172*
3:27, *71, 81*
4:4-5, *172*
4:6, *92, 95*
4:19, *71*
5, *46*
5:13-25, *172*
5:19-21, *72*
5:22, *71*
5:22-24, *178*
5:24, *72*
5:24-25, *71*
5:25, *242*
6:2, *119, 128, 172*
6:10, *148, 152*

**Ephesians**
1:13, *51*
1:13-14, *54*
2:10, *242*
4:1-2, *71*
4:1-6, *70*
4:2-3, *71*
4:13, *71*
4:16, *71*
4:22-24, *81*
4:23, *71*
4:24, *79*
4:30, *51, 54*
4:32, *71*
5:14, *192*
6, *100*
6:13, *95*

**Philippians**
2:1, *118*
2:5-11, *27*
2:6-8, *145*
2:9-11, *145*
2:17, *118*

**Colossians**
2:11-12, *74*
3:2, *71*
3:3-4, *69*
3:5, *70*
3:9-10, *74*
3:9-11, *71*
3:12-13, *71*
3:13, *119*
3:14, *71*

**1 Thessalonians**
4:14-17, *192*

**1 Timothy**
5:16, *156*

**Hebrews**
1:3, *93*
2:9-10, *94*
2:10, *94*
2:10-11, *93*
3:7-19, *173*
4:1-11, *173*
4:9-10, *173*
4:15, *93*
5, *40*
5:9, *40*
9:14, *57, 189*
12:7, *93*
12:10, *94*
13:2, *148, 149*
13:3, *147*
13:16, *119*

**1 Peter**
1:1-2, *119*
2:5, *119*
2:20, *120*
5:8, *112*

**2 Peter**
1:4, *45, 51*

**1 John**
2:7, *51*

**Revelation**
14:13, *173*